# THE DRAMATISTS GUILD RESOURCE DIRECTORY™

## 2009

The Writer's Guide
to the Theatrical Marketplace™

15th Edition

ISBN 13: 978-1-58510-328-7
ISBN 10: 1-58510-328-4

The Dramatists Guild Resource Directory and The Writer's Guide to the Theatrical Marketplace are trademarks of The Dramatists Guild.

cover image © istockphoto/Ben Taylor

Copyright in the original material, submission calendar, and compilations.
© 2009 The Dramatists Guild of America Inc. All Rights Reserved. Compiled and published by the Publications Dept. of The Dramatists Guild of America Inc. No part of this book may be reproduced without prior written permission from The Dramatists Guild of America Inc., 1501 Broadway, Suite 701, New York, NY 10036. For more information, contact Robert Ross Parker, Director of Publications at rrparker@dramatistsguild.com .

This book is published with permission by Focus Publishing/R. Pullins Company, 311 Merrimac, Newburyport MA 01950 www.pullins.com, with the expertise of Joshua Faigen of Folio Publishing Services.

10 9 8 7 6 5 4 3 2 1 0

1108TS

# Table of Contents

Preface ............................................................................. 1
Dramatists Bill of Rights ................................................. 3
Suggested Formatting for Plays and Musicals ............... 7
    Sample Format Page – Plays ..................................... 9
    Sample Format Page – Musicals .............................. 12
    Sample Letter of Inquiry ......................................... 14
    Sample Resume ........................................................ 15
DG Policy on Submission Fees ..................................... 16
Career Development Professionals ............................... 17
    Accountants.............................................................. 17
    Agents ....................................................................... 18
    Attorneys .................................................................. 23
    Commercial Producers ............................................ 25
    Publishers ................................................................. 27
Career Development Opportunities ............................... 35
    Colonies & Residencies .......................................... 35
    Conferences & Festivals.......................................... 42
    Conferences & Festivals (Fee Charged).................. 53
    Contests .................................................................... 57
    Contests (Fee Charged) ........................................... 71
    Grants & Fellowships .............................................. 79
    Theaters.................................................................... 89
    Theaters (Fee Charged) ......................................... 156
Educational Opportunities ........................................... 157
    Colleges and Universities ..................................... 157
    London, Ireland and Canadian programs ............. 169
    Workshops............................................................. 175
Writer Resources ......................................................... 183
    Emergency Funds .................................................. 183
    Membership & Service Organizations.................. 184
    Online Script Writing Software ............................ 196
    Glossary ................................................................. 201
Special Interests ........................................................... 210
    Ten-Minute Play Opportunities ............................ 210
    World Summer Theatre Festivals ......................... 222
    Index of Special Interests...................................... 235
Submission Calendar ................................................... 240
Index ............................................................................ 246

# Preface

Welcome to the 15th printed edition of *The Dramatists Guild Resource Directory*. Each year we'll add features that we think our members will find important to their lives as dramatists. This year, in addition to the standard submission opportunities and resources, you'll notice that we've added the following:

- A sample letter of inquiry/submission
- A sample writer's resume
- Educational opportunities in London, Ireland and Canada
- A summary of free script writing software available on-line
- A glossary of terms repeated in our publications
- A summary of World Summer Theater Festivals
- A special list of short play and ten-minute play opportunities

We're continuing to post the Dramatists Bill of Rights (so you'll always know your rights and protections in whatever situation you find yourself in), our statement of submission fees, and still provide you a variety of resources if you are looking for further education.

A strong word of advice about this *Resource Directory*: by the time we go to press, a number of the opportunities listed within these pages will no longer exist, will not have the same staff listed, will not have the same deadline date as printed. It is essential that you verify the information we provide either by going to the Member's Lounge at www.dramatistsguild.com and double-checking the information on our website, or, by going directly to the website of the theatre, contest, festival, etc. To repeat, we have confirmed these listings with as much accuracy as possible before going to press.

When looking for a listing in the index, please know individuals (primarily agents, attorneys, and producers) and opportunities named for individuals (primarily contests) are listed by the first letter of the individual's surname. For easier reference, we have also indicated any deadlines and fees in boldface next to the title of those opportunities that released them.

The organizations listed in the *Resource Directory* receive hundreds of inquiries, so please be considerate and responsible with your submissions.

1. Name the specific program you're interested in, since many groups sponsor multiple programs.
2. Include a self-addressed stamped envelope (SASE) with sufficient postage. Most organizations won't return material without one, while some organizations don't return material at all. You may also include a self-addressed stamped postcard (SASP) to be notified when the

organization has received your material – or if they are interested in reading your script.
3. Include your contact information in a query letter, since some organizations prefer blind submissions, with no identification on the script itself.

Please review each organization's policies carefully to ensure that all authorial rights are upheld. If you find a listing you believe is inaccurate or misleading, or if you have questions about any listing, write to the Dramatists Guild. Remember, though, listings by their nature are never complete, and any listing or omission doesn't necessarily constitute approval or disapproval by the Guild, its Council, officers, employees, agents, or affiliates.

Finally, much thanks to Joshua Levine, Madelena Ryerson, Tari Stratton, Brandon Kalbaugh, Rebecca Ballenger, Lisa Bermudez, Cara Francis, Wade German, Shoshanna Greenberg, Lauren Gunderson, Alex J. Holt, Kathryn Luckstone, Jessica Phelan, Chris Saunders, David Schultz and Bailey Stark for their invaluable contributions to this resource.

Gary Garrison
*Executive Director,*
*Creative Affairs*

# The Dramatist Bill of Rights

The Dramatists Guild is America's professional association of playwrights, librettists, lyricists and composers, with over 6,000 members around the world. The Guild is governed by our country's leading dramatists, with a fifty-five member Council that includes such dramatists as Edward Albee, Stephen Sondheim, John Patrick Shanley, Tony Kushner, Marsha Norman, Lynn Nottage, Emily Mann and Christopher Durang.

Long before playwrights or musical theatre writers join the Dramatists Guild, they often struggle professionally in small to medium-sized theatres throughout the country. It is essential, therefore, that dramatists know their rights, which the Dramatists Guild has defended for nearly one hundred years. In order to protect the dramatist's unique vision, which has always been the strength of the theatre, s/he needs to understand this fundamental principle: dramatists own and control their work.

The Guild recommends that any production involving a dramatist incorporate a written agreement in which both theatres/producers and writers acknowledge certain key rights with each other.

## In Process and Production

1. ARTISTIC INTEGRITY. No one (e.g., directors, actors, dramaturgs) can make changes, alterations, and/or omissions to your script—including the text, title, and stage directions—without your consent. This is called "script approval."
2. APPROVAL OF PRODUCTION ELEMENTS. You have the right to approve the cast, director, and designers (and, for a musical, the choreographer, orchestrator, arranger, and musical director, as well), including their replacements. This is called "artistic approval."
3. RIGHT TO BE PRESENT. You always have the right to attend casting, rehearsals, previews and performances.

## Compensations

4. ROYALTIES. You are generally entitled to receive a royalty. While it is possible that the amount an author receives may be minimal for a small- to medium-sized production, *some* compensation should always be paid if *any* other artistic collaborator in the production is being paid, or if any admission is being charged. If you are a member of the Guild, you can always call our business office to discuss the standard industry royalties for various levels of production.

5. BILLING CREDIT. You should receive billing (typographical credit) on all publicity, programs, and advertising distributed or authorized by the theatre. Billing is part of your compensation and the failure to provide it properly is a breach of your rights.

## Ownership

6. OWNERSHIP OF INTELLECTUAL PROPERTY. You own the copyright of your dramatic work. Authors in the theatre business do not assign (i.e., give away or sell in entirety) their copyrights, nor do they ever engage in "work-for-hire." When a university, producer or theatre wants to mount a production of your play, you actually license (or lease) the public performance rights to your dramatic property to that entity for a finite period of time.

7. OWNERSHIP OF INCIDENTAL CONTRIBUTIONS. You own all approved revisions, suggestions, and contributions to the script made by other collaborators in the production, including actors, directors, and dramaturgs. You do not owe anyone any money for these contributions.

    If a theatre uses *dramaturgs*, you are not obligated to make use of any ideas the dramaturg might have. Even when the input of a dramaturg or director is helpful to the playwright, dramaturgs and directors are still employees of the theatre, not the author, and they are paid for their work *by the theatre/producer*. It has been well-established in case law, beginning with "the Rent Case" (*Thompson v. Larson*) that neither dramaturgs nor directors (nor any other contributors) may be considered a co-author of a play, unless (i) they've collaborated with you from the play's inception, (ii) they've made a copyrightable contribution to the play, and (iii) you have agreed in writing that they are a co-author.

8. SUBSIDIARY RIGHTS. After the small- or medium-sized production, you not only own your script, but also the rights to market and sell it to all different media (e.g., television, radio, film, internet) in any commercial market in the world. You are not obligated to sign over any portion of your project's future revenues to any third party (fellow artist, advisor, director, producer) as a result of a production, unless that production is a professional (i.e., Actor's Equity) premiere production (including sets, costumes and lighting), of no less than 21 consecutive paid public performances for which the author has received appropriate billing, compensation, and artistic approvals.

9. FUTURE OPTIONS. Rather than granting the theatre the right to share in future proceeds, you may choose to grant a non-exclusive option to present another production of your work within six months or one year of the close of the initial production. No option should be assignable without your prior written consent.

10. AUTHOR'S CONTRACT: The only way to ensure that you get the benefit of the rights listed above is through a written contract with the producer, no matter how large or small the entity. The Guild's Department of Business Affairs offers a model "production contract" and is available to review any contracts offered to you, and advise as to how those contracts compare to industry standards.

We realize that making demands of a small theatre is a difficult task. However, you should feel confident in presenting this Bill of Rights to the Artistic Director, Producer, Literary Manager, or university administrator as a starting point for discussion. At the very least, any professional in the dramatic arts should realize that it is important for writers to understand the nature of their work—not just the artistic aspects, but the business side, as well—and that they stand together as a community, for their mutual benefit and survival, and for the survival of theatre as a viable art form in the 21st century.

# Suggested Formatting for Plays and Musicals

Included in this document are suggested formats for plays and musicals drawn from suggestions of distinguished dramatists, literary managers, teachers of dramatic writing, producers, professional theatres and publishers. It is the Guild's belief that these formats present a standard that will work for most professional opportunities. A few additional elements to consider:

1. Formatting works towards two purposes: easy reading and the ability to approximate the performance time of the written story. For plays, we've given you a traditional and a more modern format to choose from. Admittedly, not all stories or styles of writing will work within a standard format. Therefore, use your better judgment in deciding the architecture of the page.
2. There is an industry standard (though some may say old-fashioned) of using the 12-point Courier-New font; we've also noted that Times New Roman is used in more modern formatting. With the proliferation of computers and word-processing programs, there are literally hundreds of fonts to choose from. Whatever your choice, we recommend that you maintain a font size of 12 points – thereby assuring some reliable approximation of performance time.
3. Though you wrote the story, someone has to read it before anyone sees it. Therefore, make your manuscript easy to read by employing a standard format with clearly delineated page numbers, scene citations and act citations. Headers and footers are optional.
4. If you're using a software program, such as Final Draft, to format your work, be aware that you have the ability to create your own format in these programs that can be uniquely named, saved and applied to all of your manuscripts.
5. Usually, between the title page and the first page of the story and/or dialogue, there is a page devoted to a character break-down. What's important to note on this page is the age, gender and name of each character. Some dramatists write brief character descriptions beside each name.
6. While it is cost-effective for both xeroxing and mailing, realize that some institutions prefer that you don't send double-sided documents. We recommend that you inquire about preference.

7. There is no right or wrong way to signify the end of a scene or act. Some writers do nothing but end the scene; others write "black out", "lights fade down", "End Act 1" or some other signifier that the scene or act has concluded.
8. The binding margin should be 1.5 inches from the edge. All other margins (top, bottom, right) should be 1.0 inch from the edge.

## Suggested Formatting for Plays and Musicals

**Sample Title Page**

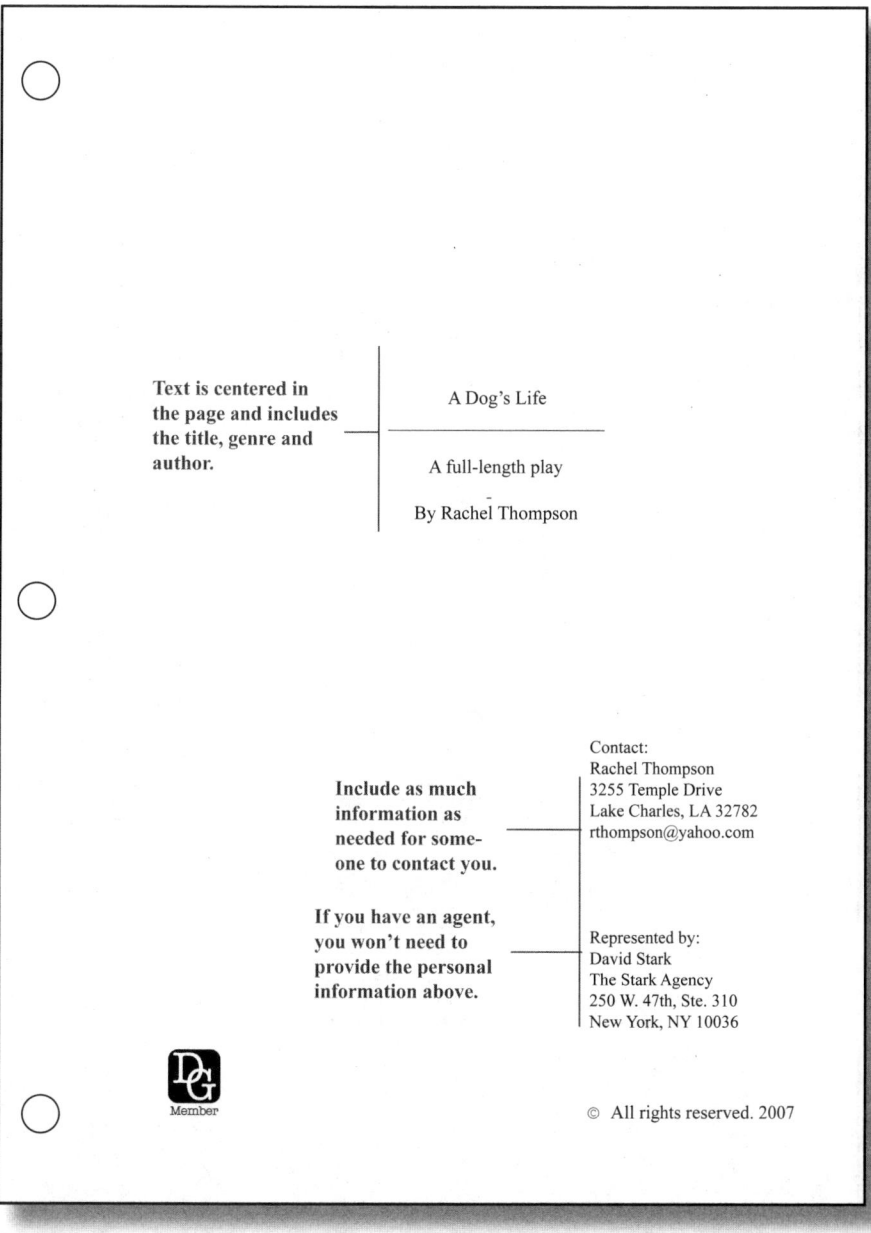

## Traditional Play Format

From Tennessee Williams' *Not About Nightingales*

> **Essential page numbering\*\***
> 16.
>
> **Dialogue begins 1.5 inches from left side to account for binding. Dialogue is single-spaced.**
>
>                             BOSS
>                 (removes cover from basket)
>     Speak of biscuits and what turns up but a nice batch of
>     homemade cookies! Have one young lady - Jim boy!
>
>                     (Jim takes two.)
>
> **Stage action is indented 3 inches from left; put in parenthesis. A blank line is inserted before and after.**
>
>                             BOSS
>     Uh-huh, you've got an awful big paw, Jimmy!
>                           (laughs)
>     Show the new Arky-what's-it to Miss Daily news - or is it
>     the Morning Star? Have a chair! I'll be right with you -
>                   (vanishes for a moment)
>     Sweat, sweat, sweat's all I do these hot breezy days!
>
> **Dialogue extends to 1.0 inch from right margin**
>
>                             JIM
>                         (sotto voce)
>     He thinks you're a newspaper woman.
>
> **Stage action reliant on the proceeding dialogue is indented to the left of the character name.**
>
>                             BOSS
>     Turn on that fan.
>                         (emerging)
>     Well, now, let's see -
>
>                             EVA
>     To begin with I'm not -
>
> **Character name in all caps; in the center of the page.**
>
>                             BOSS
>     You've probably come here to question me about that ex-
>     convicts story in that damned yellow sheet down there in
>     Wilkes county - That stuff about getting Pellagra in here
>     - Jimmy, hand me that sample menu!
>
> **Standard font for this formatting is 12.0 point, Courier New.**
>
>                             JIM
>     She's not a reporter.
>
>                             BOSS
>     Aw. - What is your business, young lady?
>
>                 (She opens her purse and spills
>                     contents on floor.)
>
> **Stage action is indented 3.0 inches from left margin and enclosed in parentheses.**
>
> \*\*There are many ways to paginate your play, from the straightforward numerical sequence of 1, 2, 3 to an older format of 1-2-16, (meaning Act 1, Scene 2, Page 16).

# Suggested Formatting for Plays and Musicals

## Modern Play Format

From Tennessee Williams' *Not About Nightingales*

---

*Essential page numbering* — 16.

**BOSS**
You've probably come here to question me about that ex-convicts story in that damned yellow sheet down there in Wilkes county – That stuff about getting Pellagra in here – Jimmy, hand me that sample menu!

**JIM**
She's not a reporter.

**BOSS**
Aw. – What is your business, young lady?

**EVA**
I understand there's a vacancy here. Mr. McBurney, my landlady's brother-in-law, told her that you were needing a new stenographer and I'm sure that I can qualify for the position. I'm a college graduate, Mr. Whalen, I've had three years of business experience – references with me – but, oh – I've – I've had such abominable luck these last six months. – the last place I worked – the business recession set in they had to cut down on their sales-force – they gave me a wonderful letter – I've got in with me.

*She opens her purse and spills contents on floor.*

**BOSS**
Anybody outside?

**EVA**
Yes. That woman.

**BOSS**
What woman?

**EVA**
The one from Wisconsin. She's still waiting –

**BOSS**
I told you I don't want to see her.
(talking into phone)
How's the track, Bert? Fast? Okay.

*Sailor Jack's mother, MRS. BRISTOL, has quietly entered. She carries a blanket.*

**MRS. BRISTOL**
I beg your pardon, I – You see I'm Jack Bristol's mother, and I've been wanting to have a talk with you so long about – about my boy!

---

*Annotations (left margin):* Dialogue begins 1.5 inches from left side to account for binding. Dialogue is single-spaced.

*Annotations (right margin):*
- Character name in all caps; in the center of the page.
- Dialogue extends to 1.0 inch from right margin.
- Stage action begins in the center of the page and scans to the right margin. A blank line is inserted before and after.
- Standard font for this formatting is 12.0 point, New Times Roman.
- Stage action reliant on the proceeding dialogue is indented to the left of the character name.

11

## Musical Format

From *APPLAUSE*, Book by Betty Comden, Adolph Green.
Music by Charles Strouse, Lyrics by Lee Adams

---

Dialogue begins 1.5 inches from left side to account for binding. Dialogue is single-spaced.

Character name in all caps; in the center of the page.

Stanzas are separated by a blank line and distinguish themselves by dramatic thought and/or changes from verse to chorus to bridges, etc.

KAREN
(to Margo)
Margo, you've been kicking us all around long enough. Someone ought to give *you* a good swift one for a change!

(She leaves.)

EVE
Miss Channing . . . if I ever dreamed that anything I did could possibly cause you any unhappiness, or come between you and your friends . . . please believe me.

MARGO
(in a low, weary voice)
Oh, I do. And I'm full of admiration for you.
(stands, approaches Eve)
If you can handle yourself on the stage with the same artistry you display off the stage . . . well, my dear, you are in the right place.

(She speaks the following lines as the music of WELCOME TO THE THEATRE begins.)

Welcome to the theater, to the magic, to the fun!

(She sings.)

WHERE PAINTED TREES AND FLOWERS GROW
AND LAUGHTER RINGS FORTISSIMO,
AND TREACHERY'S SWEETLY DONE!

NOW YOU'VE ENTERED THE ASYLUM,
THIS PROFESSION UNIQUE
ACTORS ARE CHILDREN
PLAYING HIDE-AND-EGO-SEEK . . .

SO WELCOME, MISS EVE HARRINGTON,
TO THIS BUSINESS WE CALL SHOW,
YOU'RE ON YOUR WAY
TO WEALTH AND FAME,
UNSHEATH YOUR CLAWS,
ENJOY THE GAME!
YOU'LL BE A BITCH
BUT THEY'LL KNOW YOUR NAME
FROM NEW YORK . . . TO KOKOMO

WELCOME TO THEATRE,
MY DEAR, YOU'LL LOVE IT SO!

Essential page numbering**
56.

Stage action is indented 3 inches from left; put in parentheses. A blank line is inserted before and after.

Dialogue extends to 1.0 inch from right margin

Stage action reliant on the proceeding dialogue is indented to the left of the character name.

Lyric are in all CAPS, separated line to line by either musical phrasing and/or the rhyming scheme and clearly indented from the left margin.

For duets, or characters singing counter-point, create two columns side by side, following the same format here.

**There are many ways to paginate your play, from the straight forward numerical sequence of 1, 2, 3 to an older format of 1-2-16, (meaning Act 1, Scene 2, Page 16).

## The Submission Letter and Production Resume

Though there is no right or wrong way to write a letter of introduction to your work, realize an effective submission letter should be short, professional and with just enough information so the reader knows you've submitted exactly what was called for in the solicitation. And while it's tempting to entice the reader to want to read the script with an overly expressive narrative in your submission letter, consider that this is the first exposure to your writing (of any kind) that will be read by someone in the producing organization . Be mindful, then, how you represent yourself on paper, and allow your play or musical to speak for itself.

A common question is often asked when writers construct a production resume: what do you do if you don't have a lot of readings or productions to list on your resume? Whatever you do, don't misrepresent yourself; don't say you've had a reading or a production of a play at a theatre that you haven't had. You'll eventually be found out and look worse than someone who has a thin resume. If you don't have a lot of production experience with your writing, write a brief synopsis of each of the plays you've written, cite any classes or workshops you've taken as a playwright and detail any other experience you have in the theatre (as stage manager, director, actress, dramaturg, etc.). People are more likely to be sympathetic to you being young in the theatre than they are to you being someone who misrepresents themselves.

A more accomplished playwright's resume should list the productions or readings of plays (by theatre and date), awards, grants, writers colonies attended, workshops, festivals invited to and any special recognition received as a writer. Give the reader a sense of the whole of your writing career, including memberships in theatre groups, professional organizations and related writing work. Include your address and phone number at the top or bottom of your resume, cover sheet of your play and obviously on the return envelope. Again, there are any number of variations on how to construct a writer's resume, but a template to inspire your thinking can be found on the following page.

# TAMMY STEWART

1501 Montrose
Houston, Texas 77019

tstewart@earthlink.net
713-456-2209

January 1, 2009

Terry Livingston, Literary Manager
Looking For A Name Theatre Company
1224 South Brittmorgan Lane
Dallas, Texas 22195-0989

Dear Terry Livingston:

In response to your solicitation in the *Dramatists Guild E-Newsletter* of December 15, 2008, I submit for your consideration my full-length drama, *Dearly Departed*, a play set in New Orleans in the aftermath of Hurricane Katrina. This play won the 2008 Jane Chambers Playwriting Award and was a finalist for the Sundance Theatre Institute for Playwrights. A production resume, SASE, and synopsis is enclosed.

Thank you for your consideration.

Sincerely,

Tammy Stewart

---

**Side notes:**

*If you're not absolutely sure, call and find out if a gender-ambiguous name like "Terry" is a man or woman. It's a courtesy you should afford the person you're addressing. If calling isn't possible, start the letter this way:*

*If a detailed synopsis is requested, there's no need to go on about the play in the letter. If a detailed synopsis was not requested, describe the play more fully here.*

*It's always a matter of personal preference, but you can never go wrong with a closing that is short and clean.*

*Always have your contact information somewhere to be seen and easily found.*

*Let your reader know where you saw the solicitation; they'll appreciate the feedback of their time and investment dollars.*

*Let your reader know you read the solicitation and that you're sending them the material they requested -- in this case, a full-length drama.*

*Let your reader know that you've sent all the support material requested. Send a resume, regardless if they've asked or not. That way, you don't have to include too much personal information in your letter.*

14

# Tammy Stewart

tstewart@earthlink.net
713-456-2209
1501 Montrose
Houston, Texas 77019

## PRODUCTION HISTORY

*Dearly Departed* (full-length drama)
Winner, Jane Chambers Playwriting Award                                        July 2008
Finalist, 2008 Sundance Theatre Institute for Playwrights                      May 2008
Early scenes published in *The Best Stage Scenes of 2008*, Smith & Krause, Inc.   April 2008

*Forty-Love, Roger* (full-length comedy)
Winner, Arthur W. Stone New Play Award                                    September 2007
Hedgerow Theatre Company, Summer Showcase Series, Staged Reading            June 2007
Miranda Theatre, New York City, Off-Off Broadway Equity Showcase              May 2007

*Maddie Makes a Madness* (10-minute play)
Finalist, Actors Theatre of Louisville, National Ten Minute Play Contest    December 2007

*Daily Puppy Dot Com* (10-minute play)
Summer Shorts Festival, Miami, Florida                                          May 2006
Turnip Theatre Festival, New York City, Equity showcase                     January 2006
Published in *Ten On Ten: The Best Ten Minute Plays of 2006*, Focus Publishing

## AWARDS
Residency, MacDowell Colony                                                 January 2003
Texas State Foundation for the Arts, Artist Grant                           January 2002
The Young Playwrights Award, Texas Education Theatre Association               May 1998

## MEMBER/ASSOCIATIONS
Dramatists Guild of America, Associate Member
Minneapolis Playwrights Center
Writers Focusing Writers, Houston, Texas
Scriptwriters, Houston, Texas

## EDUCATION
MFA in Playwriting, University of Houston (with Edward Albee, Lanford Wilson)   May 2002
BFA in Acting, The University of Michigan                                      May 2000

---

Cite the name of the play and genre.

Cite the name of the theatre that produced the play and where it was produced. You may want to list the kind of production presented.

Cite publications as if they were productions. Why not let whoever know that your work's been published?

Professional memberships, education, writers groups you belong to and the like should be noted.

Note your most current address, phone number and email address. If they want to contact you, you want to make it easy for them.

Because a lot of theatres are specific about the kind of second production they'll provide, note the nature of the production.

Date your events from the most recent to the least recent.

# The DG Statement on Submission Fees

The Dramatists Guild of America denounces the practice by festivals, play contests and educational events of charging excessive fees to dramatists who submit their work. Any request for submission fees should be accompanied by a complete explanation of how those fees are to be spent. The Guild also insists that contests and festivals announce the names of all finalists and winners to all participants.

It is important that members understand that submission fees are not the norm and, when required, the festival should offer something significant in return for the writer's investment, such as a large cash prize, a residency or a production. Reading fees are in no case acceptable, as most festivals receive that money from other grant sources. In no case should playwrights have to pay to simply have their work read.

The Guild also strongly disapproves of a festival's placing any encumbrances on the work as a result of the play being chosen a finalist or a participant. Any future participation in the life of the play must be earned by the festival by producing the work, and should never be granted by the writer without consultation with the Guild. If the festival expects any subsidiary income from the plays, that information should be stated clearly in all of the organization's printed and electronic materials related to the event.

The Council of the Guild feels that its members should be made aware of all legitimate opportunities available to them, and so we have listed in this section those particular contests and festivals that charge fees and have provided explanations regarding how their submission fees are spent, as well as full disclosure of any encumbrances they place on a selected writer's work, when offered by the sponsor.

# Career Development Professionals

## ACCOUNTANTS

**Giordano, Cohen, Fastiggi, Luciano, & Co., P.A.**
P.O. Box 267
147 Columbia Turnpike, Ste. 100
Florham Park, NJ 07923
Michael A. Fastiggi
Tel: (973) 377-2009 Fax: (973) 377-5535
michael@gcfl-cpa.com
    Alt. contact: John J. Luciano, C.P.A.
    john@gclf-cpa.com.

**Marks Paneth & Shron LLP**
622 3rd Ave., New York, NY 10017
David R. Marcus
Tel: (212) 503-8833
dmarcus@markspaneth.com
www.markspaneth.com
    Est. 1907. David R. Marcus, CPA, MBA, JD.

**Spielman, Koenigsberg and Parker (SKP)**
888 7th Ave., Fl. 35
New York, NY 10106
Richard Koenigsberg
    Est. 1955. Partners: Melvin Spielman, Richard Koenigsberg, Gary Parker.

April 17, 2008
From the Desk of Gary Garrison

## AGENCY

*(Reprinted from the e-newsletter)*

On the average, I get three to four phone calls or emails a day that go something like this: *"I need an agent. I know everyone needs an agent, but I <u>really need</u> an agent. Why can't the Guild help get me an agent or a director or anyone who can help promote my work? And why can't the Guild get more theatres to respond to playwrights and new plays? We need more opportunities!"* Look, I just want to get square with you once and for all: we are a member-service and advocacy organization. And while I don't want to downplay the importance for some of you to be professionally represented by an agent (or your work placed in a theatre), it is not one of the mandates of this organization to help you secure representation or production.

It doesn't matter what anyone has to say about writers and agents, the truth is having an agent is perceived – right or wrong – as a benchmark of success that comes with certain positive opportunities and a healthy amount of validation. The desire in most of us, then, is never likely to go away. But if you really want to pursue the agent thing, I want you to take a good, honest look at simple facts and figures to help you make sense of what's ahead of you.

1. The numbers: talking to my colleagues here at the Guild, and then making a few phone calls around town to some very respectable agents, to our best estimation there are approximately thirty-five agents dedicated to promoting dramatic writing for the theatre. That's thirty-five agents *total* – throughout the whole country – that represent every playwright you know by name, and then the many hundreds you don't know (yet). The simple numbers alone show the odds are against most of us having an agent.

2. Most agents that I've spoken with are rarely interested in representing a single piece of work and are far more interested in representing (and helping you grow) a body of work. To approach an agent to represent a single play or musical is not likely to get you anywhere. Agents, like all theatre business people, are as interested in the present as they are the future.

3. Twenty years ago, maybe even ten years ago, a hit production of a play or a musical and a good *New York Times* review (or any major newspaper review) would almost ensure that you'd have an agency knocking at your door. That's not true any longer; there's a glut of material and writers out there that remain unrepresented.

4. Theatre, like most arms of the entertainment industry, is ageist.

Jeeeeeez, Gary, did you have to be so . . . honest? In a word, yes, because so many of us are singularly obsessed about getting an agent. Are there exceptions to any of the points above? Of course there are exceptions; that's what makes this life interesting. Can you have a productive, successful career in the theatre without professional representation? You bet, and a heck of a lot of people do.

*Please understand that we provide a list of working literary agents as a convenience for you – nothing more. By listing these agents (which is not a comprehensive list), we do not intend to suggest that they are seeking new clients or that we are particularly endorsing them as agents. Unless indicated otherwise, send a query and synopsis to one agent at a time.*

## AGENTS

**Abrams Artists Agency**
275 7th Ave., Fl. 26
New York, NY 10001
Sarah L. Douglas, Charles Kopelman
Tel: (646) 486-4600
literary@abramsartny.com
www.abramsartists.com/literary.html
 Agents: Sarah L. Douglas, Charles Kopelman, Beth Blickers, Morgan Jenness, Maura Teitelbaum, Kate Navin, Ron Gwiazda. **Application.** What to submit: query, synopsis, SASE. We do not accept any unsolicited materials, and we are only accepting new clients by professional recommendation.

**Alan Brodie Representation Ltd.**
Fairgate House
78 New Oxford St., Fl. 6
London, England UK
Alan Brodie
Tel: 44-20-7079-7990
Fax: 44-20-70797999
info@alanbrodie.com
www.alanbrodie.com
 Staff: Alan Brodie, Sarah McNair, Lisa Foster Response Time: 3 mos. **Application.** What to submit: query, resume, SASE. Author must be resident of UK preferred. Material must be unoptioned. How to submit: professional recommendation.

**Bret Adams Ltd.**
448 W. 44th St.
New York, NY 10036
Bruce Ostler
Tel: (212) 765-5630
www.bretadamsltd.net
 Est. 1953 Staff: Bruce Ostler, Mark Orsini; Natasha Sinha (literary); Margi Rountree, Ken Melamed, Michael Golden (acting). **Preference.** Style: all styles, comedy, drama, musical. **Application.** What to submit: query. How to submit: professional recommendation.

**Ann Wright Representatives**
165 W. 46th St.,#1105
New York, NY 10036
Dan Wright
Tel: (212) 764-6770, Fax: (212) 7645125
 Est. 1961. Response Time: 5/15/04. **Preference.** Style: all styles. **Application.** What to submit: query letter (note theme addressed), submissions returned with SASE. Material must be unoptioned, unpublished, unproduced. How to submit: invitation only.

**Barbara Hogenson Agency, Inc.**
165 West End Ave., #19-C
New York, NY 10023
Barbara Hogenson
Tel: (212) 874-8084 Fax: (212) 362-3011
Est. 1994. Staff: Nicole Verity. Response Time: 2 mos. **Application.** What to submit: query, synopsis, SASE. How to submit: professional recommendation.

**Beacon Artists Agency**
120 E. 56th St., #504
New York, NY 10022
Patricia McLaughlin
Tel: (212) 736-6630
**Preference.** Length: full length plays. Style: all styles. **Application.** What to submit: query letter, synopsis, 30-pg writing sample. How to submit: professional recommendation.

**Judy Boals Inc.**
307 W. 38th St., #812
New York, NY 10018
info@judyboals.com
www.judyboals.com
Agents: Judy Boals. Response Time: 1 mo. **Application.** What to submit: query, SASE. How to submit: professional recommendation.

**Ann Elmo Agency**
60 E. 42nd St.
New York, NY 10165
Letti Lee
Tel: (212) 661-2880, Fax: (212) 661-2883
Staff: Mari Cronin, Letti Lee. Response Time: 2 mos. **Application.** What to submit: query, SASE.

**Epstein, Wyckoff, Corsa, Ross & Associates**
Gary Epstein
Tel: (212) 586-9110

**Eric Glass Ltd.**
25 Ladbroke Crescent
London, England, UK
Tel: 44-20-7229-9500
Fax: 44-20-7229-6220

**Preference.** Length: full length plays. Style: all styles. **Application.** What to submit: synopsis, 30-pg writing sample, submissions returned with SASE. How to submit: professional recommendation.

**Farber Literary Agency Inc.**
14 E. 75th St., #2-E
New York, NY 10021
Ann Farber
Tel: (212) 861-7075, Fax: (212) 861-7076
farberlit@aol.com
www.donaldfarber.com
Est.1990. Staff: Ann Farber, Donald C. Farber, Seth Farber. Response Time: 1 mo. **Preference.** Length: full length plays. **Application.** What to submit: query, synopsis, full script, SASE. Material must be unproduced.

**Fifi Oscard Agency, Inc.**
110 W. 40th St., Fl. 21
New York, NY 10018
Peter Sawyer
Tel: (212) 764-1100, Fax: (212) 840-5019
agency@fifioscard.com
www.fifioscard.com
Est. 1956. Literary Staff: Carolyn French, Carmen LaVia, Kevin McShane, Peter Sawyer.

**Gage Group Inc.**
14724 Ventura Blvd., #505
Sherman Oaks, CA 91403
Jonathan Westover
Tel: (818) 905-3800 Fax: (818) 905-3322
literary-gagegroupla@gmail.com
Est. 1975. Agents: Martin Gage, Olivia Bowe. Response Time: 3 mos. **Application.** What to submit: query, submissions not returned. Material must be unoptioned, unpublished. How to submit: professional recommendation.

**Gersh Agency Inc.**
41 Madison Ave., Fl. 33,
New York, NY 10010
Peter Hagan
Tel: (212) 997-1818, Fax: (212) 391-8459
www.gershagency.com

Agents: John Buzzetti, Seth Glewen, Peter Hagan, Joyce Ketay, Carl Mulert, Sonia Pabley, Phyllis Wender, Scott Yoselow. **Application.** What to submit: query, SASE. How to submit: professional recommendation.

**Graham Agency**
311 W. 43rd St.
New York, NY 10036
Earl Graham
Tel: (212) 489-7730
    **Preference.** Length: full length plays. Style: no adaptation, no translation. **Application.** What to submit: query, SASE. Author must be resident of US.

**GSK Talent (Grant, Savic, Kopaloff)**
6399 Wilshire Blvd., #414
Los Angeles, CA 90048
Tel: (323) 782-1854
contact@gsktalent.com
www.gsktalent.com
    Agents: Susan Grant, Ivana Savic, Don Kopaloff.

**Harden Curtis Associates**
850 7th Ave, #903
New York, NY 10019
Mary Harden
Tel: (212) 977-8502
hcassc@hardencurtis.com
www.hardencurtis.com
    Est. 1995. Contacts: Mary Harden, Scott Ewards, Christina Cox. Response Time: 2 mos. **Preference.** Length: full length plays. Style: all styles. **Application.** What to submit: query. How to submit: professional recommendation.

**International Creative Management (ICM) [UK]**
4-6 Soho Sq., London, England UK
Tel: 44-20-7432-0800
books@icmtalent.com
www.icmtalent.com/lit/lit.html
    Talent & lit agency.

**International Creative Management (ICM) [NY]**
825 8th Ave.
New York, NY 10019
Tel: (212) 556-5600
books@icmtalent.com
www.icmtalent.com
    Talent & lit agency. Staff: Patrick Herold, Buddy Thomas. **Application.** How to submit: invite.

**International Creative Management (ICM) [CA]**
10250 Constellation Blvd.
Los Angeles, CA 90067
Tel: (310) 550-4000
books@icmtalent.com
www.icmtalent.com/lit/lit.html
    Talent & lit agency.

**Kerin-Goldberg Associates**
155 E. 55th St., #5-D,
New York, NY 10022
Charles Kerin
Tel: (212) 838-7373 Fax: (212) 838-0774
kgatalent@nyc.rr.com
    Est. 1989. Staff: Ron Ross, Ellison Goldberg, Chris Nichols. **Application.** What to submit: query, SASE. Material must be unproduced. How to submit: invite.

**The Marton Agency, Inc.**
1 Union Sq. W., #815
New York, NY 10003
Tonda Marton
Tel: (212) 255-1908 Fax: (212) 691-9061
info@martonagency.com
www.martonagency.com
    Staff: Tonda Marton, Anne Reingold. Specializes in brokering foreign-language rights to US theater works. Promotes plays to associates abroad, generally after a production has been mounted in the US.

**William Morris Agency**
1325 6th Ave., New York, NY 10019
Tel: (212) 586-5100
    Staff: Val Day, Peter Franklin, Biff Liff, Roland Scahill, Jack Tantleff, Susan Weaving.

**Paradigm**
19 W. 44th St, #1410
New York, NY 10036
Tel: (212) 391-1112
  Agents: William Craver, Lucy Stille, Jack Tantleff. Response Time: 6 mos. **Application.** What to submit: query, SASE. Material must be unoptioned, unpublished, unproduced. How to submit: professional recommendation.

**Peregrine Whittlesey Agency**
279 Central Park West
New York, NY 10024
Peregrine Whittlesey
Tel: (212) 787-1802 Fax: (212) 787-4985
pwwagy@aol.com
  **Preference.** Length: full length plays. **Application.** What to submit: query, SASE. Material must be unoptioned. How to submit: professional recommendation.

**Robert A. Freedman Dramatic Agency, Inc.**
1501 Broadway, #2310
New York, NY 10036
Marta Praeger
  Est. 1917. Response Time: 4 mos. **Preference.** Length: full length plays. **Application.** What to submit: query, SASE. How to submit: invite.

**Soiree Fair Inc.**
133 Midland Ave., #10
Montclair, NJ 7042
Karen Gunn
Soireefair@yahoo.com
www.soireefair.com
  Est. 1995. **Preference.** Length: full length plays. Style: comedy, drama. Subject: woman, gay/lesbian. **Application.** What to submit: query, synopsis. Author must be resident of US. Material must be unoptioned, unpublished, unproduced. How to submit: professional recommendation.

**Stephen Pevner, Inc.**
382 Lafayette St., Fl. 8
New York, NY 10003
Stephen Pevner
Tel: (212) 674-8403

**Mark Christian Subias Agency**
331 W. 57th St, #462
New York, NY 10019
Mark Christian Subias
marksubias@earthlink.net
  Est. 2002. **Application.** What to submit: query. How to submit: professional recommendation.

**Susan Gurman Agency, LLC**
245 West 99th Street, Suite 24A
New York, NY 10025
Tel: (212) 749-4618
assistant@gurmanagency.com
www.gurmanagency.com
  Est. 1993. Response Time: 1 mo. **Preference.** Length: full length plays and musicals. Subject: All subjects, woman, T.Y.A., writers of color, disabled, gay/lesbian. **Application.** What to submit: Letter and resume only. How to submit: professional recommendation.

**Talent Representatives, Inc.**
307 E. 44th St.
New York, NY 10017
Tel: (212) 752-1835
  **Application.** What to submit: submissions returned with SASE. How to submit: professional recommendation.

**The Bohrman Agency**
8899 Beverly Blvd., #811
Los Angeles, CA 90048
Caren Bohrman
Tel: (310) 550-5444
  Agents: Caren Bohrman. **Preference.** Length: full length plays and musicals. Style: all styles. **Application.** What to submit: query, No phone queries, SASP. How to submit: professional recommendation.

## ATTORNEYS

**Brooks & Distler**
110 E. 59th St., Fl. 23
New York, NY 10022
Marsha Brooks, Esq.
Tel: (212) 486-1400 Fax: (212) 486-2266
www.brookslawyers.com

**Christensen, Glaser, Fink, Jacobs, Weil & Shapiro, LLP**
10250 Constellation Blvd., Fl. 19
Los Angeles, CA 90067
Joan Vento-Hall
Tel: (310) 556-7840 Fax: (310) 553-5336
jvento@chrisglase.com
www.chrisglase.com
    Est. 1988.

**Coblence & Associates**
200 Park Ave. S., #910
New York, NY 10003
Patricia Crown, Esq.
Tel: (212) 593-8389 Fax: (212) 358-9058
pcrown@coblence.com
www.coblence.com
    Est. 1981. Formerly Coblence & Warner.

**Cohen & Grossberg**
770 Lexington Ave.
New York, NY 10065
David Grossberg
Tel: (212) 688-6940
    Est. 1955.

**Cowan, DeBaets, Abrahams & Sheppard LLP**
41 Madison Ave., Fl. 34
New York, NY 10010
Frederick P. Bimbler, Esq.
Tel: (212) 974-7474 Fax: (212) 974-8474
fbimbler@cdas.com; www.cdas.com

**David H. Friedlander, Esq.**
81 Park Dr., Mount Kisco, NY 10549
David H. Friedlander, Esq.
Tel: (914) 241-1277 Fax: (914) 470-2244
david@dfriedlander.com
www.dfriedlander.com

**Dumler & Giroux**
488 Madison Ave., #1703
New York, NY 10022
Leigh A. Giroux, Esq.
Tel: (212) 759-4580 Fax: (212) 751-1839
lgiroux@dumlerandgiroux.com

**Fish & Richardson PC**
225 Franklin St., Boston, MA 02110
Elaine M. Rogers
Tel: (617) 521-7886
elaine.rogers@fr.com
www.fr.com

**Fitelson, Lasky, Aslan, Couture and Garmise**
551 5th Ave., #605
New York, NY 10176
Jerold Couture
Tel: (212) 586-4700 Fax: (212) 949-6746
dramalex@aol.com

**Frankfurt, Kurnit, Klein & Selz**
488 Madison Ave.
New York, NY 10022
S. Jean Ward, Esq.
Tel: (212) 826-5584 Fax: (347) 438-2167
sjward@fkks.com; www.fkks.com

**Franklin, Weinrib, Rudell & Vassallo PC**
488 Madison Ave.
New York, NY 10022
Elliot H. Brown
Tel: (212) 935-5500 Fax: (212) 308-0642
www.fwrv.com

**Graubart. Law Offices of Jeffrey L. Graubart, P.C.**
350 W. Colorado Blvd., #200
Pasadena, CA 91105
Tel: (626) 304-2800 Fax: (626) 304-2807
info@jlgraubart.com
www.lawyers.com/entertainmentlaw
    Est. 1970.

**Jay Julien, Esq.**
1501 Broadway, #1609,
New York, NY 10036
Jay Julien
Tel: (212) 221-7575 Fax: (212) 221-7386

**Kaufmann, Feiner, Yamin, Gildin & Robbins LLP**
777 3rd Ave., New York, NY 10017
Ronald Feiner, Esq.
Tel: (212) 755-3174 Fax: (212) 755-0431
rfeiner@kaufmannfeiner.com

**Law Office of John J. Tormey III, Esq.**
217 East 86th Street, PMB 221
New York, NY 10028
John L. Tormey
Tel: (212) 410-4142 Fax: (212) 410-2380
brightline@att.net
http://www.tormey.org

**Law Offices of Lloyd J. Jassin**
1560 Broadway, #400
New York, NY 10036
Lloyd J. Jassin
Tel: (212) 354-4442 Fax: (212) 840-4124
jassin@copylaw.com
www.copylaw.com
    Est. 1991.

**Lazarus & Harris LLP**
561 7th Ave., Fl. 11
New York, NY 10018
Tel: (212) 302-5252 Fax: (212) 302-8181
www.lazhar.com

**McLaughlin & Stern**
260 Madison Ave.
New York, NY 10016
Alvin Deutsch, Esq.
Tel: (212) 448-1100 Fax: (212) 448-0066
adeutsch@mclaughlinstern.com
www.mclaughlinstern.com
    Est. 1898.

**Paul, Weiss, Rifkind, Wharton & Garrison LLP**
1285 6th Ave., New York, NY 10019
John Breglio, Esq.
Tel: (212) 373-3391 Fax: (212) 373-2092
jbreglio@paulweiss.com
www.paulweiss.com

**Peter S. Cane, Esq.**
410 W. 24th St., New York, NY 10011
Tel: (212) 922-9800
peter@canelaw.com

**Robinson, Brog, Leinwand, Greene, Genovese & Gluck**
1345 6th Ave., New York, NY 10105
Richard M. Ticktin
Tel: (212) 603-6308 Fax: (212) 5815981
    What to submit: query, SASE. How to submit: professional recommendation.

**Sendroff & Baruch, LLP**
1500 Broadway, #2001
New York, NY 10036
Mark D. Sendroff, Esq.
Tel: (212) 840-6400 Fax: (212) 840-6401
msendruff@sendroffbaruch.com
www.sendroffbaruch.com
    Staff: Mark Sendroff, Jason Baruch, Eric S. Goldman.

**Law Office of Susan J. Steiger, Esq.**
60 East 42nd Street, 47th floor
New York, NY 10165
Tel: (212) 880-0865 Fax: (212) 682-1965
    Est. 1982.

**Law Office of Miriam Stern**
303 E. 83rd St., Fl. 20
New York, NY 10028
Miriam Stern, Esq.
Tel: (212) 794-1289
    Attorney represents writers, producers other creative elements involved in producing theater.

**Volunteer Lawyers for the Arts (VLA)**
1 E. 53rd St., Fl. 6
New York, NY 10022
Elena M. Paul, Esq.
Tel: (212) 319-2787 ext. 1
Fax: (212) 752-6575
vlany@vlany.org
www.vlany.org
    Est. 1969. Leading provider of pro bono legal and mediation services, educational programs and publications, and advocacy to the arts community in NYC area. Through public advocacy, VLA frequently acts on issues vitally important to the arts community in NYC and beyond. Fees: based on client's finances. Author must be under certain income ceiling.

## COMMERCIAL PRODUCERS

**Araca Group**
260 W. 44th St., #501
New York, NY 10036
Kirsten Berkman
Tel: (212) 869-0070 Fax: (212) 869-0210
www.araca.com
> Est. 1997. Matthew Rego, Michael Rego and Hank Unger are principals. *Wicked, The Wedding Singer, 'night Mother, The Good Body, Urinetown, Frankie and Johnny in the Clair de Lune, Match, Debbie Does Dallas, The Vagina Monologues, The Laramie Project.* **Application.** What to submit: full script, audio, SASE. How to submit: agent.

**Cameron Mackintosh Inc.**
1650 Broadway, #800
New York, NY 10019
Shidan Majidi
Tel: (212) 921-9290 Fax: (212) 921-9271
www.cameronmackintosh.com
> *Mary Poppins, Les Miserables, The Phantom of the Opera, Oliver!, Oklahoma!, My Fair Lady, The Witches of Eastwick.* **Application.** How to submit: agent.

**Carole Shorenstein Hays Prods. (CSHP)**
95 Fifth Ave, Fl 5,
New York, NY 10003
Duffy Anderson
> Est. 2006.

**Dodger Properties**
311 W. 43rd St., #603
New York, NY 10036
Tel: (212) 575-9710
info@dodger.com; www.dodger.com
> Est. 1978. *Jersey Boys.* **Application.** How to submit: agent.

**Frankel-Baruch-Viertel-Routh Group**
729 7th Ave., Fl. 12
New York, NY 10019
Richard Frankel
www.rfpny.com
> Est. 1985. Principals: Richard Frankel, Tom Viertel, Steven Baruch, Marc Routh. *Young Frankenstein, Hairspray, The Producers, The Fantasticks, Sweeney Todd Tour.*

**Harold Prince**
10 Rockefeller Plaza, #1004
New York, NY 10020

**Jane Harmon Associates**
One Lincoln Plaza, #280
New York, NY 10023
Jane Harmon
Tel: (212) 362-6836 Fax: (212) 362-8572
harmonjane@aol.com
> Est. 1979. Associates: Valentina Fratti, Jill Alexander. Production: drama/comedy Response Time: 4-6 wks. **Consideration.** Opportunity/Award: production. **Preference.** Length: full length plays. Style: no musical. Subject: All subjects. **Application.** What to submit: query, synopsis, SASE. Material must be preferably unoptioned, unpublished. How to submit: agent, professional reccomendation, unsolicited.

**Margery Klain**
2107 Locust St.
Philadelphia, PA 19103
Margery Klain
Tel: (215) 567-1512 Fax: (215) 567-2049
mklain1011@aol.com
> Est. 1985. Staff: Matthew Klein. *A Shanya Maidel, Mountain, Das Barbecu, Broadway Opus.* Response Time: 2 mos. **Preference.** Length: full length plays. **Application.** What to submit: query, SASE. Material must be unoptioned. How to submit: professional recommendation.

**Margo Lion Ltd.**
246 W. 44th St., Fl. 8
New York, NY 10036
Rick Hayashi
Tel: (212) 869-1112 Fax: (212) 730-0381
www.margolionltd.com
   *Hairspray, Caroline, or Change, The Cryptogram, Angels in America, Jelly's Last Jam, The Wedding Singer.* Response Time: 1 yr. **Preference.** Length: full length plays and musicals. **Application.** What to submit: synopsis,10-pg sample, audio, SASE. How to submit: agent (prefer electronically to be green).

**Nederlander Organization**
1450 Broadway, Fl. 6
New York, NY 10018
Charlene Nederlander
Tel: (212) 840-5577
www.nederlander.com
   Est. 1912. **Application.** How to submit: agent.

**New Time Productions**
311 W. 43rd St., #305
New York, NY 10036
Lauren Doll
Tel: (212) 265-9659 Fax: (212) 956-0498
www.newtimeproductions.com
   Est. 1998. Equity Broadway, Off-Broadway, MSUA., *Radio Golf, Faith Healer, Brooklyn, Squonk, Electra, On the Waterfront.* **Preference.** Length: full length plays. **Application.** What to submit: query, SASE. How to submit: agent.

**Rick Hobard**
234 W. 44th St., New York, NY 10036

**Rodger Hess Productions Inc.**
1501 Broadway
New York, NY 10036
Tel: (212) 719-2233
Est. 1973.

**Shubert Organization**
234 W. 44th St., New York, NY 10036
D.S. Moynihan
www.shubertorganization.com
   Est. 1900. *Amour, The Blue Room, Closer, Amy's View, The Ride Down Mt. Morgan, Dirty Blonde, Dance of Death.* **Application.** How to submit: agent.

**Stewart F. Lane**
200 W. 57th St., #801
New York, NY 10019
Stewart F. Lane
www.mrbroadway.com
   Formerly Stellar Productions.

**Susan Gallin Productions Inc.**
1501 Broadway, #1614
New York, NY 10036
Susan Gallin
Tel: (212) 840-1725 Fax: (212) 7684614
sgallin@aol.com
   *Spamalot, Woman Before a Glass, The Retreat From Moscow, Man of La Mancha, Hedda Gabler, The Shape of Things, Fully Committed, Burn This, The Rothschilds, Cowgirls, Other People's Money, From the Mississippi Delta, Angels in America, Stomp, The Cryptogram* (London). **Application.** What to submit: full script. Material must be unoptioned, unproduced. How to submit: agent.

**Weissberger Theater Group**
240 W. 44th St.
New York, NY 10036
Jay Harris
Fax: (212) 644-3343
jayharrisnyc@aol.com
   Est. 1992. Want scripts with plot line and edge. *Dirty Rotten Scoundrels, Never Gonna Dance, Side Man, Down the Road, Freefall, Dates and Nuts, Where the Truth Lies, Enter the Guardsman, Tamicanfly.* Production: cast limit 7. Response Time: 1 mo query, 2 mos script. **Preference.** Length: full length plays. Style: comedy, drama. **Application.** What to submit: query, synopsis. Material must be unoptioned, unproduced.

## PUBLISHERS

**Alaska Quarterly Review (AQR)**
University of Alaska Anchorage
3211 Providence Dr.
Anchorage, AK 99508
Ronald Spatz
Tel: (907) 786-6916 Fax: (907) 786-6916
ayaur@uaa.alaska.edu
www.uaa.alaska.edu/aqr
   Est. 1982. Fiction, short plays, poetry and literary nonfiction in traditional and experimental styles. Frequency: semiannual. Response Time: 6 mos. **Consideration.** Opportunity/Award: 1 contributors copy and a 1-year subscription. **Preference.** Style: open to all styles. **Application.** What to submit: application, full script.

**Alfreda's Reader's Theater**
Box 480443, Denver, CO 80248
A. Doyle
www.alfredasreaderstheater.com
   Est. 1999. **Application.** What to submit: SASE. Material must be under copyright. How to submit: invite.

**Broadway Play Publishing Inc. (BPPI)**
56 E. 81st St.
New York, NY 10028
Christopher Gould
Tel: (212) 772-8334 Fax: (212) 772-8358
sara@broadwayplaypubl.com
www.broadwayplaypubl.com
   Est. 1982. Response Time: 2 mos query, 4 mos script. **Consideration.** Opportunity/Award: 10% book, 80% amateur, 90% stock royalty; 10 complimentary copies. **Preference.** Length: full length plays. Style: comedy, drama. **Application.** What to submit: query. Material must be produced, original.

**Anchorage Press Plays Inc.**
617 Baxter Ave.
Louisville, KY 40204-1315
Marilee Hebert Miller
Tel: (502) 583-2288 Fax: (502) 583-2288
applays@bellsouth.net; www.applays.com
   Est. 1935. Performances licensed. Educational, professional and amateur venues. Response Time: 6-9 mos. **Consideration.** Opportunity/Award: royalty. **Preference.** Length: full length plays and musicals. Style: Various -original, adaptation, musical, translation. Subject: T.Y.A., writers of color. **Application.** What to submit: full play script following criteria in submission guidelines from website. (No screenplays.) Material must be for child, youth, teen, or young adult audience. How to submit: See submission guidelines on website.

**Arte Publico Press**
452 Cullen Performance Hall
Houston, TX 77204
Nicolas Kanellos
Tel: (713) 743-2988 Fax: (713) 743-2847
www.arte.uh.edu
   Est. 1979. Contemporary and recovered lit by US Hispanic authors. Response Time: 6 mos. **Consideration.** Opportunity/Award: royalty, copies. **Preference.** Length: full length plays. Subject: writers of color. **Application.** What to submit: full script, SASE. Material must be unpublished, in English or Spanish.

**Asian American Writers Workshop**
16 W. 32nd St. #10-A
New York, NY 10001
Quang Bao
Tel: (212) 494-0061 Fax: (212) 494-0062
desk@aaww.org
www.aaww.org
   Est. 1991. Semiannual paperback incl. short fiction, poems, essays, stage scripts, translations and artwork. Frequency: semiannual. Response Time: 8 mos. **Consideration.** Opportunity/Award: 2 copies. **Application.** What to submit: full script (4 copies).

### Asian Theatre Journal
2840 Kolowalu St., Honolulu, HI 96822
Tel: (808) 956-8255 Fax: (800) 650-7811
uhpjourn@hawaii.edu
www.uhpress.hawaii.edu/journals
   Dedicated to performing arts of Asia, traditional and modern, incl. original and translated plays. **Preference.** Subject: writers of color. **Application.** What to submit: query, submissions not returned.

### Audience
303 Park Ave. S., #1440
New York, NY 10010
M. Stefan Strozier
Tel: (646) 620-7406
stozier@worldaudience.org
www.worldaudience.org
   Quarterly literary journal of short stories, poetry, plays, interviews, essays, and more. Frequency: quarterly. Response Time: 2-4 wks. **Consideration.** Opportunity/Award: royalties. **Preference.** Style: all styles. **Application.** What to submit: query, synopsis, 10-page sample. How to submit: unsolicited, professional recommendation, agent.

### Baker's Plays
45 W. 25th Street, New York, NY 10010
Roxane Heinze-Bradshaw
Tel: (212) 255-8085 Fax: (212) 627-7753
publications@bakersplays.com
www.bakersplays.com
   Response Time: 8 mos. **Consideration.** Opportunity/Award: royalty. **Preference.** Length: full length plays and musicals. Subject: T.Y.A. **Application.** What to submit: full script, audio, resume, SASE. Material must be produced. How to submit: web submissions.

### Big Dog Publishing
Box 1400, Tallevast, FL 34270
Dawn Remsing
info@bigdogplays.com
www.bigdogplays.com
   Est. 2005. Plays for family and school audiences (K-12). Publishes 25-40 plays/year. Response Time: 2-3 mos. **Consideration.** Opportunity/Award: 50% royalty, 10% book, complimentary copies (50% discount on additional copies). **Preference.** Length: full length plays. **Application.** What to submit: send entire script, synopsis, cast breakdown, cover letter, production history, music, SASE, no email submissions accepted. Material must be unpublished, prefers produced works.

### Brooklyn Publishers
1841 Cord St., Odessa, TX 79762
David LeMaster
Tel: (432) 550-5532 Fax: (432) 368-0340
info@brookpub.com
www.brookpub.com
   Est. 1996. Production: performers grades 6-12. Response Time: 2 mos. **Consideration.** Opportunity/Award: royalty, 10 copies. **Preference.** Length: full length plays. Style: adaptation, comedy, drama, mystery. Subject: T.Y.A. **Application.** What to submit: full script.

### Callaloo
4212 TAMU, College Station, TX 77843
Charles H. Rowell
Tel: (979) 458-3108 Fax: (979) 4583275
callaloo@tamu.edu
www.callaloo.tamu.edu
   Quarterly journal by/about African-Americans and the African Diaspora, incl. original, unpublished essays, interviews, short fiction, poetry, drama, and visual art. Frequency: quarterly. Response Time: 6 mos. **Consideration.** Opportunity/Award: complimentary copies. **Preference.** Style: no musical. **Application.** What to submit: query, full script (3 copies), SASE.

### Capilano Review TCR
2055 Purcell Way, N.
Vancouver, BC Canada
Carol Hamshaw
Tel: (604) 984-1712
contact@thecapilanoreview.ca
www.thecapilanoreview.ca
   Est. 1972. Response Time: 4 mos. **Consideration.** Opportunity/Award:

publication, pay. **Preference.** Style: drama. **Application.** What to submit: SASE (Canadian postage). Material must be unpublished.

**Contemporary Drama Service**
885 Elkton Dr.,
Colorado Springs, CO 80907
Arthur Zapel
Fax: (719) 594-9916
merpcds@aol.com
www.contemporarydrama.com
 Est. 1970. School, college, church and amateur venues. Production: age 12-30, cast limit 20. Response Time: 1 mo. **Consideration.** Opportunity/Award: 10% royalty. **Preference.** Style: no translation. Subject: woman, T.Y.A., writers of color. **Application.** What to submit: query, SASE. Author must be age 16 or older, resident or citizen of US. Material must be unoptioned, unpublished, unproduced.

**Direct Plays**
NuComm Marketing
80 King Street, 3rd Floor
St. Catharines, ON C2R-7G1 Canada
Tel: (877) 305-1569
directplays@nucomm.net
www.directplays.com

**Drama Source**
1588 E. 361 N., St. Anthony, ID 83445
Daris Howard
Tel: (208) 6244726
info@dramasource.com
www.dramasource.com
 Est. 1997. Response Time: 3 mos. **Consideration.** Opportunity/Award: 70% royalty, 10% sales, 50% video. **Application.** What to submit: query, synopsis, audio. How to submit: email.

**Dramatic Publishing Company**
311 Washington St., #129
Woodstock, IL 60098
Linda Habjan
Tel: (800) 448-7469 Fax: (800) 3345302
plays@dramaticpublishing.com
www.dramaticpublishing.com
 Est. 1885. Performances licensed, all venues but 1st Class. Response Time: 8 mos. **Application.** What to submit: full script, SASE.

**Dramatics Magazine**
2343 Auburn Ave., Cincinnati, OH 45219
Don Corathers
Tel: (513) 421-3900 Fax: (513) 4217077
dcorathers@edta.org
www.edta.org/publications/dramatics.asp
 Est. 1929. Natl. monthly magazine for HS theater students & teachers, printing 7 one-acts and full-lengths/yr. Response Time: 5 mos. **Consideration.** Opportunity/Award: $100-$500 honorarium,5 copies. **Preference.** Length: full length plays. Style: comedy, drama. Subject: All subjects, woman, T.Y.A., writers of color, disabled, gay/lesbian. **Application.** What to submit: full script. Material must be unpublished. How to submit: email or hard copy.

**Dramatists Play Service, Inc.**
440 Park Ave. S., New York, NY 10016
Michael Q. Fellmeth
Tel: (212) 683-8960 Fax: (212) 213-1539
fellmeth@dramatists.com
www.dramatists.com
 Performances licensed. All venues except commercial. Response Time: 6 mos. **Consideration.** Opportunity/Award: 10% book, 80% amateur, 90% stock; 10 copies. **Preference.** Length: full length musicals. Style: comedy, drama, musical. **Application.** What to submit: query, synopsis.

**Eldridge Publishing Company Inc.**
Box 14367, Tallahassee, FL 32317
Nancy S. Vorhis
Tel: (850) 385-2463 Fax: (850) 385-2463
editorial@histage.com
www.histage.com
 Est. 1906. Performances licensed, all venues. Response Time: 2 mos. **Consideration.** Opportunity/Award: 10% book, 50% amateur/educational. **Preference.** Length: full length plays and musicals. Subject: All subjects, T.Y.A. **Application.** What to submit: query, full script, audio, SASE. Material must be emailed (MS Word, PDF) to newworks@histage.com.

**Empire Publishing Service**
Box 1344, Studio City, CA 91614
www.ppeps.com
> Est. 1960. Publishes performing arts books, incl. sheet music. Distributes for Players Press, Java Publications, Arte Publico Press, D-Books Intl., and others. Also distributes performing arts cassettes through direct mail and trade sales. **Consideration.** Opportunity/Award: royalty. **Application.** What to submit: query, SASE. Material must be produced.

**Freelance Press**
Box 548, Dover, MA 2030
Narcissa Campion
Tel: (508) 785-8250 Fax: (508) 785-8291
www.freelancepress.org
> Est. 1979 Response Time: 3 mos. **Consideration.** Opportunity/Award: 10% sales, 70% performance royalty. **Preference.** Style: musical. Subject: T.Y.A. **Application.** Material must be unpublished.

**Green Integer**
6022 Wilshire Blvd., #200-A
Los Angeles, CA 90036
Per Bregne
Tel: (323) 857-1115
info@greeninteger.com
www.greeninteger.com
> Works published to date incl. essays, interviews, poems, plays, speeches and novels. Response Time: 1 mo. **Consideration.** Opportunity/Award: royalty, 10 copies. **Preference.** Length: full length plays. Style: comedy, drama, translation. **Application.** What to submit: query. Material must be unpublished.

**Gumbo Media**
Box 480443, Denver, CO 80248
A. Doyle
www.gumbomedia.com
> Markets comedy scripts, e-books, stories, lyrics, film, etc. Licenses lyrics, scripts, music, content, stories, educational products, etc.

**HaveScripts.com**
204 Oakengate Turn
Virginia Beach, VA 23462
Jean Klein
www.havescripts.com
> Est. 2003. Online catalog of new plays. Response Time: 1 mo. **Preference.** Length: full length plays. **Application.** What to submit: query, submissions not returned. Material must be unpublished.

**Kalliope: A Journal of Women's Literature & Art**
11901 Beach Blvd.
Jacksonville, FL 32246
Margaret Clark
www.fccj.org/kalliope
> Kalliope publishes poetry, short fiction, interviews, reviews, and visual art by women. Copyright reverts to the author upon request. Frequency: semiannual. Response Time: 6 mos. **Consideration.** Opportunity/Award: 2 copies. **Application.** What to submit: query, full script, SASE. Author must be female. Material must be unpublished.

**Kenyon Review**
Walton House, 104 College Dr.
Gambier, OH 43022
Daniel Kramer
Tel: (740) 427-5208 Fax: (740) 427-5417
kenyonreview@kenyon.edu
www.kenyonreview.org
> Est. 1939. Response Time: 4 mos. **Consideration.** Opportunity/Award: cash payment; 2 copies. **Preference.** Style: comedy, drama. **Application.** What to submit: query. Material must be unpublished. How to submit: online. Deadline: 1/31/2009.

**Lazy Bee Scripts**
2 Wood Rd.
Ashurst, Southhampton, SO40 7BD UK
Stuart Ardern
www.lazybeescripts.co/uk
> Response Time: query response within 7 days more information at www.lazybeescripts.co.uk/Publishing.

**Consideration.** Opportunity/Award: royalties. **Preference.** Length: full length plays and musicals. Style: all styles. **Application.** What to submit: query by e-mail or SASE overseas postage. Material must be unpublished. How to submit: unsolicited query.

**Lillenas Publishing Company**
Box 419527
Kansas City, MO 64141
Kimberly R. Messer
Tel: (816) 931-1900 Fax: (816) 412-8390
drama@lillenas.com
www.lillenasdrama.com
Perfs licensed (school, church, dinner & community). Response Time: 4 mos. **Consideration.** Opportunity/Award: outright purchase or royalty. **Preference.** Length: full length plays. Style: comedy, drama. **Application.** What to submit: full script, SASE. Material must be unpublished, produced.

**Limelight Scripts**
152 Southey Hill, Sheffield, England
Dewey Willis, Jacqueline Willis
www.limelightscripts.co.uk
Est. 2005. Response Time: 24 hours. **Preference.** Style: comedy, drama, musical. **Application.** What to submit: query, synopsis, SASE. Author must be over 18. How to submit: invitation only, make inquiry.

**Meriwether Publishing Ltd.**
885 Elkton Drive
Colorado Springs, CO 80907
Arthur L. Zapel
Tel: (800) 937-5297 Fax: (888) 594-4436
editor@meriwether.com
www.meriwetherpublishing.com
**Preference.** Length: full length plays. Style: Plays and Books . Subject: All subjects, T.Y.A. **Application.** What to submit: theatre arts books written by drama educators and professionals, plus DVDs, CDs, and videos for classroom use. How to submit: Mail with SASE.

**Moose Hide Books**
684 Walls Rd.
Sault Ste. Marie, ON Canada
Richard Mousseau
Tel: (705) 779-3331 Fax: (707) 7793331
rmousseau@moosehidebooks.com
www.moosehidebooks.com
Response Time: 1 month. **Application.** What to submit: query, SASE. How to submit: unsolicited.

**Music Theatre International (MTI)**
421 W. 54th St.,
New York, NY 10019
Russell Ochocki
Tel: (212) 541-4684
www.mtishows.com
Est. 1952. Performances licensed, all venues. MTI is a secondary licensing agency and prefers musicals that have been produced. **Preference.** Length: full length musicals. Style: musical. **Application.** What to submit: query. Material must be produced.

**New Plays Inc.**
Box 5074, Charlottesville, VA 22905
Patricia Forrest
Tel: (434) 823-7555
pat@newplaysforchildren.com
www.newplaysforchildren.com
Est. 1963. Publishing house representing plays for young audiences. Response Time: 2 mos. **Consideration.** Opportunity/Award: 10% sales, 50% performance royalty. **Preference.** Subject: T.Y.A. **Application.** What to submit: query, full script, SASE. Material must be produced.

**Original Works Publishing**
4611½ Ambrose Ave.
Los Angeles, CA 90027
Jason Aaron Goldberg
info@originalworksonline.com
www.originalworksonline.com
Est. 2000. Response Time: 1-2 mos. **Consideration.** Opportunity/Award: 80% production royalty, 15% sales; 2 copies, wholesale discounts. **Preference.** Length: full length plays and musicals. Style: comedy, drama,

musical, truly original works. Subject: woman, writers of color, disabled, gay/lesbian. **Application.** What to submit: Full length, one act, ten minute collections, monologues/one-person shows, musicals. Author must be over 18. Material must be produced. How to submit: Visit website for specific guidelines.

**PAJ: A Journal of Performance and Art**
Box 532, Village Sta.
New York, NY 10014
Bonnie Marranca
Tel: (212) 243-3885 Fax: (212) 243-2885
pajpub@mac.com
www.mitpress.mit.edu/paj
Est. 1976. Response Time: 2 mos. query, 2 mos script. **Preference.** Style: plays by American authors; plays in translation. **Application.** What to submit: query, synopsis.

**Norman Maine Publishing**
Box 1400, Tallevast, FL 34270
Dawn Remsing
info@normanmaineplays.com
www.normanmaineplays.com
Est. 2005. Plays for community, professional, and university theatre. Response Time: 2-3 mos. **Consideration.** Opportunity/Award: 50% royalty, 10% book, complimentary copies (50% discount on additional copies). **Preference.** Length: full length plays. **Application.** What to submit: full script, synopsis, cast breakdown, cover letter, production history, music, SASE, no email submissions accepted. Material must be unpublished, prefers produced and/or award-winning works.

**Playscripts, Inc.**
325 W. 38th St, #305
New York, NY 10018
Tel: (866) 639-7529
submissions@playscripts.com
www.playscripts.com
Est. 1998. Acting editions sold and performances licensed to amateur/professional venues worldwide. **Preference.** Style: no musical.

**Application.** Material must be unpublished by another exclusive publisher. How to submit: see website for latest submission preferences and guidelines; electronic submissions preferred.

**Players Press Inc.**
Box 1132, Studio City, CA 91614
Robert W. Gordon
Tel: (818) 789-4980
www.ppes.com
Est. 1960. Response Time: 2 wks query, 6 mos script. **Consideration.** Opportunity/Award: royalties. **Preference.** Style: all styles. **Application.** What to submit: query, SASE. Material must be unpublished, produced.

**Poems & Plays**
MTSU English Dept.
Murfreesboro, TN 37132
Gaylord Brewer
Tel: (615) 898-2712
gbrewer@mtsu.edu
www.mtsu.edu/~english2/Journals/poemsandplays/index.html
Est. 1993. Frequency: annual Response Time: 3 mos. **Consideration.** Opportunity/Award: 1 copy. **Application.** What to submit: full script, SASE. Material must be unpublished. Deadline: 11/30/2009.

**Popular Play Service**
Box 3365, Bluffton, SC 29910
Tel: (843) 705-7981
popplays@hargray.com
www.popplays.com
Performances licensed. All venues, particularly community. **Consideration.** Opportunity/Award: feedback. **Preference.** Length: full length plays. Style: comedy, farce. **Application.** What to submit: query letter (note theme addressed), synopsis, cast 26 scene list, SASE. Material must be unoptioned, unpublished, unproduced, still in development. How to submit: professional recommendation.

## Career Development Professionals : Publishers

**Prism International**
Buchanan E462, 1866 Main Mall
Vancouver, BC Canada
Crystal Sikma
Tel: (604) 822-2514 Fax: (604) 822-3616
prismpoetry@gmail.com
www.prism.arts.ubc.ca
Est. 1959 Frequency: quarterly Response Time: 6 mos, email. **Consideration.** Opportunity/Award: $20/printed pg. **Application.** What to submit: query, full script, resume, SASE (Canadian). Material must be unpublished. How to submit: no email submissions.

**Resource Publications, Inc.**
160 E. Virginia St., #290
San Jose, CA 95112
Wiliam Burns
Tel: (408) 286-8505 Fax: (408) 287-8748
editor@rpinet.com
www.resourcepublications.com
Response Time: 2 mos. Consideration. Opportunity/Award: royalty. **Application.** What to submit: full script.

**Samuel French Inc.**
45 W. 25th St., New York, NY 10010
Roxane Heinze Bradshaw
Tel: (212) 206-8990 Fax: (212) 206-1429
publications@samuelfrench.com
www.samuelfrench.com
Est. 1830. Performances licensed for amateur, stock, professional and foreign venues in all media. Response Time: 2 mos. **Consideration.** Opportunity/Award: 10% sales, performance royalty. **Preference.** Subject: All subjects. **Application.** What to submit: Query Letter & 10-page sample, SASE.

**Seltaeb Music Pty. Ltd.**
P.O. Box 1078
Miranda NSW 2228, Sydney, Australia
Tel: (011 61) 418 229 241
Fax: (011 61) 2 9589 3272
seltaeb@bigpond.com
www.seltaeb.com.au
Australian-based publisher of plays and musicals.

**Sinister Wisdom Journal**
Box 1180, Sebastopol, CA 95473
Fran Day
fran@sonic.net
www.sinisterwisdom.org
Est. 1976. Lesbian-feminist triannual literary journal. Response Time: 6 mos. **Consideration.** Opportunity/Award: 2 copies. **Preference.** Style: drama. Subject: gay/lesbian. **Application.** What to submit: synopsis, SASE. Author must be age 21 or older. Material must be unoptioned, unproduced.

**Slavic and East European Performance**
CUNY Graduate Center, 365 5th Ave.
New York, NY 10016
Daniel Gerould
Tel: (212) 817-1866
seep@gc.cuny.edu
www.gc.cuny.edu
**Application.** Material must be unpublished. How to submit: unsolicited.

**Smith and Kraus**
Box 127, Lyme, NH 3768
Marisa Smith
Tel: (603) 643-6431 Fax: (603) 643-1831
sandk@sover.net
www.smithkraus.com
Response Time: 3 wks query; 4 mos script. **Consideration.** Opportunity/Award: payment or royalty. **Preference.** Length: full length plays. Style: no musical. Subject: T.Y.A. **Application.** What to submit: query, synopsis.

**Speert Publishing**
New York, NY
Eleanore Speert
Tel: (212) 979-7656
espeert@speertpublishing.com
www.speertpublishing.com
Self-publishing services for acting editions of original plays. Response Time: 1 wk. **Preference.** Length: full length plays. Style: no musical. **Application.** What to submit: query. How to submit: email.

**Story Time Stories That Rhyme**
Box 416, Denver, CO 80201
A. Doyle
Tel: (303) 575-5676
mail@storytimestoriesthatrhyme.net
www.storytimestoriesthatrhyme.net
Est. 1989. Educational partnership with literacy, entertainment, storytelling, bibliotherapy and poetry therapy. **Preference.** Subject: T.Y.A. **Application.** What to submit: query.

**Tams-Witmark Music Library Inc.**
560 Lexington Ave.
New York, NY 10022
Tel: (212) 688-2525 Fax: (212) 688-3232
info@tamswitmark.com
www.tams-witmark.com
Classic broadway musicals for stage performance around the world.

**Theatre Communications Group (TCG)**
520 8th Ave., Fl. 24
New York, NY 10018
Terence Nemeth
Tel: (212) 609-5900 ext. 239
Fax: (212) 609-5901
tnemeth@tcg.org
www.tcg.org
**Consideration.** Opportunity/Award: 7% 10% royalty.

**Theater Magazine**
Box 208244, New Haven, CT 6520
Tom Sellar
www.theatermagazine.org
Est. 1968. Triquarterly journal of criticism, reports, interviews and plays. Response Time: 6 mos. **Preference.** Length: full length plays. **Application.** What to submit: query. Material must be unpublished.

**Theatrefolk**
P.O. Box 1064
Crystal Beach, ON Canada
Craig Mason
Tel: (866) 245-9138 Fax: (877) 245-9138
tfolk@theatrefolk.com
www.theatrefolk.com
We publish plays specifically for student performers Production: simple. Response Time: 6-8 wks. **Consideration.** Opportunity/Award: royalties. **Preference.** Length: full length plays and musicals. Style: all styles. Subject: T.Y.A. **Application.** What to submit: full script. Material must be for student performers. How to submit: unsolicited.

**TheatreForum**
9500 Gilman Dr., 0344
La Jolla, CA 92093
Adele Edling Shank
Fax: (858) 534-1080
ashank@ucsd.edu
www.theatreforum.org
Editors: Jim Carmody, John Rouse, Adele Edling Shank, Theodore Shank. Plays must have been professionally produced. **Consideration.** Opportunity/Award: $200, 10 copies. **Preference.** Length: full length plays. Style: adventuresome. **Application.** What to submit: query with professional recommendation, submissions not returned query, submissions not returned. Material must be produced professionally. How to submit: electronically.

**Theatrical Rights Worldwide**
1359 Broadway, #914
New York, NY 10018
Steve Spiegel
Tel: (866) 378-9758 Fax: (212) 643-1322
licensing@theatricalrights.com
www.theatricalrights.com
Est. 2006. Staff: Steve Spiegel (Pres/CEO). Response Time: 3-6 mos. **Consideration.** Opportunity/Award: royalties. **Preference.** Length: full length musicals. Style: musical. **Application.** What to submit: query, full script, audio. Material must be unpublished. How to submit: professional recommendation, agent.

# Career Development Opportunities

## COLONIES AND RESIDENCIES

**Alden B. Dow Creativity Center**
4000 Whiting Dr.
Midland, MI 48640
Grover B. Procter Jr.
Tel: (989) 837-4478 Fax: (989) 837-4468
creativity@northwood.edu
www.northwood.edu/abd
  Residency of 10 wks (Jun-Aug) on campus. **Assistance:** $750 stipend,$500 travel,$1,750 per diem limit. Frequency: annual. **Application.** What to submit: application, sample, resume, SASE. Submission application fee: $10. Deadline: 12/31/2009.

**Altos de Chavon**
66 5th Ave., #604-A
New York, NY 10011
Carmen Lorente
Tel: (212) 229-5370 Fax: (212) 229-8988
altos@earthlink.net
www.altosdechavon.com
  Est. 1981. 3-mo residencies in La Romana, Dominican Rep, for visual artists, writers, musicians, and architects.

**Artward Bound Residency Program**
161 6th Ave., Fl. 14
New York, NY 10013
Patricia Burgess
Tel: (212) 691-6969 ext. 14
Fax: (212) 255-2053
patricia@thefield.org
www.thefield.org
  Residencies of 10-14 days (Jun-Sep) at rural facilities outside NYC. Fees: free ($100 refundable deposit) **Assistance:** room/board, travel Response Time: 1 mo ; Applications posted at www.thefield.org 2-3 months prior to deadline. **Preference.** Style: performing, text-based performance. **Application.** What to submit: application. Author must be resident of NYC area, 3-yr professional.

**Atlantic Center for the Arts**
1414 Art Center Ave.
New Smyrna Beach, FL 32168
James Frost
Tel: (386) 427-6975 Fax: (386) 427-5669
program@atlanticcenterforthearts.org
www.atlanticcenterforthearts.org
  Est. 1982. Residencies of 3 wks with master artists on FL's east coast. Fees: $25 application,$850 program **Assistance:** $800 limit stipend,$800 limit room/board. **Application.** What to submit: application, SASE. Submission application fee: $25.

**Blue Mountain Center**
Box 109, Blue Mt. Lake, NY 12812
Ben Strader
Tel: (518) 352-7391
bmc@bluemountaincenter.org
www.bluemountaincenter.org
  Residencies of 4 wks (Jun-Oct) in Adirondack Mts. Workspace. **Application.** What to submit: query, application, 30-pg sample, bio. Submission application fee: 20. Deadline: 2/1/2009.

**Byrdcliffe Arts Colony Artist-in-Residence (AIR)**
34 Tinker St.
Woodstock, NY 12498
Katherine Burger
Tel: (845) 679-2079 Fax: (845) 679-4529
wguild@ulster.net
www.woodstockguild.org

Est. 1980. Located in the Catskill Mountains, Woodstock, NY USA. Some use of historic Byrdcliffe Theater possible. There are four, 4-week sessions per season. Cost $300. Residents provide own food. **Consideration.** Opportunity/Award: The Handel Fellowship, awarded to one playwright per year. A free residency plus a $1000 stipend. **Application.** What to submit: application, SASE. How to submit: Download an application from our website. Work sample, work plan, CV, fee, and names of two recommendors. Submission application fee: $35. Deadline: 3/1/2009.

**Camargo Foundation**
1 ave Jermini, Cassis, 13260 France
Selig Leon
Tel: 011-334-420-1157
Fax: 011-334-420-3657
apply@camargofoundation.org
www.camargofoundation.org
Interdisciplinary residency program. Fellows are provided with accommodation on campus and a stipend of $2,500. Residencies are one semester (either early-September to mid-December or mid-January to the end of May). **Application.** What to submit: Online application form, resumé, 3 references, a 1000 word Project description, up to 3 work samples, totalling no more than 30 pages. Times New Roman, 12-point font. Work sample from proposed work preferred. Material must be specific creative project. How to submit: online. Deadline: 1/12/2009.

**Casa Karina**
casakarina@gmail.com
Fees include accommodations for twod. Weekly rates Sat. -Sat. May-November 1, 2008 $700.00. December 13 -January 3, 2009 $1,100. **Application.** Submission application fee: $700.

**Centrum Creative Residencies Program**
Box 1158, Port Townsend, WA 98368
Lisa Werner
Tel: (360) 385-3102 ext. 128
Fax: (360) 385-2470
lisa@centrum.org;
www.centrum.org
Est. 1980. Fee of $275/week includes private housing with full kitchen. Successful applicants submit 20% deposit to confirm residency dates. **Preference.** Style: New work by individuals or collaborative groups. **Application.** What to submit: Proposal of the new work you will be focused on, resume/curriculum vita application, sample, SASE. How to submit: Hard copy or by email.

**Djerassi Resident Artists Program**
2325 Bear Gulch Rd.
Woodside, CA 94062
Judy Freeland
Tel: (650) 747-1250
drap@djerassi.org
www.djerassi.org
Est. 1979. 4-5 wk residence, Mar-Nov, for writers and artists on 580-acre ranch nr San Francisco. **Application.** What to submit: application, full script, SASE. Submission application fee: $30. Deadline: 2/15/2009.

**Edward Albee Foundation**
14 Harrison St., New York, NY 10013
Jakob Holder
Tel: (212) 226-2020 Fax: (212) 226-5551
info@albeefoundation.org
www.albeefoundation.org
Est. 1966. Residencies of 1 mo (Jun-Sep) in Montauk, NY, for writers and composers. Frequency: annual. **Application.** What to submit: application, full script, SASE. Deadline: 3/1/2009.

**Envision Retreat**
520 8th Ave., #308, New York, NY 10018
Jean Wagner
Tel: (212) 268-3717 Fax: (212) 268-5462
vandv@vandv.org
www.vandv.org

Projects initiated by women in summer workshop development on Bard Coll. campus. Fees: $15 reading. **Application.** What to submit: query,1-pg synopsis, full script (2 copies), resume. Deadline: 3/31/2009.

**Gell Center of the Finger Lakes**
740 University Ave.
Rochester, NY 14607
Kathy Pottetti
Tel: (585) 473-2590 ext. 103
Fax: (585) 442-9333
Kathyp@wab.org
www.wab.org
Fees: $50/night. **Application.** What to submit: sample.

**Hall Farm Center for Arts and Education**
392 Hall Dr., Townshend, VT 5353
Philip Schoolman
Tel: (802) 365-4483
info@hallfarm.org
www.hallfarm.org
  Deadline: check website after 10/25/08. Est. 1999. Up to 4-wk residency in Jun-Jul or Aug-Sep. Fees: $20 application. **Assistance:** room/board. Frequency: annual Response Time: 2 mos. **Application.** What to submit: application,30-pg sample (4 copies), SASE. Author must be age 18 or older. Deadline: 2/1/2009.

**Hambidge Center**
Box 339, Rabun Gap, GA 30568
Bob Thomas
Tel: (706) 746-5718 Fax: (706) 746-9933
center@hambidge.org
www.hambidge.org
  Deadlines: 1/15 for May-Aug 09, 4/15 for Sep-Dec 09, 9/15 for Feb-Apr 2010. Residencies of 2-8 wks (Feb-Dec) on 600 acres in Blue Ridge Mts. Fees: $30 application,$150/wk Frequency: annual. **Application.** What to submit: application (pdf on web), 30-pg sample (3 copies), audio, resume, SASE .

**Hawthornden Castle International Retreat for Writers**
Hawthornden Castle, Lasswade, Scotland
Daniel Farrell
Tel: 44-131-440-2180
  Est. 1982. Residencies of 4 wks (Feb-Jul, Sep-Dec). **Assistance:** room/board Frequency: annual. **Application.** What to submit: application, 30-pg sample. Author must be produced or published. Deadline: 9/30/2009.

**Headlands Center for the Arts**
944 Fort Barry, Sausalito, CA 94965
Holly Blake
Tel: (415) 331-2787 ext. 24
info@headlands.org
www.headlands.org
  Est. 1987. **Assistance:** grant or stipend, room and board, travel Frequency: 30 residencies per year, 1-3 mos Response Time: 4-5 mos. **Application.** What to submit: application, SASE. How to submit: unsolicited. Deadline: 6/2/2009.

**Hedgebrook**
2197 Millman Rd., Langley, WA 98260
Amy Wheeler
Tel: (360) 321-4786 Fax: (360) 321-2171
www.hedgebrook.org
  Est. 1988. Residencies of 2 wks-2 mos in 48-acre retreat on Whidbey Island. **Assistance:** travel, stipend (low-income women w/o college degree or older than 55) Frequency: annual. **Application.** What to submit: application. Author must be female. Submission application fee: 15. Deadline: 10/15/2009.

**Helene Wurlitzer Foundation of New Mexico**
P.O. Box 1891, Taos, NM 87571
Michael Knight
Tel: (505) 758-2413 Fax: (505) 758-2559
HWF@taosnet.com
www.artistcommunities.org/wurlitzer.html
  Est. 1956. Residences of 3 mos (Jan-Nov) for visual artists, writers and composers. **Application.** What to submit: application and materials.

Material must be as requested on application -no exceptions. How to submit: send SASE in fall for application, request application via e-mail or download from website. Send SASE in fall for application. Deadline: 1/18/2009.

**William Inge Center for the Arts**
Box 708, Independence, KS 67301
Peter Ellenstein
Tel: (620) 331-7768
info@ingecenter.org
www.ingecenter.org
 Est. 2002. 2 playwrights in 9-wk residency at Inge home (Sep-Nov or Mar-May), with 1-wk Actors' Equity Reading workshop of new play, and some teaching. Assistance: $4,000 stipend, room/board, travel Frequency: semiannual Response Time: 6 mos. **Consideration.** Opportunity/Award: AEA Workshop Reading of unproduced play . **Preference.** Length: full length plays. **Application.** What to submit: query, script (best work), resume, bio and references, description of project, SASE . Author must be produced with three Equity productions. Material must be unproduced.

**Institute of Gunnar Gunnarsson -Klaustrid**
Skriduklaustur, 701 Egilsstadir,
Egilsstadir, Iceland
Halladora Tomasdohir
 Est. 1989 Assistance: room / board Response Time: 2-3 mos. **Preference.** Style: all styles. **Application.** What to submit: application. Deadline: 6/15/2009.

**International Writing Program (IWP)**
100 Shambaugh House
430 N. Clinton St., #100
Iowa City, IA 52242
Tel: (319) 335-0128
christopher-merrill@uiowa.edu
www.uiowa.edu
 Est. 1967. For writers of fiction, poetry, drama, or screenplays who are not US residents. Frequency: Aug.-Nov. **Application.** Author must be published author, proficient in English.

**Isle Royale National Park Artist-in-Residence**
800 E. Lakeshore Dr.
Houghton, MI 49931
Greg Blust
Tel: (906) 482-0984 Fax: (906) 482-8753
greg_blust@nps.gov
 Est. 1991. 2-3 wk residency (Jun-Sep). Artist conducts 1 program/wk and donates a finished piece after a year of residency. **Preference.** Length: full length plays. Style: Open to all art forms. **Application.** What to submit: application, sample, audio, SASE. How to submit: Contact the park for application. Deadline: 2/16/2009.

**Kalani Oceanside Retreat Village**
RR2, Box 4500, 12-6860 Kalapana
Kapoho Beach Road, Pahoa, HI 96778
Richard Koob
Tel: (808) 965-7828 Fax: (808) 965-0527
artists@kalani.com
www.kalani.com
 Artist residencies of 2 wks to 3 mos. Fees: $590-1690 /wk **Assistance:** stipend. **Application.** What to submit: application. How to submit: email.

**Kimmel Harding Nelson (KHN) Center for the Arts**
801 3rd Corso, Nebraska City, NE 68410
Denise Brady
Tel: (402) 874-9600 Fax: (402) 874-9600
info@khncenterforthearts.org
www.khncenterforthearts.org
 Est. 2001. 2-8 week residencies for visual artists, writers, music composers. Fees: $25 application fee. Assistance: $100/wk, housing and studio. Response Time: approx. 2 mos. **Consideration.** Opportunity/Award: Residency with weekly stipend. **Application.** What to submit: see guidelines on website. How to submit: see guidelines on website. Submission application fee: $25. Deadline: 3/1/2009. Second Deadline: 9/1/2009.

## Career Development : Colonies and Residences

**Lanesboro Residency Program Fellowships**
103 Parkway Ave. N., Box 152
Lanesboro, MN 55949
Sara Decker
Tel: (507) 467-2446 Fax: (507) 467-4446
Info@lanesboroarts.org
www.lanesboroarts.org
> **Assistance:** Residency award $625/wk; Artists' retreat space also available for rent. **Application.** What to submit: application. How to submit: Download application from website: www.lanesboroarts.org. Deadline: 6/15/2009.

**Ledig House Writers Residency Program**
55 5th Ave., Fl. 15
New York, NY 10003
DW Gibson
Tel: (212) 206-6060 Fax: (212) 206-6114
writers@artomi.org
www.artomi.org
> Est. 1992. Residencies of 1 wk-2 mos (Mar-Jun, Sep-Nov) in Catskill Mts. Frequency: Twice a year (spring/fall). **Application.** What to submit: query, 10-pg sample, bio, SASE. Deadline: 11/20/2009.

**Leighton Artists' Colony for Independent Residencies**
Box 1020 Station 28
107 Tunnel Mountain Rd
Banff, AB T1L 1H5 Canada
Tel: (800) 565-9989 Fax: (403) 762-6345
arts_info@banffcentre.ca
www.banffcentre.ca
> Residencies for writers, composers and visual artists. **Application.** What to submit: application, project description, resume, sample of work (work in progress), three letters of recommendation unless past participant of LAC. Author must be professional level. How to submit: mail, fax or email. Submission application fee: $75. Applications accepted year round.

**MacDowell Colony**
100 High St.
Peterborough, NH 3458
Courtney Bethel
Tel: (603) 924-3886 Fax: (603) 924-9142
admissions@macdowellcolony.org
www.macdowellcolony.org
> Est. 1907. Residencies up to 8 wks (Jun-Sep, Oct-Jan, Feb-May). Assistance: $1,000 stipend limit, travel. Frequency: triannual. Response Time: 10 weeks. **Consideration.** Opportunity/Award: travel and financial assistance available, based on need; aid applications mailed upon acceptance. **Application.** What to submit: project proposal, application, synopsis, full script (3 copies of all docs), SASE. How to submit: send application and materials by deadline. Submission application fee: $20. Deadlines: 1/15/ 2009, 4/15/ 2009, 9/15/2009.

**Mary Anderson Center for the Arts**
Box 12, 101 St. Francis Dr.
Mt. Saint Francis, IN 47146
Ardis Moonlight
Tel: (812) 923-8602 Fax: (888) 785-3911
macarts@onebox.com
www.maryandersoncenter.org
> Est. 1989. Residencies of 1 wk to 1 mo. Staff: LaDonna Eastman (Residency Coordinator)$60/night incl. all meals; $40/night, no meals. **Assistance:** work exchange fellowships. Frequency: annual. Response Time: 3 wks. **Application.** What to submit: application,5-pg sample, SASE. Author must be age 21 or older. Submission application fee: $10.

**Millay Colony for the Arts**
454 East Hill Rd, Box 3
Austerlitz, NY 12017
Calliope Nicholas
Tel: (518) 392-3103 Fax: (518) 392-4944
apply@millaycolony.org
www.millaycolony.org
> Est. 1973. Monthlong residencies (Apr-Nov) for writers, visual artists and composers. Fees: $30 application

**Assistance:** room/board Frequency: annual Response Time: by 2/1/09. **Application.** What to submit: application,30-pg sample (6 copies), audio (4 copies), score (4 copies), SASE. How to submit: download application on website. Deadline: 10/1/2009.

**Montana Artists Residency**
Box 8, Basin, MT 59631
Debbie Sheehan
Tel: (406) 225-3500
mar@mt.net
www.montanarefuge.org
 Est. 1993. Residencies of 1-9 mos in Nov-Jul (6/15 deadline). Fully funded residencies for Writers in Oct (5/15 deadline) and American Indian Artists in Sep (4/15 deadline). Fees: $300-550/mo. **Application.** What to submit: application, 15-pg sample (3 copies), audio, resume. Deadlines: see above.

**New York Mills Arts Retreat**
24 N. Main Ave., Box 246
New York Mills, MN 56567
Tel: (218) 385-3339
nymills@kulcher.org
www.kulcher.org
 **Application.** What to submit: query, synopsis,12-pg sample, resume, letters of recommendation, SASE.

**Ragdale Foundation**
1260 N. Green Bay Rd.
Lake Forest, IL 60045
Regin Igloria
Tel: (847) 234-1063 ext. 206
Fax: (847) 234-1063
admissions@ragdale.org
www.ragdale.org
 Est. 1976. Residencies of 2 wks-2 mos (Jun-Dec, Jan-Apr) for composers, artists, and writers. $25/day. **Assistance:** financial aid w/ demonstrated need. Response Time: 3 mos. **Application.** What to submit: query, application, synopsis, sample, SASE. Submission application fee: $30.

**Rocky Mountain National Park Artist-in-Residence Program**
1000 Hwy. 36, Estes Park, CO 80517
Tel: (970) 586-1206
www.nps.gov/romo/supportyourpark/volunteer.htm
 **Application.** What to submit: query, application, 6-pg sample (writers), audio (composers), resume (6 copies of all above), submissions not returned. Submission application fee: 35. Deadline: 12/1/2009.

**Studio for Creative Inquiry**
College of Fine Arts, #111,
Pittsburgh, PA 15213
Marge Myers
Tel: (412) 268-3454 Fax: (412) 268-2829
mmbm@andrew.cmu.edu
www.cmu.edu/studio
 Est. 1989. Currently accepting proposals for experimental and interdisciplinary arts projects that don't require full funding by CMU. Proposals should be submitted at least 6 mos in advance of the desired residency. **Application.** What to submit: query, sample, resume.

**Sundance Institute Playwrights Retreat**
8530 Wilshire Blvd., Fl. 3
Beverly Hills, CA 90211
Christopher Hibma
Tel: (310) 360-1981 Fax: (310) 360-1975
theatre@sundance.org
www.sundance.org
 Est. 2001. 18-day retreat for 5 playwrights and 1 theater composer at Ucross Foundation, Clearmont, WY. **Assistance:** $500 stipend, room/board, travel. Frequency: annual. **Application.** Material must be unproduced. How to submit: invite.

**Tyrone Guthrie Centre**
Annaghmakerrig, Newbliss, Ireland
Dr. Pat Donlon
Tel: (353) 475-4003 Fax: (353) 4754380
info@tyroneguthrie.ie
director@tyroneguthrie.ie
www.tyroneguthrie.ie

Est. 1981. Year-round residencies of varying duration. Fees: 600 euro/wk Big House, 300 euro/wk (self-catering). Response Time: 1 mo. **Application.** What to submit: application. Author must be produced or published.

**U.S./Japan Creative Artists' Program**
1201 15th St. NW, #330
Washington, DC 20005
Margaret P. Mihori
Tel: (202) 653-9800 Fax: (202) 418-9802
jusfc@jusfc.gov
www.jusfc.gov
Est. 1979. 5-mo residency in Japan for produced professional US artists. **Assistance:** up to $6,000 stipend, room/board, travel, language training and storage, 400,000 yen/mo stipend, 100,000 yen/mo housing supplement, 100,000 yen for professional services Frequency: annual. **Application.** What to submit: application. Author must be citizen or resident of US. Deadline: 2/1/2009.

**Ucross Foundation Residency Program**
30 Big Red Ln., Clearmont, WY 82835
Sharon Dynak
Tel: (307) 737-2291 Fax: (307) 737-2322
ucross@wyoming.com
www.ucrossfoundation.org
Est. 1991. Residencies of 2 weeks to 2 months (Feb-Jun, Aug-Dec) near Big Horn Mts. Residents are provided living & studio space. Frequency: semiannual. **Application.** What to submit: application, SASE. Submission application fee: 20. Deadline: 3/1/2009.

**Virginia Center for the Creative Arts (VCCA)**
154 San Angelo Dr., Amherst, VA 24521
Suny Monk
Tel: (434) 946-7236 Fax: (434) 9467239
vcca@vcca.com; www.vcca.com
Est. 1971. Residencies of 2 wks-2 mos. Fees: $30-$60/day. **Assistance:** room/board Response Time: 2 mos. **Application.** What to submit: application, full script, submissions not returned. Submission application fee: $25. Deadline: 1/15/2009.

**Women's Work Project**
456 W. 37th St.
New York, NY 10018
Melody Brooks
Tel: (212) 630-9945
www.newperspectivestheatre.org
Residencies of 9-18 mos, incl. in-house readings and directorial-dramaturgical sessions, culminating in public presentation. Frequency: annual. **Consideration.** Opportunity/Award: reading; workshop production. **Preference.** Length: full length plays. Style: comedy, drama. Subject: All subjects, woman, T.Y.A., writers of color, disabled, gay/lesbian. **Application.** What to submit: query, application, full script, bio, SASE. Author must be female, women of color encouraged. Material must be unoptioned, unpublished, unproduced. Deadline: 1/9/2009.

**Yaddo**
Box 395
Saratoga Springs, NY 12866
Candace Wait
Tel: (518) 584-0746 Fax: (518) 584-1312
yaddo@yaddo.org
www.yaddo.org
Est. 1900. Residencies of 2 wks-2 mos. **Assistance:** room/board, travel (limited) Frequency: semiannual. **Preference.** Style: professional recommendation. **Application.** What to submit: two letters of recommendation, completed application form, a professional resume, and a work sample via mail.application, synopsis, sample, SASE. How to submit: we do not accept applications online or by fax. Letters of recommendation are to be submitted separately by the people writing the letters. Submission application fee: $20. Deadline: 1/1/2009. Second Deadline: 8/1/2009, 01/01/2010.

## CONFERENCES AND FESTIVALS

**6 Women Playwriting Festival**
Box 1073, Colorado Springs, CO 80901
Donna Guthrie
www.sixwomenplayfestival.com
  Est. 2007. Frequency: annual
  Production: age 16 and older, cast
  of 2-4. Response Time: 2 mos.
  **Consideration.** Opportunity/Award:
  $75. **Application.** What to submit:
  full script, SASE. Author must be age
  16 or older, female. Material must be
  unproduced. Deadline: 12/31/2009.

**Actors Theatre of Louisville, Humana Festival**
316 W. Main St., Louisville, KY 40202
Amy Wegener
Tel: (502) 584-1265 Fax: (502) 561-3300
awegener@actorstheatre.org
www.actorstheatre.org/humana_submission.htm
  Est. 1976. Fest of 10-15 produced plays
  in Mar-Apr, incl. premieres and second
  productions. **Assistance:** room/board,
  travel, per diem. Frequency: annual.
  **Consideration.** Opportunity/Award:
  production consideration, publication.
  **Preference.** Length: full length plays.
  **Application.** What to submit: query,
  synopsis, 10-pg sample, SASE for
  return of materials; email address
  otherwise. How to submit: agent.

**Actors' Playhouse National Children's Theatre Festival**
280 Miracle Mile, Coral Gables, FL 33134
Earl Maulding
Tel: (305) 444-9293 ext. 615
Fax: (305) 444-4181
maulding@actorsplayhouse.org
www.actorsplayhouse.org
  Est. 1994. Annual 4-day fest. Winning
  show runs 4-6 wks. Non-Equity. Fees:
  $10 reading. **Assistance:** possible
  travel. Frequency: annual. Production:
  cast limit 8, touring set. Response
  Time: by 10/1/09. **Consideration.**
  Opportunity/Award: $500, production.
  **Preference.** Style: musical. Subject:
  T.Y.A. **Application.** What to submit:
  application, script, audio, SASE.
  Material must be unpublished.
  Deadline: 5/1/2009.

**Alabama Shakespeare Festival**
1 Festival Dr., Montgomery, AL 36117
Nancy Rominger
Tel: (334) 271-5300 Fax: (334) 271-5348
www.asf.net
  Est. 1972. Southern Writers' Project
  develops new plays with Southern
  or African-American themes by
  Southern or African-American
  writers. **Application.** How to submit:
  unsolicited for Southern Writers
  Project only, all else agent.

**Breaking Ground Festival**
281 Huntington Ave., Boston, MA 02115
M. Bevin O'Gara
bogara@huntingtontheatre.bu.edu
www.huntingtontheatre.org
  Est. 2001. Response Time: 1 yr.
  **Preference.** Length: full length
  plays. **Application.** What to submit:
  full script, SASE. How to submit:
  unsolicited: MA 26 RI writers only,
  agent (US, Canada, UK).

**Annual Black Theatre Festival**
5919 Hamilton Ave.
Cincinnati, OH 45224
Don Sherman
Tel: (513) 241-6060 Fax: (513) 241-6671
dsherman@cincyblacktheatre.com
www.cincyblacktheatre.com
  **Preference.** Length: full length plays
  and musicals. Subject: All subjects,
  woman, T.Y.A., writers of color,
  disabled, gay/lesbian. **Application.**
  How to submit: unsolicited, year-round
  open submissions.

**Appalachian Festival of Plays and Playwrights**
c/o Barter Theatre, Box 867
Abingdon, VA 24212
Nicholas Piper

Tel: (276) 619-3316 Fax: (276) 619-3335
apfestival@bartertheatre.com
www.bartertheatre.com/season/festival.html
Est. 2001. Plays must be written by Appalachian playwright or must contain Applachian settings & themes. Stagings of 2 plays from previous AFPP, and readings of 6 new scripts in 2-wk fest, judged by panel. Staff: Richard Rose (Artistic Dir), Nicholas Piper (Festival Director). **Consideration.** Opportunity/Award: $250-$500, 5% royalty. **Preference.** Length: full length plays. **Application.** What to submit: full script, SASE. Author must be Appalachian. Material must be unoptioned, unpublished, unproduced. Deadline: 3/31/2009.

**Attic Theatre One-Act Marathon**
5429 W. Washington Blvd.
Los Angeles, CA 90016
Laura Carson
Tel: (323) 525-0600 Fax: (323) 525-0661
litmanager@attictheatre.org
www.attictheatre.org
Entries read by ensemble, finalists read by staff, with 3-10 selected for production or reading in marathon. Panel from L.A. theater community chooses 2 winners. Fees: $15 entry Frequency: annual Production: cast limit 8, no orchestra, unit set. Response Time: 3 mos. **Consideration.** Opportunity/Award: $300 1st, $150 2nd, publication. **Preference.** Style: comedy, drama. **Application.** What to submit: query, application, synopsis, full script (2 copies), character breakdown, bio, SASE. Material must be unproduced. Deadline: 12/31/2009.

**Baldwin New Play Festival**
9500 Gilman Dr., MC0509
La Jolla, CA 92093
Allan Havis
Tel: (858) 534-3791 Fax: (858) 534-8931
ahavis@ucsd.edu
www.theatre.ucsd.edu
Est. 2006. **Assistance:** room/board, travel. Frequency: annual Response Time: by 2/28/09. **Consideration.**

Opportunity/Award: $1,000, reading. **Preference.** Length: full length plays. Style: comedy, drama. Subject: writers of color. **Application.** What to submit: application, synopsis, full script, SASE. Author must be college undergrad. Material must be unpublished, unproduced. Deadline: 1/30/2009.

**Barnstormers Theatre**
Box 434, Tamworth, NH 3886
Clayton Phillips
www.barnstormerstheatre.org
Evening of original one-acts in Oct. Frequency: annual Production: cast limit 6. **Consideration.** Opportunity/Award: $100 honorarium. **Application.** What to submit: full script. Material must be unoptioned, unpublished, unproduced. Deadline: 3/15/2009.

**Bay Area Playwrights Festival (BAPF)**
131 10th St, Third Floor
San Francisco, CA 94103
Jonathan Spector (ext. 110)
literary@playwrightsfoundation.org
www.playwrightsfoundation.org
Est. 1976. BAPF is 2-wk July fest of 5-6 full-length plays by US writers, given rehearsal and 2 readings (1 wk apart for rewrites) before production. Fees: $20 entry. **Assistance:** stipend, room/board, travel. Frequency: annual. Response Time: 4 mos. **Consideration.** Opportunity/Award: reading. **Preference.** Length: full length plays. Style: comedy, drama. **Application.** What to submit: query, full script, submissions not returned. Author must be US resident. Material must be unproduced, original, in English. Deadline: 12/15/2009.

**Bilingual Foundation of the Arts (BFA)**
421 N. Ave. 19, Los Angeles, CA 90031
Margarita Galban
Tel: (323) 225-4044 Fax: (323) 225-1250
www.bfatheatre.org
Est. 1973. Summer reading fest of new works. **Assistance:** TBA. Frequency: annual. Production: cast limit 10,

simple set. Response Time: 6 mos-1 yr. **Consideration.** Opportunity/Award: TBA. **Preference.** Length: full length plays. Style: no musical. Subject: writers of color. **Application.** What to submit: query, full script, SASE. How to submit: unsolicited.

**Black Playwrights Festival**
4520 N. Beacon, Chicago, IL 60640
Jackie Taylor
Tel: 773-4451 Fax: (773) 769-4533
blackensemble@aol.com
www.blackensemble.org
 Year-round open submissions. Clearly note script is for festival. See website for details.

**Blank Theatre Company Young Playwrights Festival**
1301 Lucile Ave.
Los Angeles, CA 90026
Stacy Reed
www.youngplaywrights.com
 Est. 1990. Winning plays assigned mentors and given professional workshop. Staff: Noah Wylie (Artistic Producer), Daniel Henning (Artistic Dir/Producer). Frequency: annual Response Time: by mid-May. **Application.** What to submit: query, full script, submissions not returned. Author must be age 19 or younger. Material must be unoptioned, unpublished. Deadline: 3/15/2009.

**Boomerang Theatre Company**
Box 237166, Ansonia Sta.
New York, NY 10023
Tim Errickson
Tel: (212) 5014069
info@boomerangtheatre.org
www.boomerangtheatre.org
 Est. 1999. Annual reading series of new plays. **Preference.** Length: full length plays. Style: no musical. Subject: woman, writers of color, disabled, gay/lesbian. **Application.** What to submit: query, synopsis,10-pg sample, resume, SASE if necessary. Material must be unproduced.

**Boston Theater Marathon**
949 Commonwealth Ave.
Boston, MA 2215
Kate Snodgrass
Tel: (617) 353-5443
newplays@bu.edu
www.bu.edu/btm
 Est. 1999. 50 10-min plays by New England playwrights by 50 New England theaters over 10 hrs in 1 day. Staff: Bill Lattanzi (Consultant), Jacob Strautmann (Managing Dir). Frequency: annual. Production: small orchestra, minimal set. Response Time: 4 mos. **Preference.** Style: comedy, drama, musical. **Application.** What to submit: full script, SASE. Author must be resident of New England. Deadline: 11/15/2009.

**Centre Stage South Carolina New Play Festival**
Box 8451, Greenville, SC 29604
Brian Haimbach
Tel: (864) 233-6733
haimbach@hotmail.com
www.centrestage.org
 Est. 2002. 5 finalists in reader's theatre during 1-week fest. Audience selects winner for full production next season. Frequency: annual Production: age 16 or older, cast limit 6, minimal set. Response Time: by 6/1/08. **Preference.** Length: full length plays. Style: adaptation, comedy, drama. **Application.** What to submit: synopsis, full script, scripts will not be returned. Material must be unpublished, unproduced. Deadline: 3/1/2009.

**Fresh Fruit Festival**
145 E. 27th St., #1-A
New York, NY 10016
Carol Polcovar
artisticdirector@freshfruitfestival.com
www.freshfruitfestival.com
 Est. 2003. Frequency: annual Response Time: 2 mos. **Consideration.** Opportunity/Award: Selected productions get a percentage of the door and a minimum guarantee.

## Career Development : Conferences and Festivals

Fresh Fruit Awards of Distinction are rewarded to outstanding festival work. **Preference.** Length: full length plays and musicals. Subject: All subjects, woman, T.Y.A., writers of color, disabled, gay/lesbian. **Application.** What to submit: SASE. Material must be unoptioned, not performed in NYC, related in some way to LGBT culture unoptioned. How to submit: application posted online . Deadline: 2/15/2009.

**Fringe of Toronto Theatre Festival**
344 Bloor St., #208
Toronto, ON Canada
www.fringetoronto.com

**Circle Theatre of Forest Park**
7300 W. Madison St.
Forest Park, IL 60130
Literary Manager
Tel: (708) 771-0700
info@circle-theatre.org
www.circletheatre.org
Est. 1985. New play fest of shorts and full-lengths. **Application.** What to submit: synopsis only, no returns. Material must be unproduced.

**Coe College Playwriting Festival & Symposia**
1220 1st Ave. NE
Cedar Rapids, IA 52402
Susan Wolverton
Tel: (319) 399-8624 Fax: (319) 399-8557
swolvert@coe.edu
www.public.coe.edu/departments/theatre
Est. 1993. Biennial spring fest. Winner of New Works for the Stage Competition receives weeklong residency, workshop with students, and staged reading. **Assistance:** room/board, travel. Frequency: biennial. Production: age 16-50, cast of 3-8 Response Time: 8 wks. **Consideration.** Opportunity/Award: $500, reading. **Preference.** Length: full length plays. Style: comedy, drama. **Application.** What to submit: 1-pg synopsis, full script, SASE. Author must be citizen of US. Material must be unpublished, unproduced, in development stage. How to submit: unsolicited. Deadline: 11/1/2009.

**Cultural Conversations**
103 Arts Bldg., University Park, PA 16802
Susan Russell
sbr13@psu.edu
www.theatre.psu.edu
Est. 2007. Readings of 3 new plays addressing themes of local and global diversity. One week rehearsal, Two week festival. Playwright residency 2-3 days. Staff: Prof. Susan Russel (Artistic Dir.) Frequency: annual. Response Time: by 1/15/09. **Consideration.** Opportunity/Award: reading. **Preference.** Length: full length plays. Style: comedy, drama. **Application.** What to submit: full script, SASE. Material must be unoptioned, unpublished, unproduced. How to submit: unsolicited. Deadline: 10/31/2009.

**Festival of New American Plays**
1609 W. Broad St., Richmond, VA 23220
Carol Piersol
Tel: (804) 355-2001 Fax: (804) 355-0999
info@firehousetheatre.org
www.firehousetheatre.org
Est. 2003. Frequency: annual Response Time: 7 mos. **Consideration.** Opportunity/Award: $1,000 1st, $500 2nd, reading. **Preference.** Length: full length musicals. Style: comedy, drama, musical, no translation. **Application.** What to submit: full script, submissions not returned. Author must be resident or citizen of USA. Material must be unproduced. How to submit: professional recommendation. Deadline: 6/30/2009.

**Florida Studio Theatre's Richard & Betty Burdick New Play Reading Series**
Florida Studio Theatre
1241 N. Palm Ave., Sarasota, FL 34236
Cristin Kelly
Tel: (941) 366-9017 Fax: (941) 9554137
ckelly@floridastudiotheatre.org
www.floridastudiotheatre.org
May workshop readings of 3 new full-length plays or musicals by

contemporary US writers. **Assistance:** stipend, room/board, travel. Frequency: annual. **Preference.** Length: full length plays and musicals. **Application.** What to submit: query, synopsis, sample, SASE , CD if musical. How to submit: E-mail or mail. Full guidelines at http://www.floridastudiotheatre.org/new_plays.php.

**FusionFest**
8500 Euclid Ave., Cleveland, OH 44106
Seth Gordon
Tel: (216) 795-7000 Fax: (216) 795-7007
www.clevelandplayhouse.com
Est. 1995. Reading series of new plays. **Assistance:** $1,000 stipend, room/board, travel. Response Time: 6 mos. **Application.** What to submit: query, synopsis, 10-pg sample, SASE. Author must be a resident of Ohio. Material must be unoptioned, unproduced. How to submit: agent.

**FutureFest**
1301 E. Siebenthaler Ave.
Dayton, OH 45414
Amy Brown
Tel: (937) 424-8477 Fax: (937) 4240062
amy@daytonplayhouse.com
www.daytonplayhouse.org
Est. 1990. Adjudicated July fest of new work with 3 full productions and 3 staged readings. Frequency: annual. Response Time: by 4/20/10. **Consideration.** Opportunity/Award: $1,000, production, reading. **Preference.** Length: full length plays. Style: no musical. **Application.** What to submit: synopsis, full script, submissions not returned. Material must be unoptioned, unpublished, unproduced. Deadline: 10/31/2009.

**GAYFEST NYC**
1 River Pl., #917
New York, NY 10036
Bruce Robert Harris
www.gayfestnyc.com
Monthlong fest (May-June) of new works by gay authors or with gay-friendly subjects, incl. three productions (2 plays, 1 musical) and reading series of works-in-progress, from hard-hitting dramas to jewel-box musicals. Fees: $20 fee. Production: cast limit 10, up to 3 settings. Response Time: 4 mos. **Consideration.** Opportunity/Award: $100 stipend. **Preference.** Length: full length musicals. Style: drama, musical theatre. Subject: gay/lesbian. **Application.** What to submit: synopsis, full script (2 copies), audio, bio, character breakdown, SASE. Material must be unoptioned, unpublished, unproduced, original. How to submit: unsolicited. Deadline: 10/31/2009.

**Genesis Festival**
P.O. Box 238, 7 Livingston Ave.
New Brunswick, NJ 8901
Marshall Jones
Tel: (732) 545-8100 Fax: (732) 907-1864
info@crossroadstheatrecompany.org
www.crossroadstheatrecompany.org
Frequency: annual. Consideration. Opportunity/Award: reading. **Preference.** Subject: writers of color. **Application.** What to submit: query letter (note theme addressed), synopsis, 30-pg writing sample, bio. How to submit: unsolicited. Deadline: 12/31/2009.

**Global Age Project (GAP)**
2081 Addison St.
Berkeley, CA 94704
Jeannette Harrison
Tel: (510) 843-4042 Fax: (510) 843-4826
tbentley@auroratheatre.org
www.auroratheatre.org
4 plays given staged readings in fest of forward-looking works on issues of the 21st century. Frequency: annual. Response Time: 5 mos. **Consideration.** Opportunity/Award: $1,000 1st, reading (finalists). **Preference.** Length: full length plays. **Application.** What to submit: full script. Material must be unproduced. How to submit: online. Deadline: 7/1/2009.

## Career Development : Conferences and Festivals

**Inspirato Festival**
124 Broadway Ave., Ste. 112
Toronto, ON M4P-1V8 Canada
Dominik Loncar
Tel: (419) 483-2222
inspirato@ca.inter.net
www.inspiratofestival.ca
   **Consideration.** Opportunity/Award: Production. **Application.** Material must be Full Script. Deadline: 1/9/2009.

**International Mystery Writers' Festival**
101 Daviess St., Owensboro, KY 42303
Kimberly Johnson
Tel: (270) 687-2770
kjohnson@riverparkcenter.org
www.newmysteries.org
   Est. 2007. Accepts Plays, Teleplays or Short Screenplays of Mystery/Thriller genre. Staff: Kimberly Johnson, Zev Buffman, Roxi Witt. **Assistance:** Travel assistance varies Frequency: annual. Response Time: 3 months. **Consideration.** Opportunity/Award: $1,000-$10,000. **Preference.** Style: adaptation, drama, Mystery. **Application.** What to submit: full script, submission not returned. Material must be unproduced. How to submit: unsolicited. Deadline: 11/30/2009.

**Jewish Ensemble Theater Festival of New Plays**
6600 W. Maple Rd.
West Bloomfield, MI 48322
Evelyn Orbach
Tel: (248) 788-2900
e.orbach@jettheatre.org
www.jettheatre.org
   Est. 1989. Staff: Pearl Orbach (Lit Desk Asst), Chris Bremer (Managing Dir). Frequency: annual Production: cast limit 8. **Consideration.** Opportunity/Award: $100, reading if selected. **Preference.** Length: full length plays. Style: no musical, no translation. **Application.** What to submit: full script, SASE. Material must be unpublished, unproduced. How to submit: hard copy by mail. Deadline: 9/1/2009.

**Kitchen Dog Theater (KDT) New Works Festival**
3120 McKinney Ave., #100
Dallas, TX 75204
Tina Parker
Tel: (214) 953-2258 Fax: (214) 953-1873
tina@kitchendogtheater.org
www.kitchendogtheater.org
   Est. 1990. Winner receives production, travel stipend, and royalty; 7 finalists receive reading. Staff: Christopher Carlos (Co-Artistic Dir). Frequency: annual. Response Time: 8 mos . **Preference.** Length: full length plays. **Application.** What to submit: full script, submissions not returned. How to submit: full scripts by mail only -no ecopies or partial scripts accepted . Deadline: 2/1/2009.

**Last Frontier Theatre Conference**
Box 97, Valdez, AK 99686
Dawson Moore
Tel: (907) 834-1614 Fax: (907) 8341611
dmoore@pwscc.edu
www.pwscc.edu/conference
   Est. 2003. Application free. See website for conference fees. Response Time: by 3/15/2010. **Consideration.** Opportunity/Award: reading. **Preference.** Style: comedy, drama. **Application.** What to submit: synopsis, full script. Material must be unproduced. How to submit: unsolicited. Deadline: 2/1/2009.

**Lavender Footlights Festival**
59 NE 46th St., Miami, FL 33137
Doug Williford
Tel: (305) 672-7818 Fax: (305) 672-7818
mdougwill@mac.com
www.caemia.org
   Est. 2000. Fest of readings with gay and lesbian themes. Staff: Ryan Capiro (artistic director). Vivian Marthell (Co-Exec. Director). Kareem Tabsch (Co-Exec. Director) Frequency: annual. Response Time: 01/15/09 . **Consideration.** Opportunity/Award: reading. **Preference.** Length: full length plays and musicals. Style: comedy, drama, musical. Subject: All subjects, gay/lesbian. **Application.** What to submit: synopsis, full script,

SASE. Material must be unproduced in FL. How to submit: Online, USPS mail Submission/Application. Deadline: 12/31/2009.

**Little Festival of the Unexpected**
Portland Stage, Box 1458
Portland, ME 04104
Daniel Burson
Tel: (207) 774-1043 Fax: (207) 774-0576
dburson@portlandstage.com
www.portlandstage.com
 Est. 1989. 1-wk fest of new plays with writers developing work thru staged readings. **Assistance:** $300 stipend. Frequency: annual. Production: cast limit 8. **Preference.** Length: full length plays. Style: adaptation, comedy, drama. Subject: All subjects. **Application.** What to submit: query, synopsis, 10-pg sample. Material must be unoptioned, unpublished, unproduced. How to submit: mail hardcopy of 10-pg sample. Deadline: 12/31/2009.

**New American Playwrights Project (NAPP)**
351 W. Center St.
Cedar City, UT 84720
Charles Metten
Tel: (435) 586-7880 Fax: (435) 865-8003
metten@bard.org
www.bard.org
 Equity LORT B+. 2000 Regional Theater Tony winner. Aug fest of 4 play readings, with writers in residence. **Assistance:** room/board, travel, tickets to USF summer season Frequency: annual. Production: cast of 8-10, set limit 2, flexible stage. **Consideration.** Opportunity/Award: reading. **Preference.** Length: full length plays. Style: no musical. Subject: woman, writers of color, disabled, gay/lesbian. **Application.** What to submit: full script, submissions not returned. Author must be resident or citizen of US. Material must be unproduced. Deadline: 12/1/2009.

**New Jersey Playwrights Festival of New Plays**
Box 1663, Bloomfield, NJ 07003
Lenny Bart
Tel: (973) 259-9187 Fax: (973) 259-9188
info@12mileswest.org
www.12mileswest.org
 Annual fest of plays by NJ playwrights. Production: cast of 2-7, unit set. Response Time: 1 yr. **Consideration.** Opportunity/Award: $500. **Preference.** Length: full length plays. **Application.** What to submit: synopsis, full script (3 copies), cast breakdown, SASE. Author must be resident of NJ.

**New Professional Theatre Writers Festival**
229 W. 42nd St., #501
New York, NY 10036
Mark D. Wood
Tel: (212) 398-2666 Fax: (212) 398-2924
newprof@aol.com
www.newprofessionaltheatre.com
 Est. 1991. Annual fest of work by African-Americans, Asians, and Latinos. Also business seminars, mentoring, and 2-wk residencies. **Assistance:** $1,000. Frequency: annual. **Preference.** Length: full length plays. **Application.** What to submit: full script, submissions not returned. Author must be African-American. Material must be unoptioned, unpublished, unproduced, original. How to submit: see website. Deadline: 6/1/2009.

**New South Play Festival**
Box 5376, Atlanta, GA 31107
J. Caleb Boyd
Tel: (404) 523-1477 ext. 113
literary@horizontheatre.com
www.horizontheatre.com
 Est. 1997. Summer fest of developmental workshops, readings and productions. Frequency: annual Production: cast limit 8 Response Time: 6 mos. **Consideration.** Opportunity/Award: production, reading. **Preference.** Length: full length plays. **Application.** What to submit: query, 10 page sample, SASE.

## Career Development : Conferences and Festivals

**New York City 15-Minute Play Fest**
145 W. 46th St., Fl. 3
New York, NY 10036
Elizabeth Keefe
Tel: (212) 869-9809
liz@americanglobe.org
www.americanglobe.org
> Est. 1993. 2-wk fest in May of 4-5 new plays each night under Equity Showcase. Staff: John Basil (Artistic Dir, AGT), Gloria Falzer (Artistic Dir, Turnip). Frequency: annual. Production: cast of 2-10, no set. Response Time: 2mos. **Consideration.** Opportunity/Award: $100 award, $25 royalty. **Application.** What to submit: full script, SASE. Material must be unpublished. Deadline: 12/31/2009.

**New York Television Festival**
39 W. 14th St., New York, NY 10011
Ned Canty
Tel: (212) 675-5840
scriptcontest@nytvf.com
www.nytvf.com
> See website for full details. **Consideration.** Opportunity/Award: Development deal with Fox. Award/Grant/Stipend: $25000. **Preference.** Style: Comedy or Variety. **Application.** What to submit: Full Script. Author must be 18. Material must be not optioned, not produced, not published. How to submit: Unsolicited. Deadline: 6/13/2009.

**Off-Off-Broadway Original Short-Play Festival**
45 W. 25 St., New York, NY 10010
Kenneth Dingledine
Tel: (212) 206-8990 Fax: (202) 2061429
oobfestival@samuelfrench.com
www.samuelfrench.com
> Est. 1976. Summer 2-wk fest in NYC of approx. 100 shows. 6 finalists chosen for publication and representation by Samuel French. Frequency: annual. **Consideration.** Opportunity/Award: publication. **Application.** What to submit: application, SASE. Material must be unpublished. How to submit: thru producing sponsor.

**Penn State New Musical Theatre Festival**
Penn State Univ., 103 Arts Bldg.
University Park, PA 16801
Raymond Sage
Tel: (814) 863-5999
raysage@psunewmusicals.org
www.psunewmusicals.org
> Est. 2006. Two week festival, 2 or more musicals in 29 hour equity format. Production: ages 18-25. **Consideration.** Opportunity/Award: cash honorarium. **Preference.** Length: full length musicals. Style: musical. **Application.** What to submit: script, recording, or any pertinent materials. How to submit: mail.

**Penobscot Theatre**
131 Main St., Bangor, ME 4401
Tel: (207) 9476618
info@penobscottheatre.org
www.penobscottheatre.org
> 2 wk. New Play Fest. featuring readings & workshops. Response Time: works selected notified by 5/1/09. **Application.** What to submit: cover letter stating how this festival will help in the development of the piece. 10-minutes, one-acts, and/or full-length plays and musicals. Material must be unpublished, unproduced. Deadline: 2/14/2009.

**Playfest -Harriett Lake Festival of New Plays**
812 E. Rollins St., #100
Orlando, FL 32803
Patrick Flick
Fax: (407) 447-1701
patrickf@orlandoshakes.org
www.orlandoshakes.org
> Est. 1989. 10 new plays receive readings, 2-3 developmental in Festival of new plays. **Assistance:** stipend, room/board, travel, actors, directors, rehearsal time, access to copiers, email, etc., while on site. **Preference.** Length: full length plays. **Application.** What to submit: 1-pg synopsis (no longer than 200 words), 10-pg sample, bio of writer, casting including doubling, name, address, email on the cover page of the submission. Please

see our website for exact, or additional submission requirements after 4/1/08, submissions not returned. Material must be unpublished, suitable to our mission. Please see website. Deadline: 8/1/2009.

**Playwrights' Week**
939 8th Ave., #301, New York, NY 10019
Andrea Hiebler
Tel: (212) 246-2676 ext. 37
andreah@larktheatre.org
www.larktheatre.org
Playwrights' Week, a Sept. fest of public readings with script in-hand. Staff: John Eisner (Producing Dir), Michael Robertson (Managing Dir). Frequency: annual. Response Time: 9 mos. **Preference.** Length: full length plays. **Application.** What to submit: application, full script (1 entry/author), SASE. Author must be age 18 or older. Material must be application, full script (1 entry/author). Deadline: 11/15/2009.

**Political Theatre Festival**
209 W. Page St., #208
St. Paul, MN 55107
Christina Akers
Tel: (651) 224-8806
teatrom@bitstream.net
www.teatrodelpueblo.org
Est. 2001. One-acts about political issues of Latino identity. **Assistance:** stipend. Production: cast limit 3, up to 3 set pieces. **Consideration.** Opportunity/Award: production, reading. **Preference.** Style: interactive encouraged. Subject: writers of color. **Application.** What to submit: synopsis, full script, resume/bio, submissions not returned. Material must be in English or Spanish. Deadline: 8/1/2009.

**Premiere Stages Play Festival**
Hutchinson Hall, 1000 Morris Ave.
Union, NJ 07083
John Wooten
www.kean.edu/premierestages
Est. 2004. Annual fest for playwrights born or living in NJ, CT, NY, PA. Three public readings in Apr, full Equity production of winner in July. Frequency: annual Production: cast limit 8. **Consideration.** Opportunity/Award: $2,000 1st, $750 2nd, $500 3rd, reading. **Preference.** Length: full length plays. Style: comedy, drama. **Application.** What to submit: synopsis,8-pg sample, cast list, production history, bio. Full script through agent only. Author must be resident of NY, NJ, CT, or PA. Material must be unoptioned, unpublished, unproduced. Deadline: 1/15/2009.

**Short Attention Span PlayFEST**
4611 Monroe St., Hollywood, FL 33021
Kimberly Davis Basso
kdb@atlantisplaymakers.com
www.atlantisplaymakers.com
Est. 1998. Frequency: annual. Response Time: 4/30/09. **Consideration.** Opportunity/Award: honorarium. **Preference.** Style: comedy, drama, musical. **Application.** What to submit: full script, submissions not returned. Material must be unpublished, unproduced. Deadline: 3/15/2009.

**ReOrient Golden Thread Fest**
131 10th St., San Francisco, CA 94103
Torange Yeghiazarian
Tel: (415) 626-4061 Fax: (415) 626-1138
www.goldenthread.org
Est. 1996. **Assistance:** $100 stipend. Frequency: annual. Length: 10-40 minutes. **Application.** What to submit: full script, submisssions not returned. Deadline: 3/1/2009.

**Scratch Pad Festival**
2911 Centenary Blvd.
Shreveport, LA 71134
Don Hooper
www.centenary.edu/theatre
Est. 2006. Frequency: annual Production: age 12-40, cast of 2-20 Response Time: by early fall. **Consideration.** Opportunity/Award: production, reading. **Preference.** Length: full length plays. **Application.**

What to submit: synopsis, 10-pg sample, submissions not returned. Material must be unoptioned, unproduced.

**Southern Appalachian Playwrights' Conference**
Box 1720, Mars Hill, NC 28754
Rob Miller
Tel: (828) 689-1384 Fax: (828) 689-1272
sart@mhc.edu
www.sartplays.org
Est. 1981. Readings & critique of 5/6 plays in 3-day conference at Mars Hill Coll. Staff: William Gregg (Artistic Dir). **Assistance:** N/C. Frequency: Annually, one-time award. Production: cast, orchestra, full. Response Time: May/July announcement. **Consideration.** Opportunity/Award: $1,000 award, possible future production. **Preference.** Length: full length. Style: no adaptation, Comedy, Drama, Musical, no translation. Subject: All subjects. **Application.** What to submit: 2 copies of full script; specific guidelines by request or on sartplays.org/guidelines.htm. Material must be unpublished, unproduced, amateur produced scripts are eligible. How to submit: unsolicited, Professional Recommendation, Agent. Deadline: 10/31/2009.

**Summer Writing Workshops**
7200 Hofstra Univ.
Hempstead, NY 11549
Kenneth Henwood
Tel: (516) 463-5737 Fax: (516) 463-4833
kenneth.a.henwood@hofstra.edu;
www.ccepa.hofstra.edu/univcollege
Opportunity to teach a 2-week workshop in Dramatic Writing at conference in July. Frequency: annual. **Consideration.** Opportunity/Award: feedback. **Application.** What to submit: query letter (note theme addressed), synopsis, submissions returned with SASE. How to submit: unsolicited.

**Teatro del Pueblo**
209 West Page St., Ste 208
St. Paul, MN 55107
Christina Akers
Tel: (651) 224-8806 Fax: (651) 298-5796
christina@teatrodelpueblo.org
www.teatrodelpueblo.org
We are looking for 15 to 50 minute one-act plays dealing with poltical issues pertaining to Latino Social Justice. **Consideration.** Opportunity/Award: Small Royalty, Production. **Application.** What to submit: Synopsis or Treatment, Full Script. Deadline: 6/15/2009.

**Theater 150 Ten-Minute Play Festival**
Box 925, Ojai, CA 93024
Gai Jones
Tel: (805) 646-4300
theater150@ojai.net
www.theater150.org
Est. 1996. Production: cast limit 8, small set. Response Time: 6 mos. **Application.** What to submit: full script, SASE. Author must be resident of Ventura/Santa Barbara counties. Material must be unpublished.

**Theatre Building Chicago**
1225 W. Belmont Ave.
Chicago, IL 60657
John Sparks
Tel: (773) 929-7367 ext. 222
Fax: (773) 327-1404
jsparks@theatrebuildingchicago.org
www.theatrebuildingchicago.org
Est. 1984. 2-day Aug fest with Equity and non-Equity actors in readings of 8 full-length musicals. Works not ready for fest are considered for development series. Theatre for Young Audiences programming must be 1-hour maximum, 5 actors maximum; age appropriate for ages 3-7. Frequency: annual Production: cast limit 16, piano only, no set. Response Time: 3 mos. **Consideration.** Opportunity/Award: reading. **Preference.** Length: full length musicals. Style: musical. Subject: All subjects, woman, T.Y.A., writers of color, disabled, gay/

lesbian. **Application.** What to submit: application, submissions not returned. Material must be considered work-in-progress. How to submit: professional recommendation. Deadline: 10/1/2009.

**Theatre Three One-Act Play Festival**
Box 512, 412 Main St.
Port Jefferson, NY 11777
Jeffrey Sanzel
Tel: (631) 928-9202 Fax: (631) 928-9120
www.theatrethree.com
Est. 1969. Festival of one-act plays in Mar. Frequency: annual. Production: 2-8, minimal set. Response Time: 8 mos. **Consideration.** Opportunity/Award: $70. **Preference.** Style: comedy, drama, experimental. **Application.** What to submit: full script, visit website for detailed guidelines, SASE. Material must be unproduced. Deadline: 9/30/2009.

**Woodstock Fringe**
Box 157, Lake Hill, NY 12448
Wallace Norman
Tel: (845) 810-0123 Fax: (212) 602-0061
wnorman@woodstockfringe.org
www.woodstockfringe.org
Est. 2003. Monthlong fest of theater and song at Byrdcliffe Arts Colony. **Assistance:** $250 stipend, travel. Frequency: annual. Production: cast of 2-6. Response Time: 6 mos. **Consideration.** Opportunity/Award: 6% royalty, $300 minimum for full-length works. **Preference.** Length: full length plays and musicals. Subject: All subjects, woman, writers of color, disabled, gay/lesbian. **Application.** What to submit: query, synopsis, 15-pg sample, SASE. How to submit: See http://www.woodstockfringe.org/participate.htm for submission guidelines.

## CONFERENCES AND FESTIVALS (*FEE CHARGED*)

**American College Theater Festival (ACTF)**
Kennedy Center, Washington, DC 20566
Susan Shaffer
www.KCACTF.org
Est. 1969. National fest of student productions, selected from regional college fests. Regional deadlines vary. Michael Kanin (1910-93) arranged for awards for the national fest (see website). **Application.** What to submit: application, 1-pg synopsis, full script. Author must be college student. Material must be original. Submission application fee: $350. Deadline: 12/1/2009.

**Ashland New Plays Festival**
Box 453, Ashland, OR
Amanda Berkeley
Tel: (541) 482-4357
playwrights@AshlandNewPlays.org
www.ashlandnewplays.org
Est. 1992. Fest in Oct. with 12 hrs rehearsal for 2 unstaged readings with professional director and actors (often from OR Shakespeare Fest). Playwrights may live outside the USA, but scripts must speak to a US-based audience. Workshops offered during fest. **Assistance:** $500 stipend, room (1 wk) Frequency: annual. Production: cast limit 8. Response Time: by 8/31/08. **Consideration.** Opportunity/Award: reading, $500. **Preference.** Length: full length plays. Style: comedy, drama, mystery, suspense. **Application.** What to submit: query, application, synopsis, full script, bio, casting list. Material must be unpublished, unproduced. Submission application fee: $15. Deadline: 1/15/2009.

**Baltimore Playwrights Festival**
Box 38537, Baltimore, MD 21231
Rich Espey
Tel: (410) 276-2153
chairman@baltimoreplaywrightsfestival.org
www.baltimoreplaywrightsfestival.org

Est. 1981. Plays chosen by 1 of 6 companies for 3-wk summer production. Selected public readings given thru year. Frequency: annual. **Consideration.** Opportunity/Award: up to $250, honoraria up to $100. **Application.** What to submit: synopsis, full script (3 copies), SASE. Author must be current or former resident or employee in MD. Material must be unpublished, unproduced. Submission application fee: $10. Deadline: 9/30/2009.

**Black Box New Play Festival**
199 14th St., Brooklyn, NY 11215
Heather S. Curran
info@galleryplayers.com
www.galleryplayers.com
Est. 1996. AEA/Non-AEA showcase. 3 week run of show plus workshop. Staff: Heather Siobhan Curran (Pres/Artistic Dir), Matt Schicker (VP). Cathy Bencivenga (Dir. of Prod.) Frequency: annual. Production: ages 20-40's, cast 5-10, unit set. Response Time: 01/01/09. **Consideration.** Opportunity/Award: production. **Preference.** Length: full length plays. Style: comedy, drama, no musical, no translation. **Application.** What to submit: synopsis, full script, resume, submissions not returned. Author must be resident of CT, NJ, NY. Material must be unproduced, readings ok. How to submit: unsolicited. Submission application fee: $10. Deadline: 11/1/2009.

**Cincinnati Fringe Festival**
1120 Jackson St., Cincinnati, OH 45202
Jason Bruffy
Tel: (513) 3005669
www.knowtheatre.com
www.cincyfringe.com
Est. 2003. Fringe Festival occurs annually late May/early June. See applications online at cincyfringe.com for specifics. Frequency: annual. Response Time: 3 mos. **Consideration.** Opportunity/Award: split box offc. **Preference.** Style: all styles. **Application.** What to submit: application, materials will not be returned. How to submit: unsolicited. Submission application fee: $25. Deadline: 12/31/2009.

**Fire Rose Prods. 10-Min. Play Festival**
11246 Magnolia Blvd.
North Hollywood, CA 91601
Kaz Mata-Mura
Tel: (818) 7663691
info@fireroseproductions.com
www.fireroseproductions.com
Est. 2000. Equity 99-seat. Frequency: annual. Response Time: 3 mos. **Application.** What to submit: full script, submissions not returned. Submission application fee: $5. Deadline: 3/31/2009.

**Juneteenth Legacy Theatre**
332 W. Broadway, #613
Louisville, KY 40202
Lorna Littleway
juneteenthlegacy@aol.com
www.juneteenthlegacytheatre.com
Est. 1999. Staged readings on African-American experience in 19th-20th centuries, incl. Harlem Renaissance, Caribbean/Native American influences, contemporary youth, and new images of women. Send 3 copies of submissions to KY address above, send 1 copy w/entry fee to JLT, 605 Water St., #21-B, New York, NY 10002. **Consideration.** Opportunity/Award: reading. **Preference.** Length: full length plays and musicals. Style: adaptation, comedy, drama. Subject: woman, writers of color, gay/lesbian. **Application.** What to submit: query, full script (4 copies: send 3 to KY, 1 to NY), SASE. Submission application fee: $15. Deadline: 3/15/2009.

**Lamia Ink! Intl. One-Page Play Competition**
Box 202, Prince St. Sta.
New York, NY 10012
Ms. Cortland Jessup
www.lamiaink.org

Est. 1989. Frequency: annual. **Consideration.** Opportunity/Award: $200, publication, reading. **Application.** What to submit: full script, 50-word bio, SASE. Submission application fee: $2. Deadline: 3/15/2009.

**Long Beach Playhouse New Works Festival**
5021 East Anaheim St.
Long Beach, CA 90804
Jo BlackJacob
Tel: (562) 494-1014 ext. 507
Fax: (562) 961-8616
joblack@dslextreme.com
www.lbph.com
Est. 1989. Fest of 4 new plays in staged readings (Spring) plus possible consideration of one world premiere prod. of previous year's winner. Staff: Gigi Fusco Meese (Exec Producer/Dir). Frequency: annual. Production: cast limit 10, limited set. Response Time: 3 mos after festival concludes. **Consideration.** Opportunity/Award: $100 reading $300 full production. **Preference.** Length: full length plays. Style: no musical. **Application.** What to submit: application, synopsis, full script, cast list, SASE. Material must be unproduced. Submission application fee: $10.

**Long Beach Playhouse New Works Festival**
5021 East Anaheim St.
Long Beach, CA 90804
Jo Black-Jacob
Tel: (562) 949-1014
Scripts are accepted year round. **Consideration.** Opportunity/Award: Reading, possible production. Award/Grant/Stipend: $100. **Preference.** Length: full length plays. Style: No Musical. **Application.** What to submit: Application, synopsis, Full script. How to submit: Unsolicited. Submission application fee: $10. Deadline: 9/30/2009.

**National Music Theater Conference (OMTC)**
305 Great Neck Rd., Waterford, CT 06385
Paulette Haupt
Tel: (860) 443-5378 ext. 301
litoffice@theoneill.org
www.theoneill.org
Est. 1978. Artistic Director, Paulette Haupt. 2-3 wk residency (Jul-Aug), with rehearsal and in-hand public readings. **Assistance:** $1,000 stipend, room/board, travel Frequency: annual Production: no orchestra, no set. **Consideration.** Opportunity/Award: professional workshop, public reading. **Preference.** Style: musical. **Application.** What to submit: application, synopsis, 30-pg sample, audio. Author must be resident or citizen of US. Material must be unproduced. How to submit: application guidelines available at www.theoneill.org. Submission application fee: $35. Deadline: 12/1/2009.

**National Playwrights Conference (OPC)**
The O'Neill, 305 Great Neck Rd.
Waterford, CT 06385
Martin Kettling
Tel: (860) 443-5378 ext. 227
litoffice@theoneill.org
www.oneill.org
Est. 1964. Artistic Director, Wendy C. Goldberg Month residency (Jun-Jul), incl. 4-day workshop and 2 in-hand readings with professional actors and directors. **Assistance:** $1,000 stipend, room/board, travel. Frequency: annual. **Consideration.** Opportunity/Award: Professional Workshop, Public Reading. **Preference.** Length: full length plays. **Application.** What to submit: application, full script (3 copies). Material must be unproduced. How to submit: application @ www.theoneill.org . Submission application fee: $35. Deadline: 10/15/2009.

**Pittsburgh New Works Festival (PNWF)**
Box 42419, Pittsburgh, PA 15203
Lora Oxenreiter
Tel: (412) 881-6888

info@pittsburghnewworks.org
www.pittsburghnewworks.org
> Est. 1991. Non-Equity 6-wk fest mid-August thru September, 6 staged readings, 12 staged productions, 18 production companies under fest umbrella. Frequency: annual. Production: age 12 and up, cast limit 8, simple set, 40 minute limit. **Consideration.** Opportunity/Award: $500 to (voted) best play, $50 to playwrights of produced scripts. **Preference.** Style: no musical. Subject: woman, writers of color, gay/lesbian. **Application.** What to submit: synopsis, 1 hard copy, electronic submission to email address, SASE. Material must be unproduced. Submission application fee: $15. Deadline: 4/1/2009.

**Old Opera House Theatre Company New Voice Play Festival**
204 N. George St.
Charles Town, WV 25414
Tel: (304) 752-4420
ooh@oldoperahouse.org
www.oldoperahouse.org
> Est. 2001. Call or email for application and deadlines. One act play festival-plays 10 to 40 minutes in length. **Consideration.** Opportunity/Award: $250 plus performance for first place, $100 plus performance for second place and $50 plus staged reading for third place. **Preference.** Length: full length plays. Subject: woman, T.Y.A., writers of color, disabled, gay/lesbian. **Application.** Submission application fee: $10. Deadline: 3/1/2009.

**Perishable Theatre Women's Playwriting Festival**
Box 23132, Providence, RI 2903
Tel: (401) 331-2695 Fax: (401) 331-7811
wpf@perishable.org
www.perishable.org
> Fall festival. Up to 3 winners produced in mainstage season. Publication in anthology. **Assistance:** travel, accommodation. Frequency: biennial. Response Time: 5/15/09. **Consideration.** Opportunity/Award: $500 award, possible future production, publication. **Preference.** Style: all styles. **Application.** What to submit: full script (up to 2 entries), cast and scene breakdown, submissions returned with SASE. Author must be female. Material must be unoptioned, unproduced. How to submit: unsolicited. Submission application fee: $10. Deadline: 1/15/2009.

**ShowOff! Playwriting Festival**
31776 El Camino Real
San Juan Capistrano, CA 92675
Tom Scott
www.caminorealplayhouse.org
> Est. 1993. Frequency: annual. Response Time: 3 mos. **Application.** What to submit: full script, submissions not returned. Material must be unpublished. Submission application fee: $10. Deadline: 10/15/2009.

**Raymond J. Flores Short Play Festival**
Around The Block, 5 E. 22nd St., #9-K
New York, NY 10010
Carlos Jerome
Tel: (212) 6739187
info@aroundtheblock.org
www.aroundtheblock.org
> Est. 2004. Theme: Life and aspirations in New York City. Part of annual Urban Arts Fest. Staff: Gloria Zelaya, Louis Vuolo (Co-dir, Theater Arts). Frequency: annual. **Consideration.** Opportunity/Award: $50, reading. **Preference.** Style: no musical. **Application.** What to submit: application, full script (2 copies, unless e-mailed),1 paragraph bio. Author must be owner of all production and publishing rights. Material must be in English, Spanish or Chinese. For Spanish and Chinese plays, we would appreciate your including a one-paragraph synopsis in English – otherwise we shall assign one of our judges to write such a synopsis. How to submit: Email, postal mail or hand delivery. Submission application fee: $5. Deadline: 11/30/2009.

**Seven Devils Playwrights Conference**
343 E. 30th St., #19-J
New York, NY 10016
Jeni Mahoney
jeni@sevendevils.org
www.sevendevils.org
Est. 2001. Equity 2-wk play development conference in McCall, ID, ending w/fully staged readings of new plays. **Preference.** Length: full length plays. **Application.** What to submit: please see website. Material must be unproduced. How to submit: please see website. Submission application fee: $5. Deadline: 12/31/2009.

**Sketchbook Festival**
437 N. Wolcott, #201, Attn: SKBK06
Chicago, IL 60622
Becky Perlman
becky@collaboraction.org
http://collaboraction.typepad.com/sketchbook/2007/01/post.html
Collaboration is accepting short play submissions (seven minutes or less in length) to be performed in May and June of 2009 in the Garage Theater at Steppenwolf Theatre Company. **Preference.** Style: audience participation. **Application.** What to submit: application, full script. Material must be unproduced. How to submit: email (rtf or doc only). Submission application fee: $10. Deadline: 12/15/2009.

**Tennessee Williams/New Orleans Literary Festival**
938 Lafayette St., #514
New Orleans, LA 70113
Laura Miller
Tel: (504) 581-1144 Fax: (504) 581-3270
info@tennesseewilliams.net
www.tennesseewilliams.net
Includes Saints and Sinners Annual Playwriting Festival. Frequency: annual. Production: small, minimal. **Consideration.** Opportunity/Award: $1,000. **Application.** Submission application fee: $25. Deadline: 11/25/2009.

**Theater Resources Unlimited (TRU)/TRU Voices**
Players Theater, 115 MacDougal St.
New York, NY 10012
Bob Ost
Tel: (212) 714-7628
Fax: (212) 864-6301
trunltd@aol.com
www.truonline.org
Deadlines: 1/1/2009 for plays, 8/31/2009 for musicals (deadlines extended a week for submissions that have a producer attached). Winter musical series (est. 1999) and spring play series (est. 1997) of 3-4 readings each. Prefer submissions from producers, but writers may submit and TRU will try to find a sponsoring producer. Frequency: annual. Production: cast limit 12 (with doubling). Response Time: 3 to 6 months. **Consideration.** Opportunity/Award: TRU Voices New Plays and New Musicals Reading Series -AEA developmental staged readings with invited industry panel. **Preference.** Length: full length plays and musicals. Style: Open to a range of work, from mainstream commercial to non-traditional. Subject: All subjects, woman, writers of color, disabled, gay/lesbian. **Application.** What to submit: Application required, plus 2 each: synopsis, letter of intention, full script, audio (CD preferred). No SASE (we do not return scripts unless specially requested). Material must have had no performances before a paying audience in the New York area. How to submit: Download application and guidelines from www.truonline.org or send an SASE to Theater Resources Unlimited/TRU Voices, 309 W. 104th Street, 1D, NYC NY 10025 (note: this is a different address than the one for script submissions). Submission application fee: $25. Deadline: 1/13/2009.

**Trustus Playwrights' Festival**
Box 11721, Columbia, SC 29211
Jon Tuttle
Tel: (803) 254-9732
trustus@trustus.org
www.trustus.org
Est. 1984. Staged reading in Aug., followed by 1-yr. development, culminating in mainstage production. Fees: $15 entry Frequency: annual. Production: ages 15-55, cast limit 8, unit set. Response Time: 3 mos. **Consideration.** Opportunity/Award: $750, production, reading. **Preference.** Length: full length plays. Style: comedy, drama. **Application.** What to submit: application, synopsis, SASE. Material must be unproduced. Submission application fee: $15. Deadline: 12/1/2008 -2/1/2009

## CONTESTS

**Brevard Little Theatre New-Play Competition**
Box 426, Brevard, NC 28712
Al Edick
Tel: (828) 890-1495
aedick@bellsouth.net
www.brevardlittletheatre.com
Production: cast limit 20, simple set. Response Time: by 9/30/09. **Consideration.** Opportunity/Award: public production. **Preference.** Length: full length plays. **Application.** What to submit: query, full script, SASE. Material must be unproduced, original. Deadline: 6/30/2009.

**Charles M. Getchell Award, SETC**
221 Brooks Center
Dept. of Performing Arts
Clemson, SC 29634
Mark Charney
Tel: (864) 656-5415 Fax: (864) 656-1013
cmark@clemson.edu
www.setc.org
**Consideration.** Opportunity/Award: $1,000. **Preference.** Length: full length plays. Style: email. **Application.** What to submit: application, full script sent electronically. Author must be resident or student in AL, FL, GA, KY, MS, NC, SC, TN, VA or WV. Material must be unpublished, unproduced. How to submit: On line application only. Deadline: 6/1/2009.

**American Scandinavian Foundation Translation Prize**
58 Park Ave., New York, NY 10016
grants@amscan.org
www.amscan.org
Est. 1979. Prize for best translation of drama written after 1800 by a Scandinavian author (Danish, Finnish, Icelandic, Norwegian, Swedish). **Consideration.** Opportunity/Award: $2,000; $1,000, publication of exerpt in Scandinavian Review. **Preference.** Length: full length plays. Style: translation. **Application.** What to submit: resume/bio. Material must be unpublished. How to submit: translation (4 copies), original (1 copy). Deadline: 6/1/2009.

**Anna Zornio Memorial Children's Theatre Playwriting Award**
UNH Theatre/Dance Dept.
PCAC, 30 College Rd.
Durham, NH 3824
Michael Wood
Tel: (603) 862-3038 Fax: (603) 862-0298
www.unh.edu/theatre-dance
Est. 1979. Quadrennial award for original children's script, selected by UNH Youth Drama Program. Students and faculty produce premiere. **Preference.** Subject: T.Y.A. **Application.** What to submit: application, full script, audio, cast/tech list, SASE. Author must be resident of US or Canada. Material must be

unoptioned, unpublished, unproduced, original. How to submit: email. Deadline: 3/3/2009.

**Arch & Bruce Brown Foundation**
2500 N. Palm Canyon Dr.
Palm Springs, CA 92262
Arch Brown
ArchWrite@aol.com
www.aabbfoundation.org
   Formed by Arch Brown in memory of Bruce Allen Brown (d. 1993). Awards for gay-positive arts projects on historic subjects. Awards rotate thru short fiction & one-act plays (2010), drama (2008), novel (2009). Frequency: annually. **Consideration.** Opportunity/Award: $1,000. **Preference.** Length: full length plays. Subject: gay/lesbian. **Application.** What to submit: full script, submissions not returned. Material must be unpublished. How to submit: unsolicited. Deadline: 11/30/2009.

**Arthur W. Stone New Play Award**
Box 8608, Ruston, LA 71272
Louisiana Tech University
Tel: (318) 257-2711 Fax: (318) 257-4571
stoneplaywritingaward@yahoo.com
http://performingarts/latech.edu
   Est. 2006. **Assistance:** room/board, travel. Frequency: biennial. Opens for submissions: 10/1/08. Production: college age. Response Time: 5/1/09. **Consideration.** Opportunity/Award: $500, plus production. **Preference.** Length: full length plays and musicals. **Application.** What to submit: full script, bio, SASE. For musicals -book, score, and recording. How to submit: email (DOC, FDR, RTF). Deadline: 3/1/2009.

**Aurora Theatre Company: Global Age Project**
2081 Addison St., Berkeley, CA 94704
J Harrison
Tel: (510) 843-4042
litman@auroratheatre.org
www.auroratheatre.org
   **Consideration.** Opportunity/Award: Reading, Workshop. Award/Grant/ Stipend: $1000. Travel Stipend provided. **Preference.** Length: full length plays. Style: Comedy, Variety, Drama. **Application.** What to submit: Material must be from U.S., Canada, Mexico. How to submit: Deadline: 7/1/2009.

**Award Blue**
Box 445, Buckley, IL 60918
Steven Packard
buntville@yahoo.fr
   Est. 1999. Frequency: annual. **Consideration.** Opportunity/Award: $200. **Application.** What to submit: full script, bio. Author must be IL high school student. Deadline: 5/31/2009.

**Babes With Blades Joining Sword and Pen**
Babes with Blades
2050 W. Addison, #3
Chicago, IL 60618-6126
Beth Cummings
newplays@BabesWithBlades.org
www.babeswithblades.org
   See website for updated info and deadline. Contest est. 2005; company est. 1997. **Consideration.** Opportunity/Award: $1000 cash prize. **Preference.** Subject: woman. **Application.** Material must include fighting roles for women! How to submit: via mail or email -see website for details.

**Baker's Plays High School Playwriting Contest**
45 W. 25th St., New York, NY 10010
Roxane Heinze-Bradshaw
Tel: (212) 255-8085 Fax: (212) 627-7753
www.bakersplays.com
   Est. 1989. For student plays, preferably about HS experience. Plays must be accompanied by signature of HS English or drama teacher. Response Time: TBA. **Consideration.** Opportunity/Award: $500 1st, $250 2nd, $100 3rd, publication, royalty. **Application.** What to submit: full script, SASE. Author must be HS student. Material must be produced.

## Beverly Hills Theatre Guild Julie Harris Playwright Awards
Box 148, Beverly Hills, CA 90213
Candace Coster
Tel: (310) 273-3390
www.beverlyhillstheatreguild.org
Frequency: annual. **Consideration.** Opportunity/Award: $3,500 1st, $2,500 2nd, $1,500 3rd. **Preference.** Length: full length plays. Style: comedy, drama. **Application.** What to submit: query, application, full script. Author must be citizen or resident of US. Material must be unoptioned, unpublished, unproduced, original, in English. Deadline: 11/1/2009.

## Beverly Hills California Musical Theatre Award
Box 148, Beverly Hills, CA 90213
Patricia Mock
Tel: (310) 273-3390
www.beverlyhillstheatreguild.org
**Consideration.** Opportunity/Award: $4,000. **Preference.** Style: musical. **Application.** What to submit: query, application, full script, audio. Author must be resident of CA, citizen of US. Material must be unproduced, original, in English. Deadline: 11/15/2009.

## Beverly Hills Theatre Guild Youth Theatre Marilyn Hall Awards
Box 148, Beverly Hills, CA 90213
Candace Coster
www.beverlyhillstheatreguild.org
Frequency: annual. **Consideration.** Opportunity/Award: $700 1st, $300 2nd. **Preference.** Subject: T.Y.A. **Application.** What to submit: query, application, full script. Author must be citizen or resident of US. Material must be unoptioned, unpublished, unproduced, in English. Deadline: 2/28/2009.

## California Young Playwrights Contest
Playwrights Project
2356 Moore St., #204
San Diego, CA 92110
Deborah Salzer
Tel: (619) 239-8222 Fax: (619) 239-8225
write@playwrightsproject.com
www.playwrightsproject.com
Est. 1984. All entrants receive evaluation. Winners work with a dramaturg and receive 4 performances at Old Globe. **Assistance:** room/board, travel. Frequency: annual. **Consideration.** Opportunity/Award: $100, production. **Preference.** Style: comedy, drama. **Application.** What to submit: query, full script (2 copies). Author must be age 18 or younger, resident of CA. Material must be unoptioned, unpublished, original. Deadline: 6/1/2009.

## Canadian Jewish Playwriting Competition
Jewish Theater
750 Spadina Ave., fl. 2
Toronto, ON M5R-3B2 Canada
Esther Arbeid
Tel: (416) 924-6211 ext. 606
esthera@mnjcc.org; www.mnjcc.org
Frequency: annual. Response Time: no reponse unless play is chosen as winner, no feedback from jury. **Consideration.** Opportunity/Award: 4 hour workshop with public reading, professional artists only. **Preference.** Length: full length plays and musicals. Subject: All subjects, woman, T.Y.A., writers of color, disabled, gay/lesbian. **Application.** Author must be Canadian or have strong Canadian ties. Material must be unpublished, unproduced. Deadline: 6/30/2009.

## Christopher Brian Wolk Award
312 W. 36th St., 6th floor
New York, NY 10018
Kim T. Sharp
Tel: (212) 868-2055 Fax: (212) 868-2056
ksharp@abingdontheatre.org
www.abingdontheatre.org
Est. 2001. Frequency: annual Production: cast limit 8. Response Time: 3 mos. **Consideration.** Opportunity/Award: $1,000, reading. **Preference.** Length: full length plays. Style: comedy, drama. Subject: All subjects, woman, writers of color. **Application.** What to submit: Mail

printed and bound copy of entire script, character breakdown, synopsis, production history, bio, see website for updates. Author must be resident or citizen of US. Material must be unoptioned, unproduced in NYC. Deadline: 6/1/2009.

**Cincinnati Playhouse in the Park Mickey Kaplan New American Play Prize**
Box 6537, Cincinnati, OH 45206
Tel: (513) 345-2242 Fax: (513) 345-2254
www.cincyplay.com
 Est. 2004. Frequency: annual. **Consideration.** Opportunity/Award: $15,000, production. **Preference.** Length: full length plays and musicals. Style: drama, comedy, musical, adaptation; no translation. **Application.** What to submit: See website for details. Agent submission of full script. Non-agent: synopsis, 10 pages dialog, character breakdown, playwright bio, production history. Include audio tape or CD of selections from score for musicals. SASE. Author must be citizen of US. Material must be unoptioned, unpublished, unproduced. Deadline: 12/31/2009.

**City Attic Theatre CAT Tales Festival**
19-25 Ditmars Blvd., 3rd Floor
Astoria, NY 10032
Melissa Gawlowski
cityattic@gmail.com
www.myspace.com/cityattic
 Est. 2004. Frequency: biennial Production: cast limit 6. Response Time: 4 mos. **Preference.** Length: full length plays. **Application.** What to submit: synopsis, 15-page sample. Material must be unpublished. Deadline: 2/1/2010.

**Cunningham Commission for Youth Theatre**
2135 N. Kenmore Ave., Chicago, IL 60614
Anna Ables
Tel: (773) 325-7938
aables@depaul.edu
www.theatreschool.depaul.edu

Est. 1991. Commission to write theater for youth that affirms the centrality of religion, broadly defined, and the human quest for meaning, truth and community. Frequency: annual. **Consideration.** Opportunity/Award: $6,000 commission. **Preference.** Subject: T.Y.A. **Application.** What to submit: 20-pg sample, resume. Author must be resident of Chicago (100 miles of Loop), not Cunningham winner in last 5 yrs. Deadline: 12/1/2009.

**Dorothy Silver Playwriting Competition**
26001 S. Woodland Ave.
Beachwood, OH 44122
Deborah Bobrow
Tel: (216) 831-0700 Fax: (216) 831-7796
dbobrow@clevejcc.org
www.clevejcc.org
 Award for original works of significant, fresh perspective on Jewish experience. Frequency: annual. Response Time: 4 mos. **Consideration.** Opportunity/Award: $1,000, reading. **Preference.** Length: full length plays. **Application.** What to submit: full script, audio, SASE. Material must be unoptioned, unpublished, unproduced. Deadline: 12/31/2009.

**Dr. Floyd Gaffney Playwriting Award on the African-American Experience**
9500 Gilman Drive, MC 0344
La Jolla, CA 92093
Tel: (858) 534-4791
www.theatre.ucsd.edu/playwritingcontest
 Est. 2007. Contest seeking scripts highlighting the African-American experience in contemporary or historical terms. No adaptations. Response Time: announced by 2/28/08. **Consideration.** Opportunity/Award: $1,000. **Application.** What to submit: application, full script. Author must be undergraduate, enrolled student. How to submit: unsolicited.

**Edgar Allan Poe Award for Best Play**
1140 Broadway, St. 1507
New York, NY 10001
Margery Flax

Tel: (212) 888-8171
mwa@mysterywriters.org
www.mysterywriters.org
   Est. 1945. Frequency: annual.
**Preference.** Length: full length musicals. Style: comedy, drama, musical. **Application.** What to submit: application, full script (5 copies), submissions not returned. Material must be produced. Deadline: 11/30/2009.

**Eileen Heckart Drama For Seniors Competition**
Ohio State University
1430 Lincoln, 1800 Cannon Drive
Columbus, OH 43210
Alan Wood
Tel: (614) 292-6614
woods.1@osu.edu
www.heckartdrama.blogspot.com
   Est. 2003. Biennial.

**Essential Theatre Playwriting Award**
1414 Foxhall Lane #10, Atlanta, GA 30316
Peter Hardy
Tel: (404) 2120815
pmhardy@aol.com
www.essentialtheatre.com
   Please put contact info on front page; number pages. **Consideration.** Opportunity/Award: $500, production. **Preference.** Length: full length plays and musicals. Style: Any style. Subject: All subjects. **Application.** What to submit: full script. Author must be resident of GA. Material must be unproduced. How to submit: email or regular mail. Deadline: 4/23/2009.

**Firehouse Center for the Arts**
Market Square, Newburyport, MA 01950
Tel: (978) 462-7336
kimm@firehouse.org
www.firehouse.org
   Deadline: August each year. **Consideration.** Award/Grant/Stipend: $150. **Preference.** Length: full length plays. Subject: woman, writers of color, disabled, gay/lesbian. **Application.** What to submit: new work. Author must be New England resident. How to submit: guidelines on website. Deadline: 8/8/2009.

**Fort Wayne Civic Theatre-Northeast Indiana Playwright Contest**
303 E. Main St.
Fort Wayne, IN 46802
Phillip H. Colglazier
Tel: (260) 422-8641 Fax: (260) 4226900
pcolglazier@fwcivic.org
www.fwcivic.org
   Author must be 19 or older. Current or former resident of Northeast Indiana within a 90 mile radius of Fort Wayne, IN. **Consideration.** Opportunity/Award: Reading, Production, 1st Place-$1,000, 2nd Place-$750, 3rd Place-$500 . Award/Grant/Stipend: $1000. **Preference.** Length: full length plays. Style: Adaptation, Comedy or Variety, Drama. Subject: All subjects, woman, writers of color, disabled, gay/lesbian. **Application.** What to submit: Application, Synopsis or Treatment, 10 page sample. Submit an entry form, play synopsis (1 page), 10 pages of script, and playwright's bio. Additional Guidelines: Suggested sets or unit set, cast limit of 10, 1 submission per playwright. The playwright's name should only appear on the title page and not on the subsequent pages of the script. Entry form available on-line at www.fwcivic.org. Material must be not optioned, not produced, not published. How to submit: Unsolicited Usolicited. Deadline: 9/1/2009.

**Fred Ebb Award**
231 W. 39th St., #1200
New York, NY 10018
info@fredebbfoundation.org
www.fredebbfoundation.org
   Est. 2005. Named for lyricist Fred Ebb (1928-2004), award recognizes excellence by a songwriter or songwriting team that hasn't yet achieved significant commercial success. Frequency: annual. Response Time: by 11/30/09. **Consideration.** Opportunity/Award: $50,000. **Preference.** Style: musical. **Application.** What to submit: application, audio (up to 4 songs), lyrics and context for songs. Author must be produced, published,

or professional workshop member. Deadline: 6/29/2009.

**Goshen College Peace Playwriting Contest**
1700 S. Main St.
Goshen, IN 46526
Douglas Caskey
Tel: (574) 535-7393 Fax: (574) 535-7660
douglc@goshen.edu
www.goshen.edu
> Renumeration: 1st Place: $500, production, room and board to attend rehearsals and/or production. 2nd Place: $100, possible production. Frequency: biennial. **Consideration.** Opportunity/Award: $500 1st; $100 2nd, production. **Preference.** Style: One Act play. **Application.** What to submit: 1-paragraph synopsis, full script, resume. Material must be unproduced preferred. Deadline: 12/31/2009.

**Green Light**
1819 JFK BLVD, #400
Philadelphia, PA 19103
A. Pandola
> Currently seeking submissions of one-act plays written by women for GLO 2008. For full details, please visit website. **Consideration.** Opportunity/Award: Production. **Preference.** Style: Comedy or Variety, Drama. Subject: woman. **Application.** What to submit: Full Script. Author must be Female, U.S. Resident. Material must not be produced or published. How to submit: Unsolicited. Deadline: 4/30/2009.

**Harold Morton Landon Translation Award**
584 Broadway, #604
New York, NY 10012
Ryan Murphy
Tel: (212) 274-0343 ext. 17
Fax: (212) 274-9427
academy@poets.org
www.poets.org
> Est. 1976. Recognizes translation of poetry (incl. verse drama) from any language into English. A noted translator chooses the winning book published that year. Frequency:

annual. **Consideration.** Opportunity/Award: $1,000. **Preference.** Length: full length plays. Style: translation of poetry. **Application.** What to submit: full script (3 copies). Author must be citizen of US. Material must be plays in verse; translation of poetry. How to submit: unsolicited. Deadline: 12/31/2009.

**Hawai'i Prize**
46 Merchant St.
Honolulu, HI 96813
Harry Wong III
Tel: (808) 536-4222 Fax: (808) 536-4226
kumukahuatheatre@hawaiiantel.net
www.kumukahua.org
> Frequency: annual. **Consideration.** Opportunity/Award: $600. **Preference.** Length: full length plays. **Application.** What to submit: full script (3 copies). Deadline: 1/2/2008.

**Henrico Theatre Company One-Act Playwriting Competition**
P.O. Box 90775, Henrico, VA 23273
Amy Perdue
Tel: (804) 5015138
per22@co.henrico.va.us
www.co.henrico.va.us/rec
> Est. 1984. Frequency: annual. **Consideration.** Opportunity/Award: $300, production. **Application.** What to submit: full script (2 copies), SASE. Material must be unpublished, unproduced, original. Deadline: 7/1/2009.

**International Radio Playwriting Competition**
Rm 118 East Wing, Bush House
London, England UK
intradioplaycomp@bbc.co.uk
www.bbc.co.uk
> **Assistance:** travel Frequency: biennial Production: cast limit 6. **Consideration.** Opportunity/Award: £2,500. **Application.** What to submit: application, full script. Author must be resident outside UK. Material must be unoptioned, unpublished, unproduced professionally, original, in English. Deadline: 4/30/2009.

## Intersection for the Arts James D. Phelan Literary Award
446 Valencia St.
San Francisco, CA 94103
Chida Chaemchaeng, Kevin Chen
Tel: (415) 626-2787
chida@theintersection.org
www.theintersection.org
>Est. 1937. Named for James Duval Phelan (1861-1930). Frequency: annual. **Consideration.** Opportunity/Award: $2,000. **Application.** What to submit: application, full script (3 copies). Author must be age 20-35, in March 2009. Material must be unpublished. Deadline: 3/31/2009.

## Jackie White Memorial National Children's Play Writing Contest
309 Parkade Blvd., Columbia, MO 65202
Betsy Phillips
Tel: (573) 874-5628
bybetsy@yahoo.com
www.cectheatre.org
>Est. 1988. In memory of Jackie Pettit White (1947-91). All scripts read by at least 3, finalists by at least 12. All receive written evaluation. Fees: $20 entry. Frequency: annual. Production: at least 7, speaking roles, sets appropriate for community theaters. Response Time: by 8/31/08. **Consideration.** Opportunity/Award: $500. **Preference.** Length: full length plays and musicals. **Application.** What to submit: application, full script, SASE. Material must be unpublished. Deadline: 6/1/2009.

## Jacksonville Univ. Helford Prize
2800 University Blvd. N.
Jacksonville, FL 32211
Laura Porter
lporter1@ju.edu
www.arts.ju.edu
>Production: cast of 5-10.
>**Consideration.** Opportunity/Award: $10,000. **Preference.** Length: full length plays. **Application.** What to submit: query, full script (3 blind copies), audio, score, submissions not returned. Author must be resident of US. Material must be unpublished, unproduced, original, in English. Deadline: 5/15/2009.

## Jacksonville University
2800 University Blvd.
Jacksonville, FL 32211
Dean Hill
Tel: (904) 256-7337 Fax: (904) 256-7375
whill@ju.edu
http://www.art.ju.edu
>Cast size 5-10. **Consideration.** Opportunity/Award: $10,000 stipend and possible production. **Preference.** Style: Plays, Musicals. Must be full-length. **Application.** What to submit: 3 copies of the full script. Author must be U.S. resident. Material must be unoptioned, unproduced. How to submit: Unsolicited. Deadline: 5/15/2008.

## L. Arnold Weissberger Award
Box 428, Williamstown, MA 1267
Suzanne Agins
Tel: (413) 458-3200 Fax: (413) 458-3147
sagins@wtfestival.org
www.wtfestival.org
>Est. 1988. Honors theater attorney and supporter L. Arnold Weissberger (1907-81). Frequency: annual. **Consideration.** Opportunity/Award: $10,000, publication. **Preference.** Length: full length plays. Style: drama, no musical, no screenplay. **Application.** What to submit: query, SASE. Material must be unpublished, professionally unproduced. How to submit: invite. Deadline: 6/15/2009.

## Lewis Galantiere Award
225 Reinekers Ln., #590
Alexandria, VA 22314
Tel: (703) 683-6100 Fax: (703) 683-6122
ata@atanet.org
www.atanet.org
>Est. 1982. Biennial award (even yrs) for outstanding published translation from language other than German into English. **Assistance:** $500 travel. Frequency: biennial (even yrs). **Consideration.** Opportunity/Award: $1,000. **Preference.** Length: full length plays. Style: translation. **Application.** What to submit: query, 10-pg sample of original and translation (2 copies), full script of translation (2 copies), bio. Material must be published. Deadline: 5/1/2009.

**Little Theatre of Alexandria National One-Act Playwriting Competition**
600 Wolfe St., Alexandria, VA 22314
Tel: (703) 683-5778 Fax: (703) 683-1378
asklta@thelittletheatre.com
www.thelittletheatre.com
> LTA reserves the right to produce selected script without payment of royalties. Frequency: annual Production: unit set. **Consideration.** Opportunity/Award: $350 1st; $250 2nd; $150 3rd, reading. **Preference.** Style: comedy, drama. Fees: $20 **Application.** What to submit: synopsis, full script, character breakdown, SASE. Material must be unpublished, unproduced, original. How to submit: unsolicited. Deadline: 10/31/2009.

**LiveWire Chicago Theatre**
P.O. Box 11226, Chicago, IL 60611
Josh Weinstein
Tel: (312) 533-4666
livewirechicago@gmail.com
www.livewirechicago.com/vision
> LiveWire presents VisionFest, an annual short play festival surrounding a central theme. See website for theme guidelines, submission criteria and more info. **Consideration.** Opportunity/Award: Reading. **Preference.** Style: Adaptation, Comedy or Variety, Drama. Subject: All subjects. **Application.** What to submit: Full Script. How to submit: Unsolicited. Deadline: 5/15/2009.

**Macy's New Play Prize for Young Audiences**
Box 6537, Cincinnati, OH 45206
Tel: (513) 345-2242 Fax: (513) 345-2254
education@cincyplay.com
www.cincyplay.com
> Est. 1999. Frequency: annual. Production: cast of 3-5, touring set. **Consideration.** Opportunity/Award: $5,000 commission. **Preference.** Style: no musical. Subject: T.Y.A. **Application.** What to submit: synopsis, 3-pg sample, full script (of another TYA), resume, SASE. Material must be unproduced. Deadline: 3/31/2009.

**Met Life Nuestras Voces Playwriting Competition**
138 E. 27th St., New York, NY 10016
Allison Astor-Vargas
Tel: (212) 225-9950
aav@repertorio.org
www.repertorio.org
> Est. 1999. Frequency: annual. Response Time: 6 mos. **Consideration.** Opportunity/Award: production, reading. **Preference.** Length: full length plays. Style: comedy, drama. Subject: writers of color. **Application.** What to submit: application, full script, submissions not returned. Author must be age 18 or older, resident or citizen of US. Material must be unpublished. Deadline: 6/1/2008.

**Mildred & Albert Panowski Playwriting Award**
701 W. College Ave.
Marquette, MI 49855
Matthew W. Hudson
Tel: (906) 227-2559 Fax: (906) 227-2567
www.nmu.edu/theatre
> Est. 1977. Winning playwright expected to participate in script development workshop during summer. **Assistance:** room/board, travel Frequency: annual. **Consideration.** Opportunity/Award: $2,000, production. **Preference.** Length: full length plays. Style: comedy, drama. **Application.** What to submit: 1-pg synopsis, full script, SASE. Material must be unoptioned, unpublished, unproduced. Deadline: 10/31/2009.

**Mountain Playhouse Playwriting Contest**
7713 Somerset Pike, Box 205
Jennerstown, PA 15547
Teresa Stoughton Marafino
Tel: (814) 629-9201 ext. 118
Fax: (814) 629-9201
erica@mountainplayhouse.com
www.mountainplayhouse.org
> Frequency: annual. Production: cast limit 8. **Consideration.** Opportunity/Award: $3,000, reading. **Preference.** Length: full length plays. Style: comedy. **Application.** What to submit: full script. Material must be

unproduced, not previously submitted for this award unless revised 70% or more. Deadline: 12/31/2009.

**Naples Players ETC**
701 5th Ave. S., Naples, FL 34102-6662
Joe Moran
Tel: (239) 434-4192
> 10 to 30 minutes in length. Writer must reside in Collier, Lee, Charlotte, Glades or Hendry county in Florida and may not be a member of the anonymous judging panel. **Consideration.** Opportunity/Award: Reading. **Preference.** Style: Comedy or Variety, Drama. Subject: All subjects. **Application.** Material must not be produced or published. Deadline: 5/31/2009.

**Nathan Miller History Play Contest**
1614 20th St. NW, Washington, DC 20009
Laura VanDruff
Tel: (202) 518-5357 ext. 2
> Frequency: annual. **Consideration.** Opportunity/Award: $2000. **Preference.** Length: full length plays. **Application.** Material must be unproduced. How to submit: Contact Sprenger Land Foundation for submission guidelines. Deadline: 12/31/2009.

**National New Play Network NNPN Smith Prize**
c/o InterAct Theatre, 2030 Sansom St.
Philadelphia, PA 19103
Toni Press-Coffman
tpplay@cox.net
www.nnpn.org
> Est. 2006. Prize for a play on issues of national or global import that examines our civic institutions. NNPN is an alliance of nonprofit professional theaters aiding the development, production and continued life of new plays for American theater. Fees: $10 entry **Assistance:** travel. Frequency: annual. **Consideration.** Opportunity/Award: $2,500, reading. **Preference.** Length: full length plays. Style: comedy, drama. **Application.** What to submit: full script, submissions not returned. Material must be

unproduced in LORT or NYC Equity venue. How to submit: unsolicited. Deadline: 7/1/2009.

**National Playwriting Competition**
Box 5134, New York, NY 10185
Sheri Goldhirsch
Tel: (212) 594-5440 Fax: (212) 684-4902
admin@youngplaywrights.org
www.youngplaywrights.org
> Winning playwrights receive full Off-Broadway productions in Young Playwrights Festival. Frequency: annual. **Preference.** Style: drama, musical. **Application.** What to submit: full script. Author must be age 18 or younger. Material must be original. Deadline: 1/2/2009.

**National Ten-Minute Play Contest**
316 W. Main St., Louisville, KY 40202
Amy Wegener
Tel: (502) 561-3300 Fax: (502) 561-3300
ahansel@actorstheatre.org
www.actorstheatre.org/humana_contest.htm
> Est. 1989. Frequency: annual. **Consideration.** Opportunity/Award: $1,000, production consideration. **Application.** What to submit: full script (1 entry/author), SASE. Author must be citizen or resident of US. Material must be full script (1 entry/author). How to submit: unsolicited. Deadline: 11/1/2009.

**New Playwrights Competition**
Box 22372, Santa Fe, NM 87502
N. Sabato
Tel: (505) 582-7992 Fax: (505) 982-7993
www.sfperformingarts.org
> Frequency: annual. **Preference.** Length: full length plays. Style: comedy, drama. **Application.** What to submit: synopsis, cast list. Author must be citizen of US. Material must be unproduced. Deadline: 9/1/2009.

**Pacific Rim Prize**
46 Merchant St., Honolulu, HI 96813
Harry Wong III
Tel: (808) 536-4222 Fax: (808) 536-4226
kumukahuatheatre@hawaiiantel.net
www.kumukahua.org

Frequency: annual. **Consideration.** Opportunity/Award: $450. **Preference.** Length: full length plays. Subject: writers of color. **Application.** What to submit: full script (3 copies). Deadline: 1/2/2009.

**None of the Above Playwriting Contest**
Box 2373, Astoria, NY 11102
Robert Liebowitz
liebo12360@yahoo.com
Est. 1981. New short plays using the last words of Dutch Schultz. Response Time: 1 mo. **Consideration.** Opportunity/Award: $100. **Application.** What to submit: full script, SASE. Deadline: 3/31/2009.

**North Carolina New Play Project (NCNPP)**
200 N. Davie St., Box 2
Greensboro, NC 27401
Stephen Hyers
Tel: (336) 335-6426 Fax: (336) 373-2659
drama@greensboro-nc.gov
www.playwrightsforum.org
Frequency: annual Production: small cast, simple set Response Time: 6 mos. **Consideration.** Opportunity/Award: $500. **Application.** What to submit: application, synopsis, full script, cast/scene list, submissions not returned. Author must be resident of NC. Material must be unpublished, unproduced professionally, original. How to submit: email (DOC, PDF, RTF). Deadline: 8/15/2009.

**Towngate Theatre Playwriting Contest**
Stifel FAC, 1330 National Rd.
Wheeling, WV 26003
Kate H. Crosbie
Tel: (304) 242-7700 Fax: (304) 242-7747
kcrosbie@oionline.com
www.oionline.com
Est. 1976. check website for programs and contest details.**Assistance:** $500 room/board limit, travel. Frequency: annual. Response Time: by 5/15/09. **Consideration.** Opportunity/Award: $300, production. **Preference.** Length: full length plays. Style: comedy, drama. **Application.** What to submit: full script, SASE. Material must be unpublished, unproduced. Deadline: 1/1/2009.

**Ohioana Career Award**
274 E. 1st Ave., #300
Columbus, OH 43201
Linda Hengst
Tel: (614) 466-3831 Fax: (614) 7286974
ohioana@ohioana.org
www.ohioana.org
Est. 1943. Award to native Ohioan for outstanding professional accomplishments in arts and humanities. Recipient is honored guest at Ohioana Day and must be present to receive award. **Assistance:** room/board Frequency: annual. **Application.** What to submit: query, application, 10-pg sample, 2-pg resume, submissions not returned. Author must be native of OH. Deadline: 12/31/2009.

**Ohioana Citations**
274 E. 1st Ave., #300
Columbus, OH 43201
Linda Hengst
Tel: (614) 466-3831 Fax: (614) 728-6974
ohioana@ohioana.org
www.ohioana.org
Est. 1945. Award for outstanding contributions and accomplishments in specific area of arts and humanities. Four citations may be given each year. **Assistance:** room/board Frequency: annual. **Application.** What to submit: query, application,10-pg sample, 2-pg resume, submissions not returned. Author must be native or 5-yr resident of OH. How to submit: professional recommendation. Deadline: 12/31/2009.

**Ohioana Pegasus Award**
274 E. 1st Ave., #300
Columbus, OH 43201
Linda Hengst
Tel: (614) 466-3831 Fax: (614) 728-6974
ohioana@ohioana.org
www.ohioana.org
Est. 1964. Award for unique or outstanding contributions or achievements in arts and humanities, given at discretion of trustees. **Assistance:** room/board Frequency: annual. Response Time: by 5/31/09. **Application.** What to submit:

query, application, 10-pg sample, 2-pg resume, submissions not returned. Author must be native or 5-yr resident of OH. How to submit: professional recommendation. Deadline: 12/31/2009.

**One-Act Playwriting Competition**
900 N. Benton Ave.
Springfield, MO 65802
Dr. Mick Sokol
Tel: (417) 873-6821
msokol@drury.edu
www.drury.edu
> Est. 1984. Frequency: biennial. Response Time: by 4/1/10. **Consideration.** Opportunity/Award: $300 1st, $150 2nd, $150 3rd. **Application.** What to submit: full script, SASE. Material must be unpublished, unproduced. Deadline: 12/1/2009.

**PEN/Laura Pels Foundation Awards for Drama**
588 Broadway, #303
New York, NY 10012
Nick Burd
Tel: (212) 334-1660 ext. 108
awards@pen.org
www.pen.org
> Est. 1998. Award to US playwright in mid-career writing in English with professional productions of at least 2 full-lengths (excl. musicals, translations) in theaters of at least 299 seats. Playwrights don't apply on their own behalf but are nominated by peers. Frequency: annual. **Consideration.** Opportunity/Award: $7,500. **Application.** How to submit: professional recommendation. Deadline: 1/16/2009.

**Playwrights First Award**
15 Gramercy Park S.
New York, NY 10003
Emily Andrew
Tel: (212) 744-1312
www.playwrightsfirst.com
> Est. 1993. Frequency: annual. Production: in English. Response Time: by 5/01/09. **Consideration.** Opportunity/Award: $1,000 award, reading. **Preference.** Length: full length plays. Style: comedy, drama.

**Application.** What to submit: full script, resume, submissions not returned. Material must be unproduced, in English, by 1 author. Deadline: 10/15/2009.

**Public Access Television Corporation**
PATV
1111 Marcus Ave., Suite LL27
Lake Success, NY 11042
Shirley Bruno
Tel: (516) 629-3710 Fax: (516) 629-3704
pachannel@aol.com
www.patv.org
> Submit typed manuscript to: The Public Access Television Corporation ATTN: "New Playwrights" Competition. **Consideration.** Opportunity/Award: Production. Award/Grant/Stipend: $100. **Preference.** Style: comedy or variety, drama. Subject: All subjects. **Application.** What to submit: full script. How to submit: see website for details. Deadline: 2/1/2009.

**Robert Chesley Award**
828 N. Laurel Ave.
Los Angeles, CA 90046
Victor Bumbalo
VictorTom@aol.com
> Est. 1991. In honor of Robert Chesley (1943-90) to recognize gay and lesbian themed work. Nominations open in early fall. Frequency: annual. **Consideration.** Opportunity/Award: $2,000. **Preference.** Subject: gay/lesbian. **Application.** What to submit: full script, SASE. Material must be gay themed.

**Robert J. Pickering Award for Playwriting Excellence**
89 Division St., Coldwater, MI 49036
J. Richard Colbeck
Tel: (517) 2797963
> Est. 1984. Award for unproduced plays and musicals. Frequency: annual. **Consideration.** Opportunity/Award: $200 1st, $50 2nd, $25 3rd. **Preference.** Length: full length plays. **Application.** What to submit: full script, SASE. Material must be unproduced. Deadline: 12/31/2009.

**Resident Prize**
46 Merchant St., Honolulu, HI 96813
Harry Wong III
Tel: (808) 536-4222 Fax: (808) 536-4226
kumukahuatheatre@hawaiiantel.net
www.kumukahua.org
Frequency: annual. **Consideration.**
Opportunity/Award: $250.
**Application.** What to submit: full script (3 copies). Author must be resident of HI. Deadline: 1/2/2009.

**Richard Rodgers Awards for Musical Theater**
633 W. 155th St., New York, NY 10032
Jane E. Bolster
Tel: (212) 368-5900 Fax: (212) 491-4615
www.artsandletters.org
Est. 1978. Awards for musicals by writers and composers not already established in this field. Staff: Virginia Dajani (Exec. Dir.), Ezra Laderman (Pres.) Frequency: annual. Response Time: 3/01/10. **Preference.** Length: full length musicals. Style: musical. **Application.** What to submit: application, synopsis, full script, audio, SASE. Author must be citizen or resident of US. Deadline: 11/1/2009.

**Ruby Lloyd Apsey Award**
ASC 255, 1530 3rd Ave. S.
Birmingham, AL 35294
Lee Shackleford
Tel: (205) 975-8755 Fax: (205) 934-8076
leeshack@uab.edu
www.theatre.hum.uab.edu
In even-number years, UAB seeks new, original full-lengths on racial or ethnic issues, with ethnically diverse casting. Frequency: biennial (even yrs). Next deadline in 2010. Production: college age. **Consideration.** Opportunity/Award: full-length. **Preference.** Length: full length plays. Style: comedy, drama. **Application.** What to submit: full script. How to submit: Electronic OK but prefer recyclable hard copy. Winner announced on web site.

**Scholastic Art & Writing Awards**
557 Broadway, New York, NY 10012
Bryan Doerries
Tel: (212) 343-7783 Fax: (212) 3893939
A&WGeneralInfo@scholastic.com
www.artandwriting.org
Est. 1923. National awards in 2 categories (grades 7-8; grades 9-12), selected from regional contests. Regional deadlines vary. Regional Gold Key works are considered for national awards. **Preference.** Style: comedy, drama. **Application.** What to submit: application (2 copies), full script. Author must be student (grades 7-12) in US or Canada. Material must be by 1 author.

**Southern Playwrights Competition**
700 Pelham Rd. N
Jacksonville, AL 36265
Joy Maloney
Tel: (256) 7825469
jmaloney@jsu.edu
www.jsu.edu/depart/english/southpla.htm
Est. 1991. Frequency: annual.
**Consideration.** Opportunity/Award: $1,000, production. **Preference.** Length: full length plays. Style: no musical. **Application.** What to submit: application, synopsis, full script, SASE. Author must be native or resident of South. Material must be unoptioned, unproduced professionally. Deadline: 1/15/2009.

**STAGE International Script Competition**
CNSI, MC 6105, 3241 Elings Hall -Bl
Santa Barbara, CA
Nancy Kawalek
stage@csni.ucsb.edu
www.cnsi.ucsb.edu/stage
Est. 2005. The Professional Artists Lab and California NanoSystems Institute (CNSI) at UCSB collaborate on Scientists, Technologists and Artists Generating Exploration (STAGE), Competition for best new play about science and technology. Frequency: annual Response Time: 7/09. **Consideration.** Opportunity/Award: $10,000, reading. **Preference.**

Length: full length plays. Style: adaptation, comedy, drama, nontraditional, multimedia; no musicals or translations. **Application.** What to submit: query, application, synopsis, full script (3 copies), cover letter, written statement, bio/resume, submissions not returned. Material must be unoptioned, unpublished, unproduced, not reviewed, in English. Deadline: 12/21/2009.

**Summerfield G. Roberts Award**
1717 8th St., Bay City, TX 77414
Janet Hickl
Tel: (979) 245-6644 Fax: (979) 2443819
www.srttexas.org
  Award for creative writing about the Republic of Texas, to encourage literature & research about the events and personalities of 1836-46. Frequency: annual. **Consideration.** Opportunity/Award: $2,500. **Application.** What to submit: full script (5 copies), SASE. Deadline: 1/15/2009.

**Susan Smith Blackburn Prize**
3239 Avalon Pl., Houston, TX 77019
Emilie Kilgore
www.blackburnprize.org
  Est. 1978. Plays accepted only from specified source theaters in US, UK and Ireland. Writers should bring their work to the attention of those listed on website. Frequency: annual. Response Time: by 1/30/10, see www.blackburnprize.org. **Consideration.** Opportunity/Award: $20,000 winner; $5,000 special commendation; $1,000 finalists. **Preference.** Length: full length. Style: comedy, drama, musical. **Application.** What to submit: full script (2 copies), SASE. Author must be female. Material must be unproduced or produced within a year of deadling submission, in English. Deadline: 9/20/2009.

**Towson Univ. Prize for Literature**
8000 York Rd., Towson, MD 21252
Edwin Duncan
Tel: (410) 704-2871 Fax: (410) 7043999
drjohnson@towson.edu
www.towson.edu/english
  Est. 1979. Frequency: annual. **Consideration.** Opportunity/Award: $1,000. **Preference.** Length: full length plays. **Application.** What to submit: application, full script (5 copies). Author must be resident of MD. Material must be published. Deadline: 6/15/2009.

**VSA arts Playwright Discovery Program**
818 Connecticut Ave. NW, #600
Washington, DC 20006
Elena Widder
Tel: (202) 628-2800
www.vsarts.org
  Est. 1984. Annual contest for one-acts by students grades 6-12 on how disability affects a person's life. Frequency: annual. Response Time: 2 mos. **Consideration.** Opportunity/Award: $1500, production, trip to Washington DC. **Preference.** Subject: disabled. **Application.** What to submit: application, full script. Author must be resident or citizen of US, grades 6-12. Material must be unoptioned, unpublished, unproduced. How to submit: online. Deadline: 4/15/2009.

**The Ten Minute Musicals Project**
Box 461194, West Hollywood, CA 90046
Michael Koppy
info@TenMinuteMusicals.org
www.TenMinuteMusicals.org
  Est. 1989. Frequency: annual Production: cast limit 10. **Consideration.** Opportunity/Award: $250. **Preference.** Style: musical. Subject: All subjects, woman, T.Y.A., writers of color, disabled, gay/lesbian. **Application.** What to submit: full script, audio, lead sheets/score, SASE. How to submit: by mail. Deadline: 8/31/2009.

**Theodore Ward Prize**
72 E. 11th St., #413, Chicago, IL 60605
Chuck Smith
Tel: (312) 344-6136
csmith@colum.edu
www.colum.edu

Frequency: annual. **Consideration.** Opportunity/Award: $2,000 1st, $500 2nd, production. **Preference.** Length: full length plays. Subject: writers of color. **Application.** What to submit: full script, SASE. Author must be resident of US, African-American. Material must be unproduced. Deadline: 7/1/2009.

**Turtle Shell Productions**
300 W. 43rd St, #403
New York, NY 10036
John Cooper
Tel: (646) 765-7670
jcooper@turtleshellproductions.com
www.turtleshellproductions.com
   **Consideration.** Opportunity/Award: Renumeration. Production. **Preference.** Style: Plays for children focusing on 21st century themes. **Application.** What to submit: Full Script. Material must be one-act for kids. 10-30 mins. How to submit: Unsolicited. Deadline: 6/2/2009.

**Ungar German Translation Award**
225 Reinekers Ln., #590
Alexandria, VA 22314
Marilyn Gaddis Rose
Tel: (703) 683-6100 Fax: (703) 683-6122
ata@atanet.org
www.atanet.org
   Biennial award (odd yrs) for outstanding published translation from German into English. **Assistance:** $500 travel. Frequency: biennial (odd yrs). **Consideration.** Opportunity/Award: $1,000. **Preference.** Length: full length plays. Style: translation. **Application.** What to submit: query,10-pg sample of original and translation (2 copies), full script of translation (2 copies), bio. Material must be published, from German original. Deadline: 5/1/2009.

**Valencia Character Company**
Box 3028, Orlando, FL 32802
Julia Gagne
Tel: (407) 582-2296
jgagne@valenciacc.edu
www.valenciacharacterco.com
   Est. 1991. Winning script receives development and full production by college. **Assistance:** $800 stipend. Frequency: annual. Production: some college age Response Time: 2 mos. **Preference.** Length: full length plays. Style: comedy, drama. **Application.** What to submit: 15-pg sample, sample will not be returned. electronic transmission preferred. Author must be resident of FL. Deadline: 10/15/2009.

**Vermont Playwrights Award**
Valley Players, P.O. Box 441
Waitsfield, VT 05673
Sharon Kellermann
valleyplayers@madriver.com
www.valleyplayers.com
   Est. 1982. Frequency: annual. **Consideration.** Opportunity/Award: $1,000, production or reading. **Preference.** Length: full length plays. Style: full-length non-musical, comedy, drama comedy, drama. **Application.** What to submit: application, full script, SASE. Author must be resident of ME, NH, VT. Material must be unoptioned, unpublished, unproduced. Deadline: 2/1/2009.

**Full-Length Play Competition**
Box 38728, Los Angeles, CA 90038
Les Hanson
Tel: (323) 876-9337
www.wcensemble.org
   ON HOLD. Est. 1989.

**Whiting Writers' Awards**
1133 6th Ave., Fl. 22
New York, NY 10036
www.whitingfoundation.org
   Est. 1985. Annual awards of $50,000 each to 10 emerging writers in fiction, nonfiction, poetry and drama, based on accomplishment and promise. Writers cannot apply for the awards. **Consideration.** Opportunity/Award: $50,000.

**Wichita State Univ. (WSU) New Play Competition**
1845 Fairmount, Campus Box 153
Wichita, KS 67260
Steve Peders
Tel: (316) 978-3360 Fax: (316) 978-3202
finearts.wichita.edu/performing
  Contest for original plays of at least 90 min. by undergrad or graduate students enrolled in any US college. ACTF production of new, unproduced script. Frequency: annual. Response Time: by 3/15/09. **Preference.** Length: full length plays. Style: comedy, drama. **Application.** What to submit: query, full script, SASE. Author must be US college student. Material must be unpublished, unproduced, original. Deadline: 1/15/2009.

**Write a Play! NYC Contest**
Young Playwrights Inc, PO Box 5134
New York, NY 10185
Sheri Goldhirsch
Tel: (212) 594-5440
admin@youngplaywrights.org
www.youngplaywrights.org
  Open to all NYC students in 3 categories: elementary, middle, and high school. All receive certificate of merit, written evaluation, and invitation to awards ceremony. Frequency: annual. **Consideration.** Opportunity/Award: Cash prize awarded to winners in each division. All playwrights receive an evaluation of their play. **Preference.** Style: comedy, drama. **Application.** What to submit: full script, submissions not returned. Author must be resident of NYC, student in elementary, middle or high school. Material must be original. How to submit: Visit www.youngplaywrights.org for submission instructions. Early Bird Postmark Deadline: February 1, 2009 Final Postmark Deadline: April 1, 2009

## CONTESTS (*FEE CHARGED*)

**Actors' Theatre Full-Length Play Contest**
1001 Center St., #12
Santa Cruz, CA 95060
Wendy Adler
Tel: (831) 425-1003 Fax: (831) 425-7560
actors@sbcglobal.net
www.actorssc.org
  Est. 1985. Frequency: annual. **Consideration.** Opportunity/Award: $200, reading. **Preference.** Length: full length plays. **Application.** What to submit: full script (2 copies), submissions not returned. Material must be unpublished, unproduced, original. Submission application fee: $15. Deadline: 10/1/2009.

**Actors' Theatre Ten-Minute Play Contest**
1001 Center St., #12
Santa Cruz, CA 95060
Wendy Adler
Tel: (831) 425-1003 Fax: (831) 425-7560
actors@sbcglobal.net
www.actorssc.org
  Est. 1985. Frequency: annual. **Consideration.** Opportunity/Award: production, reading. **Application.** What to submit: full script (5 copies), cover letter, submissions not returned. Material must be full script (5 copies), cover letter, submissions not returned; do not identify author on scripts. Submission application fee: $10. Deadline: 6/1/2009.

**Arts & Letters Prize in Drama**
GCSU Campus Box 89
Milledgeville, GA 31061
David Muschell
Tel: (478) 445-1289 Fax: (478) 445-5961
al@gcsu.edu
http://www.al.gcsu.edu/
  Est. 1999. Response Time: 3 mos. **Consideration.** Opportunity/Award: $1,000, production, publication,1-yr subscription (2 issues). **Application.**

What to submit: query, full script. Material must be unpublished, original, in English. Submission application fee: $15. Deadline: 3/15/2009.

**Aurand Harris Memorial Playwriting Award**
NETC, 215 Knob Hill Dr.
Hamden, CT 06518
Joseph Juliano
Tel: (617) 851-8535
mail@netconline.org
www.netconline.org
> Est. 1997. Honors Aurand Harris for his lifetime dedication to all aspects of professional theater for young audiences. Frequency: annual. Response Time: by 11/1/09. **Consideration.** Opportunity/Award: $1,000 1st, $500 2nd. **Preference.** Length: full length plays. Style: comedy, drama. Subject: T.Y.A. **Application.** What to submit: application, full script. Material must be unpublished, unproduced. Submission application fee: $10. Deadline: 5/1/2009.

**Laity Theatre Company**
343 E. Palmdale Blvd, Ste. 8
Palmdale, CA 93551
James Goins
Tel: (661) 223-5585 Fax: (661) 430-5423
contact@laityarts.org
www.laityarts.org
> Submit query, synopsis or treatment, 15 page sample. Subject: women, theatre for young adults, writers of color, disabilities. **Consideration.** Opportunity/Award: Reading, Workshop. Award/Grant/Stipend: $100. **Preference.** Length: full length plays. Style: comedy, variety, drama, musical, translation. Subject: woman, T.Y.A., writers of color, disabled. **Application.** What to submit: full-length plays, full-length musicals, one-act plays, one-act musicals. Material must be not produced, not published. How to submit: Unsolicited. Submission application fee: $25. Deadline: 1/15/2009.

**National Children's Theatre Festival**
280 Miracle Mile, Coral Gables, FL 33134
Earl Maulding
Tel: (305) 444-9293 ext. 615
www.actorsplayhouse.org
> Response Time: 10/01/09. **Application.** Submission application fee: $10. Deadline: 4/1/2009.

**Community Theatre Association of Michigan**
4026 Lester, Oscoda, MI 48750
Vincent Weiler
vweiler@iresa.k12.mi.us
www.communitytheatre.org
> Frequency: annual. **Consideration.** Opportunity/Award: $500. **Preference.** Length: full length plays. Style: comedy, drama. **Application.** What to submit: full script, SASE. Author must be resident of Michigan. Material must be full evening's entertainment; several one-acts will meet requirement. How to submit: U. S. Mail; check website for details. Submission application fee: $20. Deadline: 5/15/2009.

**Das Goldkiel**
Box 445, Buckley, IL 60918
Steven Packard
buntville@yahoo.fr
> Est. 1999. Frequency: annual. **Consideration.** Opportunity/Award: $250. **Preference.** Length: full length plays. **Application.** What to submit: full script, resume. Material must be unpublished, unproduced, original; in English, French, German, Italian, Portuguese or Spanish. Submission application fee: $8. Deadline: 5/31/2009.

**David C. Horn Prize**
Box 209040, New Haven, CT 6520
Keith Condon
www.yalebooks.com
> Est. 2006. **Consideration.** Opportunity/Award: $10,000, publication by Yale Press, staged reading at Yale Rep. **Preference.** Length: full length plays. Style: no musical. **Application.** What to submit: full script (unbound), cover pg (w/title, contact info, pg count), cast/

scene list, submissions not returned. Author must be citizen of US, Canada, UK or Ireland, not published in full-length. Material must be unpublished, unproduced professionally, original, in English. Submission application fee: $25. Deadline: 8/15/2009.

**Eric Bentley New Play Competition**
95 Johnson Park, Buffalo, NY 14201
Richard Lambert
Tel: (716) 853-1334 Fax: (716) 853-1334
newphnxtheatre@aol.com
www.newphoenixtheatre.com
Frequency: annual. **Consideration.** Opportunity/Award: production. **Preference.** Subject: gay/lesbian. **Application.** What to submit: full script, SASE. Material must be unproduced. Submission application fee: $25. Deadline: 5/1/2009.

**FirstStage One-Act Play Contest**
Box 38280, Los Angeles, CA 90038
Dennis Safren
Tel: (323) 3506271
firststagela@aol.com
www.firststagela.org
Est. 1983. Staged readings of 3 finalists. Frequency: annual. Response Time: 3 wks. **Consideration.** Opportunity/Award: $300 1st, $100 2nd/3rd, reading. **Application.** What to submit: full script, submissions not returned. Material must be unproduced. Submission application fee: $10. Deadline: 11/15/2009.

**Francesca Primus Prize**
773 Nebraska Ave. W., St. Paul, MN 55117
Katie Burger
Tel: (651) 261-7804
www.americantheatrecritics.org/awards.html
In memory of Francesca Primus (d.1992). Frequency: annual. **Consideration.** Opportunity/Award: $10,000. **Preference.** Length: full length plays. Style: comedy, drama. **Application.** What to submit: query, full script (6 copies). Author must be female. Material must be professionally produced in previous yr. How to submit: professional recommendation.

Submission application fee: $25. Deadline: 2/15/2009.

**Fremont Centre Theatre New Playwright Contest**
1000 Fremont Ave.
South Pasadena, CA 91030
Carol Doehring
Tel: (626) 441-5977 Fax: (626) 441-5976
fct@fremontcentretheatre.com
www.fremontcentretheatre.com
Frequency: annual. Production: cast limit 10. **Consideration.** Opportunity/Award: $350 1st, $250 2nd, $100 3rd, reading. **Preference.** Length: full length plays. Subject: writers of color. **Application.** What to submit: 1-pg synopsis, full script, cast list, resume. Material must be unpublished, unproduced professionally. Submission application fee: $15. Deadline: 4/30/2009.

**FUSION Theatre Co.**
700 1st Street NW
Albuquerque, NM 87102
Jen Grigg
Tel: (505) 7669412
jeng@fusionabq.org
www.fusionabq.org
One playwright will be provided with round trip airfar to Albuqueque to attend the festival. See website for guidelines. **Consideration.** Opportunity/Award: Production. **Preference.** Style: All. **Application.** What to submit: Full script. Material must not be produced or published. Submission application fee: $5. Deadline: 5/15/2009.

**Georgia College and State University**
Porter Hall CBX66
Milledgeville, GA 31061
Karen Berman
Tel: (478) 445-1980 Fax: (478) 445-1633
kbermanth@aol.com
www.gcsu.edu/musicandtheatre
Please submit cover letter and biography of two pages or less. **Consideration.** Opportunity/Award: Production/$2000. Award/Grant/Stipend: $2000. **Preference.** Length:

full length plays. Style: comedy or variety, drama. **Application.** What to submit: full script. Author must be available for short residency. Material must not be optioned, published, or produced. How to submit: separate cover sheet with author's name and address. Submission application fee: $20. Deadline: 12/1/2009.

**Grawemeyer Award for Music Composition**
University of Louisville School of Music
Louisville, KY 40292
Marc Satterwhite
GrawemeyerMusic@louisville.edu
www.grawemeyer.org
Est. 1984. **Consideration.** Opportunity/Award: $200,000. **Application.** What to submit: application, full score, audio, bio. Material must have been premiered between 1/1/04 and 12/31/08. How to submit: professional recommendation. Submission application fee: $40. Deadline: 1/12/2009.

**High School New Play Award**
700 Cobb Pkwy. N., Marietta, GA 30062
Katie Watts
wattsk@thewalkerschool.org
www.setc.org/scholarship
**Consideration.** Opportunity/Award: $250, reading. **Application.** What to submit: full script, SASE. Author must be student in AL, FL, GA, KY, MS, NC, SC, TN, VA or WV. Material must be unpublished, unproduced. Submission application fee: $10. Deadline: 12/1/2009.

**Irish American Theatre Co.**
PO Box 1647, New York, NY 10028
Thomas Henry
Tel: (917) 9290169
iatc@excite.com
**Consideration.** Opportunity/Award: reading, workshop. **Preference.** Style: comedy or variety, drama, translation. **Application.** What to submit: query, synopsis or treatment, 10 page sample. Please provide a brief bio. Author must be 18 or older. Material must not be optioned, produced, or published. How to submit: Unsolicited. Submission application fee: $10. Deadline: 10/31/2009.

**Jane Chambers Playwriting Award**
Georgetown University
108 Davis Center, Box 571063
Washington, DC 20057
Maya Roth
www.athe.org/wtp/html/chambers.html
Named in honor of lesbian playwright Jane Chambers, and administered by the Women and Theatre Program of ATHE. **Consideration.** Opportunity/Award: $500 and a public reading at the annual ATHE Conference. **Preference.** Length: full length plays and musicals. Style: Feminist plays and performance texts written by women with a majority of roles for female performers. We welcome experimentations in style and form, and understand feminism varies in relation to experiences of race, sexuality, class, geography, ability and identity. Subject: All subjects, woman, T.Y.A., writers of color, disabled, gay/lesbian. **Application.** What to submit: In 2009, send application, synopsis, full script (3 copies), resume. Submissions are not returned. Author must be female. Material must be original work, and not yet published. How to submit: Consult the WTP website each December for current guidelines, as organizers/submission addresses rotate. Submission application fee: $15. Deadline: 2/15/2009.

**Jane Chambers Student Playwriting Award**
230 W. 56th St., #65-A
New York, NY 10019
Jen-Scott Mobley
Tel: (646) 662-5702
www.athe.org/wtp/html/chambers.html
Award for plays and texts by female students that reflect a feminist perspective and contain a majority of opportunities for women performers. Frequency: annual. **Consideration.** Opportunity/Award: $150, reading $250, reading. **Preference.** Subject: woman. **Application.** What to submit:

# Career Development : Contests (Fee Charged)

application, synopsis, full script (3 copies), resume, submissions not returned. Author must be female student. Material must be original. Submission application fee: $10. Deadline: 2/25/2009.

**Jewel Box Theatre Playwriting Award**
3700 N. Walker Ave.
Oklahoma City, OK 73118
Chuck Tweed
Tel: (405) 521-1786
www.jewelboxtheatre.org
 Est. 1986. Frequency: annual Response Time: by 5/30/08. **Consideration.** Opportunity/Award: $500. **Preference.** Length: full length plays. Style: adaptation, comedy, drama. **Application.** What to submit: application, full script, SASE. Material must be unoptioned, unpublished, unproduced. Submission application fee: $15. Deadline: 1/19/2008.

**John Gassner Memorial Playwriting Award**
NETC, 215 Knob Hill Dr.
Hamden, CT 06518
Joseph Juliano
Tel: (617) 851-8535
mail@NETConline.org
www.NETConline.org
 Est. 1967. Honors theater historian John Gassner for his lifetime dedication to all aspects of professional and academic theater. Frequency: annual. Response Time: by 11/01/09. **Consideration.** Opportunity/Award: $1,000 1st, $500 2nd. **Preference.** Length: full length plays. Style: comedy, drama. **Application.** What to submit: application, full script. Material must be unpublished, unproduced. Submissions not returned. Submission application fee: $10. Deadline: 4/15/2009.

**Maxim Mazumdar New Play Competition at Alleyway Theatre**
1 Curtain Up Alley, Buffalo, NY 14202
Joyce Stilson
www.alleyway.com
 Est. 1990. Named for Maxim Mazumdar (1953-87). Winning full-length receives premiere production in mainstage season. Winning one-act receives premiere in Buffalo Quickies fest. Frequency: annual. Response Time: 5 mos. **Consideration.** Opportunity/Award: $400 (full-length), $100 (one-act). **Preference.** Length: full length plays. **Application.** What to submit: full script, SASE. Material must be unoptioned, unproduced. Submission application fee: $25. Deadline: 7/1/2009.

**McLaren Memorial Comedy Playwriting Competition**
2000 W. Wadley Ave.
Midland, TX 79705
Ken Tumlin
Tel: (432) 682-2544
mclaren1@mctmidland.org
www.mctmidland.org
 Est. 1989. Staff: Marla Cooper, Brenda Tumlin. Frequency: annual. **Consideration.** Opportunity/Award: $400 (full-length), $200 (one-act). **Preference.** Length: full length plays. Style: comedy, no musical. **Application.** What to submit: full script, SASE. Material must be unoptioned, unpublished, unproduced. Submission application fee: $15. Deadline: 2/28/2009.

**Mississippi Theatre Association**
206 Yeates St., Starkville, MS 39759
Kris Lee
Tel: (812) 320-3534
tklee1976@gmail.com
www.mta-online.org
 This competition is designed to recognize and promote the works of Mississippi playwrights and is open to all Mississippi writers either in state or abroad. **Consideration.** Opportunity/Award: Reading. Award/Grant/Stipend: $500. **Preference.** Style: Comedy or Variety, Drama. **Application.** What to submit: Application, Synopsis or Treatment, Full script. Author must be 18 or older. Material must not be produced, published, or optioned. How to submit: Unsolicited. Submission application fee: $10. Deadline: 9/1/2009.

**Moving Arts Premiere One-Act Competition**
Box 481145, Los Angeles, CA 90048
Trey Nichols
www.movingarts.org
> Frequency: annual Production: cast limit 8, unit set. **Consideration.** Opportunity/Award: $200, production. **Preference.** Style: comedy, drama. **Application.** What to submit: query, full script, SASE. Material must be unproduced in L.A. Submission application fee: $10. Deadline: 2/1/2009.

**National New Play Network**
2030 Sansom St., Philadelphia, PA 19103
David Golston
Tel: (215) 568-8077 Fax: (215) 568-8095
davidg@nnpn.org
www.nnpn.org
> **Consideration.** Opportunity/Award: $2500, production. Award/Grant/Stipend: $2500. **Preference.** Style: comedy, drama, translation, adaptation. **Application.** What to submit: Full Script. Material must be unproduced. How to submit: unsolicited. Submission application fee: $10. Deadline: 8/1/2009.

**National One-Act Playwriting Contest**
1686 Lawndale St., Dubuque, IA 52001
Gary Arms
gary.arms@clarke.edu
> Est. 1977. Frequency: annual Production: cast of 2-5, unit set Response Time: 6 mos. **Consideration.** Opportunity/Award: $600 1st, $300 2nd, $200 3rd. **Application.** What to submit: application, full script (2 copies), SASE. Material must be unpublished, unproduced. Submission application fee: $10. Deadline: 1/31/2009.

**New Play Festival**
Yellow Taxi Productions, Box 1515
Nashua, NH 03061
Suzanne Delle
sdelle@yellowtaxiproductions.org
www.yellowtaxiproductions.org
> Est. 2002. Multi-day new-play fest of readings and productions with talkbacks. Production: cast limit 5. Response Time: 3 mos. **Consideration.** Opportunity/Award: production at festival. **Preference.** Length: full length plays. Style: drama. **Application.** What to submit: ten-minute play. Material must be unpublished, unproduced. Submission application fee: $10. Deadline: 12/15/2009.

**New Rocky Mountain Voices**
Box 790, Westcliffe, CO 81252
Dick Senff
wcpa@ris.net
www.westcliffecenter.org
> Est. 1999. Winning plays staged at Jones Theater in Westcliffe, CO. Authors asked to speak afterward. Staff: Anne Kimbell Relph (Artistic Dir). Frequency: annual. Production: cast of 4-8, unit set. Response Time: 2 mos. **Consideration.** Opportunity/Award: $200, production. **Preference.** Style: comedy, drama. **Application.** What to submit: query, synopsis, full script, no author name on title page (on letter only), SASE. Author must be resident of Rocky Mts (AZ, CO, ID, MT, NM, UT). Material must be unproduced professionally. Submission application fee: $5. Deadline: 4/15/2009.

**Next Generation Playwriting Contest**
520 8th Ave, #317
New York, NY 10018
Kimberly Wadsworth
Tel: (212) 244-7803 Fax: (212) 244-7813
info@ReverieProductions.org
www.ReverieProductions.org
> Est. 2004. New work from established & emerging writers on socio-political issues in highly theatrical contexts. Finalists recieve public staged reading; grand prize receives workshop production and possible full production in NYC. Staff: Colin D. Young (Artistic Dir). Frequency: annual. **Consideration.** Opportunity/Award: $500. **Preference.** Length: full length plays and musicals, at least 60 min long - no one acts! Style: comedy, drama, radio. Subject: woman, writers of color, disabled,

gay/lesbian. **Application.** What to submit: application, full script, SASE. Material must be unpublished, not produced in NY, NJ or CT. How to submit: Please follow guidelines on website. Submission application fee: $18. Deadline: 12/15/2009.

**PEN Center USA Literary Awards**
c/o Antioch University
Los Angeles, 400 Corporate Pointe
Culver City, CA 90230
Tel: (310) 862-1555 ext. 361
Fax: (310) 862-1556
awards@penusa.org
www.penusa.org
 Est. 1982. Prizes for plays, teleplays, and screenplays. Frequency: annual. **Consideration.** Opportunity/Award: $1,000. **Application.** What to submit: application, full script (4 copies), submissions not returned. Author must reside west of the Mississippi River, or in the states of Minnesota or Louisiana. Submission application fee: $35. Deadline: 1/31/2009.

**PEN Translation Prize**
588 Broadway, #303
New York, NY 10012
Nick Burd
Tel: (212) 334-1660 ext. 108
awards@pen.org
www.pen.org
 Est. 1963. **Consideration.** Opportunity/Award: $3,000. **Preference.** Length: full length plays. Style: translation. **Application.** What to submit: full script (3 copies), submissions not returned. Material must be published in US. Submission application fee: $50. Deadline: 12/15/2009.

**Plays for the 21st Century**
6732 Orangewood Dr., Dallas, TX 75248
Jack Marshall
www.playwrightstheater.org
 Est. 1995. Staff: Alberto Rubio (Dir. of Operations), John Luis Navarro (Artistic Dir. -Theatrical Prod.) Frequency: annual. **Consideration.** Opportunity/Award: $750 1st, $500 2nd, $250 3rd (full-length); $250 (one-act). **Preference.** Length: full length plays. Style: no musical. **Application.** What to submit: synopsis, full script (DOC, HTML, RTF). Material must be unoptioned, unpublished, unproduced professionally, original, in English. How to submit: email to 2.act.play@sbcglobalnet or 1.act.play@sbcglobal.net. Submission application fee: $20. Deadline: 3/15/2009.

**Prix Hors Pair**
Box 445, Buckley, IL 60918
Steven Packard
buntville@yahoo.fr
 Est. 1999. Frequency: annual. **Consideration.** Opportunity/Award: $200. **Application.** What to submit: full script, resume. Material must be original; in English, French, German, Italian, Portuguese or Spanish. Submission application fee: $8. Deadline: 5/31/2009.

**Reva Shiner Full-Length Play Contest**
107 W. 9th St., Bloomington, IN 47404
Sonja Johnson
Tel: (812) 334-1188
bpplitma@newplays.org
www.bloomingtonplays.org
 BPP is a development group. Winning writers are expected to be part of development process. Frequency: annual. **Consideration.** Opportunity/Award: $500, production. **Preference.** Length: full length plays and musicals. **Application.** What to submit: query, full script, audio. Material must be unpublished, unproduced. How to submit: unsolicited. Submission application fee: $10. Deadline: 10/31/2009.

**Reverie Productions**
520 Eighth Ave., #317
New York, NY 10018
Kimberly Wadsworth
Tel: (212) 244-7803
kimberly@reverieproductions.org
www.reverieproductions.org
 Est. 2002 check website for guidelines. Frequency: annual. Response Time: April. **Consideration.** Opportunity/Award: $500. **Preference.** Length: full length plays. Style: comedy,

drama. Subject: All subjects, woman, writers of color, disabled, gay/lesbian. **Application.** What to submit: application, full script, SASE. Material must be unoptioned, unpublished, unproduced. Submission application fee: $18. Deadline: 12/15/2009.

**W. Keith Hedrick Playwriting Contest**
Box 940, Hudson, NY 12534
Jan M. Grice
Tel: (518) 851-7244
jangrice2002@yahoo.com
www.hrc-showcasetheatre.org
Est. 1993. 1 winner and 4 finalists receive public staged reading by professional actors. Frequency: annual. Production: cast limit 8 Response Time: 3 mos. **Consideration.** Opportunity/Award: $500 1st, $100 finalist, reading. **Application.** What to submit: full script, SASE. Author must be resident of Northeast. Material must be unpublished. Submission application fee: $5. Deadline: 5/1/2009.

**TeCo Theatrical Productions New Play Competition**
215 S. Tyler St., Dallas, TX 75208
Teresa Coleman Walsh
Tel: (214) 948-0716 Fax: (214) 948-3706
teresa@tecotheater.org
www.tecotheater.org
TeCo not accepting submissions this year. Est. 1993. Multicultural theater promoting quality theatre through dramatic artistic expression. Assistance: travel. Frequency: annual. Production: cast limit 4, minimal set Response Time: 2 mos. **Application.** Submission application fee: $10.

**Theatre in the Raw Playwriting Contest**
3521 Marshall St., Vancouver, BC Canada
Jay Hamburger
Tel: (604) 708-5448 Fax: (604) 708-1454
theatreintheraw@telus.net
www.theatreintheraw.ca
Est. 1994. Frequency: biennial Production: cast limit 6, set limit 2 (scene limit 3). **Consideration.** Opportunity/Award: CA$150 1st, CA$75 2nd, CA$50 3rd. **Preference.** Style: comedy, drama, radio.

**Application.** What to submit: full script, SASE. Material must be unoptioned, unpublished, unproduced. Submission application fee: $25. Deadline: 12/31/2009.

**Theatre Oxford 10-Minute Play Contest**
Box 1321, Oxford, MS 38655
Dinah Swan
www.10minuteplays.com
Est. 1998. Frequency: annual. Production: cast limit 5, minimal set. Response Time: 3 mos. **Consideration.** Opportunity/Award: $1,000, production. **Preference.** Style: no musicals. **Application.** What to submit: full script, submissions not returned. Material must be unoptioned, unpublished, unproduced. Submission application fee: $10.

**Urban Stages Emerging Playwright Award**
17 E. 47th St., Fl. 6
New York, NY 10017
Frances Hill
www.urbanstages.org
Est. 1986. Frequency: annual. Production: cast limit 7. Response Time: 3 mos. **Consideration.** Opportunity/Award: $500 (in lieu of royalty), production. **Preference.** Length: full length plays. Style: comedy, drama. **Application.** What to submit: full script, SASE. Material must be unoptioned, unpublished, unproduced. Submission application fee: $10.

**Writer's Digest Writing Competition**
700 East State St., Iola, WI 54990
Tel: (715) 445-4612 ext. 13430
Fax: (715) 445-4067
writing-competition@fwpubs.com
www.writersdigest.com
Est. 1931. Assistance: travel. Frequency: annual. **Consideration.** Opportunity/Award: $3,000 1st. **Application.** What to submit: application, 1-pg synopsis, 15-pg sample. Material must be unpublished, unproduced. Submission application fee: $15. Deadline: 2009 deadline to be announced.

## GRANTS AND FELLOWSHIPS

**Alabama State Council on the Arts**
201 Monroe St., Montgomery, AL 36130
Randy Shoults
Tel: (334) 242-4076 ext. 224
Fax: (334) 240-3269
randy.shoults@arts.alabama.gov
www.arts.state.al.us
> Opportunities incl. Artist Fellowships and Artist in Education Residency in performing artists (music, dance, theater), literature (fiction, creative nonfiction, poetry, screenwriting, playwriting), and visual artists. **Application.** Author must be 2-yr resident of AL. Deadline: 3/1/2009.

**Alaska State Council on the Arts (ASCA)**
411 W. 4th Ave., #1-E
Anchorage, AK 99501
Tel: (888) 278-7424 Fax: (907) 269-6601
aksca_info@eed.state.ak.us
www.eed.state.ak.us/aksca
> Est. 1966. Opportunities incl. quarterly Career Opportunity Grants and biennial Connie Boochever Artist Fellowships (Aug 31 deadline, odd yrs). Staff: Andrea Noble (Dir, Career Grants), Charlotte Fox (Dir, Artist Fellowships). **Application.** What to submit: 10-pg sample, audio. Author must be age 18 or older, resident of AK. Deadline: 3/1/2009.

**Allen Lee Hughes Fellowship Program**
1101 6th St. SW, Washington, DC 20024
Katherine Keefe
> **Preference.** Subject: writers of color.

**American Antiquarian Society Fellowships**
185 Salisbury St., Worcester, MA 01609
Cheryl McRell
Tel: (508) 471-2149 Fax: (508) 7549069
cmcrell@mwa.org; www.americanantiquarian.org
> Up to 4 fellowships to creative and performing artists and writers for 4-wk residency to research works about pre-20th century US history. Assistance: $1,200/mo, travel. Response Time: by 12/5/09. **Application.** How to submit: see directions on website. Deadline: 10/5/2009.

**American-Scandinavian Foundation (ASF)**
58 Park Ave., New York, NY 10016
Tel: (212) 879-9779 Fax: (212) 249-3444
grants@amscan.org
www.amscan.org
> Grants for short visits and fellowships for full year of study or research in Denmark, Finland, Iceland, Norway or Sweden. Fees: $20 application. Frequency: annual. Response Time: by 3/15/08. **Consideration.** Opportunity/Award: $20,000 fellowship limit; $4,000 grant limit. **Application.** What to submit: application. Author must be citizen or resident of US, college graduate, proficient in host language preferred. How to submit: online. Deadline: 11/1/2008.

**Arizona Commission on the Arts (ACA)**
417 W. Roosevelt St., Phoenix, AZ 85003
Claire West
Tel: (602) 771-6501 Fax: (602) 256-0282
cwest@azarts.gov
www.azarts.gov
> Est. 1966. Artist Career Advancement Grants (ACAG) and Artist Project Grants. Check website for deadlines. **Application.** Author must be age 18 or older, resident of AZ, not a student. How to submit: online.

**Arkansas Arts Council**
323 Center St., #1500
Little Rock, AR 72201
Sally A. WIlliams
Tel: (501) 324-9348 Fax: (501) 324-9207
sally@arkansasheritage.org
www.arkansasarts.com
> Est. 1971. Check website for 2009 fellowship categories. **Application.** What to submit: application, SASE. Author must be age 25 or older, resident of AR, not a former fellow.

**Artist Trust**
1835 12th Ave., Seattle, WA 98122
Monica Miller
Tel: (206) 467-8734 Fax: (206) 467-9633
info@artisttrust.org
www.artisttrust.org
  Grants for Artist Projects (GAP) program. **Assistance:** $1,500 stipend Frequency: annual Response Time: 4mos. **Application.** What to submit: application, 12-pg sample, audio, SASE. Author must be age 18 or older, resident of WA, not a student. Deadline: 2/20/2009.

**Artists' Fellowships**
New York City Arts Fellows
155 Avenue of the Americas, Fl. 6
New York, NY 10013
Margie Lempert
Tel: (212) 366-6900 Fax: (212) 366-1778
fellowships@nyfa.org
www.nyfa.org
  Est. 1984. Artistists Fellowships are intended to fund an artists vision or voice, regardless of the level of her or his artistic development. Grants are given to individual originating artists living in New York State. **Assistance:** $7,000 grant Frequency: biennial. **Application.** What to submit: application. Author must be age 18 or older, resident of NYS, not a student. Deadline: 10/3/2009.

**Asian Cultural Council**
6 West 48th Street, 12th Fl
New York, NY 10036
Cecily D. Cook
Tel: (212) 843-0403 Fax: (212) 843-0343
acc@accny.org
www.asianculturalcouncil.org
  Est. 1963. Support for cultural exchange in performing/visual arts between US and Asia, primarily fellowships for artists from Asia to pursue projects in US, but some support for Americans for research and creative work in Asia. Frequency: annual. **Consideration.** Opportunity/Award: individual fellowship. **Application.** What to submit: Letter of inquiry followed by application. Author must be citizen of US or Asian country. How to submit: Submit letter of inquiry by 10/15 and application postmarked by 11/15.

**Aurand Harris Fellowship**
617 Baxter Ave., Louisville, KY 40204
Marilee Miller
www.childrenstheatrefoundation.org
  Est. 1958. For individuals with specific projects or with specific plans for developing excellence in children's theater. Frequency: annual. **Consideration.** Opportunity/Award: $5,000 max. **Preference.** Subject: T.Y.A. **Application.** What to submit: application, info on websites, submissions not returned. Author must be age 18 or older, resident or citizen of US. Material must be unoptioned. Deadline: 4/30/2009.

**Berlin Artists-in-Residence**
Markgrafenstrasse 37
Lindsborg, KS 10117
Tel: 49-030-202-2080
Fax: 49-030-204-1267
bkp.berlin@daad.de
www.daad-berlin.de
  1-yr residency for authors/composers to produce work and contribute to Berlin's cultural life. Grant incl. rent for furnished living/work area. **Application.** What to submit: application, sample. Deadline: 1/1/2008.

**CEC ArtsLink**
435 Hudson St, Fl. 8
New York, NY 10014
Chelsey Morell
Tel: (212) 643-1985 ext. 22
Fax: (212) 6431996
al@cecartslink.org; www.cecartslink.org
  Est. 1992. Grants for collaborative projects with colleagues in Central and Eastern Europe, Russia, Central Asia and the Caucasus alternating between visual/media arts (2009) and performing arts or literature (2010). **Assistance:** grants up to

$10,000. **Application.** What to submit: Application available on-line. How to submit: Mail application. Deadline: 1/15/2010.

**Fulbright Program for US Scholars**
3007 Tilden St. NW, #5-L
Washington, DC 20008
Anne Clift Boris
info@cies.iie.org
www.cies.org
   Est. 1947. Grants for US faculty or professionals to research or lecture abroad for 2-12 mos. in 140 countries. **Assistance:** grant / stipend varies, Room / board varies, travel varies Frequency: annual. **Consideration.** Opportunity/Award: award varies. **Application.** What to submit: application, SASE. Author must be citizen of US. Deadline: 8/1/2009.

**Fund for New Work**
150 Convent Avenue
New York, NY 10030
Tel: (212) 281-9240 Fax: (212) 281-9318
www.harlemstage.org
   Grants & funding for emerging artists. See website for application and details.

**Colorado Council on the Arts**
1625 Broadway, #2700
Denver, CO 80202
Jeanette Albert
Tel: (303) 892-3802 Fax: (303) 892-3848
coloarts@state.co.us
www.coloarts.state.co.us
   Grants only. We do not offer fellowships. **Application.** Material must be online only. Deadline: 3/15/2009.

**Connecticut Commission on Culture & Tourism (CCT)**
One Constitution Plaza, 2nd Fl.
Hartford, CT 06103
Tamara Dimitri
Tel: (860) 256-2720
tamara.dimitri@ct.gov
www.cultureandtourism.org
   Artistic fellowships alternating between visual art (odd yrs) and choreography, fiction, music composition and film/video, playwriting, and poetry (even yrs). **Application.** Deadline: 9/1/2009.

**Delaware Division of the Arts**
820 N. French St.
Wilmington, DE 19801
Kristin Pleasanton
Tel: (302) 577-8278 Fax: (302) 577-6561
paul.weagraff@state.de.us
www.artsdel.org
   Invidual artists fellowships. Frequency: annual. **Application.** What to submit: application, 10-20 pg sample, SASE. Author must be age 18 or older, resident of DE, not a student. Deadline: 8/1/2009.

**Fiscal Sponsorship**
155 Ave. of the Americas
New York, NY 10013
Mary Six Rupert
Tel: (212) 366-6900 Fax: (212) 366-1778
msrupert@nyfa.org
www.nyfa.org/fs
   Deadlines: First Friday of May and November. Est. 1971. Allows artists to apply for funds usually available only to nonprofits. Fees: $100 contract fee (if accepted), 4%-8% admin fee. Frequency: semiannual. Response Time: 2 mos. **Application.** What to submit: application, SASE. Author must be not a student. Deadline: 5/2/2009. Second Deadline: 11/7/2009.

**George Bennett Fellowship**
20 Main St., Exeter, NH 3833
Charles Pratt
english@exeter.edu
www.exeter.edu
   Est. 1968. Fellowship for academic year to early-career writer, who will live in Exeter and be available to students, but not be on faculty nor be required to teach. **Assistance:** $10,000 stipend, room/board. Frequency: annual. **Application.** What to submit: application, 50-pg sample, SASE. Author must be writing a work in process. Submission application fee: $5.

**Hodder Fellowship**
Lewis Center for the Arts
Princeton University
185 Nassau St., Princeton, NJ 08544
Janine Braude
Tel: (609) 258-4096 Fax: (609) 258-2230
jbraude@princeton.edu
www.princeton.edu/arts/lewis_center/society_of_fellows/
> 1-yr fellowship for Academic Year 2010-11 for individuals outside academia to pursue independent projects. **Assistance:** $62,000 stipend. **Consideration.** Opportunity/Award: $62,000 stipend. **Application.** What to submit: query, 10-pg sample, resume. Authors must be poets, playwrights, novelists, creative nonfiction writers and translators who have published one highly acclaimed book and are undertaking significant new work. How to submit: by mail. Deadline: 11/1/2009.

**Humanities Projects in Media**
1100 Pennsylvania Ave. NW
Washington, DC 20506
Margaret Scrymser
Tel: (202) 606-8269
publicpgms@neh.gov
www.neh.gov
> Development and production grants for humanities projects of broad appeal. **Assistance:** $30,000-$500,000 grant. Frequency: January and August each year Response Time: 6 mos. **Preference.** Length: full length plays. Style: documentary. **Application.** What to submit: application, submissions not returned. How to submit: online. Deadline: 1/28/2009.

**Indiana Arts Commission (IAC)**
150 W. Market St., #618
Indianapolis, IN 46204
Monica R. Peterson
Tel: (317) 232-1283
mpeterson@iac.in.gov
www.state.in.us/iac
> Est. 1969. Individual Artist Program (IAP). See website for deadlines. **Assistance:** $2,000 grant limit Frequency: annual. **Application.** What to submit: application, 10-pg sample (10 copies). Author must be age 18 or older, resident of IN, not a student. Deadline: 2/1/2009.

**Iowa Arts Council**
600 E. Locust, Des Moines, IA 50319
Linda Lee
Tel: (515) 2426194
Linda.lee@iowa.gov
www.iowaartscouncil.org
> **Assistance:** $10,000 grant/ $1,500 minor grant Response Time: Appx. 4-6 wks. **Consideration.** Opportunity/Award: Project Grants: Major Grant up to $10,000; Mini Grant up to $1,500. **Application.** Author must be age 18 or older, resident of IA, not a student. How to submit: See information on web site . Deadlines: Major Grants: April 1 and October 1; Mini Grants: 1st business day of each month.

**Japan Foundation**
152 W. 57th St., Fl. 17
New York, NY 10019
Kenji Matsumoto
Tel: (212) 489-0299 Fax: (212) 489-0409
info@jfny.org
www.jfny.org
> Touring Grants help U.S. nonprofit organizations present Japanese performing arts in the U.S. and Canada. Collaboration Grants help American and Japanesse artists develop new works, which will further an appreciation of Japanese culture when presented to American audiences. **Preference.** Subject: writers of color. **Application.** What to submit: application. How to submit: unsolicited.

**Jerome Playwright-in-Residence Fellowships**
2301 Franklin Ave. E.
Minneapolis, MN 55406
Kevin McLaughlin
Tel: (612) 332-7481 Fax: (612) 332-6037
info@pwcenter.org
www.pwcenter.org
> Fellowships to emerging playwrights for 1-yr residency (Jul-Jun) in MN using Center services. **Assistance:**

$10,000 fellowship + $1,000 in development support. Frequency: annual. **Application.** What to submit: application. Author must be citizen or resident of US, not produced professionally more than twice. How to submit: online. Deadline: 9/12/2009.

**John D. and Catherine T. MacArthur Fund Grant**
1001 E. Indiantown Rd.
c/o Maltz Jupiter Theatre
Jupiter, FL 33477
Tel: (561) 743-2666
www.jupitertheatre.org/
    **Consideration.** Opportunity/Award: Staged Reading. **Preference.** Length: full length musicals. Style: Musical. **Application.** What to submit: cover letter, a signed letter from the author(s) and underlying rights representative stating that the rights to the piece have been fully secured (in the case where the musical is based on copyrighted material), or is within the public domain. Demo CD with songs from show, short synopsis of the piece, playwright's theatre resume. Deadline: 9/30/2009.

**John Simon Guggenheim Memorial Foundation**
90 Park Ave., New York, NY 10016
Keith B. Lewis
Tel: (212) 687-4470 Fax: (212) 697-3248
fellowships@gf.org
www.gf.org
    Est. 1925. Fellowship to scholars and artists for research or creation. **Application.** What to submit: query, application, sample. Deadline: 9/15/2009.

**Kleban Award**
424 W. 44th St.
New York, NY 10036
Tel: (212) 757-6960 Fax: (212) 265-4738
newdramatists@newdramatists.org
www.newdramatists.org/kleban_award.htm
    Award to lyricists and librettists working in the American musical theater. Frequency: annual.
    **Consideration.** Opportunity/Award: $100,000 each to a lyricist and a librettist. **Preference.** Style: musical. **Application.** What to submit: See application for guidelines. Author must be produced or member of a professional musical theater workshop. How to submit: See application for guidelines. Deadline: 9/15/2010.

**Literature Fellowships: Translation Projects**
1100 Pennsylvania Ave. NW
Washington, DC 20506
Tel: (202) 682-5400
www.arts.gov

**Louisiana Division of the Arts**
Box 44247, Baton Rouge, LA 70804
Vanessa Ledbetter
Tel: (225) 342-8184 Fax: (225) 342-8173
arts@crt.state.la.us
www.crt.state.la.us/arts
    Deadline: 3/3/2009.

**Ludwig Vogelstein Foundation, Inc.**
Box 510, Shelter Island, NY 11964
Diana Braunschweig
lvf@earthlink.net
    Provides one-time grants to individuals working in playwriting, fiction/non-fiction, and the arts (paint sculpture, prints). **Consideration.** Opportunity/Award: $1,000-$3,000. **Application.** How to submit: email inquiries.

**Maine Arts Commission**
25 State House Station
Augusta, ME 4333
Donna McNeil
Tel: (207) 287-2724 Fax: (207) 287-2725
donna.mcneil@maine.gov
www.mainearts.maine.gov
    **Application.** Author must be age 18 or older, resident of ME, not a student. See website for 2009 deadline.

**Many Voices Playwriting Residency Awards**
2301 Franklin Ave. E.
Minneapolis, MN 55406
Kevin McLaughlin
Tel: (612) 332-7481 Fax: (612) 332-6037
info@pwcenter.org
www.pwcenter.org

Grants, education, and development opportunities to writers of color living in MN. **Assistance:** Two beginning playwrights receive a $1,000 stipend and $250 in development funds. Three emerging playwrights receive a $3,500 stipend and $1,000 in development funds. Frequency: annual. **Application.** What to submit: application. Author must be resident of MN. How to submit: online. Deadline: 7/25/2009.

**Marin Arts Council Fund for Artists**
555 Northgate Dr., #270
San Rafael, CA 94903
Tel: (415) 499-8350 Fax: (415) 499-8537
marinarts@marinarts.org
www.marinarts.org
Est. 1985. Career Development Grants ($1,500) to individual artists for professional development. **Application.** What to submit: Application plus 4 copies of narrative, resume and work sample application. Author must be age 18 or older, resident of Marin Co, not a student. Deadline: 2/15/2009. Second Deadline: 5/15/2009. 1/15/10 plus late spring 2010 TBA. Check website for upcoming deadlines.

**Massachusetts Cultural Council (MCC)**
10 St. James Ave., Fl. 3
Boston, MA 02116
Dan Blask
Tel: (617) 727-3668 ext. 329
Fax: (617) 727-0044
dan.blask@art.state.ma.us
www.massculturalcouncil.org
Grants alternating between dance, drawing, prose, painting, poetry, traditional arts (2010) and crafts, film/video, music, photography, playwriting, sculpture (2009). **Assistance:** $10,000 grant. **Application.** What to submit: application. Author must be age 18 or older, resident of MA. How to submit: online.

**McKnight Advancement Grants**
2301 Franklin Ave. E.
Minneapolis, MN 55406
Kevin McLaughlin
Tel: (612) 332-7481 Fax: (612) 332-6037
info@pwcenter.org
www.pwcenter.org
Grants to advance a writer's art and career. Author must be 2-yr resident of MN, professionally produced, not recipient of this grant in past 3 yrs. **Assistance:** $25,000 grant. Frequency: annual. **Application.** What to submit: application. How to submit: online. Deadline: 2/1/2009.

**McKnight National Playwriting Residency and Commission**
2301 Franklin Ave. E.
Minneapolis, MN 55406
Kevin McLaughlin
Tel: (612) 332-7481 Fax: (612) 332-6037
info@pwcenter.org; www.pwcenter.org
Commissioning and production of new works from nationally recognized playwrights. Recipient in residence at Center while play is in development. Author must be nationally recognized playwright with 2 full professional productions. **Assistance:** $12,500 grant Frequency: annual. **Application.** What to submit: application. How to submit: agent. Deadline: 12/7/2009.

**Meet the Composer Grant Programs**
90 John Street, Suite 312
New York, NY 10038
Dereck Geary
Tel: (212) 645-6949 Fax: (212) 645-9669
eficklin@meetthecomposer.org
www.meetthecomposer.org
Est. 1988.**Assistance:** $10,000 $25,000. Frequency: biennial. Response Time: Varies, consult guidelines . **Preference.** Style: all styles. Subject: All subjects, woman, T.Y.A., writers of color, disabled, gay/lesbian. **Application.** What to submit: application, audio. Author must be U.S. citizen or permanent resident. How to submit: unsolicited. Deadline: 3/14/2009. Deadline varies -consult website.

**Michener Center for Writers**
702 E. Dean Keeton St.
Austin, TX 78705
Graduate Coordinator
Tel: (512) 471-1601 Fax: (512) 471-9997
mcw@www.utexas.edu
www.utexas.edu/academic/mcw
    Est. 1993. Financial assistance for full-time students in MFA program. **Assistance:** $25,000 stipend, free tuition. Frequency: annual. **Application.** Author must be holder of a BA degree.

**Nebraska Arts Council**
1004 Farnam St., Plaza Level
Omaha, NE 68102
Suzanne Wise
Tel: (402) 595-2122 Fax: (402) 595-2334
info@nebraskaartscouncil.org
www.nebraskaartscouncil.org
    Individual Artist Fellowship (IAF). Frequency: annual. **Application.** What to submit: application, SASE. Author must be resident of NE. Deadline: 11/15/2009.

**Nevada Arts Council**
716 N. Carson St., Ste. A
Carson City, NV 89701
Fran Morrow
Tel: (775) 687-7106
fkmorrow@clan.lib.nv.us
www.dmla.clan.lib.nv.us/docs/arts
    Artist Fellowships. Author must be age 21 or older, 1-yr resident of NV, citizen of US, not a student. **Assistance:** $5,000 grant. **Application.** What to submit: application, full script (5 copies), resume, SASE. Deadline: 4/6/2009.

**New Generations Program: Future Collaborations**
520 8th Ave., Fl. 24
New York, NY 10018
David Nugent
Tel: (212) 609-5900 Fax: (212) 609-5901
grants@tcg.com
www.tcg.org
    Early-career theatre professionals in any discipline are given 2-yr paid ($35,000/yr) mentorship at a theater. In addition, grants of $15,000 available to repay student loans. **Application.** Theaters submit application. Deadline: 10/1/2009.

**New Hampshire State Council on the Arts**
2½ Beacon St., Suite 225
Concord, NH 03301-4447
Jane Elklund
Tel: (603) 271-0791
yvonne.m.stahr@dcr.nh.gov
www.state.nh.us/nharts
    Criteria are: Artistic excellence based on work sample, and professional commitment based on resume. **Assistance:** $5,000 Fellowships awarded to up to 6 individual artists annually. **Application.** What to submit: application, 20-pg sample (6 copies). Author must be age 18 or older, resident of NH. How to submit: professional commitment based on resume. Deadline: 4/10/2009.

**New Jersey State Council on the Arts**
Box 306, Trenton, NJ 08625
Tom Moran
Tel: (609) 292-6130 Fax: (609) 989-1440
tom@arts.sos.state.nj.us
www.njartscouncil.org
    Artists fellowships in 14 disciplines, 7/yr (playwrights in odd yrs, composers in even yrs) thru Mid-Atlantic Arts Foundation (midatlanticarts.org). See website for details. **Application.** Author must be age 18 or older, resident of NJ, not a student. Deadline: 7/8/2009.

**P73 Playwriting Fellowship**
138 S. Oxford St. #5C
Brooklyn, NY 11217
Liz Jones
Tel: (718) 598-2099 Fax: (718) 398-2794
info@p73.org
www.p73.org
    Est. 1997. Committed to developing and producing the work of emerging playwrights. Fellowship program applicants considered for future projects, incl. writing group, summer residency, and mainstage production.

Author must be resident of US, have 2 full-lengths or 3 one-acts, never had production budgeted above $65k, not a student. **Assistance:** $2,000 stipend. Frequency: annual. **Application.** What to submit: query, application, 10-pg sample, resume, SASE. How to submit: unsolicited, professional recommendation.

**New York State Council on the Arts (NYSCA)**
175 Varick St., Fl. 3, New York, NY 10014
Heather Hitchens
Tel: (212) 627-4455 Fax: (212) 620-5911
www.nysca.org

**New York Theatre Workshop (NYTW) Playwriting Fellowship**
83 E. 4th St., New York, NY 10003
Geoffrey Scott
Tel: (212) 780-9037 Fax: (212) 460-8996
www.nytw.org
   Visit website for list of Fellowships and opportunities.

**North Dakota Council on the Arts**
1600 E. Century Ave., #6
Bismarck, ND 58503
Jan Webb
Tel: (701) 328-7590 Fax: (701) 328-7595
www.nd.gov/arts
   Est. 1984. Individual Artist Fellowship. Author must be age 18 or older, resident of ND. Rotates thru literary and musical arts (2007), traditional, dance, and theater arts (2008), visual arts/crafts and media arts (2009). **Assistance:** $2,500 grant Frequency: triennial. Response Time: 3 mos. **Application.** What to submit: application, SASE. Material must be unpublished, new work. Deadline: 2/15/2009.

**Ohio Arts Council**
727 E. Main St., Columbus, OH 43205
Ken Emerick
Tel: (614) 466-2613 Fax: (614) 466-4494
www.oac.state.oh.us
   Individual Excellence Awards in choreography, crafts, fiction/nonfiction, poetry, play/screen writing, criticism, design/illustration, performance/interdisciplinary art, media art, music composition, photography, and visual art. Author must be 1-yr resident of OH, not a student. **Assistance:** $5,000-$10,000 grants. Frequency: annual. **Preference.** Length: full length plays. **Application.** What to submit: application, full script (4 copies), audio. Deadline: 9/1/2009.

**Oklahoma Arts Council**
Box 52001-2001
Oklahoma City, OK 73152
Suzanne Tate
Tel: (405) 521-2931 Fax: (405) 521-6418
okarts@arts.state.ok.us
www.oklaosf.state.ok.us/~arts

**Pennsylvania Council on the Arts**
Finance Bldg, #216
Harrisburg, PA 17120
Lori Frush Schmelz
Tel: (717) 787-6883 Fax: (717) 783-2538
www.pacouncilonthearts.org
   Est. 1966. Frequency: annual Response Time: 8 mos. **Application.** What to submit: application. Author must be resident of PA. Deadline: 8/1/2009.

**Pew Fellowships in the Arts (PFA)**
Philadelphia Center for Arts
1608 Walnut St., 18th Floor
Philadelphia, PA 19103
Melissa Franklin
Tel: (267) 350-4920 Fax: (267) 350-4997
pfa@pcah.us
www.pewarts.org
   Est. 1991. Awards rotate in 4-yr cycle (3 disciplines chosen each Aug), incl. choreography, crafts, fiction/creative nonfiction, folk/traditional arts, media arts, music composition, painting, performance art, poetry, sculpture/installation, stage/screen scripts, and works on paper. Author must be age 25 or older, 2-year resident of eastern PA (Bucks, Chester, Delaware, Montgomery, Philadelphia cos.), not a student. **Assistance:** $1,000 grant. **Consideration.** Opportunity/

Award: $60,000. **Application.** What to submit: application. How to submit: On-line application at www.pewarts.org.

**Pilgrim Project**
156 5th Ave., #400
New York, NY 10010
Davida Goldman
Tel: (212) 627-2288 Fax: (212) 627-2184
davida@firstthings.com
 Est. 1987. Small grants for a reading, workshop or full production of plays that deal with questions of moral significance. Grants are for production of plays and not administrative costs. **Assistance:** $1,000-$7,000 grant Response Time: 5mos. **Preference.** Length: full length plays. **Application.** What to submit: full script, SASE.

**Princess Grace Foundation USA Playwriting Fellowship**
150 E. 58th St., Fl.25
New York, NY 10155
Kathleen Richards
Tel: (212) 317-1470 Fax: (212) 317-1473
grants@pgfusa.org
www.pgfusa.org
 Est. 1982. 10-wk residency with New Dramatists; $7,500 stipend; and publication/representation by Samuel French for 1 winning playwright. **Assistance:** $7,500 grant. Frequency: annual. Response Time: by 9/30/09. **Consideration.** Opportunity/Award: publication, residency. **Preference.** Length: full length plays. Style: comedy, drama. **Application.** What to submit: application, full script. Author must be resident or citizen of US. Material must be unpublished, unproduced, original. How to submit: Application online. Deadline: 3/31/2009.

**Radcliffe Institute Fellowships**
8 Garden St., Cambridge, MA 02138
Application Office
Tel: (617) 496-1324
fellowships@radcliffe.edu
www.radcliffe.edu/fellowships
 To support scholars, scientists, artists, and writers of exceptional promise and demonstrated accomplishments to pursue work in academic and professional fields and in the creative arts. **Application.** Deadline: 10/1/2009.

**Rhode Island State Council on the Arts**
1 Capitol Hill, Fl. 3, Providence, RI 02908
Cristina Di Chiera
Tel: (401) 222-3880 Fax: (401) 422-3018
cristina@arts.ri.gov
www.arts.ri.gove
 Fellowships in: crafts, film/video, poetry, fiction, play/screenwriting, sculpture, and photography (Apr 1); choreography, design, painting, and music (Oct 1). **Assistance:** $5,000 Fellowship, $500-$10,000 Project Grant. Frequency: annual. **Application.** What to submit: application. Author must be age 18 or older, resident of RI, not a student. Deadline: 4/1/2009.

**Rome Prize**
7 E. 60th St., New York, NY 10022
Tel: (212) 751-7200
www.aarome.org
 Est. 1894. Annual yearlong fellowships to 15 emerging artists (literature, music, etc.) and 15 scholars (Italian studies). Literature candidates must be nominated through the American Academy of Arts and Letters. Music candidates may apply themselves. **Application.** What to submit: application, 2-3 orchestral scores, CDs of included scores, resume, 1-pg proposal, 3 reference letters. Author must be recipient of BA in music. Deadline: 11/1/2009.

**South Carolina Arts Commission**
1800 Gervais St., Columbia, SC 29201
Jeanette Guinn
Tel: (803) 734-8677
jguinn@arts.state.sc.us
www.southcarolinaarts.com
 Fellowships in three categories each yr, rotating between prose/poetry (odd yrs) and visual arts/crafts (even

yrs), with third changing category, incl. music (2007), dance (2008), theater (2009). **Assistance:** $5,000 grant. **Application.** What to submit: application, support materials, SASE. Author must be age 18 or older, 2-yr resident of SC, not a student. Deadline: 10/1/2009.

**South Dakota Arts Council**
711 E. Wells Ave., Pierre, SD 57501
Dennis Holub
Tel: (605) 773-3301 Fax: (605) 773-5657
sdac@state.sd.us
www.artscouncil.sd.gov
  Est. 1966. **Assistance:** $3,000 grant Frequency: annual Response Time: 3 mos. **Application.** What to submit: application, 30-pg sample, SASE. Author must be resident of SD. Deadline: 3/1/2009.

**TCG/ITI Intl. Fellowship**
520 8th Ave., Fl. 24, New York, NY 10018
Casey Baltes
Tel: (212) 609-5900 Fax: (212) 6095901
grants@tcg.org
www.tcg.org
  Travel grants in fall/winter and spring/summer for travel to Russia and Eastern and Central Europe, to foster cultural exchange and artistic partnerships. **Assistance:** $3,000 grant Frequency: semiannual Response Time: 2 months. **Application.** What to submit: application. Deadline: 10/26/2009.

**Travel & Study Grant Program**
400 Sibley St., #125, St. Paul, MN 55101
Cynthia Gehrig
Tel: (651) 224-9431 Fax: (651) 224-3439
www.jeromefdn.org
  **Application.** Author must be resident of MN or NYC, emerging artist. Deadline: 2/15/2009.

**The Public Theater/Emerging Writers Group**
425 Lafayette St., New York, NY 10003
ewgquestions@publictheater.org
www.publictheater.org
  Seeks to target playwrights at the earliest stages in their careers. The Public hopes to create an artistic home for a diverse and exceptionally talented group of up-and-coming writers. See website for further details. **Assistance:** $3,000. **Application.** See website.

**U.S. Dept. of State Fulbright Program for US Students**
809 United Nations Plaza
New York, NY 10017
Tel: (212) 984-5330
www.iie.org/fulbright/us
  Est. 1946. Funds for graduate study, research, or teaching. Students in US colleges must apply thru campus Fulbright Advisers. Those not enrolled in US may apply directly to IIE. Frequency: annual. **Application.** What to submit: application. Deadline: 10/1/2009.

**Utah Arts Council**
617 E. South Temple
Salt Lake City, UT 84102
Margaret Hunt
Tel: (801) 236-7555 Fax: (801) 236-7556
www.arts.utah.gov
  Deadline: 1/5/2009.

**Vermont Arts Council**
136 State St., Drawer 33
Montpelier, VT 5633
Sonia Rae
Tel: (802) 828-3293 Fax: (802) 828-3363
srae@vermontartscouncil.org
www.vermontartscouncil.org
  Est. 1994. Opportunity Grants for creation and for artist development. **Assistance:** $1,000-$3,000 grant. Frequency: annual. Response Time: 2 mos. **Application.** What to submit: application, synopsis, 10-pg sample, SASE. Author must be age 18 or older, resident of VT, not a student. Material must be original. How to submit: online. Submission application fee: $20. Deadline: 10/1/2009.

**The Villar-Hauser Theatre Development Fund**
188 E. 93rd St., #2-B
New York, NY 10128
Ludovica Villar-Hauser
Tel: (917) 304-6823
lvillarhauser@aol.com

**Virginia Commission for the Arts**
223 Governor St., Fl. 2
Richmond, VA 23219
Peggy J. Baggett
Tel: (804) 225-3132 Fax: (804) 225-4327
arts@arts.virginia.gov
www.arts.state.va.us
  Artists Fellowships in rotating disciplines announced each Jun (photography, fiction in 2006). Frequency: annual. **Consideration.** Opportunity/Award: $5,000. **Application.** What to submit: application. Author must be age 18 or older, resident of VA. Deadline: 8/1/2009.

**Wisconsin Arts Board**
101 E. Wilson St., Fl. 1
Madison, WI 53702
Mark Fraire
Tel: (608) 264-8191 Fax: (608) 267-9629
mark.fraire@arts.state.wi.us
www.arts.state.wi.us/static
  Artist Fellowship Awards of unrestricted funds to professional WI artists. Rotating between Lit Arts, Music Composition, Choreography/Performance Art (even yrs), and Visual/Media Arts (odd yrs). **Assistance:** $8,000 grant. Frequency: biennial. **Application.** What to submit: online application, 2-pg statement, 25-pg sample, 3-track audio (composers only), 3-pg resume, SASE. Author must be 1-yr resident of WI, not a fine arts student. Deadline: 9/17/2009.

## THEATERS

**12 Miles West Theatre Company**
Box 1663, Bloomfield, NJ 7003
Lenny Bart
Tel: (973) 259-9187 Fax: (973) 259-9187
info@12mileswest.org
www.12mileswest.org
  Est. 1992. Equity SPT-1. Production: cast of 2-7, simple set Response Time: 1 yr. **Consideration.** Opportunity/Award: $500 or 5% royalty. **Preference.** Length: full length plays. **Application.** What to submit: query, synopsis, full script, SASE.

**16th St. Theater**
6420 16th. St., Berwyn, IL 60402
Ann Filmer
Tel: (708) 795-6704
info@16thstreettheater.org
www.16thstreettheater.org
  We give preference to writers residing in Illinois who are able to commit to being a "playwright-in-residence" for the season. We happily welcome "second productions." No musicals please. We are an Equity CAT Tier N 49-seat new theater 10 miles west of downtown Chicago dedicated to writers. See web site for production history. **Preference.** Length: full length plays. Style: adaptation, comedy or variety, drama. Strong preference for IL residents.

**1812 Productions**
421 N. 7th St., #218
Philadelphia, PA 19123
Jennifer Childs
Tel: (215) 592-9560 Fax: (215) 592-9580
jen@1812productions.org
www.1812productions.org
  Est. 1997. Response Time: 6 mos. **Preference.** Length: full length plays and musicals. Style: comedy, musical comedy. **Application.** What to submit: synopsis, character breakdown, 10-page excerpt, musicals please include cd.

**3S Theatre Collective**
297 4th St #4, Jersey City, NJ 10302
Marc Eardley
Tel: (917) 628-0363
literary@3stc.com
www.3stc.com
Deadline: ongoing. Alt. contact: marc@3stc.com – Marc Eardley Artistic Director. **Consideration.** Opportunity/Award: Reading. Possible production. **Preference.** Length: full length plays. Style: All. Subject: All subjects. **Application.** What to submit: Synopsis or treatment, full script. How to submit: Via email or regular mail.

**40th Street Stage**
809 W. 40th St., Norfolk, VA 23508
Frankie Little Hardin
frankielhardin@aol.com
www.40thstreetstage.com
Production: cast limit 6, minimal set. Response Time: 6 mo. **Preference.** Style: plays for young audiences. **Application.** What to submit: query, full script, SASE. Material must be unpublished.

**5th Avenue Theatre**
1308 5th Ave., Seattle, WA 98101
Bill Berry
Tel: (206) 625-1418 Fax: (206) 292-9610
admin@5thavenuetheatre.org
www.5thavenuetheatre.org
Est. 1980. Production: cast of 8 or more. Response Time: 6 mos. **Preference.** Style: musical. **Application.** What to submit: full script, audio. Material must be unproduced. How to submit: agent.

**Abingdon Theatre Company**
312 W. 36th St., Fl. 6
New York, NY 10018
Kim T. Sharp
Tel: (212) 868-2055 Fax: (212) 868-2056
ksharp@abingdontheatre.org
www.abingdontheatre.org
Est. 1993. Equity readings and full productions. Staff: Jan Buttram (Artistic Dir). Production: cast limit 8 Response Time: 3 mos. **Preference.**

Length: full length plays. Style: comedy, drama. No musicals. Subject: All subjects, woman, writers of color. **Application.** What to submit: Mail printed and bound copy of entire script, character breakdown, synopsis, production history, bio, see website for updates. Author must be permanent resident or citizen of US. Material must be unoptioned, unproduced in NYC.

**About Face Theatre (AFT)**
1222 W. Wilson Ave., Fl. 2
Chicago, IL 60640
Bonnie Metzgar, Art. Dir.
Rick Dildine, Mgr. Dir.
Tel: (773) 784-8565 Fax: (773) 784-8557
rick@aboutfacetheatre.com
www.aboutfacetheatre.com
Est. 1995. New plays exploring gender and sexuality. Opportunities incl. production and workshop/reading. Production: no fly space. Response Time: 6 mos query, 3 mos script. **Preference.** Length: full length plays and musicals. Style: performance art considered. Subject: All subjects, woman, writers of color, gay/lesbian. **Application.** What to submit: query, synopsis, 10-pg sample, cast list, SASE.

**Absinthe-Minded Theatre Company**
1484 Stadium Ave., Bronx, NY 10465
Ralph Scarpato
Tel: (212) 714-4696
rscarp@aol.com

**Act II Playhouse**
56 E. Butler Pike, Ambler, PA 19002
Bud Martin
bud@act2.org
www.act2.org
Est. 1998. 130-seat SPT. Staff: Bud Martin (Producing Artistic Director), Harriet Power (Associate Artistic Director), Steve Blumenthal (Founding Artistic Director). **Preference.** Length: full length musicals. Style: comedy, drama, musical. **Application.** What to submit: synopsis, full script, SASE. Material must be unproduced.

**ACT Theater (A Contemporary Theatre)**
700 Union St., Seattle, WA 98101
Anita Montgomery
Tel: (206) 292-7660 Fax: (206) 292-7670
www.acttheatre.org
   Est. 1965. Equity LORT C. Special programs incl. new play award and new play development workshops. Response Time: 6 mos. **Preference.** Length: full length plays. **Application.** How to submit: agent.

**Acting Company**
Box 898, Times Sq. Sta.
New York, NY 10108
Margot Harley
Tel: (212) 258-3111 Fax: (212) 258-3299
mail@theactingcompany.org
www.theactingcompany.org
   Est. 1972. Prefer solo one-acts on US historical figures for HS tours and full-length adaptations of classic novels. Production: cast limit 13, touring theater. **Preference.** Length: full length plays. **Application.** How to submit: agent.

**Actors Art Theatre (AAT)**
6128 Wilshire Blvd., #110
Los Angeles, CA 90048
Jolene Adams
actorsart@actorsart.com
www.actorsart.com
   Est. 1994. 32-seat theater developing plays thru workshops and labs. Produces 1 original play each year, plus one-acts and solos under Equity. 99-seat. Production: no orchestra Response Time: 1 yr. **Consideration.** Opportunity/Award: 6% royalty. **Preference.** Style: no musical. **Application.** What to submit: query, synopsis, 10-pg sample, submissions not returned. Material must be unoptioned, unproduced on West Coast. How to submit: email.

**Actors Collective**
447 W. 48th St., Ste. 1W
New York, NY 10036
Catherine Russell
Tel: (212) 445-1016 Fax: (212) 445-1015
postarvis@aol.com
www.perfect-crime.com
   Est. 1981. Equity Off-Broadway. Production: cast limit 8. Response Time: 1 mo. **Application.** What to submit: query, SASE. How to submit: professional recommendation.

**Actor's Express**
887 W. Marietta St. NW, #J-107
Atlanta, GA 30318
Freddy Ashley
www.actors-express.com
   Est. 1988. AEA Guest Artist Contract. Opportunities incl. readings, workshops, production. **Assistance:** room/board, travel. Response Time: 6 mos. **Consideration.** Opportunity/Award: 6%-8% royalty. **Preference.** Length: full length plays. Style: no adaptation. Subject: writers of color, disabled, gay/lesbian. **Application.** What to submit: full script. How to submit: agent.

**Actors' Guild of Lexington**
141 E. Main St., Lexington, KY 40507
Richard St. Peter
Tel: (859) 233-7330 Fax: (859) 233-3773
actorsguild@qx.net
www.actorsguildoflexington.org
   Est. 1984. Production: cast limit 6, unit set, no fly space Response Time: 1 mo query, 6 mos script. **Preference.** Length: full length plays. **Application.** What to submit: query, synopsis. How to submit: email.

**A. D. Players**
2710 W. Alabama St., Houston, TX 77098
Tel: (713) 5262721 Fax: (713) 439-0905
lee@adplayers.org
www.adplayers.org
   Est. 1967. Production: cast limit 12 (mainstage)/8 (children's), piano only, limited sets. Response Time: 3-6 mos. **Preference.** Length: full length plays. **Application.** What to submit: query, synopsis, 10-pg sample. Material must be query, synopsis, 10-pg sample. How to submit: email professional recommendation.

**Actors Theatre of Louisville**
316 W. Main St., Louisville, KY 40202
Amy Wegener
Tel: (502) 584-1265 Fax: (502) 561-3300
ahansel@actorstheatre.org
www.actorstheatre.org
> Est. 1964. Reading cycle April-Oct; best time to submit: April-August. Equity LORT B, C and D. 1980 Regional Theater Tony winner. Staff: Marc Masterson (Artistic Dir), Jennifer Bielstein (Managing Dir). Response Time: 9 mos. **Preference.** Length: full length plays. **Application.** What to submit: query, synopsis, 10-pg sample. Material must be unproduced. How to submit: agent.

**Actors Theatre of Phoenix**
P.O. Box 1924, Phoenix, AZ 85001
Matthew Wiener
Tel: (602) 253-6701 Fax: (602) 254-9577
info@actorstheatrePHX.org
www.actorstheatrephx.org
> Est. 1985. Production: cast limit 8 Response Time: 10 mos. **Preference.** Length: full length plays. Style: contemporary, political, comedy, drama. **Application.** How to submit: professional recommendation.

**Adirondack Theatre Festival**
Box 3203, Glens Falls, NY 12801
Mark Fleischer
Tel: (518) 798-7479 Fax: (518) 793-1334
atf@ATFestival.org
www.atfestival.org
> Est. 1995. Production: cast limit 10, no fly space Response Time: 6 mos query, 6 mos script. **Preference.** Length: full length plays. **Application.** How to submit: synopsis, 10 sample pages and professional recommendation.

**Adventure Stage Chicago (ASC)**
1012 N. Noble St., Chicago, IL 60622
Tom Arvetis
Tel: (773) 342-4141 Fax: (773) 278-2621
info@vittumtheater.org
www.vittumtheater.org
> Est. 1998. Annual TYA season. Production: ages 18 and older, cast limit 10 Response Time: 1 mo. Consideration. Opportunity/Award: 6% royalty. **Application.** What to submit: synopsis, 10-pg sample.

**African Continuum Theatre Co. (ACTCo)**
3523 12th St. NE, Fl. 2
Washington, DC 20017
Jennifer L. Nelson
Tel: (202) 529-5764 Fax: (202) 529-5782
info@africancontinuumtheatre.com
www.africancontinuumtheatre.com
> Est. 1996. Fresh Flavas Reading Series: staged readings of three-works-in-progress per year. Production: small cast, unit set. **Preference.** Subject: writers of color.

**AfroSolo Theatre Company**
762 Fulton St. #307
San Francisco, CA 94102
Thomas R. Simpson
www.afrosolo.org
Tel: (415) 771-2376 Fax: (415) 771-2312
> Solo work only, usually to be performed by writer. Send up to 10pg synopsis, bio, photo.

**Algonkuin Theatre Company**
1231 Pulaski Blvd.
Bellingham, MA 02019
Marty BlackEagle-Carl
algonkuintheatre@comcast.net
www.hometown.aol.com/algonkuin
> Est. 1993. Production: unit set Response Time: 1 mo. **Preference.** Length: full length plays. Style: no musical. **Application.** What to submit: query. How to submit: email.

**All Arts Matter**
Box 513, Greenville, NY 10283
Tony DeVito
Tel: (518) 966-4038
allartsmatter@juno.com
www.allartsmatter.org
> Est. 2000. Producing unit of diversified arts organization. Reading series and play productions. **Assistance:** room/board, travel. Response Time: 6 wks. **Preference.** Subject: woman, T.Y.A. **Application.** What to submit: full script, SASE. How to submit: agent.

**Allenberry Playhouse**
Box 7, Boiling Springs, PA 17007
Claude Giroux
Tel: (717) 960-5273
www.allenberry.com
   Production: age 20-60, cast of 6-10, orchestra limit 5. **Consideration.** Opportunity/Award: royalty. **Preference.** Length: full length musicals. Style: adaptation, comedy, musical, farce. Subject: woman, T.Y.A., disabled. **Application.** What to submit: query, 20-pg sample, submissions not returned.

**Alley Theatre**
615 Texas Ave., Houston, TX 77002
Mark Bly
Tel: (713) 228-9341 ext. 369
webmaster@alleytheatre.org
www.alleytheatre.org
   Est. 1947. 1996 Regional Theater Tony winner. Response Time: 3 mos. **Preference.** Length: full length plays. Style: Open. No restrictions. Subject: All subjects, woman, writers of color, disabled, gay/lesbian. **Application.** How to submit: Professional recommendation or inquiry letter.

**Alliance Theatre**
1280 Peachtree St. NE
Atlanta, GA 30309
Freddie Ashley
Tel: (404) 733-4650 Fax: (404) 733-4625
ATCliterary@woodruffcenter.org
www.alliancetheatre.org
   Est. 1968. Equity LORT B and D, TYA. 2007 Regional Theater Tony winner. 11 shows in 2 spaces: 800-seat proscenium, 200-seat black box. Staff: Susan Booth (Artistic Dir), Celise Kalke (Artistic Assoc/Dramaturg). Response Time: 1 yr. **Preference.** Length: full length plays. **Application.** What to submit: query, 10-pg sample, full script, SASE. How to submit: agent.

**Allied Theater Group/Stage West**
821 West Vickery Blvd.
Fort Worth, TX 76107
Jim Covault
Tel: (817) 784-9378 Fax: (817) 348-8392
boxoffice@stagewest.org
www.stagewest.org
Equity SPT. Formerly Stage West & Fort Worth Shakespeare Festival. Production: cast limit 9. Response Time: 1 mo query, 3 mos script. **Preference.** Length: full length plays and musicals. Style: adaptation, comedy, drama, musical, translation. Subject: All subjects. **Application.** What to submit: query, synopsis.

**Altarena Playhouse / Alameda Little Theater**
1409 High St., Alameda, CA 94501
Susan Dunn
www.altarena.org
   Est. 1938. Non-Equity volunteer community theater offering readings, new works by local playwrights. Production: cast limit 16, orchestra limit 10, minimal set, in the round Response Time: 6 mos. **Preference.** Length: full length musicals. Style: comedy, drama, musical, solo. **Application.** What to submit: query, full script. Author must be resident of Bay Area. How to submit: professional recommendation.

**Amas Musical Theatre**
115 MacDougal St., #2-B
New York, NY 10012
Donna Trinkoff
Tel: (212) 563-2565 Fax: (212) 239-8332
amasevents@aol.org
www.amasmusical.org
   Est. 1968. Most productions begin in Six O'Clock Musical Theater Lab, featuring 1-hr staged readings of new musicals (3 in spring, 3 in fall). Production: small cast (multi-ethnic encouraged). Response Time: 6 mos. **Preference.** Style: musical. **Application.** What to submit: synopsis, full script, audio, scene list, SASE.

**American Folklore Theatre (AFT)**
Box 273, Fish Creek, WI 54212
Jeffrey Herbst
Tel: (920) 854-6117 Fax: (920) 854-9106
aft@folkloretheatre.com
www.folkloretheatre.com
   Est. 1990. Equity LOA, LORT D. Original musical works for families. Production: cast of 3-10.

Consideration. Opportunity/Award: royalty. **Preference.** Style: musical. **Application.** What to submit: synopsis, SASE. How to submit: professional recommendation.

**Brat Productions**
56 S. 2nd St., Philadelphia, PA 19106
Tel: (215) 627-2577 Fax: (215) 627-4304
info@bratproductions.org
www.bratproductions.org
> Est. 1996. Production: cast limit 7, unit set. Response Time: 1 mo query, 6 mos script. **Preference.** Length: full length plays. **Application.** What to submit: query, synopsis, sample.

**Brava! for Women in the Arts**
2781 24th St., San Francisco, CA 94110
Ellen Gavin
Tel: (415) 641-7657 Fax: (415) 641-7684
ellen@brava.org
www.brava.org
> Est. 1986. Response Time: 6 mos query, 8 mos script. **Preference.** Length: full length plays. **Application.** What to submit: query, synopsis, sample. Author must be lesbian or woman of color.

**Bristol Riverside Theatre**
Box 1250, Bristol, PA 19007
Keith Baker
Tel: (215) 785-6664 Fax: (215) 7852762
Keith@brtstage.org
www.brtstage.org
> Est. 1986. Production: cast limit 10 (plays) or 18 (musicals), orchestra limit 9. Response Time: 18 mos. **Application.** What to submit: full script.

**Chameleon Theatre Company Ltd.**
25-26 42nd St., #3-B
Astoria, NY 11103
Robert D. Carver
tdcarver 2526 @hotmail
robertcarver@yahoo.com
> Est. 1987. Dedicated to developing new plays and musicals, primarily originated in-house or recommended by professional associates. Staff: Cash Tilton (Co-Artistic Dir). Response Time: 2 mos. **Application.** What to submit: query, SASE. Material must be unoptioned, unpublished, unproduced. How to submit: professional recommendation.

**Charleston Stage**
Box 356, Charleston, SC 29402
Julian Wiles
Tel: (843) 577-5967 Fax: (843) 577-5422
cstage@charlestonstage.com
www.charlestonstage.com
> Est. 1977. In residence at the Historic Dock Street Theater. Production: small cast. Response Time: 2 mos. **Preference.** Length: full length plays. **Application.** How to submit: professional recommendation.

**American Musical Theatre of San Jose (AMT)**
1717 Technology Dr., San Jose, CA 95110
Tel: (408) 453-1543 Fax: (408) 453-7123
newworks@amtsj.org
www.amtsj.org
> Equity WCLO. New Works program devoted to new talent in musical theater. Songwriters and librettists with production history may submit scripts and demo tapes of new projects. **Preference.** Length: full length musicals. Style: musical. **Application.** What to submit: synopsis, audio, SASE. Author must be age 21 or older. How to submit: agent.

**American Repertory Theatre**
64 Brattle St., Cambridge, MA 2138
Arthur Holmberg
Tel: (617) 495-2668
www.amrep.org
> Est. 1979. 1986 Regional Theater Tony winner. Response Time: 6 mos. **Preference.** Length : full length plays. Style: non-realistic material. **Application.** What to submit: SASE. How to submit: agent.

**American Stage**
211 3rd St. S., St. Petersburg, FL 33731
Todd Olson
Tel: (727) 823-1600 Fax: (727) 821-2444
www.americanstage.org

Est. 1977. Production: cast limit 4, unit set. **Preference.** Length: full length plays. Subject: T.Y.A.

**American Theater Company**
1909 W. Byron St., Chicago, IL 60613
Tel: (773) 929-5009 Fax: (773) 929-5171
info@atcweb.org
www.atcweb.org
 Est. 1985. Production: cast limit 20. Response Time: 4 mos query, 1 yr script. **Preference.** Length: full length musicals. Style: musical or, play. **Application.** What to submit: query, synopsis, 10-pg sample, SASE.

**American Theatre of Actors, Inc. (ATA)**
314 W. 54th St., New York, NY 10019
James Jennings
Tel: (212) 581-3044
www.americantheatreofactors.org
 Est. 1976. New plays by new writers for 1-4 wks, both Equity and non-Equity. Plays rehearse 3-4 wks. Staff: Jane Culley. Production: age 20-80, cast of 3-6, set limit 2. Response Time: 3 wks. **Preference.** Length: full length plays. Style: comedy, drama. **Application.** What to submit: full script, SASE. Author must be age 20 or older, resident of US. Material must be unoptioned, unpublished, unproduced.

**Amherst Players/Upstage NY**
56 Bright St., Lockport, NY 14094
Debra Cole
Tel: (716) 713-2649
colebuffalo@aol.com
www.amherstplayers.org
 **Preference.** Style: comedy, musical. **Application.** What to submit: full script, submissions not returned. Author must be age 21 or older, resident of US. Material must be unoptioned, unpublished, unproduced.

**Amphibian Productions**
1300 Gendy St., Fort Worth, TX 76107
Kathleen Culebro
info@amphibianproductions.org
www.amphibianproductions.org
 Est. 2000. Produces plays and readings in Ft. Worth and New York City. Production: cast limit 6, set limit 2. Response Time: 8 mos. **Consideration.** Opportunity/Award: production, reading. **Preference.** Length: full length plays. **Application.** What to submit: query, SASE. How to submit: professional recommendation via snail mail, do not email.

**Animated Theaterworks Inc.**
240 Central Park S., #13-B
New York, NY 10019
Elysebeth Kleinhans
info@animatedtheaterworks.org
www.animatedtheaterworks.org
 Est. 1999. Readings and showcase productions of new and developing works. Production: cast limit 6, unit set. Response Time: 6 mos. **Preference.** Length: full length plays. Style: comedy, drama. **Application.** What to submit: query, synopsis, 10-15 pg sample, SASE for return of materials if desired. Material must be unpublished, unproduced.

**Aquila Theatre Company**
4 Washington Square N., #452
New York, NY 10003
Peter Meineck
Tel: (212) 998-8017
aquila@aquilatheatre.com
www.aquilatheatre.com
 Est. 1991. Response Time: 3 mos. **Preference.** Length: full length plays. Style: no musical. **Application.** How to submit: professional recommendation.

**Arden Theatre Company**
40 N. 2nd St., Philadelphia, PA 19106
Dennis Smeal
dsmeal@ardentheatre.org
www.ardentheater.org
 Est. 1988. Equity LORT D, TYA. 7 shows/yr in 360-seat and 175-seat house. Response Time: 10 wks. **Preference.** Length: full length musicals. Style: adaptation, drama, musical. **Application.** What to submit: synopsis, 10-pg sample, submissions not returned.

**Arena Players Repertory Theatre**
296 Rte. 109, E. Farmingdale, NY 11735
Fred De Feis
Tel: (516) 293-0674 Fax: (516) 777-8688
arena109@aol.com
www.arenaplayers.org
> Est. 1950. Production: cast of 2-10. Response Time: 6 mos. **Consideration.** Opportunity/Award: $600. **Preference.** Length: full length plays. **Application.** What to submit: query, synopsis, full script, SASE. Material must be unoptioned, unpublished, unproduced.

**Arena Stage**
1101 6th St. SW, Washington, DC 20024
Mark Bly
Tel: (202) 554-9066
www.arenastage.org
> Est. 1950. Equity LORT B+, B and D. 1976 Regional Theater Tony winner. Staff: Molly Smith (Artistic Dir), Stephen Richard (Exec Dir), Mark Bly (Sr Dramaturg). Response Time: 3 mos. **Consideration.** Opportunity/Award: royalty. **Preference.** Length: full length plays. **Application.** What to submit: query, synopsis, 10-pg sample, SASE. Prefer unproduced. How to submit: professional recommendation.

**Arizona Theatre Company**
Box 1631, Tucson, AZ 85702
Jennifer Bazzell
Tel: (520) 884-8210 ext. 8510
jbazzell@arizonatheatre.org
www.arizonatheatre.org
> Est. 1966. Equity LORT B. Response Time: 6 mos. **Preference.** Length: full length plays. **Application.** What to submit: query, synopsis, 10-pg sample, SASE. How to submit: Out-of-state writers must submit query packet before sending entire script; does not accept material via email.

**Arkansas Arts Center Children's Theatre**
Box 2137, Little Rock, AR 72203
Bradley Anderson
Tel: (501) 372-4000
banderson@arkarts.com
www.arkarts.com/childrens_theatre
> Est. 1979. Response Time: 4 mos. **Preference.** Length: full length musicals. Style: adaptation, musical. Subject: T.Y.A. **Application.** How to submit: professional recommendation.

**Arkansas Repertory Theatre**
Box 110, Little Rock, AR 72201
Brad Mooy
Tel: (866) 6TH-EREP
Fax: (501) 378-0012
www.therep.org
> Production: small cast. Response Time: 3 mos query, 6 mos script. **Preference.** Length: full length plays. **Application.** What to submit: query, synopsis.

**Ars Nova**
511 W. 54th St., New York, NY 10019
Jason Eagan
www.arsnovanyc.com
> Ars Nova is committed to developing and producing eclectic theater, comedy and music to feed today's popular culture. To that end, Ars Nova strives to meld disciplines and give clear voice to a new generation of artists. Ars Nova was founded in memory of Gabe Weiner. **Consideration.** Opportunity/Award: music series, comedy series, and a playwrights group.

**ART Station**
Box 1998, Stone Mountain, GA 30086
Jon Goldstein
Tel: (770) 469-1105 Fax: (770) 4690355
jon@artstation.org
www.artstation.org
> Est. 1986. Equity SPT. Works representing Southern experience. Staff: David Thomas (Artistic Dir.). Production: cast limit 6. Response Time: 1 yr. **Consideration.** Opportunity/Award: 7% royalty. **Preference.** Length: full length musicals. Style: comedy, musical. **Application.** What to submit: synopsis, 10-pg sample, SASE. How to submit: through regular mail, no emails please.

**Artists Repertory Theatre**
1516 SW Alder St., Portland, OR 97205
Stephanie Mulligan
Tel: (503) 241-9807 ext. 110

Fax: (503) 241-8268
stephanie@artistsrep.org
www.artistsrep.org
> Est. 1981. Equity SPT-8, with 7 shows per season on 2 stages, plus staged readings. Staff: Alen Nause (Artistic Dir), Jon Kretzu (Assoc Artistic Dir). Response Time: 2 mos query, 6 mos script. **Preference.** Length: full length plays. Style: no musical. **Application.** What to submit: query, synopsis, SASE.

**ArtsPower National Touring Theatre**
39 S. Fullerton Ave., Montclair, NJ 07042
Gary Blackman
gblackman@artspower.org
www.artspower.org
> Tourable theater presenting one-act plays and musicals for young and family audiences. Production: cast limit 4. **Preference.** Style: adaptation, drama, musical. Subject: T.Y.A. **Application.** What to submit: synopsis, audio, SASE. Material must be unpublished.

**Asian American Theater Company**
690 Fifth St., #211
San Francisco, CA 94107
Sean Lim
Tel: (415) 543-5738
www.asianamericantheater.org
> Est. 1973. **Preference.** Subject: writers of color. **Application.** What to submit: synopsis, 30-pg sample, submissions not returned.

**Asolo Repertory Theatre**
5555 N. Tamiami Tr., Sarasota, FL 34243
Sasso Lauryn
Tel: (941) 351-9010
corinne_gabrielson@asolo.org
www.asolo.org
> Est. 1960. **Preference.** Length: full length plays. **Application.** What to submit: Letter of inquiry through agency only. How to submit: invite.

**Asylum Theatre**
4441 Rockaway Beach St.
Las Vegas, NV 89129
Sarah O'Connell
Tel: (702) 604-3417 Fax: (702) 650-0242
sarah@asylumtheatre.org
www.asylumtheatre.org
> Est. 1997. **Assistance:** $100-$200. **Preference.** Length: full length plays and musicals. Style: all styles. **Application.** What to submit: full script, SASE. Material must be unoptioned, prefer non-produced but not required. How to submit: email.

**Atlantic Theater Company**
76 9th Ave., #537, New York, NY 10011
Christian Parker
Tel: (212) 691-5919 Fax: (212) 645-8755
www.atlantictheater.org
> Est. 1985. Off-Broadway, LOA. 4-show mainstage season, 2-show second stage season. Staff: Neil Pepe (Artistic Dir). Response Time: 6 mos. **Preference.** Length: full length plays. Style: all styles. **Application.** What to submit: query, synopsis, 20 pg sample, full script, audio, SASE. How to submit: professional recommendation, agent.

**Attic Ensemble**
83 Wayne St., Jersey City, NJ 07302
Mary Anne Murphy
Tel: (201) 413-9200
www.atticensemble.org
> Est. 1970. Fees: none. Production: cast 4-8, character ages 15-65, unit set or conceptual. Response Time: 5/15/09. **Preference.** Length: full length plays. Style: comedy, drama, no musical. **Application.** What to submit: full script, submissions returned with SASE. Author must be ages 15-65. How to submit: unsolicited. Deadline: 1/31/2009.

**August Wilson New Play Initiative**
2936 N. Southport Avenue, # 210
Chicago, IL 60657
Daniel Bryant
www.congosquaretheatre.org/augustwilson.asp
> **Application.** What to submit: query, synopsis, 10-15 pg. sample, SASE.

**Aurora Theatre, Inc. [GA]**
128 E Pike St., Lawrenceville, GA 30045
Anthony Rodriguez
Tel: (678) 226-6222
info@auroratheatre.com

www.auroratheatre.com
Established in 1996, Aurora Theatre has a 100 studio and 248 Main Stage. **Preference.** Length: full length plays and musicals. Style: Musicals, Plays that help create a new generation of theatre goers. Subject: All subjects, T.Y.A., writers of color. **Application.** What to submit: full script, audio, bio. How to submit: Send an inquiry email to info@auroratheatre.com.

**Austin Playhouse**
Box 50533, Austin, TX 78763
Don Toner
Tel: (512) 476-0084 Fax: (512) 476-3063
austinplayhouse@aol.com
www.austinplayhouse.com

**Axis Theatre Company**
1 Sheridan Sq., New York, NY 10014
Randy Sharp
Tel: (212) 807-9300 Fax: (212) 807-9039
www.axiscompany.org
Est. 1997. **Application.** What to submit: query. Material must be unpublished. How to submit: invite.

**b current**
720 Bathurst St, #402
Toronto, ON M5S 2R4 Canada
Tel: (416) 533-1500 Fax: (416) 533-1560
office@bcurrent.ca
www.bcurrent.ca
Toronto-based arts company that presents and supports performance works emerging from the Canadian and International Black Diaspora. b current hosts annual themed festival. See website for details. **Preference.** Style: cultural, contemporary. Subject: T.Y.A. **Application.** What to submit: Plays or other performance creations. How to submit: By mail, or email. See web for deadline.

**B Street Theatre**
2711 B St., Sacramento, CA 95816
Buck Busfield
Tel: (916) 443-5391 Fax: (916) 443-0874
www.bstreettheatre.org
Est. 1991. Equity SPT & TYA. 220 seat thrust. Production: cast limit 6, no fly. **Preference.** Length: full length plays. Style: comedy, drama. **Application.** How to submit: agent.

**Bailiwick Repertory Theatre**
1229 W. Belmont Ave., Chicago, IL 60657
David Zak
Tel: (773) 883-1090
Bailiwick@Bailiwick.org
www.bailiwick.org
Est. 1982. Mainstage Series; Deaf Bailiwick Artists; The Lesbian Initiative; College/University Playwriting Festival. **Preference.** Length: full length plays. Subject: gay/lesbian. **Application.** How to submit: online.

**Barksdale Theatre**
7 1/2 West Marshall St.
Richmond, VA 23220
Janine Serresseque
Tel: (804) 783-1688 Fax: (804) 288-6470
TheatreIVandBarksdale@gmail.com
www.barksdalerichmond.org
Est. 1953. Production: small cast, no fly or wing space. Response Time: 6 mos query, 1 yr script. **Preference.** Length: full length plays. **Application.** What to submit: query, synopsis. How to submit: email, regular mail.

**Barrington Stage Company**
30 Union St., Pittsfield, MA 1201
Tel: (413) 499-5446 Fax: (413) 499-5447
bsc@berkshire.net
www.barringtonstageco.org
Est. 1995. Production: cast of 4-8 (plays) or 10-12 (musicals), modest set. Response Time: 1 mo query, 6 mos script. **Preference.** Length: full length plays. **Application.** What to submit: query, 1-pg synopsis, 10-pg sample, audio.

**Barrow Group**
312 W. 36th St., #4-W
New York, NY 10018
Literary Dept.
Tel: (212) 760-2615
www.barrowgroup.org
Est. 1986. Equity Nonprofit Tier 2. Offers 1-2 mainstage shows/yr, plus

readings and workshops. **Response Time:** 1 mo query, 4 mos script. **Application.** What to submit: no unsolicited, agents only.

**Barter Theatre**
Box 867, Abingdon, VA 24212
Richard Rose
Tel: (276) 628-2281 Fax: (276) 619-3335
barterinfo@bartertheatre.com
www.bartertheatre.com
Est. 1933. Equity LORT D. 1948 Regional Theater Tony winner. Staff: Nicholas Piper (Assoc. Dir.), Katy Brown (Art. Dir. of Children's Theatre) Catherine Bush (Dramaturge). Response Time: 6-8 months. **Consideration.** Opportunity/Award: reading, royalties. **Preference.** Length: full length plays and musicals. Style: all styles. **Application.** Best to submit June through December. What to submit: query, synopsis, 10-pg. sample, audio, submission returned with SASE. How to submit: professional recommendation, agent, invite.

**Bay Street Theatre**
Box 810, Sag Harbor, NY 11963
Mia Grosjean
Tel: (631) 725-0818 Fax: (631) 725-0906
www.baystreet.org
Est. 1991. Equity LORT C. Opportunities incl. mainstage season and play reading series. Production: cast limit 9, unit set, no fly or wing space. Response Time: 6 mos. **Preference.** Length: full length plays. **Application.** How to submit: agent.

**Berkeley Repertory Theatre**
2025 Addison St., Berkeley, CA 94702
Madeleine Oldham
Tel: (510) 647-2900
www.berkeleyrep.org
Est. 1968. 1997 Regional Theater Tony winner. Staff: Tony Taccone (Artistic Dir), Les Waters (Assoc Artistic Dir). Response Time: 8 mos. **Preference.** Length: full length plays. **Application.** What to submit: full script, SASE. How to submit: professional recommendation.

**Berkshire Theatre Festival**
P.O. Box 797, Stockbridge, MA 01262
Kate Maguire
Tel: (413) 298-5536 Fax: (413) 298-3368
www.berkshiretheatre.org
Est. 1928. Equity LORT B. Opportunities incl. new works, small musicals. Production: cast of up to 8. Response Time: only if interested. **Preference.** Length: full length plays. **Application.** What to submit: submissions not returned. How to submit: agent.

**Black Ensemble Theater**
4520 North Beacon, Chicago, IL 60640
Jackie Taylor
blackensemble@aol.com
www.blackensembletheater.org
Est. 1976. **Preference.** Length: full length musicals. Style: musicals only, except for Black Playwrights Fest. Subject: writers of color.

**Black Rep**
1717 Olive St., Fl. 4, St. Louis, MO 63103
Ron Himes
Tel: (314) 534-3807 Fax: (314) 534-4035
www.theblackrep.org
est. 1976. **Preference.** Length: full length plays. Subject: T.Y.A., writers of color. **Application.** What to submit: query, synopsis, 3-5 pg. sample, resume to Ameer Harper, Assistant to Executive Director, at ameerh@theblackrep.org.

**Black Spectrum Theatre**
Roy Wilkins Park, 177 St. & Baisley
Mailing Only: 119-07 Merrick Blvd., Jamaica, NY 11434
Tel: (718) 723-1800 Fax: (718) 723-1806
info@blackspectrum.com
www.blackspectrum.com
**Application.** How to submit: Mail full script and contact information.

**Black Swan Theater**
825-C Merrimon Ave., #318
Asheville, NC 28804
David B. Hopes
Fax: (828) 251-6603
swanthtre@aol.com
www.blackswan.org

Est. 1988. Non-Equity theater specializing in developing new scripts or revisiting classics. Production: modest cast, simple set. Response Time: 3 mos. **Application.** What to submit: full script. Material must be unpublished.

**Blinn College Theatre Arts Program**
902 College Ave., Brenham, TX 77833
Bradley Nies
www.blinn.edu/finearts/theatre

**Bloomsburg Theatre Ensemble (BTE)**
266 Center St., Bloomsburg, PA 17815
Gerard P. Stropnicky
Tel: (570) 784-5530 Fax: (570) 784-4912
www.bte.org
Est. 1978. Production: small to mid-sized cast, unit set. Response Time: 3 mos query, 6 mos script. **Preference.** Length: full length plays. Style: adaptation, translation. **Application.** What to submit: query, synopsis, sample. How to submit: professional recommendation.

**Blowing Rock Stage Company**
Box 2170, Blowing Rock, NC 28605
Kenneth Kay
Tel: (828) 2959168
info@blowingrockstage.com
www.blowingrockstage.com
Est. 1986. Equity SPT. Opportunities incl. New Voices of the South reading series (est. 2001). Production: cast limit 10, orchestra limit 8. Response Time: 1 yr. **Application.** What to submit: query, 10-pg sample, audio, submissions not returned.

**Blue Coyote Theater Group (BCTG)**
380 Broadway, Fl. 4
New York, NY 10013
Stephen Speights
Tel: (212) 966-1047 Fax: (212) 966-1047
readings@bluecoyote.org
www.bluecoyote.org
Resident company at Access Theater. Equity Showcase productions, workshops, and readings. **Application.** What to submit: electronic submission or full script, SASE.

**BoarsHead Theatre: Michigan Public Theater**
425 S. Grand Ave., Lansing, MI 48933
Jonathan Courtemanche
Tel: (517) 484-7800 Fax: (517) 484-2564
www.boarshead.org
Est. 1966. Equity SPT-6, 250 seat house. Staff: Kristine Thatcher (Artistic Dir), Marlene Shelton (Managing Dir). Response Time: 6 mos. **Consideration.** Opportunity/ Award: royalty. **Application.** What to submit: query, synopsis, SASE.

**Bond Street Theatre**
2 Bond St., New York, NY 10012
Joanna Sherman
Tel: (212) 254-4614 Fax: (212) 4609378
info@bondst.org
www.bondst.org
Response Time: 1 mo. **Preference.** Style: nonverbal scripts (dance, masks, music, circus arts, gestural arts). **Application.** What to submit: query, synopsis, SASE.

**Borderlands Theater**
Box 2791, Tucson, AZ 85702
Toni Press-Coffman
Tel: (520) 882-8607 Fax: (520) 884-4264
tpplay@cox.net
www.borderlandstheater.org
Est. 1986. Production: cast limit 12, minimal set. Response Time: 1 mo query, 6 mos script. **Preference.** Length: full length plays. Style: adaptation, translation. **Application.** What to submit: query, synopsis.

**Boston Playwrights' Theatre**
949 Commonwealth Ave.
Boston, MA 2215
Michael Duncan Smith
Tel: (617) 353-5443 Fax: (617) 353-6196
newplays@bu.edu
www.bu.edu/bpt
Est. 1981. Equity SPT. Opportunities incl. production and workshop. Production: cast limit 8, black box set. Response Time: 6 mos. **Consideration.** Opportunity/Award: $500 honorarium. **Application.** What to submit: query, SASE. Author must be student or alum of Boston

Univ. Material must be unoptioned, unpublished, unproduced. How to submit: unsolicited.

**Broken Watch Theatre Company**
311 W. 43rd St., #602
New York, NY 10036
Drew DeCorleto
Tel: (212) 397-2935 Fax: (775) 263-6024
contact@brokenwatch.org
www.brokenwatch.org
 Est. 2001. Equity Showcase. Staff: Stephen P. Brumble Jr (Development Dir). **Preference.** Length: full length plays. Style: comedy, drama. **Application.** What to submit: synopsis, SASE. Author must be resident or citizen of US. Material must be unoptioned, unpublished, unproduced. How to submit: professional recommendation.

**Bryant-Lake Bowl Theater**
810 W. Lake St., Minneapolis, MN 55408
Kristin Van Loon
Tel: (612) 825-8949 Fax: (612) 825-7109
www.bryantlakebowl.com
 Cabaret performance space of 90 seats that facilitates performance through active collaboration between producer and staff. **Preference.** Style: all styles. **Application.** What to submit: query letter (note theme addressed), submissions returned with SASE. How to submit: unsolicited.

**Buntville Crew**
118 North Railroad, Buckley, IL 60918
Steven Packard
buntville@yahoo.fr
 Est. 1999. **Application.** What to submit: full script. Material must be unoptioned, unpublished. How to submit: unsolicited.

**Burning Coal Theatre Company**
Box 90904, Raleigh, NC 27675
Marc Williams
Tel: (919) 834-4001
burning_coal@ipass.net
www.burningcoal.org
 Est. 1995. 4 staged readings/yr. Response Time: 6 mos. **Consideration.** Opportunity/Award: reading. **Application.** What to submit: full script, SASE. Author must be resident of, or connected to NC. Material must be unpublished, unproduced. Deadline: 12/16/2009.

**Caffeine Theatre**
PO Box 1904, Chicago, IL 60690
Jennifer Shook
Tel: (312) 409-4778
info@caffeinetheatre.com
www.caffeinetheatre.com
 Please see mission and recent programming at www.caffeinetheatre.com: plays in conversation with the poetic tradition. **Consideration.** Opportunity/Award: Reading, workshop, production, royalties. **Preference.** Length: full length plays. Style: Adaptation, comedy or variety, drama, musical, translation. **Application.** What to submit: Query, synopsis or treatment, 10 page sample. How to submit: Unsolicited, professional recommendation.

**Caldwell Theatre Company**
7901 N. Federal Hwy.
Boca Raton, FL 33487
New Plays
www.caldwelltheatre.com
 Est. 1975. Equity LOA. Playsearch series reads 4 plays annually with 500-600 people in audience. **Assistance:** Travel assistance Production: cast of up to 8. Response Time: varies. **Preference.** Length: full length plays. Style: all styles. **Application.** What to submit: synopsis. How to submit: professional recommendation, agent submission.

**California Theatre Center**
Box 2007, Sunnyvale, CA 94087
Will Huddleston
Tel: (408) 245-2979 Fax: (408) 245-0235
resdir@ctcinc.org
www.ctcinc.org
 Est. 1976. Nonprofit for youth. Theatre for young audiences, non-equity. Two types of scripts sought: cast of 4-8 one hour plays performed for children; cast

of 15-30 one-hour plays performed by children. Response Time: 4 mos. **Consideration.** Opportunity/Award: neg. fee. **Preference.** Subject: T.Y.A. **Application.** What to submit: query, synopsis, SASE. How to submit: unsolicited.

**Capital Repertory Theatre**
111 N. Pearl St., Albany, NY 12207
Maggie Mancinelli-Cahill
Tel: (518) 462-4531 Fax: (518) 465-0213
info@capitalrep.org
www.capitalrep.org
Est. 1981. LORT D.

**Caribbean American Repertory Theatre**
114-13 Ovid Pl., St. Albans, NY 11412
Rudolph Shaw
Tel: (718) 4544234
shawcart@aol.com
www.offbroadwayonline.com
Est. 1975. Equity showcase contract. Plays addressing Afrocentric themes. Production: cast size 6. Response Time: 3 weeks. **Preference.** Length: full length plays. Style: comedy, drama. Subject: writers of color. **Application.** What to submit: full script. Author must be resident of NY. How to submit: unsolicited.

**Casa Manana Inc.**
930 W. 1st St., #200, Ft. Worth, TX 76102
Denton Yockey

**Celebration Theatre**
7985 Santa Monica Blvd., #109-1
Los Angeles, CA 90046
Efrain Schunior
Tel: (323) 957-1884 Fax: (323) 957-1826
celebrationthtr@earthlink.net
www.celebrationtheatre.com
Est. 1982. Equity 99-seat. Accepting scripts for Celebrating New Works, a workshop series for unproduced works. Work must fall within Celebration Theatre's Mission Statement. Production: cast limit 12. Response Time: none unless interested. **Preference.** Length: full length plays. Subject: gay/lesbian. **Application.** What to submit: 1-pg synopsis, full script, bio. Material must be original, unproduced. How to submit: hard copy via mail. Deadline rolling.

**Center Stage Community Playhouse**
Box 138, Bronx, NY 10461
Nick Leshi
Tel: (212) 823-6434
info@centerstageplayhouse.org
www.centerstageplayhouse.org
Est. 1969. Nonprofit community theater. Response Time: 2mos. **Preference.** Length: full length plays and musicals. Style: adaptation, comedy, drama. **Application.** What to submit: query, SASE. Material must be unoptioned, unpublished, unproduced. How to submit: invite.

**Center Stage**
700 N. Calvert St., Baltimore, MA 21202
Otis Ramsey-Zoe
Tel: (410) 9864042
oramseyz@centerstage.org
www.centerstage.org
Est. 1963. Equity LORT B, C. **Preference.** Length: full length plays. **Application.** What to submit: query, synopsis, 10-pg sample, audio, SASE. Material must be unproduced.

**Center Theatre Group (CTG)**
601 W. Temple St.
Los Angeles, CA 90012
Pier Carlo Talenti
www.centertheatregroup.org
Est. 1967. Incl. Ahmanson Theatre and Mark Taper Forum (1977 Regional Theater Tony winner) at Music Center in L.A. and Kirk Douglas Theatre in Culver City. Response Time: 6 wks. **Preference.** Length: full length plays. **Application.** What to submit: query, synopsis, 5-10 pg sample, SASE. How to submit: professional recommendation.

**Contemporary American Theatre Company (CATCO)**
77 S. High St., Fl. 2, Columbus, OH 43215
Jonathan Putnam
writers@catco.org
www.catco.org

Est. 1984. Equity SPT 6, LORT B. 5-6 plays/season. Production: cast limit 10, set limit 2 Response Time: 6 mos. **Consideration.** Opportunity/Award: royalty. **Preference.** Length: full length plays. **Application.** What to submit: synopsis, 10-pg sample.

**Illinois Theatre Center**
Box 397, Park Forest, IL 60466
Tel: (708) 481-3510 Fax: (708) 481-3693
ilthctr@bigplanet.com
www.ilthctr.org
Est. 1976. Production: cast limit 9 (play) or 14 (musical) Response Time: 1 mo query, 2 mos script. **Preference.** Length: full length plays. **Application.** What to submit: query, synopsis, SASE.

**Illusion Theater**
528 Hennepin Ave., #704
Minneapolis, MN 55403
Michael Robins
Tel: (612) 339-4944 Fax: (612) 337-8042
info@illusiontheater.org
www.illusiontheater.org
Est. 1974. Response Time: 1 yr. **Preference.** Length: full length plays. **Application.** How to submit: professional recommendation.

**Imagination Stage**
4908 Auburn Ave., Bethesda, MD 20814
Janet Stanford
Tel: (301) 961-6060 Fax: (301) 718-9526
kbryereimaginationstage.org
www.imaginationstage.org
Est. 1979 Production: cast of 4-10. **Preference.** Style: drama, musical. Subject: T.Y.A. **Application.** What to submit: query, sample.

**Court Theatre**
5535 S. Ellis Ave., Chicago, IL 60637
Kate Bredeson
Tel: (773) 702-7005 Fax: (773) 834-1897
www.courttheatre.org
Est. 1955. Equity LORT D. In residence at Univ. of Chicago. New adaptations and translations of classical material or new work that corresponds to a classical-based repertory. Production: cast of 8-10, thrust stage, limited fly. **Preference.**

Length: full length plays. Style: adaptation, translation. **Application.** What to submit: query, synopsis, 30-pg sample. How to submit: invite.

**Children's Theatre Company (CTC)**
2400 3rd Ave. S., Minneapolis, MN 55404
Elissa Adams
Tel: (612) 874-0500 Fax: (612) 874-8119
www.childrenstheatre.org
Est. 1965. 2003 Regional Theater Tony winner. **Preference.** Length: full length plays. Subject: T.Y.A. **Application.** How to submit: agent.

**Childsplay**
900 S. Mitchell Dr., Tempe, AZ 85281
David Saar
Tel: (480) 350-8101 Fax: (480) 350-8584
info@childsplayaz.org
www.childsplayaz.org
Est. 1977. Non-Equity TYA. 6 mainstage and 3 touring productions/ yr. Opportunities incl Whiteman New Plays Program. Production: cast of 2-12. **Preference.** Length: full length plays and musicals. Family/ children. Subject: T.Y.A., writers of color, disabled. **Application.** What to submit: synopsis, 10 pg sample, SASE.

**Chinese Theatre Works**
34-23 Steinway St., #241
Long Island City, NY 11101
Tel: (718) 392-3493
chinesethrwks@aol.com

**Cincinnati Black Theatre Company**
5919 Hamilton Ave.
Cincinnati, OH 45224
Don Sherman
Tel: (513) 241-6060 Fax: (513) 2416671
dsherman@cincyblacktheatre.com
www.cincyblacktheatre.com

**Cincinnati Playhouse in the Park**
Box 6537, Cincinnati, OH 45206
Attn: Literary
Tel: (513) 345-2242 Fax: (513) 345-2254
www.cincyplay.com
Est. 1960. Equity LORT B+ and D. 2004 Regional Theater Tony winner. Response Time: 8 mos. **Preference.** Length: full length plays. Subject: All

subjects. **Application.** How to submit: Agent submission of full script. Non-agent: synopsis, 10 pages dialog, character breakdown, playwright bio, production history. Include audio tape or CD of selections from score for musicals. SASE.

**Cinnabar Theater**
3333 Petaluma Blvd. N.
Petaluma, CA 94952
Elly Lichenstein
Tel: (707) 763-8920 ext. 104
Fax: (707) 763-8929
www.cinnabartheater.org
   Est. 1970. Equity MBATT. Will consider operas. **Application.** What to submit: no unsolicited submissions.

**City Theatre Company**
1300 Bingham St., Pittsburgh, PA 15203
Carlyn Aquiline
Tel: (412) 431-4400 Fax: (412) 431-5535
caquiline@citytheatrecompany.org
www.citytheatrecompany.org
   Est. 1974. Prefer plays of substance and ideas; fresh use of language or form; plays by underrepresented voices. Production: cast limit 10, prefers 6 or fewer. **Preference.** Length: full length plays and musicals. Style: Full-length plays, musicals, translations, adaptations, solo pieces. **Application.** What to submit: Query including the name and contact info for a professional reference, synopsis, 10 pg sample, audio, cast list, resume, production history, SASE. How to submit: Query by mail.

**City Theatre**
444 Brickell Ave., #229, Miami, FL 33131
Marco Ramirez
Tel: (305) 755-9401 Fax: (305) 755-9404
info@citytheatre.com
www.citytheatre.com
   Est. 1996. Opportunities incl. Winter Shorts and Summer Shorts fests (thru Actors Theater of Louisville), as well as Short Cuts educational tours, Festival Reading Series, and Kid Shorts Project. Summer Shorts also incl. City Dialogues guest artist residency. Production:
age 20-65, cast limit 10, unit set. **Consideration.** Opportunity/Award: royalty. **Application.** What to submit: full script, submissions not returned. Bilingual encouraged.

**Clarence Brown Theatre (CBT)**
206 McClung Tower
Knoxville, TN 37996
Calvin MacLean
Tel: (865) 974-6011 Fax: (865) 974-4867
cbt@utk.edu
www.clarencebrowntheatre.org
   Est. 1974. Response Time: 1 mo. **Preference.** Length: full length plays. Style: comedy, drama. **Application.** What to submit: query, synopsis, 1-2 pg sample.

**Classical Theatre of Harlem**
520 Eighth Ave., #313
New York, NY 10018
Tel: (212) 564-9983
www.classicaltheatreofharlem.com

**Cleveland Play House**
8500 Euclid Ave., Cleveland, OH 44106
Seth Gordon
Tel: (216) 795-7000 Fax: (216) 795-7005
www.clevelandplayhouse.com
   Est. 1916. Response Time: 2 mos query, 6 mos script. **Preference.** Length: full length plays. **Application.** What to submit: query, synopsis, 10-pg sample, resume, SASE.

**Cleveland Public Theatre**
6415 Detroit Ave., Cleveland, OH 44102
Raymond Bobgan
Tel: (216) 631-2727 Fax: (216) 631-2575
rbobgan@cptonline.org
www.cptonline.org
   Est. 1983. Response Time: 9-12 mos. **Consideration.** Opportunity/Award: production. **Preference.** Style: experimental, poetic; politically, intellectually, or spiritually challenging. **Application.** What to submit: query, 1-pg synopsis, 10-pg sample, SASE.

**Clubbed Thumb**
312 E. 23rd St., #4B, New York, NY
Tel: (212) 802-8007 Fax: (212) 533-9286
info@clubbedthumb.org

www.clubbedthumb.org
See website for details.

**Colony Theatre Company**
555 N. Third St., Burbank, CA 91502
Michael David Wadler
Tel: (818) 558-7000 Fax: (818) 558-7110
michaelwadler@colonytheatre.org
www.colonytheatre.org
Est. 1975. Equity LOA. Production: cast limit 5. **Preference.** Length: full length plays. **Application.** What to submit: query, synopsis, first 10 pages, breakdown, resume. How to submit: US mail only.

**Columbus Children's Theatre (CCT)**
177 E. Naghten St., Columbus, OH 43215
William Goldsmith
Tel: (614) 224-6673 Fax: (614) 224-8844
BGShows@aol.com
www.colschildrenstheatre.org
Est. 1963. Production: cast limit 4, touring set. Response Time: 4 mos. **Preference.** Subject: T.Y.A. **Application.** What to submit: 45-55 min script.

**Commonweal Theatre Company**
Box 15, Lanesboro, MN 55949
Hal Cropp
hal@commonwealtheatre.org
www.commonwealtheatre.org
Est. 1989. Non-Equity company producing at least 1 new work/season. Production: cast of 3-10. Response Time: 6 mos. **Consideration.** Opportunity/Award: 8% royalty. **Preference.** Length: full length plays. Style: adaptation, comedy, drama. **Application.** What to submit: query, synopsis, 10-pg sample, SASE. Material must be unproduced.

**Conejo Players Theatre**
351 S. Moorpark Rd.
Thousand Oaks, CA 91361
Dick Johnson
Tel: (805) 495-3715 Fax: (805) 435-8100
www.conejoplayers.org
Est. 1958. Mainstage productions run 5 wks; Afternoon series, 4 wks; Children's series, 2 wks. Response Time: 3 mos. **Consideration.** Opportunity/Award: royalty. **Preference.** Length: full length musicals. Style: comedy, drama, musical. **Application.** What to submit: full script, SASE.

**Coney Island, USA**
1208 Surf Ave., Brooklyn, NY 11224
Dick D. Zigun
Tel: (718) 372-5159 Fax: (718) 372-5101
dzigun@coneyisland.com
www.coneyisland.com
Est. 1980. Response Time: 1 mo query, 6 mos script. **Preference.** Style: vaudeville, Americana sideshow. **Application.** What to submit: query, synopsis, resume, reviews.

**Congo Square Theatre Company**
2936 N. Southportt #210
Chicago, IL 60657
Derrick Sanders
Tel: (773) 296-1108 Fax: (773) 472-6634
atdouglas125@congosquaretheatre.org
www.congosquaretheatre.org

**Contemporary American Theater Festival (CATF)**
Box 429, Shepherdstown, WV 25443
Ed Herendeen
Tel: (304) 876-3473 Fax: (304) 876-5443
eherende@shepherd.edu
www.catf.org
Est. 1991. Equity LORT D.
**Preference.** Length: full length plays. **Application.** What to submit: query, synopsis. How to submit: agent.

**Cornerstone Theater Company**
708 Traction Ave.
Los Angeles, CA 90013
Laurie Woolery
Tel: (213) 613-1700 Fax: (213) 613-1714
mgarces@cornerstonetheater.org
www.cornerstonetheater.org
Est. 1986. Primaily interested in collaborating with playwrights to develop new work. Response Time: 4 mos. **Preference.** Length: full length plays. **Application.** What to submit: query.

**Coterie Theatre**
2450 Grand Ave., #144
Kansas City, MO 64108
Jeff Church
Fax: (816) 474-7112
www.coterietheatre.org
> Est. 1979. Equity TYA. Production: cast limit 10, orchestra limit 3, no fly or wing space. Response Time: 1 mo query. **Preference.** Style: adaptation, drama, musical. Subject: T.Y.A. **Application.** What to submit: query, synopsis, 1-scene sample, audio, SASE. How to submit: prefer email unless a musical.

**Creative Evolution**
21-70 Crescent St., #A-1
Astoria, NY 11105
Michelle Colletti
Tel: (718) 821-2682
cevolution@mindspring.com
www.creativeevolution.org
> Est. 2000. Nonprofit for women to present work in development. Staff: Lisa Haas (Treasurer). **Application.** What to submit: query, 1-pg proposal, sample, resume, SASE. How to submit: email.

**Crossroads Theatre Company**
P.O. Box 238, 7 Livingston Ave.
New Brunswick, NJ 08901
Marshall Jones
Tel: (732) 249-5581
info@crossroadstheatrecompany.org
www.crossroadstheatrecompany.org
> Est. 1978. **Preference.** Subject: writers of color. **Application.** How to submit: no unsolicited scripts.

**CTA Crossroads Theatre**
1277 Boulevard Way
Walnut Creek, CA 94595
Claire Yarrington
Tel: (925) 944-0551
www.ctacrossroads.org
> Est. 1984. Production: orchestra limit 8. Response Time: 2 mos. **Preference.** Subject: T.Y.A. **Application.** What to submit: full script, audio, submissions not returned.

**Cumberland County Playhouse**
Box 484, Crossville, TN 38557
Jim Crabtree
Tel: (931) 484-4324 Fax: (931) 484-6299
www.ccplayhouse.com
> Est. 1965. Response Time: 2 wks query, 1 yr script. **Preference.** Length: full length plays. Subject: T.Y.A. **Application.** What to submit: query, synopsis.

**Curan Repertory Company**
561 Hudson St., #88
New York, NY 10014
Ken Terrell
Tel: (212) 479-0821
kenatcuran@hotmail.com
www.curan.org
> Est. 1990. Non-Equity. 5 original full-length plays and one-act fest each season. Production: cast of 2-15, small set. Response Time: 4 mos. **Preference.** Style: adaptation, comedy, drama, translation. Subject: gay/lesbian. **Application.** What to submit: query, 10-pg sample, SASE. How to submit: unsolicited, agent.

**Cyrano's Theatre Company (CTC)**
413 D St., Anchorage, AK 99501
Sandy Harper
Tel: (907) 274-2599 Fax: (907) 277-4698
cyrano@ak.net
www.cyranos.org
> Est. 1992. Formerly Eccentric Theatre Company. Response Time: 8 mos. **Preference.** Length: full length plays. Style: adaptation, comedy, drama. **Application.** How to submit: professional recommendation.

**Dad's Garage Theatre Co.**
280 Elizabeth St., #C-101
Atlanta, GA 30307
Kate Warner
kate@dadsgarage.com
www.dadsgarage.com
> Est. 1995. **Consideration.** Opportunity/Award: royalty. **Preference.** Style: adaptation, comedy, musical. **Application.** What to submit: query, synopsis, sample. How to submit: professional recommendation.

**Dallas Children's Theater**
5938 Skillman St., Dallas, TX 75231
Artie Olaisen
artie.olaisen@dct.org; www.dct.org
    Est. 1984. Professional family theater. **Preference.** Length: full length plays. Subject: T.Y.A. **Application.** What to submit: query, synopsis, cast/scene list.

**Dallas Theater Center**
3636 Turtle Creek Blvd., Dallas, TX 75219
Kevin Moriarty
Tel: (214) 526-8210 Fax: (214) 521-7666
www.dallastheatercenter.org
    Est. 1959. Response Time: 1 yr. **Preference.** Length: full length plays. **Application.** What to submit: synopsis, 10-pg sample. How to submit: professional recommendation.

**Danisarte**
PO Box 286146, 1617 Third Ave.
New York, NY 10128
Alicia Kaplan
Tel: (212) 561-0191
Danisarte@aol.com
www.danisarte.org
    Est. 1992. Production: cast limit 6. **Preference.** Subject: woman, T.Y.A., writers of color. **Application.** What to submit: query, SASE. Material must be unpublished, unproduced. How to submit: invite.

**Delaware Theatre Company**
200 Water St., Wilmington, DE 19801
David Stradley
Tel: (302) 594-1104 Fax: (302) 594-1107
literary@delawaretheatre.org
www.delawaretheatre.org
    Est. 1978. Equity LORT D. Opportunities incl. reading and production. Season is usually 5-6 productions. Production: cast limit 10, small orchestra, unit set Response Time: 6 mos. **Preference.** Length: full length plays. **Application.** How to submit: agent submission only.

**Dell'Arte Company**
Box 816, Blue Lake, CA 95525
Michael Fields
Tel: (707) 668-5663 Fax: (707) 668-5665
dellarte@aol.com
www.dellarte.com
    Est. 1977. Equity LOA. Topical and issue-oriented comedy for touring performers. Production: cast of 3-4, touring set. **Preference.** Length: full length plays. Style: adaptation. Subject: T.Y.A. **Application.** What to submit: query, synopsis.

**Detroit Repertory Theatre**
13103 Woodrow Wilson St.
Detroit, MI 48238
Tel: (313) 868-1347 Fax: (313) 868-1705
detrepth@aol.com
www.detroitreptheatre.com
    Est. 1957. Equity SPT-3. Production: age 18-65, cast of 5-7, non-traditional casting. Response Time: 6 mos. **Consideration.** Opportunity/Award: 8% royalty. **Preference.** Length: full length plays. **Application.** What to submit: full script, SASE. Material must be unproduced. How to submit: no online submissions.

**Detroit Repertory Theatre/Millan Theatre Company**
13103 Woodrow Wilson, Detroit, MI
Barbara Busby
    Production: no children. **Preference.** Style: comedy, drama.

**Discovery Theater**
Box 23293, Washington, DC 20026
Roberta Gasbarre
Tel: (202) 633-8700 Fax: (202) 343-1073
gasbaro@si.edu
www.discoverytheater.org
    Commissions 4-5 productions each year. **Preference.** Style: all styles. Subject: T.Y.A. **Application.** What to submit: synopsis, full script, cast, scene breakdown, submissions returned with SASE. How to submit: unsolicited.

**District of Columbia Arts Center (DCAC)**
2438 18th St., NW
Washington, DC 20009
    Rolling deadline. Est. 1989. Nonprofit in Adams Morgan neighborhood that supports emerging artists trying to

get a foothold in the public arena. **Application.** What to submit: Proposals for performances in the theater space. How to submit: http://www.dcartscenter.org/submit_theater.htm.

**Diversionary Theatre**
4545 Park Blvd., #101
San Diego, CA 92116
Dan Kirsch
Tel: (619) 220-0097 Fax: (619) 220-0148
www.diversionary.org
Est. 1986. 3rd oldest LGBT theater in US. 6-show season and new-work readings in 106-seat space. Staff: Bret Young (Managing Dir). Response Time: 6 mos. **Consideration.** Opportunity/Award: royalty. **Preference.** Subject: gay/lesbian. **Application.** What to submit: application, synopsis,15-pg sample. How to submit: online.

**Dixon Place**
258 Bowery, Fl. 2, New York, NY 10012
Ellie Covan
Est. 1986. Nonprofit laboratoty theater for NY-based performing and literary artists to create and develop new works in front of a live audience.

**Do Gooder Productions**
359 W. 54th St., #4-FS
New York, NY 10019
Tel: (212) 581-8852
dgp@dogooder.org
www.dogooder.org
**Application.** How to submit: only per theater's request.

**Dobama Theatre**
2490 Lee Blvd., #325
Cleveland Heights, OH 44118
Joyce Casey
Tel: (216) 932-6838 Fax: (216) 9323259
dobama@dobama.org
www.dobama.org
Est. 1959. Production: cast limit 9, no fly. **Preference.** Length: full length plays. **Application.** What to submit: query, synopsis, sample. Author must be resident of OH.

**Doorway Arts Ensemble**
5904 Beech Ave., Bethesda, MD 20817
Claire Myles
Tel: (301) 530-4349 Fax: (301) 530-4349
info@doorwayarts.org
www.DoorwayArts.org
See website for details. **Preference.** Length: full length plays. Style: All. **Application.** What to submit: Full script.

**Double Edge Theatre**
948 Conway Rd., Ashfield, MA 01330
Mathew Glassman
Tel: (413) 628-0277 Fax: (831) 307-6159
office@doubleedgetheatre.org
www.doubleedgetheatre.org
Est. 1982. Opportunities incl. Individual Artist Retreats. Response Time: 6 mos. **Preference.** Style: original ensemble performance, physical theatre. **Application.** What to submit: video.

**Downstage Left (DSL)**
3408 North Sheffield, Chicago, IL 60657
David Alan Moore
Tel: (773) 883-8830 ext. 3
david@stagelefttheatre.com
www.stagelefttheatre.com
**Assistance:** travel. **Consideration.** Opportunity/Award: royalty. **Preference.** Length: full length plays. **Application.** What to submit: full script,1 page synopsis, resume, SASE. How to submit: submit application online. Deadline: 3/15/2009.

**Dream Theatre**
484 W. 43rd St., #14-Q
New York, NY 10036
Andrea Leigh
Tel: (212) 564-2628
andrealeigh88@hotmail.com
Deadline: ongoing. Est. 2001. New works, esp. by/for women, that have not been optioned or produced in NYC. Response Time: 6 mos. **Preference.** Length: full length plays and musicals. Style: drama, comedy, adaptation. Subject: All subjects, woman, writers of color, disabled, gay/lesbian. **Application.** What to submit: synopsis,

full script, submissions not returned. How to submit: e-mail, US mail.

**Drilling Company**
107 W. 82nd St., #1-A
New York, NY 10024
Hamilton Clancy
Tel: (212) 877-4234 Fax: (212) 877-0099
DrillingCompany@aol.com
www.drillingcompany.org
> Est. 1999. Commissions for shorts produced in NYC, workshops for full-lengths. Staff: Dave Marantz (Asst Artistic Dir). Response Time: 3 mos. **Consideration.** Opportunity/Award: $100. **Preference.** Style: comedy, drama, musical. **Application.** What to submit: 10-pg sample, submissions not returned. Material must be unoptioned, unpublished, unproduced. How to submit: professional recommendation.

**East West Players**
120 N. Judge John Aiso St.
Los Angeles, CA 90012
Jeff Liu
Tel: (213) 625-7000 ext. 27
Fax: (213) 6257111
jliu@eastwestplayers.org
www.eastwestplayers.org
> Est. 1965. 4 mainstage productions/season in addition to readings. Especially interested in work by Asian-Americans. Response Time: 9 mos. **Preference.** Length: full length plays and musicals. Subject: writers of color. **Application.** What to submit: no query required; send synopsis, full script, resume, SASE. How to submit: by regular mail only; no e-submissions.

**Egyptian Theatre Company**
328 Main St., Box 3119
Park City, UT 84060
Terence Goodman
Tel: (435) 645-0671 Fax: (435) 649-0446
terence@parkcityshows.com
www.egyptiantheatrecompany.org
> Est. 1981. Response Time: 6 mos. **Preference.** Length: full length musicals. Style: musical. **Application.** How to submit: professional recommendation.

**El Centro Su Teatro**
4725 High St., Denver, CO 80216
Tony Garcia
Tel: (303) 296-0219 Fax: (303) 296-4614
elcentro@suteotro.org
www.suteatro.org
> Est. 1971. Production: cast of 6-8 Response Time: 6 mos. **Preference.** Length: full length plays. Style: no musical. Subject: T.Y.A., writers of color. **Application.** What to submit: full script. Material must be bilingual or Spanish.

**Electric Theatre Company**
Literary Manager, PO Box 854
Scranton, PA 18501
John Beck
Tel: (570) 558-1520
jbeck@electrictheatre.org
www.electrictheatre.org
> Est. 1992. Production: cast limit 6. Response Time: 3 mos. **Preference.** Length: full length plays. Style: comedy, drama. Subject: All subjects, woman, writers of color. **Application.** What to submit: 10 page dialogue sample, short synopsis. How to submit: mail or email. Deadline: 12/1/2009.

**Emelin Theatre for the Performing Arts**
153 Library Ln., Mamaroneck, NY 10543
Lisa Dozier
Tel: (914) 698-3045 Fax: (914) 698-1404
info@emelin.org
www.emelin.org
> Est. 1972. Production: small cast, no fly. Response Time: 6 mos. **Preference.** Length: full length plays. **Application.** How to submit: professional recommendation.

**Emerging Artists Theatre (EAT)**
464 West 25th St. # 4
New York, NY 10001-6501
Paul Adams
Tel: (212) 247-2429
eattheatre@gmail.com
www.eatheatre.org
> Deadline: For Illuminating Artists New Works Series -Nov 15th, Fall Eatfest -April 1st, Spring Eatfest -July 1st. Est. 1993. Develop and produce new work from shorts to full-lengths.

Production: 20-70, cast 2-10. Response Time: 3-6 mos. **Preference.** Length: full length plays and musicals. Style: comedy, drama, musical. Subject: All subjects, woman, writers of color, disabled, gay/lesbian. **Application.** What to submit: query, synopsis (full-lengths), by email, SASE. Material must be unproduced. How to submit: call for scripts thru DG and InsightforPlaywrights.com .

**Encompass New Opera Theatre**
138 S. Oxford St., #1-A
Brooklyn, NY 11217
Roger Cunningham
Tel: (718) 398-4675 Fax: (718) 398-4684
encompassopera@yahoo.com
www.encompassopera.org
Est. 1975. Contemporary opera and music theater. Staff: Lisa E. Harris (Mgr.). **Preference.** Style: musical. **Application.** What to submit: query, synopsis, audio, SASE. How to submit: professional recommendation.

**Enrichment Works**
5605 Woodman Ave., # 207
Van Nuys, CA 91401
Abraham Tetenbaum
Tel: (818) 780-1400 Fax: (818) 780-0300
atetenbaum@enrichmentworks.org
www.enrichmentworks.org
Est. 1999. Nonprofit presenting tours in L.A. schools, libraries and museums and community venues of works to inspire learning. Also accepts musical plays. Production: cast limit 3, touring set. Response Time: 6 mos. **Consideration.** Opportunity/Award: 10% royalty. **Preference.** Style: comedy, drama, musical. Subject: All subjects, woman, T.Y.A., writers of color, disabled. **Application.** What to submit: full script, SASE.

**The Ensemble Theatre**
3535 Main St., Houston, TX 77002
Eileen J. Morris
Tel: (713) 520-0055 Fax: (713) 520-1269
ejmorris@ensemblehouston.com
www.ensemblehouston.com

The Ensemble Theatre produces contemporary and classical works devoted to the portrayal of the African-American experience. Est. 1976. Production: cast limit 5, touring set. Response Time: 3 mos. **Consideration.** Opportunity/Award: work that has been produced; one-act plays. **Preference.** Length: full length plays and musicals. Subject: All subjects, woman, T.Y.A., writers of color. **Application.** What to submit: query, synopsis, sample, audio, resume, SASE. How to submit: between March and August.

**Ensemble Theater**
Box 181309, Cleveland Heights, OH 44118
Tel: (216) 321-2930
ensembletheater@sbcglobal.net

**Ensemble Theatre Company of Santa Barbara**
Box 2307, Santa Barbara, CA 93120
Jonathan Fox
Tel: (805) 965-5400 Fax: (805) 568-3806
info@ensembletheatre.com
www.ensembletheatre.com
Est. 1979. Production: cast limit 8, unit set. Response Time: 9 mos. **Preference.** Length: full length plays. **Application.** What to submit: query, synopsis, 10-pg sample, submissions not returned. How to submit: invite.

**Ensemble Theatre of Cincinnati**
1127 Vine St., Cincinnati, OH 45202
D. Lynn Meyers
Tel: (513) 421-3555 Fax: (513) 562-4104
administration@cincyetc.com
www.cincyetc.com
ETC Est. 1986. Production: cast limit 10, simple set. **Preference.** Length: full length plays and musicals. Subject: All subjects, woman, T.Y.A., writers of color, disabled, gay/lesbian. **Application.** What to submit: Query letter, synopsis, sample, resume, & SASE. Material must be A world or regional premiere. How to submit: Please inquire ahead of sending as to whether or not ETC is currently accepting new scripts.

## Career Development : Theaters

**eta Creative Arts Foundation Inc.**
7558 S. Chicago Ave., Chicago, IL 60619
Runako Jahi
email@etacreativearts.org
www.etacreativearts.org
> Est. 1971. Playwrights Speak Reading Series: staged readings followed by discussion, plays considered for mainstage productions. **Preference.** Subject: writers of color. **Application.** What to submit: synopsis, full script, bio, submissions returned with SASE. How to submit: unsolicited.

**Express Children's Theatre**
446 Northwest Mall, Houston, TX 77092
Pat Silver
Tel: (713) 682-5044
expresstheatre@sbcglobal.net
www.expresstheatre.com
> Est. 1991. In residence at Houston Community Coll. Central Fine Arts Dept. Production: cast of 3-4, touring set Response Time: 2 wks query, 8 ws script. **Preference.** Style: multi-ethnic. Subject: T.Y.A. **Application.** What to submit: query, synopsis. Bilingual encouraged.

**First Light Festival**
4400 University Dr., MS 6B8
Fairfax, VA 22030
Suzanne Maloney
Tel: (703) 993-2195 Fax: (703) 993-2191
smaloney@gmu.edu
www.gmu.edu/cfa/tfa
> Annual fest of new play readings. Response Time: 2 wks query, 6 mos script. **Preference.** Length: full length plays. Style: no musical. **Application.** What to submit: query, sample. Deadline: 11/15/2009.

**First Stage Children's Theater**
325 W. Walnut St., Milwaukee, WI 53212
Jeff Frank
Tel: (414) 267-2929 Fax: (414) 267-2930
jfrank@firststage.org
www.firststage.org
> Est. 1987. Response Time: 1 mo query, 3 mos script. **Preference.** Style: adaptation, musical, translation. Subject: T.Y.A. **Application.** What to submit: query, synopsis, resume.

**Flat Rock Playhouse**
Box 310, Flat Rock, NC 28731
Robin R. Farquhar
> **Preference.** Length: full length plays and musicals. Subject: All subjects, T.Y.A. **Application.** How to submit: hard copy by mail.

**Florida Repertory Theatre**
2267 1st St., Fort Myers, FL 33901
Bari Newport
www.floridarep.org
> Est. 1989. Equity LORT D. 8 mainstage plays Sep-Jun. Staff: Robert Cacioppo (Producing Artistic Dir). Production: cast limit 10, orchestra of 4-5, sets limit 2. Response Time: 1 yr. **Preference.** Length: full length plays. Style: all styles. Subject: woman, T.Y.A. **Application.** What to submit: synopsis, full script, SASE. How to submit: agent.

**Florida Stage**
262 S. Ocean Blvd., Manalapan, FL 33462
Javier Chacin
Tel: (561) 585-3404 Fax: (561) 5884708
javier@floridastage.org
www.floridastage.org
> New work. Est. 1987. Equity LORT C. Thought-provoking, issue-oriented material. Opportunities incl New Works Fest. Production: cast of 2-6, unit set. Response Time: 4 mos. **Preference.** Length: full length plays. Style: comedy, drama. **Application.** What to submit: query, synopsis, 10-page sample, playwright bio. Material must be agent only submissions. How to submit: email.

**Florida Studio Theatre**
1241 N. Palm Ave., Sarasota, FL 34236
Cristin Kelly
Tel: (941) 366-9017 Fax: (941) 955-4137
ckelly@floridastudiotheatre.org
www.floridastudiotheatre.org
> Response Time: 2 months query, 6 mos script. **Preference.** Length: full length plays. **Application.** What to submit: query, synopsis, 5-pg sample, SASE. CD if musical. How to submit: email (Word or PDF) or mail.

**Foothill Theatre Company**
Box 1812, Nevada City, CA 95959
Gary Wright
Tel: (530) 265-9320 Fax: (530) 265-9325
gary@foothilltheatre.org
www.foothilltheatre.org
   Est. 1977. Opportunities incl New Voices of the West staged readings. Frequency: annual Production: cast limit 6. Response Time: 1 yr. **Consideration.** Opportunity/Award: reading. **Preference.** Length: full length plays. **Application.** What to submit: query, synopsis, 10-pg sample, SASE. Material must be unproduced.

**Ford's Theatre Society**
511 10th St., NW, Washington, DC 20004
Paul Tetreault
www.fordstheatre.org
   Est. 1968. Equity LORT. 4-5 shows/yr, incl. perhaps 1 original play or musical. Staff: Mark Ramont (Assoc Prod/Artistic Dir). Production: orchestra limit 7. Response Time: 1 yr. **Consideration.** Opportunity/Award: royalty. **Preference.** Length: full length plays. **Application.** What to submit: query, synopsis, 10-pg sample, SASE. How to submit: professional recommendation.

**Fountain Theatre**
5060 Fountain Ave.
Los Angeles, CA 90029
Simon Levy
Tel: (323) 663-2235 Fax: (323) 663-1629
www.fountaintheatre.com
   Equity 99 seat. Production: cast limit 12, unit set, no fly. Response Time: 3 mos. **Consideration.** Opportunity/Award: 6% royalty. **Preference.** Length: full length plays. Style: no translation. **Application.** What to submit: query, synopsis. How to submit: professional recommendation.

**Fountainhead Theatre**
2003 Columbia Pike, #218
Arlington, VA 22204
Charlotte Akin
Tel: (703) 920-5923 Fax: (703) 920-5923
   Est. 1992 as New Theater Company (NTC).

**Free Street Programs**
1419 W. Blackhawk St.
Chicago, IL 60622
Bryn Magnus
www.freestreet.org
   Est. 1969. Creates experimental work in collaboration with youth, emerging and professional artists. Staff: Ron Bieganski (Artistic Director), Anita Evans (Creative Director). **Application.** What to submit: query with project ideas, submissions not returned.

**Freed-Hardeman University**
Theater Dept., 158 E. Main St.
Henderson, TN 38340
Cliff Thompson
Tel: (731) 989-6780
cthompson@fhu.edu
   **Preference.** Length: full length plays. Style: all styles. Subject: woman, T.Y.A. **Application.** What to submit: synopsis, 30-pg writing sample, submissions returned with SASE. How to submit: unsolicited.

**Freedom Repertory Theatre**
1346 N. Broad St., Philadelphia, PA 19121
Walter Dallas
Tel: (215) 765-2793 Fax: (215) 765-4191
www.freedomtheatre.org
   Est. 1966. Response Time: 3 mos. **Preference.** Length: full length plays. Subject: writers of color. **Application.** How to submit: professional recommendation.

**GableStage**
1200 Anastasia Ave.
Coral Gables, FL 33134
Joseph Adler
Tel: (305) 446-1116 Fax: (305) 445-8645
jadler@gablestage.org
www.gablestage.org
   Est. 1979. Equity SPT-5. 6 productions/yr. **Preference.** Length: full length plays. Subject: writers of color, gay/lesbian. **Application.** What to submit: query.

**Geffen Playhouse**
10886 LeConte Ave.
Los Angeles, CA 90024
Amy Levinson Millan

www.geffenplayhouse.com
   Est. 1995. Response Time: 6 mos.
   **Preference.** Length: full length plays.
   **Application.** How to submit: agent.

**Genesis Repertory Ensemble**
23-23 30th Ave., Fl. 2, Astoria, NY 11102
J. Michaels
Tel: (646) 226-0370
genesisnyc@gmail.com
www.genesis-repertory.org
   Est. 1999. New works, non-Equity and Equity Showcase. Response Time: 2 mos. **Application.** What to submit: full script.

**George Street Playhouse**
9 Livingston Ave.
New Brunswick, NJ 8901
Jeremy Stoller
www.georgestplayhouse.org
   Est. 1974. Equity LORT C. Productions, readings, tours of issue-oriented 40-min one-acts for schools, and Next Stage Fest workshops. Prefer fresh perspectives on society, compelling personal and human stories that entertain, challenge, and stretch the imagination. Production: cast limit 7. Response Time: 10 mos. **Preference.** Length: full length plays. Style: no translation. **Application.** What to submit: query, synopsis, 10-pg sample, cast/scene list, tech needs. How to submit: professional recommendation.

**Georgia Shakespeare**
4484 Peachtree Rd. NE
Atlanta, GA 30319
   Est. 1985. Staff: Richard Garner (Producing Artistic Dir); Stacy Shaw (Managing Dir).

**Germinal Stage Denver**
2450 W. 44th Ave., Denver, CO 80211
Ed Baierlein
Tel: (303) 455-7108
gsden@privatei.com
www.germinalstage.com
   Est. 1974. Production: cast limit 10 Response Time: 2 wks query, 6 mos script. **Preference.** Length: full length plays. **Application.** What to submit: query, synopsis, 5-pg sample.

**Geva Theatre Center**
75 Woodbury Blvd., Rochester, NY 14607
Marge Betley
Tel: (585) 232-1366 Fax: (585) 232-4031
www.gevatheatre.org
   Est. 1972. Equity LORT B and D. Produces classics to musicals to new works, incl. readings and workshops. Staff: Jean Gordon Ryon (New Plays Coord.). **Assistance:** stipend, room/board, travel Response Time: 3 mos query; 6 mos script. **Preference.** Length: full length plays. **Application.** What to submit: query, synopsis, 10-pg sample, SASE. How to submit: professional recommendation.

**Golden Fleece Ltd.**
70-A Greenwhich Ave., #256
New York, NY 10011
Lou Rodgers
Tel: (212) 691-6105
info@goldenfleeceltd.org
www.goldenfleeceltd.org
   Est. 1974. Golden Fleece Ltd. nurtures, develops and produces new works by emerging American composers as well as playwrights, lyricists and librettists. The Composers Chamber Theatre; annual commissioned opera/music theater production; Square One Series of works by composers, lyricists and librettists in progress; Argonaut Series of new works by poets and playwrights in progress. Production: all ages, cast limit of 8, orchestra of 4, set varies. Response Time: varies. **Preference.** Style: all styles. **Application.** What to submit: synopsis or treatment, resume, submission returned if SASE provided. Material must be unpublished, unproduced. How to submit: unsolicited, professional recommendation.

**Goodman Theatre**
170 N. Dearborn St., Chicago, IL 60601
Tanya Palmer
www.goodmantheatre.org
   Est. 1925. Equity LORT B+ and C. 1992 Regional Theater Tony winner. Staff: Robert Falls (Artistic Dir.), Roche Schulfer (Exec. Dir.). Response Time: 6 mos. **Preference.** Length: full length

plays. **Application.** What to submit: 10 pg sample. How to submit: agent.

**Goodspeed Musicals**
6 Main St, P.O. Box A
East Haddam, CT 06423-0281
Donna Lynn Cooper Hilton
Tel: (860) 873-8664 Fax: (860) 873-2329
info@goodspeed.org
www.goodspeed.org
 Est. 1959. 1995 Regional Theater Tony winner. Staff: Michael P. Price (Exec. Dir.). **Preference.** Length: full length musicals. Style: musical. **Application.** What to submit: submit a synopsis, demo and bios of the authors, and a SASE. How to submit: agent.

**Great Lakes Theater Festival**
1501 Euclid Ave., # 300
Cleveland, OH 44115
Charles Fee
Tel: (216) 241-5490
www.greatlakestheater.org
 Est. 1961. Response Time: 3 mos. **Preference.** Length: full length plays. Style: adaptation, translation, relevant to classical repertoire. **Application.** How to submit: professional recommendation.

**Greenbrier Valley Theatre**
113 E. Washington St.
Lewisburg, WV 24901
Cathey Sawyer
Tel: (304) 645-3838 Fax: (304) 645-3818
www.gvtheatre.org
 Est. 1967. Equity LOA. Production: age 7 and older, cast of 6-10, orchestra of 1-4, set limit 1. Response Time: 6 mos. **Preference.** Length: full length musicals. Style: adaptation, comedy or variety, drama, musical. Subject: woman, T.Y.A., writers of color. **Application.** What to submit: synopsis, 5-pg sample, submissions not returned. Author must be resident of US. Material must be unoptioned, unproduced. How to submit: professional recommendation, agent.

**Gretna Theatre**
Box 578, Mt. Gretna, PA 17064
Larry Frenock
Tel: (717) 964-3322
www.gretnatheatre.com
 Est. 1927. Equity Guest Artists LOA. Opportunities incl. reading. Response Time: 1 mo query, 3 mos script. **Preference.** Length: full length plays. **Application.** What to submit: synopsis, 5-pg sample, audio.

**Growing Stage The Children's Theatre of New Jersey**
P.O. Box 36, Netcong, NJ 7857
Stephen L. Fredericks
Tel: (973) 347-4946 Fax: (973) 691-7069
exdir@growingstage.com
www.growingstage.com
 We review submissions between May – August only Est. 1982. Response Time: 4 mos. **Preference.** Length: full length plays and musicals. Subject: T.Y.A. **Application.** What to submit: Synopsis, character breakdown, sample scene; SASE. Material must be for young audiences and/or families.

**Guthrie Theater**
818 S. 2nd St., Minneapolis, MN 55415
Michael Kinghorn
www.guthrietheater.org
 Est. 1963. Equity LORT A, B, D. 1982 Regional Theater Tony winner. New Play Program has over 110 commissions, workshops, publications or productions. New 3-theater complex opened 2006, incl. 1100-seat thrust, 700-seat proscenium, and 199-seat studio. Response Time: 6 mos. **Preference.** Length: full length plays. **Application.** What to submit: full script. How to submit: agent only.

**Hadley Players**
207 W. 133rd St., New York, NY 10030
Tel: (212) 368-9314
hadleyplayers@yahoo.com
 **Application.** What to submit: 10 pg. sample, SASE.

**Halcyon Theatre**
1906 W. Winnemac, #2, Chicago, IL 60640
Tony Adams
Tel: (312) 458-9170
submissions@halcyontheatre.org
www.halcyontheatre.org
> **Consideration.** Opportunity/Award: Reading, Workshop, Production. **Preference.** Length: full length plays and musicals. Style: All. Subject: All subjects, woman, T.Y.A., writers of color, disabled, gay/lesbian. **Application.** What to submit: Full script. How to submit: Unsolicited, Professional recommendation, Agent. For submissions policies go to halcyontheatre.org/submissions. Deadline: rolling.

**Hangar Theatre KIDDSTUFF**
Box 205, Ithaca, NY 14851
Literary Asst.
literary@hangartheatre.org
www.hangartheatre.org
> Staff: Peter Flynn, Artistic Dir. Response Time: 6 mos. **Consideration.** Opportunity/Award: royalty. **Preference.** Subject: T.Y.A. **Application.** What to submit: full script, SASE.

**Harlem Stage at The Gatehouse**
150 Convent Ave., New York, NY 10031
Tel: (212) 281-9240 Fax: (212) 281-9318
> Sunday Works reading Series.

**Harlequin Productions**
197 Franklin St., Auburn, NY 13021
Robert Frame
framer@cayuga-cc.edu
www.cayugacc.edu
> Est. 1958. 6 perfs over 2 weekends (fall and spring) with college students in high-quality extracurricular program. Production: age 16-35, cast of 7-14. Response Time: 1 yr. **Consideration.** Opportunity/Award: flat fee. **Preference.** Style: adaptation, comedy, drama. **Application.** What to submit: full script, SASE.

**Hartford Stage**
50 Church St., Hartford, CT 6103
Jeremy B. Cohen
www.hartfordstage.org
> Est. 1963. Equity LORT B. 1989 Regional Theater Tony winner. **Preference.** Length: full length plays. **Application.** What to submit: full script. How to submit: agent, unsolicited (CT residents only).

**Harwich Junior Theatre (HJT)**
Box 168, 105 Division St.
West Harwich, MA 2671
hjt@capecod.net
www.hjtcapecod.org
> Est. 1951. New plays for intergenerational casts and audiences. Production: no fly. Response Time: 6 mos. **Consideration.** Opportunity/Award: royalty. **Preference.** Subject: T.Y.A. **Application.** What to submit: synopsis, SASE.

**Hedgerow Theatre**
64 Rose Valley Rd., Media, PA 19063
Penelope Reed
www.hedgerowtheatre.org
> Est. 1923. Readings of new plays by Delaware Valley writers in readings and workshops. Production: cast of 2-8. Response Time: 2 mos query, 4 mos script. **Preference.** Length: full length plays. Style: comedy, mystery. **Application.** What to submit: query, synopsis. Author must be resident of NJ, PA, DE. Material must be unpublished, unproduced.

**Hip Pocket Theatre**
Box 136758, Ft. Worth, TX 76136
Johnny Simons
Tel: (817) 246-9775
www.hippocket.org
> Est. 1977. Production: simple set, outdoor amphitheater. Response Time: 2 mos. **Preference.** Length: full length plays. **Application.** What to submit: synopsis, sample, audio.

**Hippodrome State Theatre**
25 SE 2nd Pl., Gainesville, FL 32601
Tamerin Dygert
Tel: (352) 373-5968
www.thehipp.org
> Est. 1973. Equity SPT. Production: cast limit 6, unit set. Response Time: 5 mos. **Preference.** Length: full length

plays. **Application.** How to submit: agent.

**Honolulu Theatre for Youth**
229 Queen Emma Sq.
Honolulu, HI 96813
Eric Johnson
Tel: (808) 839-9885 Fax: (808) 839-7018
htyeric@gmail.com
www.htyweb.org
  Est. 1955. Producing and commissioning new plays, Sep-May. Production: cast limit 5. **Preference.** Subject: T.Y.A., writers of color. **Application.** What to submit: query, submissions not returned.

**Horizon Theatre Rep**
41 E. 67th St., New York, NY 10021
Rafael De Mussa
Tel: (212) 737-3357 Fax: (212) 737-5103
info@htronline.org
www.htronline.org
  Est. 2000. Equity Showcase. Staff: Andrew Cohen (Managing Dir). Production: ages 16-75, cast size 4-15 Response Time: 1 mo. **Preference.** Length: full length plays. Style: no musical. **Application.** What to submit: synopsis, submissions not returned. Material must be unoptioned, unproduced.

**Horse Trade Theater Group**
85 E. 4th St., New York, NY 10003
Erez Ziv
Tel: (212) 777-6088
www.horsetrade.info
  Horse Trade is a self-sustaining theater development group; with a focus on new work, it has produced a massive quantity of stimulating downtown theater. Horse Trade's Resident Artist Program offers a home to a select group of Independent Theater artists, pooling together a great deal of talent and energy. It is also the home of FRIGID New York – the first and only festival of its kind in New York City. **Application.** What to submit: full scriptquery, sample, SASE. Material must be full script, query, sample, SASE. How to submit: See instructions on website, professional recommendation.

**Hubris Productions**
724 W. Roscoe Street, #3S
Chicago, IL 60657
Jacob Green
Tel: (773) 398-3273
jacob@hubrisproductions.com
www.hubrisproductions.com
  **Preference.** Length: full length plays and musicals. Style: All. Subject: All subjects, woman, writers of color, disabled, gay/lesbian. **Application.** What to submit: query. 10-page sample. Material must not be optioned, produced, or published.

**Hudson Theatres**
6539 Santa Monica Blvd.
Los Angeles, CA 90038
Elizabeth Reilly
Tel: (323) 856-4252 Fax: (323) 856-4316
ereilly@hudsontheater.com
www.hudsontheatre.com
  Est. 1991. Primarily rental house Equity 99-seat. Hollywood Theatre Row complex incl. Mainstage, and Backstage (Comedy Central in residence); 43-seat Guild; and Caffe Bacio. Response Time: 6 mos query, 1 yr script. **Application.** What to submit: query, synopsis, sample.

**Hyde Park Theatre**
511 W. 43rd St., Austin, TX 78751
Peck Phillips
peck@hydeparktheatre.org
www.hydeparktheatre.org
  Est. 1992. Southwest premieres of alternative and classic works that challenge modern audiences. Also Frontera Fest, 5-wk unjuried fringe fest. Play Development Reading Series. Response Time: 3 mos query, 6 mos script. **Preference.** Length: full length plays. Style: no musical. **Application.** What to submit: query, synopsis, SASE.

**Hypothetical Theatre Company**
344 E. 14th St., New York, NY 10003
Amy Feinberg

Tel: (212) 780-0800 ext. 254
htc@hypotheticaltheatre.org
www.hypotheticaltheatre.org
   Est. 1986. Response Time: 6 mos.
   **Preference.** Length: full length plays.
   Style: adaptation, comedy, drama.
   **Application.** What to submit: full script,
   SASE. Material must be unproduced in
   NYC. How to submit: agent.

**Idaho Repertory Theater (IRT)**
University of Idaho, Box 442008
Moscow, ID 83844
Jere Hodgin
theatre@uidaho.edu
www.idahorep.org
   Production: ages 13-35, cast of 2-10.
   Response Time: 4 mos. **Consideration.**
   Opportunity/Award: royalty.
   **Application.** What to submit: query.
   Author must be new/emerging writer.
   Material must be unpublished. How to
   submit: email.

**Immigrants' Theatre Project**
44 Douglass St., Brooklyn, NY 11231
Marcy Arlin
Tel: (347) 512-5572 Fax: (718) 237-4545
immigrantstheat@aol.com
www.immigrantstheat.org
   **Immigrants' Theatre Project will
   be taking a hiatus on new work in
   2009. For 2010, we will only work
   on co-productions and co-funding
   situations.** Est. 1988. **Consideration.**
   Opportunity/Award: reading, royalties
   by agreement. **Preference.** Style: all
   styles, no musical. **Application.** What
   to submit: query letter (note theme
   addressed), synopsis, 20-pg writing
   sample, submissions returned with
   SASE. How to submit: unsolicited,
   email okay.

**Impact Theatre Company**
190 Underhill Ave., Brooklyn, NY 11238
E. K. Rivera
Tel: (718) 3907163
impacttheaternyc@yahoo.com
www.geocities.com/impacttheaternyc
   Staff: Tim Lewis (Exec Producer).
   **Application.** What to submit: query,
   SASE. Material must be unoptioned.

**Impact Theatre**
Box 12666, Berkeley, CA 94712
Melissa Hillman
melissa@impacttheatre.com
www.impacttheatre.com
   Est. 1996. Response Time: varies.
   **Preference.** Length: full length
   plays. Style: all styles. **Application.**
   What to submit: synopsis, 20
   page sample, full script, SASE.
   Material must be unoptioned. How
   to submit: unsolicited, professional
   recommendation, agent.

**Indiana Repertory Theatre**
140 W. Washington St.
Indianapolis, IN 46204
Richard J. Roberts
Tel: (317) 635-5277 Fax: (317) 236-0767
rroberts@irtlive.com
www.irtlive.com
   Est. 1972. Equity LORT, 6-show
   Signature Series (Sep-May) in 600-
   seat proscenium mainstage, 2-show
   Discovery Series for family/youth in
   300-seat thrust upperstage. Production:
   cast limit 10. Response Time: 6 mos.
   **Preference.** Length: full length plays.
   Style: adaptation, translation, solo; no
   musical. **Application.** What to submit:
   query, synopsis, resume; all via email.
   Material must be Midwest voice. How
   to submit: email.

**Infamous Commonwealth Theatre**
4845 North Harding, Unit 1
Chicago, IL 60625
Genevieve Thompson
Tel: (312) 458-9780
gthompson@infamouscommonwealth.org
www.infamouscommonwealth.org
   Est. 2001.

**InnerAct Productions**
138 S. Oxford St., #2-C
Brooklyn, NY 11217
John Shevin Foster
Tel: (718) 230-1323
mail@inneractpd.com
www.inneractpd.com
   Est. 1998. Equity. Theater by/for
   artists of color. Production: cast
   limit 8. **Consideration.** Opportunity/

Award: 5% royalty. **Preference.** Style: no revues. Subject: writers of color. **Application.** What to submit: query, synopsis. Author must be age 18 or older. How to submit: email.

**INTAR (International Arts Relations) Theatre**
Box 756, New York, NY 10108
Lorenzo Mans
Tel: (212) 695-6134
submissions@intartheatre.org
www.intartheatre.org
> Est. 1966. Equity LOA. Opportunities incl. workshops, productions of works in progress, and mainstage productions. Response Time: 3 mos. **Preference.** Length: full length plays. Style: comedy, drama. Subject: writers of color. **Application.** What to submit: full script. Material must be unproduced.

**InterAct Theatre Company**
2030 Sansom St., Philadelphia, PA 19103
Rebecca Wright
Tel: (215) 568-8077 Fax: (215) 568-8095
bwright@interacttheatre.org
www.interacttheatre.org
> Est. 1988. Resident company at Adrienne Theatre. Production: cast 1-8. Response Time: 6-12 months. **Preference.** Length: full length plays. **Application.** What to submit: query, synopsis, writing sample, bio, SASE. How to submit: unsolicited.

**Interborough Repertory Theater Inc. (IRT)**
154 Christopher St., #3-B
New York, NY 10014
Jonathan Fluck
Tel: (212) 206-6875 Fax: (212) 206-7037
www.irt.dreamhost.com
> Est. 1986. Equity Showcase. Provdes accessible theater to schools and families of diverse cultural backgrounds in an atmosphere where theater professionals can grow and develop. **Preference.** Length: full length plays. Subject: T.Y.A., disabled. **Application.** What to submit: query, SASE.

**International City Theatre**
1 World Trade Center, #300
Long Beach, CA 90831
Shashin Desai
Tel: (562) 495-4595 Fax: (562) 436-7895
shashinict@earthlink.net
www.ictlongbeach.org
> Est. 1985. Equity SPT, Long Beach PAC resident company, 349-seat venue. Staff: Caryn Desai (Gen Mgr). Production: cast limit 9, orchestra limit 6 Response Time: 6 mos. **Consideration.** Opportunity/Award: 7% royalty. **Preference.** Length: full length plays. **Application.** What to submit: synopsis, sample, full script, SASE. How to submit: professional recommendation.

**Interplayers Ensemble Theatre**
174 S. Howard St., Spokane, WA 99210
Tel: (509) 455-7529
office@interplayers.com
www.interplayers.com
> Est. 1981. Production: cast limit 8, unit set, thrust stage. **Preference.** Length: full length plays. **Application.** What to submit: query, synopsis, 10-pg sample, full script, SASE. Author must be age 21 or older. Material must be unoptioned.

**Intiman Theatre**
201 Mercer St., Seattle, WA 98109
Kate Godman
Tel: (206) 269-1901 Fax: (206) 269-1928
literary@intiman.org
www.intiman.org
> Est. 1972. Equity LORT C. 2006 Regional Theater Tony winner. 6-play season (Apr-Dec) in 450-seat theater. Response Time: 8 mos. **Preference.** Length: full length plays. Style: no musical. **Application.** What to submit: query, synopsis, SASE. How to submit: professional recommendation.

**Irish Classical Theatre Company (ICTC)**
625 Main St., Buffalo, NY 14203
Fortunato Pezzimenti
Tel: (716) 853-1380 Fax: (716) 853-0592
vinco@irishclassical.com
www.irishclassicaltheatre.com

Est. 1990. Equity Buffalo-Rochester Special Agreement, 5-play season. Response Time: 3 mos. **Consideration.** Opportunity/Award: royalties. **Preference.** Length: full length plays. Style: adaptation, comedy, drama. **Application.** What to submit: synopsis, sample. Author must be Irish or Irish-American. How to submit: professional recommendation.

**Irish Repertory Theatre**
132 W. 22nd St., New York, NY 10011
Kara Manning
Tel: (212) 255-0270 Fax: (212) 255-0281
kara@irishrep.org
www.irishrep.org
Ongoing new works reading series reflecting the Irish and Irish American experience. Female playwrights and writers of color encouraged. **Preference.** Length: full length plays. **Application.** What to submit: Unsolicited: 20 page sample, synopsis, cover letter, audio if musical, SASE Agent or solicited submissions: entire script, cast breakdown, cover letter. No email submissions unless solicited as such. Material must be unpublished, not produced in the U.S. (Ireland/UK productions permissible).

**Irondale Ensemble Project**
Box 150604, Brooklyn, NY 11215
Jim Niesen
Tel: (718) 488-9233 Fax: (718) 788-0607
irondalert@aol.com
www.irondale.org
Est. 1983. Equity LOA. Classic work in unorthodox production and original work combining new and classic styles of performance, music, dance and design. Production: cast limit 9. Response Time: 10 wks. **Preference.** Length: full length plays. **Application.** What to submit: query.

**Jefferson Performing Arts Society**
1118 Clearview Pkwy., Metairie, LA 70001
Dennis G. Assaf
Tel: (504) 885-2000 ext. 201
Fax: (504) 885-3437
www.jpas.org
Est. 1978. **Application.** Material must be any. How to submit: mail.

**Jewish Ensemble Theatre**
6600 W. Maple Rd.
West Bloomfield, MI 48322
Evelyn Orbach
Tel: (248) 788-2900
e.orbach@jettheatre.org
www.jettheatre.org
Est. 1989. In addition to a 4-5 production annual subscription season (Equity SPT), JET sponsors an annual fest of new plays, presented for 2 perfs in staged readings. Response Time: 1/31/09. **Preference.** Length: full length plays. Style: all styles. **Application.** What to submit: full script, SASE. Material must be unproduced. How to submit: unsolicited. Deadline: 9/1/2009.

**Jewish Theater of New York**
Box 845, Times Sq. Sta.
New York, NY 10108
Liz Lauren
thejtny@aol.com
www.jewishtheater.org
Est. 1994. Staff: Tuvia Tenenbom (Artistic Dir). Response Time: 3 mos. **Preference.** Length: full length musicals. Style: comedy, drama, musical. **Application.** What to submit: synopsis, submissions not returned. Material must be unoptioned, unpublished, unproduced. How to submit: invite.

**John Capo Productions**
PMB 112, 222 Guideboard Rd.
Clifton Park, NY 12065
Jack Dowd
Tel: (518) 383-0743
est. 2001 Response Time: 3-6 mos. **Consideration.** Opportunity/Award: production. **Preference.** Length: full length plays. Style: all styles. **Application.** What to submit: query, synopsis, full script, SASE. Material must be unpublished, unproduced. How to submit: unsolicited.

**Jubilee Theatre**
506 Main St., Forth Worth, TX 76102
Ed Smith
Tel: (817) 338-4204 Fax: (817) 338-4206
ed.smith@jubileetheatre.org
www.jubileetheatre.org
> **Application.** What to submit: query,10 pg. sample, resume, SASE.

**Judith Shakespeare Company NYC**
367 Windsor Hwy., #409
New Windsor, NY 12553
Joanne Zipay
Tel: (212) 592-1885
www.judithshakespeare.org
> Est. 1995. Offers RESURGENCE concert reading series and full productions of new plays with heightened language and significant roles for women. **Consideration.** Opportunity/Award: Reading/Possible production. **Preference.** Length: full length plays. Style: Classical with emphasis on roles for women. Subject: woman, writers of color, disabled, gay/lesbian. **Application.** What to submit: must be heightened language with significant roles for women. How to submit: regular mail.

**Kairos Italy Theater (KIT)**
50 E. 8th Street, #12B
New York, NY 10003
Laura Caparrotti
Fax: (801) 749-6727
info@kitheater.com
www.kitheater.com
> Est. 2002. KIT's mission is to produce plays by and about Italian authors and Italian themes. Production: cast of 5. **Preference.** Style: all styles. **Application.** What to submit: send email with synopsis, sample pages. How to submit: send email with synopsis, sample pages.

**Kansas City Repertory Theatre**
4949 Cherry St., Kansas City, MO 64110
Eric Rosen
Tel: (816) 235-2727 Fax: (816) 235-5367
www.kcrep.org
> Est. 1964. Formerly Missouri Repertory Theatre. Equity LORT B. **Application.** How to submit: invite.

**Karamu House Inc.**
2355 E. 89th St., Cleveland, OH 44106
Tel: (216) 795-7070
www.karamu.com
> Nonprofit community-based arts and educational organization to encourage and support the preservation, celebration and evolution of African-American culture and provide a vehicle for social, economic and educational development.

**Kavinoky Theatre**
320 Porter Ave., Buffalo, NY 14221
David Lamb
Tel: (716) 829-7668
www.kavinokytheatre.com
> Est. 1981 Production: cast limited 7, no fly, limited wing. Response Time: 1 mo. **Preference.** Length: full length plays. **Application.** How to submit: professional recommendation.

**Kentucky Repertory Theatre at Horse Cave**
Box 215, 101 E. Main St.
Horse Cave, KY 42749
Robert Brock
Tel: (270) 786-1200 Fax: (270) 786-5298
rbrock@kentuckyrep.org
www.kentuckyrep.org
> Est. 1977. Equity LOA. Formerly Horse Cave Theater. Production: cast limit 10, unit set. **Preference.** Length: full length plays. **Application.** What to submit: query. Author must be resident of KY. Material must be unproduced. How to submit: professional recommendation.

**Kidworks Touring Theatre Co.**
5215 N. Ravenswood Ave., #307
Chicago, IL 60640
Andrea Salloum
Tel: (773) 907-9932
kidworkstheatre@aol.com
www.kidworkstheatre.org
> Est. 1987.

**Killing Kompany**
21 Turn Ln., Levittown, NY 11756
Jon Avner
Tel: (212) 772-2590 Fax: (212) 2026495
killingkompany@killingkompany.com
www.killingkompany.com
> Interactive shows for dinner theater.

**Kumu Kahua Theatre**
46 Merchant St., Honolulu, HI 96813
Harry Wong III
Tel: (808) 536-4222 Fax: (808) 536-4226
kumukahuatheatre@hawaiiantel.net;
www.kumukahua.org
   Est. 1971. Response Time: 4 mos.
   **Preference.** Length: full length plays.
   Style: adaptation, comedy, drama.
   **Application.** What to submit: full script, SASE.

**Kuntu Repertory Theatre**
Dept. of Africana Studies
4140 S. Bouquet St., Pittsburgh, PA 15260
Dr. Vernall A. Lillie
Tel: (412) 624-7298
www.kuntu.org
   Est. 1974. **Application.** What to submit: full script.

**Kuumba Ensemble Heritage House Community Theater**
1021 Hartmont Road, #755
Baltimore, MA 21228
www.kuumbaensemble.org
info@kuumbaensemble.org
   **Application.** What to submit: query, synopsis, 10 pg. sample.

**L.A. Theatre Works (LATW)**
681 Venice Blvd., Venice, CA 90291
Brendon Fox
Tel: (310) 827-0808
www.latw.org
   Est. 1974. Live performances and studio recordings for broadcast over public radio. Some published as Plays on Tape, for which authors receive a percentage of gross sales. Response Time: 6 mos. **Preference.** Length: full length plays. Style: adaptation, comedy, drama. **Application.** How to submit: agent.

**La Jolla Playhouse**
Box 12039, La Jolla, CA 92039
Gabriel Greene
Tel: (858) 550-1070 Fax: (858) 550-1075
www.lajollaplayhouse.org
   Est. 1947. LORT B, C. 1993 Regional Theater Tony winner. Commissions playwrights and provides developmental support thru Page to Stage readings (est. 2001). Response Time: 2 mos query, 1 yr script.
   **Preference.** Length: full length plays.
   **Application.** What to submit: 10-page sample accepted from Southern California-based playwrights. Include SASE. Material must be West Coast premiere. How to submit: full script from agent only.

**La MaMa Experimental Theater Club**
74-A E. 4th St., New York, NY 10003
Ellen Stewart
Tel: (212) 254-6468
web@lamama.org
www.lamama.org
   Est. 1961. Response Time: 6 mos.
   **Preference.** Length: full length plays. **Application.** How to submit: professional recommendation.

**Laguna Playhouse**
Box 1747, Laguna Beach, CA 92652
Donna Inglima
www.lagunaplayhouse.com
   Est. 1920. Staff: Andrew Barnicle (Artistic Dir). **Application.** How to submit: invite.

**LaMicro Theater**
Box 20019, London Ter.
New York, NY 10011
Pietro Gonzalez
Tel: (212) 979-5744
info@lamicrotheater.org
www.lamicrotheater.org
   Est. 2003. Staff: Martin Balmaceda (Exec Dir), Berioska Ipinza (Exec Dir). Production: cast of 2-4.
   **Preference.** Style: comedy, drama, translation. Subject: woman, T.Y.A., writers of color. **Application.** What to submit: sample, full script, submissions not returned. Material must be unproduced.

**Latin American Theater Ensemble (LATE) / El Portón del Barrio**
Box 18, Radio City Sta.
New York, NY 10101
Margarita Toirac
Tel: (212) 397-3262 Fax: (212) 397-3262

elportonlatenyc@aol.com
www.lateny.org
> Est. 1970. Production: cast limit 3. **Preference.** Style: comedy, drama. Subject: writers of color. **Application.** What to submit: full script.

**Lifeline Theatre**
6912 N. Glenwood Ave.
Chicago, IL 60626
Dorothy Milne
www.lifelinetheatre.com
> Est. 1982. Production: cast limit 9. **Preference.** Style: adaptation. **Application.** What to submit: query, synopsis, SASE. Author must be resident of Chicago. How to submit: invite.

**Lincoln Center Theater**
150 W. 65th St., New York, NY 10023
Anne Cattaneo
Tel: (212) 362-7600
www.lct.org
> Est. 1966. Equity LORT A & B. Response Time: 2 mos. **Preference.** Length: full length plays. **Application.** How to submit: agent.

**Little Fish Theatre (LFT)**
397 W 11th St., San Pedro, CA 90731
Lisa Coffi Melanie Jones
Tel: (310) 512-6030
lisa@littlefishtheatre.org
melanie@littlefishtheatre.org
www.littlefishtheatre.org
> Est. 2002. Equity 99-seat. Offers full-length plays that are innovative and thought-provoking, socially and culturally relevant, challenging and entertaining. Staff: Lisa Coffi (Producing Artistic Director) Melanie Jones (Artistic Dir). Production: cast limit 7, minimal set. **Preference.** Length: full length plays. Subject: All subjects. **Application.** What to submit: query, synopsis, 10-pg sample, SASE.

**Live Bait Theater**
3914 N. Clark St., Chicago, IL 60613
Tel: (773) 871-1212
info@livebaittheater.org
www.livebaittheater.org
> Est. 1987. Opportunities incl. Fresh Bait reading series. Production: cast limit 9, unit set, no fly/wing space. Response Time: 6 wks query, 6 mos script. **Preference.** Length: full length plays. Style: no musical. **Application.** What to submit: query, synopsis. Author must be resident of Chicago area.

**Looking Glass Theatre**
422 W. 57th St., New York, NY 10019
Erica Nilson
Tel: (212) 307-9467
admin@lookingglasstheatrenyc.com
www.lookingglasstheatrenyc.com
> Est. 1993. Off-Off Broadway Showcase Theatre. Production: minimal. Response Time: 6 mos-1 yr. **Preference.** Style: all styles. Subject: woman. **Application.** What to submit: full script. How to submit: unsolicited.

**Lorraine Hansberry Theater**
777 Jones St., San Francisco, CA 94109
Stanley Williams
Tel: (415) 345-3980 Fax: (415) 345-3983
theatre@lhtsf.org
www.lhtsf.org
> **Preference.** Length: full length plays and musicals. Style: all styles. Subject: writers of color. **Application.** What to submit: synopsis, full script, submissions returned with SASE. How to submit: unsolicited.

**Lost Nation Theater**
39 Main St., Montpelier, VT 5602
Mr. Kim Bent
Tel: (802) 229-0492
info@lostnationtheater.org
www.lostnationtheater.org
> Est. 1977. Production: cast limit 8, unit set, no fly. Response Time: 2 mo query, 4 mos script. **Preference.** Length: full length plays. Subject: T.Y.A. **Application.** What to submit: query, synopsis, sample, resume.

**Luna Stage**
695 Bloomfield Ave., Montclair, NJ 07042
Cheryl Katz
Tel: (973) 744-3309 Fax: (973) 509-2388
cheryl@lunastage.org
www.lunastage.org

Est. 1992. Equity SPT-2. 3-6 new plays/season. Staff: Jane Mandel (Artistic Dir), Mona Hennessy (Managing Dir). Response Time: 3-6 mos. **Consideration.** Opportunity/Award: $1,000 in lieu of royalty. **Preference.** Length: full length plays. **Application.** What to submit: see website for guidelines. Deadline: 4/15/2009.

**Lyric Stage Company of Boston**
140 Clarendon St., Boston, MA 2116
Rebecca Curtiss
www.lyricstage.com
Est. 1974. Opportunities incl. Growing Voices new work development program. Production: cast limit 6 (plays) or 12 (musicals), modest orchestra, unit set. Response Time: 2 mos query, 6 mos script. **Preference.** Length: full length musicals. Style: comedy, musical. **Application.** What to submit: query, 1-pg synopsis, 15-pg sample, audio, cast list, SASE. Author must be resident of MA, women and minorities encouraged.

**Ma-Yi Theatre Company**
520 8th Ave, #309, New York, NY 10018
Ralph B. Pena
info@ma-yitheatre.org
www.ma-yitheatre.org
Est. 1989. **Preference.** Length: full length plays. Style: original new plays. Subject: All subjects, writers of color. **Application.** What to submit: query, synopsis, submissions not returned. Material must be unoptioned, unpublished, unproduced. How to submit: send 1-page synopsis and bio.

**Madison Repertory Theatre**
1 S. Pinckney St., Suite LL100
Madison, WI 53703
Trevin Gay
Tel: (608) 256-0029 Fax: (608) 256-7433
tgay@madisonrep.org
www.madisonrep.org
Est. 1969. Production: cast limit 15, no fly Response Time: 6 mos. **Preference.** Length: full length plays. **Application.** How to submit: agent.

**Magic Theatre**
Ft. Mason Ctr., Bldg. D
San Francisco, CA 94123
Erin Gilley
Tel: (415) 441-8001 Fax: (415) 771-5505
www.magictheatre.org
Rolling deadline. Production: cast limit 8. Response Time: 8 mos script . **Preference.** Length: full length plays. Style: comedy, drama. **Application.** What to submit: script and cover letter. Author must be represented by agent or a Bay Area local. Material must be unproduced.

**Main Street Theater**
2540 Times Blvd., Houston, TX 77005
Rebecca Greene Udden
Tel: (713) 524-3622 Fax: (713) 524-3977
rudden@mainstreettheater.com
www.mainstreettheater.com
Est. 1975. Production: cast limit 9. **Consideration.** Opportunity/Award: royalty. **Preference.** Length: full length plays. Subject: woman. **Application.** What to submit: query, synopsis, 20 pg sample.

**Marin Theater Company (MTC)**
397 Miller Ave., Mill Valley, CA 94941
Margot Melcon
Tel: (415) 388-5200 Fax: (415) 388-1217
margot@marintheatre.org
www.marintheatre.org
Est. 1966, Jasson Minadakis (Artistic Director) Ryan Rilette (Managing Director) Response Time: 8 months. **Preference.** Length: full length plays. **Application.** What to submit: full script, SASE. How to submit: agent.

**MCC Theater**
311 W. 43rd St., #206
New York, NY 10036
Stephen Willems
Tel: (212) 727-7722 Fax: (212) 727-7780
literary@mcctheater.org
www.mcctheater.org
Est. 1986. Equity ANTC. Staff: Jaime Green (Asst Lit Mgr). Production: cast limit 10. Response Time: 2 mos. **Application.** What to submit: query, synopsis, 10-pg sample,

SASE. Material must be unoptioned, unproduced in NYC.

**McCarter Theater Center**
91 University Pl., Princeton, NJ 08540
Carrie Hughes
Tel: (609) 258-6500
www.mccarter.org
Equity LORT B+, C, and D. 1994 Regional Theater Tony winner. Staff: Emily Mann (Artistic Dir). Response Time: 6 mos . **Preference.** Length: full length plays. Subject: All subjects, woman, writers of color, disabled, gay/lesbian. **Application.** What to submit: full script, SASE. How to submit: agent.

**Meadow Brook Theatre**
207 Wilson Hall, Oakland University
Rochester, MI 48309
David L. Regal
Tel: (248) 370-3322
jm@mbtheatre.com
www.mbtheatre.com
Est. 1967. Equity LORT C. 600-seat venue. Production: no fly. **Preference.** Length: full length plays. **Application.** What to submit: synopsis, SASE.

**Melting Pot Theatre Company**
2440 Broadway, #197
New York, NY 10024
Larry Hirschhorn
larry@meltingpottheatre.com
www.meltingpottheatre.com
**We do not accept unsolicited submissions of any kind.** Est. 1998. Equity LOA. Production: cast limit 10, orchestra limit 6, sets limit 3.

**Merrimack Repertory Theatre**
132 Warren St., Lowell, MA 01852
Literary Department
Tel: (978) 654-7550 Fax: (978) 654-7575
info@merrimackrep.org
www.merrimackrep.org
Est. 1979. Equity LORT D. Production: cast limit 7. Response Time: 12 mos. **Preference.** Length: full length plays. Style: no musical. **Application.** What to submit: full script, SASE. How to submit: agent only.

**Merry-Go-Round Playhouse**
17 Williams St., Fl. 2
Auburn, NY 13021
Amy Simolo
Tel: (315) 255-1305 Fax: (315) 252-3815
youthinfo@merry-go-round.com
www.merry-go-round.com
Est. 1958. Production: cast of 2-4, unit set. **Consideration.** Opportunity/Award: royalty. **Preference.** Subject: T.Y.A. **Application.** What to submit: synopsis, full script, submissions not returned.

**MetroStage**
1201 N. Royal St., Alexandria, VA 22314
Carolyn Griffin
Tel: (703) 548-9044 Fax: (703) 548-9089
info@metrostage.org
www.metrostage.org
Est. 1984. Equity SPT. Production: cast limit 6-8, orchestra limit 5, unit set. **Consideration.** Opportunity/Award: royalty. **Preference.** Length: full length plays and musicals. Style: drama, musical. Subject: All subjects. **Application.** What to submit: synopsis, 10-pg sample, SASE. How to submit: agent.

**Metro Theater Company**
8308 Olive Blvd., St. Louis, MO 63132
Carol North
Tel: (314) 997-6777 Fax: (314) 9971811
carol@metrotheatercompany.org
www.metrotheatercompany.org
Est. 1973. Mainstage shows, tours and commissions of theater for children and family audiences. Production: cast limit 10. Response Time: 3 mos. **Consideration.** Opportunity/Award: 6% royalty. **Preference.** Subject: T.Y.A. **Application.** What to submit: synopsis, sample, SASE. How to submit: professional recommendation.

**Milk Can Theatre Company**
260 West 52nd St., No. 23A
New York, NY 10019
Julie Fei Fan Balzer
www.milkcantheatre.org
Est. 2003. Staff: Julie Fei-Fan Balzer (Artistic Dir.). **Application.** What to submit: full length by invitation only.

**Mill Mountain Theatre**
1 Market Sq., Fl. 2, Roanoke, VA 24011
Patrick Benton
Tel: (540) 342-5730 Fax: (540) 342-5745
www.millmountain.org
> Est. 1964. Equity LOA. Center Piece program offers monthly lunchtime staged readings of one-acts. Submission to other programs by invitation. Production: small cast favored. Response Time: 6 months. **Consideration.** Opportunity/Award: reading. **Preference.** Style: all styles. **Application.** What to submit: full script, submissions returned with SASE. Material must be unpublished. How to submit: unsolicited, invitation (all other programs).

**Milwaukee Chamber Theatre**
158 N. Broadway, Milwaukee, WI 53202
Jacque Troy
Tel: (414) 276-8842 Fax: (414) 277-4477
jacque@chamber-theatre.com
www.chamber-theatre.com
> Est. 1975. Equity SPT. Production: small cast, unit set. Response Time: 6 mos. **Preference.** Length: full length plays. Style: no musical. Subject: woman, writers of color, disabled, gay/lesbian. **Application.** What to submit: query, synopsis, 10-pg sample, SASE. Author must be from Wisconsin or writing about Wisconsin themes (this material will be given first consideration). How to submit: professional recommendation.

**Milwaukee Repertory Theater**
108 E. Wells St., Milwaukee, WI 53202
Tel: (414) 224-1761 Fax: (414) 224-9097
www.milwaukeerep.com
> Est. 1954. Response Time: 4 mos. **Preference.** Length: full length plays. Style: no musical. **Application.** How to submit: professional recommendation.

**Miracle Theatre Group**
425 SE 6th Ave., Portland, OR 97214
Olga Sanchez
Tel: (503) 236-7253
www.milagro.org
> Est. 1985. Production: cast limit 10, no fly. Response Time: 5 mos. **Preference.** Length: full length plays. Style: no musical. Subject: writers of color. **Application.** What to submit: full script. Author must be Hispanic.

**Mixed Blood Theatre Company**
1501 S. 4th St., Minneapolis, MN 55454
Aditi Kapil
Tel: (612) 338-0937
literary@mixedblood.com
www.mixedblood.com
> Est. 1976. Response Time: 4 mos. **Preference.** Length: full length plays. Subject: disabled, gay/lesbian. **Application.** What to submit: query, synopsis, 10-pg sample, SASE.

**Montana Repertory Theater**
Dept. of Drama & Dance
Missoula, MT 59812
Salina Chatlain
Tel: (406) 243-6809 Fax: (406) 243-5726
salina.chatlain@mso.umt.edu
www.montanarep.org
> Est. 1967. Production: touring set Response Time: 3 mos query, 6 mos script. **Preference.** Length: full length plays. **Application.** What to submit: query, synopsis, resume.

**Moving Arts**
Box 481145, Los Angeles, CA 90048
Trey Nichols
www.movingarts.org
> Est. 1992. 99-seat. Response Time: 3 mos query, 5 mos script. **Preference.** Length: full length plays. Style: no musical. **Application.** What to submit: query, synopsis, 20-pg sample, resume, SASE. Material must be unproduced in L.A.

**Mu Performing Arts**
2700 NE Winter St., #4
Minneapolis, MN 55413
Rick Shiomi
Tel: (612) 824-4804 Fax: (612) 824-3396
info@muperformingarts.org
www.muperformingarts.org
> Est. 1992. Formerly Theater Mu. Equity and non-Equity. Production: cast limit 15, simple set. Response Time: 2 mos query, 3 mos script. **Preference.** Length: full length plays. Style: no

translation. Subject: T.Y.A., writers of color. **Application.** What to submit: query, full script. How to submit: Contact Artistic Director Rick Shiomi at ricks@muperformingarts.org.

**NACL Theatre (North American Cultural Laboratory)**
Box 2201, Times Sq. Sta.
New York, NY 10108
Brad Krumholz
Tel: (845) 557-0694
nacl@nacl.org
www.nacl.org
Est. 1997. Production: cast of 4-8, minimal set. Response Time: 10 wks. **Preference.** Style: no musical. **Application.** What to submit: no unsolicited scripts. How to submit: professional recommendation.

**National Theatre of the Deaf**
139 N. Main St., West Hartford, CT 6107
Aaron M. Kubey
akubey@ntd.org
www.ntd.org
Est. 1967. Production: cast limit 10, touring set. Response Time: 1 mo query, 6 mos script. **Preference.** Length: full length plays. Style: adaptation, comedy, drama. Subject: T.Y.A., disabled. **Application.** What to submit: query, synopsis, sample, SASE. Material must be unproduced professionally.

**Near West Theatre (NWT)**
6514 Detroit Ave., Cleveland, OH 44102
Bob Navis Jr.
Tel: (216) 961-9750 Fax: (216) 961-6381
www.nearwesttheatre.org

**Nebraska Theatre Caravan**
6915 Cass St., Omaha, NE 68132
Lara Marsh
Tel: (402) 553-4890 ext. 135
Fax: (402) 553-6288
caravan@omahaplayhouse.com
www.nebraskatheatrecaravan.com
Est. 1975. Seasonal touring theater. Production: age 8 and older, cast limit 25, touring set. **Preference.** Length: full length plays. Style: adaptation. **Application.** What to submit:

video. How to submit: professional recommendation.

**Negro Ensemble Company**
303 West 42nd St, #501
New York, NY 10036
Charles Weldon
Tel: (212) 582-5862 Fax: (212) 582-9639
info@necinc.org
www.negroensemblecomany.org
**Application.** How to submit: unsolicited.

**New Conservatory Theatre Center**
25 Van Ness Ave., Lower Lobby
San Francisco, CA 94102
Ed Decker
Tel: (415) 861-4914 Fax: (415) 861-6988
www.nctcsf.org
Est. 1981. Response Time: 3-6 mos. **Consideration.** Opportunity/Award: 6%-8 % royalty. **Preference.** Length: full length plays. Style: no translation. Subject: T.Y.A., gay/lesbian. **Application.** What to submit: query, synopsis, character breakdown. Author must be resident of US. Material must be un-optioned. How to submit: visit website for up-to-date submission policy.

**New Federal Theatre**
292 Henry St., New York, NY 10002
Woodie King Jr.
Tel: (212) 353-1176 Fax: (212) 353-1088
newfederal@aol.com
www.newfederaltheatre.org
Est. 1970. Equity Showcase. Production: cast limit 5, unit set. Response Time: 6 mos. **Consideration.** Opportunity/Award: $500 option fee. **Preference.** Length: full length plays. Style: drama. Subject: writers of color. **Application.** What to submit: full script, SASE. Material must be unoptioned, unpublished, unproduced. How to submit: professional recommendation.

**New Georges**
109 W. 27th St., #9-A
New York, NY 10001
Kara-Lynn Vaeni
info@newgeorges.org

www.newgeorges.org
  Est. 1992. Equity Tiered Showcase.
  Staff: Susan Bernfield (Artistic Dir).
  Response Time: 1 yr. **Consideration.**
  Opportunity/Award: royalty.
  **Preference.** Length: full length plays.
  Style: comedy, drama. **Application.**
  What to submit: full script, SASE.
  Author must be female.

**New Ground Theatre**
2822 Eastern Ave., Davenport, IA 52803
Chris Jansen
Tel: (563) 326-7529
www.newgroundtheatre.org
  Est. 2001. Production: cast limit 6, unit set, no fly. Response Time: 6 mos. **Application.** What to submit: full script. Author must be resident of Midwest.

**New Jersey Repertory Company**
179 Broadway, Long Branch, NJ 07740
Suzanne Barabas
Tel: (732) 229-3166 Fax: (732) 229-3167
info@njrep.org
www.njrep.org
  Est. 1997. Equity SPT 4. Production: cast limit 5 for plays, 4 for musicals. 6-7 full length plays produced each year. 15-25 staged readings. Theatre Brut Festival of Short Plays. **Consideration.** Opportunity/Award: royalty. **Preference.** Length: full length plays. Style: comedy, drama, and musical. Subject: woman, writers of color, disabled, gay/lesbian. **Application.** What to submit: Prefers full script via email with cast breakdown and synopsis. For musicals send disk with songs, or email mp3 files. Material must be unproduced. How to submit: Email. Hard copy may be mailed, but will not be returned.

**New Jomandi Productions, Inc.**
675 Ponce de Leon Ave., Fl. 8
Atlanta, GA 30308
Carol Mitchell-Leon
Tel: (404) 784-1587
jomandiproductions@yahoo.com
www.jomandi.org
  Est. 1978. Formerly Jomandi Prods. Production: small cast, unit set Response Time: only if interested. **Preference.** Length: full length plays. Subject: writers of color. **Application.** What to submit: query, synopsis, sample, resume.

**New Perspectives Theatre Company**
456 W. 37th St., New York, NY 10018
Melody Brooks
Tel: (212) 630-9945
www.newperspectivestheatre.org
  Est. 1992. Staged reading workshops and full productions provided to new scripts in development whenever possible. Response Time: 3 mos. **Preference.** Length: full length plays. Style: comedy, drama, translation. Subject: woman, writers of color, disabled. **Application.** What to submit: synopsis, 15-pg sample, SASE. Material must be unoptioned, unpublished, unproduced.

**Organic Theater Company**
Box 578189, Chicago, IL 60657
Alexander Gelman
Tel: (312) 634-0199
dhadley@organictheater.org
www.organictheater.org
  Equity CAT-2. **Preference.** Style: all styles. **Application.** What to submit: query letter (note theme addressed),10-pg writing sample, submissions returned with SASE. How to submit: agent submission.

**Pan Asian Repertory Theatre**
520 8th Ave., #314, New York, NY 10018
Tisa Chang
Tel: (212) 868-4030 Fax: (212) 868-4033
panasian@aol.com
www.panasianrep.org
  Est. 1977. Equity LOA. Production: cast limit 5, unit set. Response Time: 6 mos query, 9 mos script. **Preference.** Length: full length plays. Style: comedy, drama. Subject: writers of color. **Application.** What to submit: query, synopsis, 10-pg sample, bio, SASE. How to submit: email.

**Pittsburgh Public Theater**
621 Penn Ave., Pittsburgh, PA 15222
Heather Helinsky
hhelinsky@ppt.org
www.ppt.org
   Est. 1975. Equity LORT B. Response Time: 6 mos. **Preference.** Length: full length plays. Style: comedy, drama. **Application.** What to submit: query, synopsis, 10-pg sample, SASE. How to submit: professional recommendation.

**Piven Theatre**
927 Noyes St., #110, Evanston, IL 60201
Jodi Gottberg
Tel: (847) 866-8049
jgottberg@piventheatre.org
www.piventheatre.org
   **Preference.** Length: full length plays. Style: Adaptation, Drama, Translation. **Application.** What to submit: query, synopsis or treatment, 15-pg sample.

**Plan-B Theatre Company**
138 W. 300 S., Salt Lake City, UT 84101
Jerry Rapier
Tel: (801) 297-4200 Fax: (801) 466-3840
jerry@planbtheatre.org
www.planbtheatre.org
   Est. 1995. Equity SPT-2, Production: cast limit 5, minimal set. Response Time: 3 mos. **Consideration.** Opportunity/Award: royalty. **Preference.** Style: drama. Subject: gay/lesbian. **Application.** What to submit: full script, SASE. Material must be full script. How to submit: email (PDF) only.

**Prop Thtr**
3502-4 N. Elston Ave., Chicago, IL 60618
Diane M. Honeyman
www.propthtr.org
   Est. 1981.

**Prospect Theater Company**
520 8th Ave., Suite 307, 3rd fl.
New York, NY 10018
Cara Reichel
Tel: (212) 594-4476 Fax: (212) 594-4478
www.prospecttheater.org
   Est. 1998. Small company of emerging artists, producing a 3-show season OOB under Equity Transition Contract. **Consideration.** Opportunity/Award: royalty. **Preference.** Style: primarily new musicals. **Application.** What to submit: full script, demo CD, SASE. How to submit: for full productions, professional recommendation only. Dark Nights series productions applications are available periodically in the summer / fall through our website.

**Providence Black Repertory Company**
276 Westminster St., Providence, RI 02903
Donald W. King
Tel: (401) 351-0353 Fax: (401) 621-7136
elephant@blackrep.org
www.blackrep.org
   See mission and submission details on website before submitting.

**New Repertory Theatre**
200 Dexter Ave., Watertown, MA 02472
Bridget Kathleen O'Leary
artistic@newrep.org
www.newrep.org
   Est. 1984. Equity. Production: cast limit 12. **Consideration.** Opportunity/Award: 5%-10% royalty. **Preference.** Length: full length plays. Subject: All subjects. **Application.** What to submit: full-length plays. Author must be agented or local playwright. Material must be unoptioned. How to submit: professional recommendation.

**New Stage Theatre**
1100 Carlisle St., Jackson, MS 39202
Francine Thomas Reynolds
Tel: (601) 948-3533 Fax: (601) 948-3538
mail@newstagetheatre.com
www.newstagetheatre.com
   Est. 1965. Production: cast limit 8. Response Time: 3 mos query, 6 mos script-no guaranteed response. **Preference.** Length: full length plays. Style: comedy, drama, musicals. **Application.** What to submit: query, synopsis.

**New Theatre**
4120 Laguna St., Coral Gables, FL 33146
Tara Vodihn
Tel: (305) 443-5373 Fax: (305) 443-1642
tvodihn@new-theatre.org

www.new-theatre.org
> Est. 1986. Equity SPT-4. Production: cast limit 6, minimal set. Response Time: 2-3 mos. **Consideration.** Opportunity/Award: 5%-7% royalty. **Preference.** Length: full length musicals. Style: Check history of productions on website All styles, small cast/ piano musicals accepted. Subject: woman, writers of color, disabled, gay/lesbian. **Application.** What to submit: query, synopsis, sample pages, SASE check website for full instructions. Material must be unpublished, unproduced, second and third productions are also welcome. How to submit: Check website for full instructions.

**New WORLD Theater (NWT)**
100 Hicks Way, #16 Curry Hicks
Amherst, MA 1003
Andrea Assaf
Tel: (413) 545-1972 Fax: (413) 545-4414
nwt@admin.umass.edu
www.newworldtheater.org
> We host New WORKS for a New WORLD every summer & invite four artists for a development residency. See website for details. **Application.** What to submit: query. How to submit: professional recommendation.

**New York Stage and Film (NYSAF)**
315 W. 36th St., #1006
New York, NY 10018
Johanna Pfaelzea
Tel: (212) 736-4240 Fax: (212) 736-4241
info@newyorkstageandfilm.org
www.newyorkstageandfilm.org
> Est. 1985. Summer season (Jun-Aug) in residence as part of Powerhouse program at Vasser Coll. **Assistance:** $100 stipend,$30 travel. Response Time: 6 mos. **Consideration.** Opportunity/Award: $550. **Preference.** Length: full length musicals. Style: comedy, drama, musical. **Application.** What to submit: full script, SASE. Material must be unpublished, unproduced. How to submit: no unsolicited scripts; unsolicited queries and synopsis, agent.

**New York State Theatre Institute (NYSTI)**
37 1st St., Troy, NY 12180
Patricia Di Benedetto Snyder
Tel: (518) 274-3200
www.nysti.org
> Est. 1974. Equity TYA. **Assistance:** room/board, travel Response Time: 6 mos. **Preference.** Length: full length plays. **Application.** What to submit: full script, SASE. Material must be unproduced. How to submit: agent.

**New York Theatre Workshop (NYTW)**
83 E. 4th St., New York, NY 10003
Tel: (212) 780-9037 Fax: (212) 460-8996
info@nytw.org
www.nytw.org
> Est. 1979. Works of innovative form & language about socially relevant issues. Response Time: 3 mos query, 8 mos script. **Application.** What to submit: query, synopsis, 10-pg sample, resume, SASE.

**Next Act Theatre**
342 N. Water St., Fl. 2
Milwaukee, WI 53202
David Cecsarini
Tel: (414) 278-7780 Fax: (414) 278-5930
cez@nextact.org
www.nextact.org
> Est. 1990. Equity SPT-8. Production: cast limit 8 Response Time: 1 yr. **Preference.** Length: full length plays. Style: contemporary, no musical. **Application.** What to submit: query, synopsis, 10-pg sample, email ok. Deadline: 9/1/2009.

**Next Theater Company**
927 Noyes St., Evanston, IL 60201
Jason Loewith
Tel: (847) 475-1875 Fax: (847) 475-6767
info@nexttheatre.org
www.nexttheatre.org
> Est. 1981. Equity CAT 1/2. Commissions 1 world premiere per season. Production: cast limit 10. **Preference.** Length: full length plays. **Application.** What to submit: query, synopsis, 10-pg sample, SASE.

**Noise Within (ANW)**
234 S. Brand Blvd., Glendale, CA 91204
Geoff Elliot
Tel: (818) 240-0910 Fax: (818) 240-0826
www.anoisewithin.org
> Est. 1991. Equity Special Agreement. Response Time: 8 mos. **Preference.** Length: full length plays. Style: adaptation, translation. **Application.** What to submit: full script.

**North Shore Music Theatre (NSMT)**
Box 62, Beverly, MA 1915
Barry Ivan
Fax: (978) 921-7874
www.nsmt.org
> Est. 1955. Equity COST. 1,500-seat arena, 100-seat studio. Readings, workshops, commisssions and productions. **Assistance:** per diem, room/board, travel Production: cast of 5 or more, orchestra of 2 or more. Response Time: 6 mos. **Consideration.** Opportunity/Award: Royalty: negotiable. **Preference.** Length: full length plays. **Application.** What to submit: query, synopsis, 25-pg sample, audio, SASE. Material must be unoptioned. How to submit: professional recommendation.

**Northern Stage**
Box 4287, White River Junction, VT 05001
Brooke Ciardelli
www.northernstage.org
> Est. 1997. Equity LORT-D. **Application.** What to submit: query, SASE. How to submit: professional recommendation.

**Northlight Theatre**
9501 N. Skokie Blvd., Skokie, IL 60077
Meghan Beals McCarthy
www.northlight.org
> Est. 1975. Equity LORT C. Response Time: 1 mo query, 8 mos script. **Preference.** Length: full length plays. **Application.** What to submit: query, 10-pg sample, SASE.

**Northside Theatre Company**
848 E. William St., San Jose, CA 95116
Richard Orlando
www.northsidetheatre.com
> Equity BAPP. Production: thrust stage, no fly. **Preference.** Length: full length plays. Style: no musical. **Application.** What to submit: synopsis, sample, SASE.

**Not Merely Players**
173 14th St., NE, Atlanta, GA 30309
Gene-Gabriel Moore
Tel: (404) 872-8940 Fax: (404) 522-1903
ggmnmp@bellsouth.net
> Est. 1998. Nonprofit professional theater of inclusion. **Assistance:** travel. Production: cast limit 8. **Consideration.** Opportunity/Award: royalty. **Preference.** Style: no musical. Subject: woman, disabled. **Application.** What to submit: query, synopsis, SASE. Material must be unoptioned, unproduced. How to submit: professional recommendation.

**Obsidian Theatre Company**
943 Queen St. East
Toronto, ON M4M-1J6 Canada
Philip Akin
Tel: (416) 463-8444
obsidiantheatre@bellnet.ca
www.obsidian-theatre.com
> Check website for submission details. **Preference.** Length: full length plays.

**Odyssey Theatre Ensemble**
2055 S. Sepulveda Blvd.
Los Angeles, CA 90025
Sally Essex-Lopresti
Tel: (310) 477-2055
www.odysseytheatre.com
> Est. 1969. Equity 99-seat. Response Time: 2 wks query, 6 mos script. **Preference.** Length: full length plays. **Application.** What to submit: query, synopsis, 10-pg sample, SASE.

**Old Globe**
Box 122171, San Diego, CA 92112
Kim Montelibano Heil
www.theoldglobe.org
> Est. 1935. Equity LORT B, C. 1984 Regional Theater Tony winner. Response Time: 3 mos query, 6 mos script. **Preference.** Length: full length

plays. **Application.** What to submit: query, synopsis, 10-pg sample, SASE. How to submit: agent.

**Old Log Theater**
Box 250, Excelsior, MN 55331
Don Stolz
Tel: (952) 474-5951 Fax: (952) 474-1290
info@oldlog.com
www.oldlog.com
Est. 1940. Equity theater. Production: cast limit 8. Response Time: 2 wks. **Consideration.** Opportunity/Award: royalty. **Preference.** Length: full length plays. Style: comedy, drama. **Application.** What to submit: full script, SASE.

**Oldcastle Theatre Company**
Box 1555, Bennington, VT 5201
Eric Peterson
Tel: (802) 447-1267 Fax: (802) 442-3704
vtpeterson@adelphia.net
www.oldcastletheatreco.org
Est. 1972. Equity LOA. Productions and workshops. **Preference.** Length: full length plays. **Application.** What to submit: full script, SASE.

**Olney Theatre Center for the Arts**
2001 Olney-Sandy Spring Rd.
Olney, MD 20832
Jim Petosa
Tel: (301) 924-4485 Fax: (301) 9242654
www.olneytheatre.org
Est. 1937. Production: cast limit 8 Response Time: 6 mos. **Preference.** Length: full length plays. Style: no musical. **Application.** How to submit: professional recommendation.

**Omaha Theater Company**
2001 Farnam St., Omaha, NE 68102
James Larson
Tel: (402) 502-4618
www.otcyp.org
Est. 1949. Production: cast limit 10, unit set. Response Time: 6 mos. **Preference.** Style: adaptation, comedy, drama. Subject: T.Y.A. **Application.** How to submit: professional recommendation.

**Open Circle Theater (OCT)**
429 Boren Ave. N., Seattle, WA 98109
Ron Sandahl
Tel: (206) 382-4250
www.octheater.com
Est. 1992. Response Time: 3 mos query, 6 mos script. **Preference.** Length: full length plays. **Application.** What to submit: query, synopsis, 10-pg sample, resume. How to submit: local professional recommendation.

**Open Eye Theater**
Box 959, Margaretville, NY 12455
Amie Brockway
Tel: (845) 586-1660 Fax: (845) 586-1660
openeye@catskill.net
www.theopeneye.org
Est. 1972. Readings and productions for a multigenerational audience. Production: small cast, modest set. Response Time: 6 mos. **Application.** What to submit: query, synopsis. Material must be unproduced or seeking a second production. How to submit: professional recommendation.

**OpenStage Theatre & Company**
Box 617, Fort Collins, CO 80522
Denise Burson Freestone
Tel: (970) 484-5237 Fax: (970) 482-0859
denisef@openstagetheatre.org
www.openstagetheatre.org
Est. 1973. Response Time: 1 year. **Consideration.** Opportunity/Award: staged workshop production, minimal tech . **Preference.** Length: full length plays. Style: no musicals or one-act plays (unless latter is full evening of entertainment) . Subject: All subjects, woman, writers of color, disabled, gay/lesbian. **Application.** What to submit: plot summary; script samples of first 2 pages, 2 pages from the middle, last 2 pages query, resume. Material must be full evening of entertainment . How to submit: mail. Rolling submissions.

**Opera Cleveland**
1422 Euclid Ave, #1052
Cleveland, OH 44115
Dean Williamson
Tel: (216) 575-0903

www.operacleveland.org
  Est. 2006 (merger of Lyric Opera Cleveland, Cleveland Opera). Spring-fall season and summer fest of 5 full-length operas. **Assistance:** room/board, travel. Response Time: 1 mo. **Preference.** Length: full length musicals. Style: opera. **Application.** What to submit: query, synopsis, full script, audio, SASE. How to submit: agent.

**Oregon Shakespeare Festival**
Box 158, Ashland, OR 97520
Lue Morgan Douthit
Tel: (541) 482-2111 Fax: (541) 482-0446
literary@osfashland.org
www.osfashland.org
  Est. 1935. Equity LORT B+. 1983 Regional Theater Tony winner. Staff: Bill Rauch (Artistic Dir). Response Time: 6 mos. **Preference.** Length: full length plays. **Application.** What to submit: query. Author must be women/minorities encouraged. How to submit: agent.

**Pangea World Theater**
711 W. Lake St., #101
Minneapolis, MN 55408
Meena Natarajan
Tel: (612) 822-0486 Fax: (612) 821-1070
pangea@pangeaworldtheater.org
www.pangeaworldtheater.org
  Est. 1995. Response Time: 6 mos. **Preference.** Length: full length plays. Style: no musical. **Application.** What to submit: query.

**Pasadena Playhouse**
39 S. El Molino Ave., Pasadena, CA 91101
Tel: (626) 737-2857
www.pasadenaplayhouse.org
  Est. 1917. Equity LORT B. Year-round season in 670-seat and 99-seat theaters. **Preference.** Length: full length plays. Subject: woman, T.Y.A., writers of color, disabled, gay/lesbian. **Application.** The Pasadena Playhouse does not accept unsolicited manuscripts unless submitted by an agent or by invitation. However, each year from June 1-30, we do accept inquiry letters with a synopsis and 10-page sample. Scripts sent unsolicited will not be read. Please do not call or email to follow up on the status of your submission. If you wish your material returned, please include a S.A.S.E. with your submission. What to submit: query, 10-pg sample, SASE.

**Passage Theatre**
P.O. Box 967, Trenton, NJ 08605
Tel: (609) 392-0766 Fax: (609) 392-0318
info@passagetheatre.org
www.passagetheatre.org
  Deadline: ongoing. Est. 1985. Production: Modest cast size, 4-6 actors, no fly. Response Time: 5 mos. **Preference.** Length: full length plays and musicals. Style: Boundary-pushing & stylistically adventurous new works for the theatre that entertain and challenge a diverse audience. Subject: writers of color. **Application.** What to submit: Full length if professional recommendation, sample work if unrepresented; see website for details. How to submit: professional recommendation, website.

**PCPA Theatrefest**
800 S. College Dr.
Santa Maria, CA 93454
Patricia M. Troxel
Tel: (805) 928-7731 Fax: (805) 928-7506
literary@pcpa.org
www.pcpa.org
  Est. 1964. Response Time: 3 mos query, 6 mos script. **Preference.** Length: full length plays. **Application.** What to submit: query, synopsis.

**Pegasus Players**
1145 W. Wilson Ave., Chicago, IL 60640
Alex Levy
Tel: (773) 878-9761 Fax: (773) 271-8057
info@pegasusplayers.org
www.pegasusplayers.org
  Est. 1978. Response Time: 1 mo query, 6 mos script. **Preference.** Length: full length plays. **Application.** What to submit: query, synopsis.

**Pegasus Theater Company**
Box 942, Monte Rio, CA 95462
Tel: (707) 522-9243
www.pegasustheater.com
   Est. 1998.

**Pendragon Theatre**
15 Brandy Brook Ave.
Saranac Lake, NY 12983
Molly Pietz-Walsh
www.pendragontheatre.com
   Est. 1980. **Preference.** Length: full length plays. No musicals please. **Application.** What to submit: query, 10-pg sample, SASE. Material must be unpublished, unproduced.

**Penguin Repertory Company**
Box 91, Stony Point, NY 10980
Staci Swedeen
www.penguinrep.org
   Est. 1977. Equity Guest Artist. Staff: Joe Brancato (Artistic Dir), Andrew Horn (Exec Dir). Full length plays, small sets, four characters or fewer. Response Time: up to one year. **Preference.** Length: full length plays and musicals. If play is selected for reading series, author must be able to attend rehearsal and reading. If play is selected for production, author availability is flexible. **Application.** What to submit: full script, submissions not returned. How to submit: Mail full play to address listed above.

**Penumbra Theatre Company**
270 N. Kent St., St. Paul, MN 55102
Dominic Taylor
Tel: (651) 288-6790 Fax: (651) 2886789
sarah.bellamy@penumbratheatre.org
www.penumbratheatre.org
   Est. 1976. Response Time: 9 mos. **Preference.** Length: full length plays. Subject: T.Y.A., writers of color. **Application.** No unsolicted submissions.

**People's Light and Theatre Company**
39 Conestoga Rd., Malvern, PA 19355
Alda Cortese
cortese@peopleslight.org
www.peopleslight.org

Est. 1974. Equity LORT. **Consideration.** Opportunity/Award: royalty. **Preference.** Length: full length plays. Style: adaptation, comedy, drama. **Application.** What to submit: query, synopsis, 10-pg sample.

**Performance Network Theatre**
120 E. Huron St., Ann Arbor, MI 48104
Carla Milarch
Tel: (734) 663-0696 Fax: (734) 663-7367
info@performancenetwork.org
www.performancenetwork.org
   Est. 1981. Production: cast limit 10, no fly Response Time: 6 mos. **Preference.** Length: full length plays. **Application.** What to submit: synopsis, 10-pg sample, SASE.

**Perseverance Theatre (PT)**
914 3rd St, Douglas, AK 99824
Tel: (907) 364-2421 Fax: (907) 364-2603
info@perseverancetheatre.org
www.perseverancetheatre.org
   Est. 1979. Staff: Art Rotch (Artistic Dir), Elizabeth Davis (Managing Dir). Response Time: 1 mo query, 3 mos script. **Preference.** Length: full length plays. Subject: gay/lesbian. **Application.** What to submit: query, synopsis, sample. Author must be resident of AK, women encouraged.

**Philadelphia Theatre Company (PTC)**
230 S. 15th St., Fl. 4
Philadelphia, PA 19102
Warren Hoffman
Tel: (215) 985-1400 Fax: (215) 985-5800
www.phillytheatreco.com
   Est. 1974. Equity LORT D. 4 contemporary US plays/season (Sep-July). Production: cast limit 10. Response Time: 6 mos. **Preference.** Length: full length musicals. Style: comedy, drama, musical, family shows. **Application.** What to submit: full script. How to submit: agent or local writers only.

**Phoenix Arts Association Theatre**
414 Mason St., #601
San Francisco, CA 94103
Linda Ayres Frederick

Tel: (415) 759-7696 Fax: (415) 664-5001
Lbaf23@aol.com
www.phoenixtheatresf.org
Est. 1985. Production: cast limit 7, unit set. Response Time: 6 wks query, 6 mos script. **Preference.** Length: full length plays. Style: no musical. Subject: woman. **Application.** What to submit: query, synopsis.

**Phoenix Theatre [AZ]**
100 E. McDowell Rd., Phoenix, AZ 85004
Daniel Schay
Tel: (602) 258-1974 Fax: (602) 899-5297
www.phoenixtheatre.net
Est. 1920. **Assistance:** $200 Response Time: 6 mos. **Preference.** Length: full length plays. **Application.** What to submit: query, full script. Material must be unproduced. Deadline: 1/15/2009.

**Phoenix Theatre [IN]**
749 N. Park Ave., Indianapolis, IN 46202
Tony McDonald
Tel: (317) 635-7529 Fax: (317) 635-0010
tmcdonald@phoenixtheatre.org
www.phoenixtheatre.org
Est. 1983. Staff: Bryan Foseca (Producing Dir). Production: cast limit 6. Response Time: 6 mos. **Preference.** Length: full length plays. Subject: woman, writers of color, gay/lesbian. **Application.** What to submit: query, synopsis, 10-pg sample, SASE. How to submit: professional recommendation.

**Pier One Theatre**
Box 894, Homer, AK 99603
Lance Petersen
lance@xyz.net
www.pieronetheatre.org
Est. 1973. Non-Equity community theater. Response Time: 6 mos. **Consideration.** Opportunity/Award: 4% royalty. **Preference.** Length: full length plays and musicals. Subject: All subjects. **Application.** What to submit: full script, SASE.

**Pillsbury House Theatre**
3501 Chicago Ave. S.
Minneapolis, MN 55407
Tel: (612) 825-0459 Fax: (612) 827-5818

www.puc-mn.org/theatre.html
Est. 1992. Production: cast limit 10. Response Time: 5 mos query, 6 mos script. **Preference.** Length: full length plays. Style: no musical. Subject: All subjects, woman, T.Y.A., writers of color, disabled, gay/lesbian. **Application.** What to submit: Invitation only. How to submit: agent.

**Pioneer Theatre Company**
300 South 1400 East, #205
Salt Lake City, UT 84112
Charles Morey
Tel: (801) 581-6356 Fax: (801) 581-5472
www.pioneertheatre.org
Est. 1962. Equity LORT B. Response Time: 1 mo query, 6 mos script. **Preference.** Length: full length plays. **Application.** How to submit: agent submissions only at this time.

**Playhouse on the Square**
51 S. Cooper St., Memphis, TN 38104
Jackie Nichols
Tel: (901) 725-0776 Fax: (901) 726-4498
www.playhouseonthesquare.org
Est. 1968. **No longer accepting submissions.**

**PlayMakers Repertory Company**
CB-3235, Center for Dramatic Art
Chapel Hill, NC 27516
Adam Versenyi
www.playmakersrep.org
Est. 1976. Equity LORT D. Staff: Joseph Haj (Producing Artistic Dir). Response Time: 6 mos. **Preference.** Length: full length plays. Style: no musical. **Application.** What to submit: submissions not returned. How to submit: agent.

**Playwrights Horizons**
416 W. 42nd St., New York, NY 10036
Adam Greenfield
Tel: (212) 564-1235 Fax: (212) 594-0296
literary@playwrightshorizons.org
www.playwrightshorizons.org
Est. 1971. Equity Off-Broadway nonprofit dedicated to new American voices, offering 6 productions/season and numerous readings. Production: cast limit 10. Response Time: 6-7 mos

Contacts: Adam Greenfield (plays), Christie Evangelisto (musicals). **Preference.** Length: full length plays and musicals. Style: no adaptation, no jukebox musical. **Application.** What to submit: full script, audio, bio, SASE. Author must be citizen of US. Material must be unpublished, unproduced in NYC. How to submit: open submission policy.

**Playwrights' Forum**
Box 11265, Memphis, TN 38111
Billy Pullen
Tel: (901) 725-2040
www.playwrights-forum.org
Est. 1991. 3-weekend run in 100-seat theater. **Assistance:** $300 travel Frequency: semiannual. Production: ages 18-90, cast of 2-6. Response Time: 8 mos. **Preference.** Length: full length plays. Style: adaptation, comedy, drama. Subject: woman, writers of color, gay/lesbian. **Application.** What to submit: query, 10-pg sample. Material must be unpublished. How to submit: professional recommendation.

**Polarity Ensemble Theatre**
135 Asbury Ave., Evanston, IL 60202
Richard Engling
Tel: (847) 475-1139
richard@petheatre.com
www.petheatre.com
**Consideration.** Opportunity/Award: Workshop/Production. **Preference.** Length: full length plays. Style: All. **Application.** What to submit: Full Script. Author must be Chicago Area. How to submit: We only accept script when we put out a call for submissions. We do not read year round. Visit our website and register on our auditions list.

**Porchlight Music Theatre Chicago**
2814 N. Lincoln Ave., Chicago, IL 60657
L. Walter Stearns
Tel: (773) 325-9884
porchlighttheatre@yahoo.com
www.porchlighttheatre.com
Est. 1994. Response Time: 6 mos. **Preference.** Style: musical. **Application.** What to submit: synopsis, audio, bio, SASE. Material must be unoptioned.

**Portland Center Stage**
128 NW 11th Ave., Portland, OR 97209
Mead Hunter
Tel: (503) 445-3792 Fax: (503) 445-3721
www.pcs.org
Est. 1988. Production: cast limit 12. Response Time: 3 mos query, 6 mos script. **Preference.** Length: full length plays. Style: comedy, drama. **Application.** What to submit: query, 10-pg sample, resume.

**Portland Stage Company**
Box 1458, Portland, ME 4104
Daniel Burson
Tel: (207) 774-1043 Fax: (207) 774-0576
dburson@portlandstage.com
www.portlandstage.com
Est. 1970. Response Time: 3 mos query, 6 mos script. **Preference.** Length: full length plays. Style: comedy, drama. Subject: All subjects. **Application.** How to submit: agent. Rolling submissions.

**Primary Stages**
307 W. 38th St, #1510
New York, NY 10018
Tessa LaNeve
info@primarystages.com
www.primarystages.com
Est. 1984. Equity Off-Broadway, ANTC. In residence at 59E59 Theaters. Founded to produce new plays and develop playwrights. Staff: Andrew Leynse (Artistic Dir.) Response Time: 1 yr. **Preference.** Length: full length plays. **Application.** Material must be unproduced. How to submit: agent. We no longer accept unsolicited scripts.

**Prime Stage Theatre**
Box 1849, Pittsburgh, PA 15230
Wayne Brinda
Tel: (412) 771-7373 Fax: (412) 771-8585
wbrinda@primestage.com
www.primestage.com
Literature based youth and adult theatre. Production: age 12 through senior citizen. **Preference.**

Style: adaptation. **Application.** What to submit: query, synopsis, 30-pg sample, submissions returned with SASE. How to submit: unsolicited.

**Prince Music Theater**
100 S. Broad St., #650
Philadelphia, PA 19110
Tel: (215) 9721000
info@princemusictheater.org
www.princemusictheater.org
Est. 1984. Formerly American Music Theater Festival. Production: cast of 2-12 Response Time: 8 mos. **Preference.** Style: musical. **Application.** What to submit: query, synopsis, 30-pg sample, audio, SASE. Material must be unproduced. How to submit: professional recommendation.

**Public Theater**
425 Lafayette St., New York, NY 10003
Liz Frankel
Tel: (212) 539-8530 Fax: (212) 539-8505
www.publictheater.org
Est. 1954. Response Time: 6 mos. **Preference.** Length: full length plays. **Application.** What to submit: query, synopsis, 10-pg sample. How to submit: agent.

**Puerto Rican Traveling Theatre**
141 W. 94th St., New York, NY 10025
Allen Davis
Tel: (212) 354-1293 Fax: (212) 307-6769
est. 1997. Workshops for beginning and professional playwrights.

**Purple Rose Theatre Company**
137 Park St., Chelsea, MI 48118
Guy Sanville
Tel: (734) 433-7782 Fax: (734) 475-0802
www.purplerosetheatre.org
Est. 1991. Equity SPT-7. Production: ages 18-80, cast of 2-10. Response Time: 6 mos. **Consideration.** Opportunity/Award: 6%-8% royalty. **Preference.** Length: full length plays. **Application.** What to submit: synopsis, 15-pg sample, SASE. Author must be age 18 or older. Material must be unoptioned, unpublished, unproduced. How to submit: agent.

**Shakespeare Theatre Company**
516 8th St. SE, Washington, DC 20003
Akiva Fox
Tel: (202) 547-3230 Fax: (202) 547-0226
afox@shakespearetheatre.org
www.shakespearetheatre.org
Est. 1986. Classical theatre dedicated to works of Shakespeare and other classical writers in new translations and adaptations. Fees: royalty. **Preference.** Length: full length plays. Style: adaptation, translation. **Application.** What to submit: query, SASE. How to submit: agent.

**Shotgun Productions Inc.**
165 E. 35 St., #7-J, New York, NY 10016
Patricia Klausner
Tel: (212) 689-2322 Fax: (718) 291-9354
literary@shotgun-productions.org
www.shotgun-productions.org
Est. 1989. Equity. 3-step development, incl. staged readings, workshops and full productions. Response Time: 1 yr. **Preference.** Length: full length plays. **Application.** What to submit: query, synopsis. Material must be unoptioned, unproduced. How to submit: professional recommendation.

**Stage One: The Louisville Children's Theater**
501 W. Main, Louisville, KY 40202
J. Daniel Herring
Tel: (502) 589-5946 Fax: (502) 588-5910
stageone@stageone.org
www.stageone.org
Est. 1946. Equity TYA. Classic and contemporary tales of childhood with strong social and emotional content. Production: cast limit 12, touring set Response Time: 3 mos. **Preference.** Style: adaptation, comedy, drama. Subject: T.Y.A. **Application.** What to submit: query, sample.

**Queens Theatre in the Park**
Box 520069, Flushing, NY 11352
Rob Urbinati
Tel: (718) 760-0064
urbinati@aol.com
www.queenstheatre.org

Est. 2001. New play development series incl. Immigrant Voices Project and Plays a Mother Would Love. Production: cast limit 6. Response Time: 6 mos. **Preference.** Length: full length musicals. Style: comedy, drama, musical. **Application.** What to submit: No unsolicited submissions. Check our website, www.queenstheatre.org for submission policies.

**Rainbow Dinner Theatre**
3065 Lincoln Hwy East, Box 56
Paradise, PA 17562
David DiSavino
david@rainbowdinnertheatre.com
www.rainbowdinnertheatre.com
Est. 1984. Professional non-Equity dinner theater. Production: ages 18 and older, cast of 2-12, set limit 2. Response Time: 6 mos. **Consideration.** Opportunity/Award: 3% royalty. **Preference.** Length: full length plays. Style: mainstream comedy. **Application.** What to submit: synopsis, sample, SASE. How to submit: agent.

**Red Barn Theatre**
319 Duval St., Rear, Key West, FL 33040
Mimi McDonald
Tel: (305) 296-9911 Fax: (305) 293-3035
www.redbarntheatre.org
Est. 1981. Production: cast limit 8, small band, no fly. Response Time: only if interested. **Preference.** Length: full length plays. **Application.** What to submit: query, synopsis. How to submit: professional recommendation.

**Red Bull Theater**
Literary Submission, P.O. Box 250863
New York, NY 10025
Jesse Berger
Tel: (212) 414-5168
info@redbulltheater.com
www.redbulltheater.com
Est. 2003. Produces reading series, annual full production, and new play workshop. **Preference.** Length: full length plays and musicals. Style: adaptation, translation, classically inspired. Subject: All subjects. **Application.** What to submit: synopsis, sample, SASE. How to submit: BY REGULAR MAIL ONLY WITH AN SASE. See website.

**Red Orchid Theatre**
1531 N. Wells St., Chicago, IL 60610
Kristen Lahey
Tel: (312) 9438722
literary@aredorchidtheatre.org
www.aredorchidtheatre.org
Est. 1993. Accepts Synopsis with 10 page sample or Full Length Plays. **Application.** How to submit: Electronic preferred.

**Repertory Theatre of St. Louis**
P. O. Box 191730, St. Louis, MO 63119
Susan Gregg
Tel: (314) 968-7340
sgregg@repstl.org
www.repstl.org
Est. 1966. Equity LORT B, D. Production: small cast. Response Time: 4 mos query, 2 yrs script. **Preference.** Length: full length plays. Style: comedy, drama. **Application.** What to submit: query, synopsis.

**Riant Theatre**
The Black Experimental Theatre
Box 1902, New York, NY 10013
Tel: (646) 623-3488
TheRiantTheatre@aol.com
www.therianttheatre.com
Opportunities incl. semiannual Strawberry One-Act Fest, Core Project workshop. Staff: Van Dirk Fisher (Artistic Dir.), Richard Mover (Assoc. Dir.).

**Riverlight and Company**
75 Wendell St., Battle Creek, MI 49017
J. Kline Hobbs
Tel: (269) 962-2453
riverlightbc@yahoo.com
www.willard.lib.mi.us/npa/rlight
Est. 1981. School tours (grades 7-12). **Assistance:** room/board, travel Production: ages 21-85, cast limit 5, piano only, touring set. Response Time: 2 mos. **Preference.** Style: documentary. **Application.** What to submit: query, resume, reviews, SASE. Author must be age 21 or older,

citizen of US, resident of MI preferred. Material must be unoptioned, unpublished, unproduced. How to submit: invite.

**Riverside Theatre [IA]**
213 N. Gilbert St., Iowa City, IA 52245
Jody Hovland
Tel: (319) 887-1360 Fax: (319) 887-1362
artistic@riversidetheatre.org
www.riversidetheatre.org
> Also accepts submissions for annual monologue Festival. Est. 1981. Production: small cast, simple set. Response Time: only if interested. **Preference.** Length: full length plays and musicals. Style: all styles. **Application.** What to submit: query, synopsis, first 10 pages.

**Riverside Theatre [FL]**
3250 Riverside Park Dr.
Vero Beach, FL 32963
Allen D. Cornell
Tel: (772) 231-5860
backstage@riversidetheatre.com
www.riversidetheatre.com
> Est. 1985. Production: cast limit 10. **Riverside Theatre no longer accepts submissions.**

**Roots & Branches Theater**
315 Hudson St., New York, NY 10013
Arthur Strimling
Tel: (212) 366-8032 Fax: (212) 3668033
roots&branches@fegs.org

**Ross Valley Players**
Box 437, Ross, CA 94957
raw@rossvalleyplayers.com
www.rossvalleyplayers.org
> Opportunities incl. RAW (Ross Alternative Works) staged readings. **Application.** Author must be Greater San Francisco Bay Area Playwrights.

**Round House Theatre**
Box 30688, Bethesda, MD 20824
Tel: (240) 644-1099 Fax: (240) 644-1090
www.roundhousetheatre.org
> Est. 1978. Literary Works Project in Bethesda, and New Works Series in Silver Spring. Production: cast limit 8, piano only, unit set. Response Time: 2 mos query, 1 yr script. **Preference.** Length: full length plays. Subject: T.Y.A. **Application.** What to submit: synopsis, 10-pg sample.

**Roxbury Crossroads Theatre**
37 Vine St., Roxbury, MA 2119
Ed Bullins
Tel: (617) 4426627
rct9@verizon.net
http://www.roxburycrossroadstheatre.com

**Royal Court Theatre**
Sloane Sq., London, England UK
www.royalcourttheatre.com
> Est. 1956. Opportunities incl. production and development for both international writers (international@royalcourttheatre.com) and young writers (ywp@royalcourttheatre.com). **Application.** What to submit: 1/2-page synopsis, SASE (intl. reply coupon). How to submit: by snail mail only.

**Ryan Repertory Company Inc.**
2445 Bath Ave., Brooklyn, NY 11214
Barbara Parisi
Tel: (718) 996-4800
ryanrep@juno.com
> Est. 1972. Staff: John Sannuto, Artistic Dir. **Application.** What to submit: full script, audio, submissions not returned.

**Sacramento Theatre Company**
1419 H St., Sacramento, CA 95814
Peggy Shannon
Tel: (916) 446-7501 Fax: (916) 446-4066
www.sactheatre.org
> Est. 1942. Equity LORT D. Production: cast limit 10. Response Time: 6 mos. **Preference.** Length: full length plays. Style: adaptation, comedy, drama, revue. Subject: T.Y.A., writers of color. **Application.** How to submit: agent.

**Salt Lake Acting Company**
168 West 500 North
Salt Lake City, UT 84103
David Mong
Tel: (801) 363-0526 Fax: (801) 532-8513
mong@saltlakeactingcompany.org
www.saltlakeactingcompany.org

Est. 1970. Four staged readings/year of new plays and some commissions. Response Time: 6 mos. **Preference.** Length: full length plays. **Application.** What to submit: query, SASE. Material must be unproduced. How to submit: professional recommendation.

**San Diego Repertory Theatre**
79 Horton Plz., San Diego, CA 92101
Angela Rasbeary
Tel: (619) 231-3586 Fax: (619) 2350939
arasbeary@sandiegorep.com
www.sandiegorep.com
 Est. 1976. **Preference.** Length: full length plays. **Application.** What to submit: full script. Deadline: rolling.

**San Jose Repertory Theatre**
101 Paseo de San Antonio
San Jose, CA 95113
Kirsten Beandt
Tel: (408) 367-7206 Fax: (408) 367-7237
www.sjrep.com
 Est. 1980. Equity LORT C. Works begin in New America Playwrights Fest of mid-career playwrights. Interested in ethnic plays, plays by women, and plays with music. Staff: Nick Nichols (Managing Dir). Response Time: 6-9 mos. **Preference.** Length: full length plays. **Application.** How to submit: professional recommendation.

**Santa Monica Playhouse**
1211 4th St., Santa Monica, CA 90401
Cydne Moore
Tel: (310) 394-9779 Fax: (310) 393-5573
theatre@SantaMonicaPlayhouse.com
www.santamonicaplayhouse.com
 Est. 1960. Production: cast limit 10 Response Time:9 mos query, 12 mos script . **Preference.** Length: full length plays. Style: no musical. **Application.** What to submit: query,1-pg synopsis, 10-pg sample, resume, submissions not returned.

**Seacoast Repertory Theatre**
125 Bow St., Portsmouth, NH 3801
John McCluggage
Tel: (603) 433-4793 ext. 128
Fax: (603) 431-7818
www.seacoastrep.org
 Est. 1986. Offers 8 mainstage and 6 youth works each year. Response Time: 6 mos. **Preference.** Length: full length plays. Style: all styles. **Application.** What to submit: 1-pg synopsis, 10 page sample, SASE. Material must be unoptioned. How to submit: agent.

**Seaside Music Theater (SMT)**
Box 2835, Daytona Beach, FL 32120
Lester Malizia
Tel: (386) 252-3394 Fax: (386) 252-8991
www.seasidemusictheater.org
 Est. 1977. Production: cast limit 10 (youth) or 30 (adult), small combo (youth) or orchestra limit 25 (adult) Response Time: 3 mos query, 6 mos script. **Preference.** Style: musical (youth; adult), revue. **Application.** What to submit: query, synopsis, audio.

**Seattle Children's Theatre**
201 Thomas St., Seattle, WA 98109
Torrie McDonald
Tel: (206) 443-0807 Fax: (206) 443-0442
torriem@sct.org
www.sct.org
 Est. 1975. Innovative and professional theater for family and school audiences, Sep-Jun. Response Time: 6 mos. **Preference.** Length: full length plays and musicals. Subject: T.Y.A. **Application.** What to submit: synopsis, 10-pg sample, SASE. How to submit: No unsolicited works, professional recommendation only.

**Seattle Repertory Theatre**
155 Mercer St., Box 900923
Seattle, WA 98109
Braden Abraham
Tel: (206) 443-2210 Fax: (206) 443-2379
bradena@seattlerep.org
www.seattlerep.org
 Est. 1963. Equity LORT B+, C. 1990 Regional Theater Tony winner. 8-9 plays/yr on 2 proscenium stages: 850-seat Bagley Wright; 300-seat Leo K. Staff: David Esbjornson (Artistic Dir). **Assistance:** room/board, travel. Response Time: 6 mos. **Consideration.** Opportunity/

Award: royalty. **Preference.** Length: full length plays. Style: adaptation, comedy, drama. **Application.** What to submit: full script, SASE. How to submit: agent.

**Second Stage Theatre**
307 W. 43rd St., New York, NY 10036
Sarah Bagley
Tel: (212) 787-8302 Fax: (212) 397-7066
sbagley@secondstagetheatre.com
www.secondstagetheatre.com
   Est. 1979. Two Off-Broadway theaters, six shows per season. Full-length plays and musicals of heightened realism and sociopolitical issues, particularly by women and minority writers. Prefer work with contemporary setting. No historical biography or one person shows. Staff: Carole Rothman (Artistic Dir), Ellen Richard (Exec Dir). Response Time: 1 mo query, 6 mos script . **Preference.** Length: full length plays and musicals. **Application.** What to submit: query, synopsis, 10 pg sample.

**Serendipity Theatre Company**
2936 N. Southport Ave.
Chicago, IL 60657
Tel: (773) 296-0163 Fax: (773) 296-0165
Literary@serendipitytheatre.com
www.serendipitytheatre.org
   Est. 1999. Response Time: 6 mos. **Preference.** Length: full length plays. Style: adaptation, comedy, drama. **Application.** What to submit: query, synopsis, sample, SASE. Author must be early-career or lesser-known writer.

**Seven Angels Theatre**
Box 3358, Waterbury, CT 6705
Semina DeLaurentis
Tel: (203) 591-8223 Fax: (203) 757-1807
www.sevenangelstheatre.org
   Est. 1990. Production: cast limit 10, unit set, no fly. Response Time: only if interested. **Preference.** Length: full length plays. **Application.** How to submit: professional recommendation.

**Seventh Street Playhouse, LLC**
PO Box 15414
Washington, DC 20003
Anthony Gallo
seventheatre@verizon.net
www.geocities.com/aegallores/ssp.html
   **Consideration.** Opportunity/Award: Reading, workshop. **Preference.** Length: full length plays. Style: All. **Application.** What to submit: Synopsis or Treatment, 10-page sample. Material must be not published. How to submit: prior professional recommendations only. Email submissions only.

**ShadowBox: The Sketch Comedy Rock 'n' Roll Club**
164 Easton Town Center
Columbus, OH 43219
Tom Cardinal
Tel: (614) 416-7625 Fax: (614) 4167600
tomcardinal@earthlink.net
www.shadowboxcabaret.com
   Est. 1989 Production: age 15-50, cast of up to 5, minimal set. Response Time: 10 months. **Preference.** Style: comedy / drama / musicals. **Application.** What to submit: full script. Scripts will not be returned. How to submit: unsolicited.

**Shadowlight Productions**
22 Chattanooga St.
San Francisco, CA 94114
Larry Reed
Tel: (415) 648-4461 Fax: (415) 641-9734
info@shadowlight.org
www.shadowlight.org
   Est. 1972. Production: cast limit 15 Response Time: 1 mo. **Preference.** Length: full length plays. Subject: T.Y.A. **Application.** Material must be suitable for shadow theater (puppets and live actors). How to submit: professional recommendation.

**Shakespeare & Company**
70 Kemble St., Lenox, MA 01240
Michael Hammond
Tel: (413) 637-1199 ext. 118
mhammond@shakespeare.org

www.shakespeare.org
Est. 1978. Production: cast of 2-8. Response Time: 3 mos. **Preference.** Length: full length plays. Style: no musical. **Application.** What to submit: query, synopsis, 10-pg sample, by post only, SASE. How to submit: By post only.

**Shakespeare Festival at Tulane**
215 McWilliams Hall
New Orleans, LA 70118
Ron Gural
Tel: (504) 865-5105 Fax: (504) 865-5205
www.neworleansshakespeare.com
Est. 1993. Production: unit set, no fly. Response Time: 2 mos query, 3 mos script. **Preference.** Length: full length plays. Style: adaptation, comedy, drama. **Application.** What to submit: query, synopsis, sample, resume, SASE. Author must be resident of LA.

**Signature Theatre**
4200 Campbell Ave., Arlington, VA 22206
Marcia Gardner
Tel: (703) 820-9771
www.signature-theatre.org
Est. 1990. Production: cast limit 10, no fly Response Time: 4 mos. **Preference.** Length: full length musicals. Style: musical. **Application.** Material must be professionally unproduced. How to submit: agent.

**Signature Theatre Company**
630 9th Ave., #1106, New York, NY 10036
Kristen Bowen
Tel: (571) 527-1838 Fax: (703) 845-0236
kbowen@signaturetheatre.org
www.signaturetheatre.org
Est. 1990. Production: small and large cast shows. Response Time: 4 mos. **Preference.** Length: full length plays and musicals. Style: Musicals; plays; cabarets. Subject: woman, writers of color, disabled, gay/lesbian. **Application.** How to submit: Due to the nature of our programming, Signature Theatre Company does not accept unsolicited submissions.

**SignStage**
11206 Euclid Ave., Cleveland, OH 44106
William Morgan
Tel: (216) 231-8787 ext. 302
Fax: (216) 231-7141
wmorgan@chsc.org
www.signstage.org
Est. 1975. In-school residencies, educational performances about deaf awareness. Response Time: only if interested. **Application.** What to submit: synopsis, SASE.

**Simpatico Theatre Project**
Box 2277, Philadelphia, PA 19103
Angela S. Zuck
www.simpaticotheatre.org
Production: cast size 1-10. Response Time: varies. **Preference.** Length: full length plays. Style: comedy, drama. **Application.** What to submit: synopsis, SASE. Material must be unproduced.

**SITI Company**
520 8th Ave., #310, New York, NY 10018
Megan Szalla
Est. 1992. Staff: Anne Bogart (Artistic Dir).

**Skylight**
158 N. Broadway, Milwaukee, WI 53202
Diana Carl
Tel: (414) 291-7811 Fax: (414) 291-7815
dianac@skylightopera.com
www.skylightopera.com
Est. 1959. Formerly Skylight Opera Theatre. Production: cast limit 22, orchestra limit 18 Response Time: 2 mos query, 1 yr script. **Preference.** Style: musical, revue. **Application.** What to submit: query, synopsis, audio.

**Society Hill Playhouse**
507 S. 8th St., Philadelphia, PA 19147
Tel: (215) 923-0210 Fax: (215) 923-1789
shp@erols.com
www.societyhillplayhouse.org
Production: cast of up to 8. Response Time: 3 months. **Preference.** Length: full length plays. Style: no adaptation, no translation. **Application.** What

to submit: query letter (note theme addressed), submissions returned with SASE.

**SoHo Repertory Theatre Inc.**
86 Franklin St, Fl. 4, New York, NY 10013
Tania Camargo
Tel: (212) 941-8632 Fax: (212) 941-7148
sohorep@sohorep.org
www.sohorep.org
 Est. 1975. Apply thru Writer/ Director Lab. Staff: Sarah Benson (Artistic Director), Rob Marcato (Producer). **Preference.** Length: full length plays. Style: contemporary plays. **Application.** How to submit: invitation only.

**Sonoma County Repertory Theater**
104 N. Main St., Sebastopol, CA 95472
www.the-rep.com
 Est. 1993. Staff: Jennifer King (Exec./ Art. Dir.), Scott Phillips (Prod./Art. Dir), Jack Weaver (Dev./Marketing Mang.). **Application.** What to submit: 1-pg synopsis, full script, cast list, SASE.

**South Camden Theatre Company**
318 Hudson St., Gloucester City, NJ 8030
Joseph M. Paprzycki
joep@southcamdentheatre.org
www.southcamdentheatre.org
 Est. 2004. Non-Equity. Opportunities incl. one-act fest. **Consideration.** Opportunity/Award: honorarium. **Preference.** Length: full length plays. Style: drama. **Application.** What to submit: synopsis, SASE. How to submit: invite.

**South Coast Repertory Theatre**
Box 2197, Costa Mesa, CA 92628
Tel: (714) 708-5500
www.scr.org
 Est. 1964. 1988 Regional Theater Tony winner. Mainstage programming in 507-seat Segerstrom and 335-seat Argyros; family series in Argyros. Also NewSCRipts reading series and Pacific Playwrights Festival (PPF) of new work. Response Time: 2 mos query; 6 mos script.

**Consideration.** Opportunity/Award: royalty. **Preference.** Length: full length plays and musicals. Subject: All subjects, woman, T.Y.A., writers of color. **Application.** What to submit: query, synopsis, 10-pg sample, SASE; for more information please see submission guidelines on website. How to submit: please see submission guidelines on website.

**Springer Opera House**
103 10th St., Columbus, GA 31901
Paul Pierce
Tel: (706) 324-5714 Fax: (706) 324-4461
p_pierce@springeroperahouse.org
www.springeroperahouse.org
 Est. 1871. Production: small cast, unit set Response Time: 2 mos query, 6 mos script. **Preference.** Length: full length musicals. Style: comedy, musical. Subject: T.Y.A. **Application.** What to submit: query, synopsis.

**Square Mama Productions**
63 El Pavo Real, San Rafael, CA 94903
Randy Warren
Tel: (415) 225-3258 Fax: (415) 444-0766
info@squaremama.com
www.squaremama.com
 Produce revivals of overlooked plays, but always ready for a new play offer we can't refuse. **Consideration.** Opportunity/Award: Workshop, Production. **Preference.** Length: full length plays. Style: Comedy or Drama. **Application.** What to submit: Query, 10 page sample. How to submit: Unsolicited. Email submission preferred.

**St. Louis Black Repertory Company**
1717 Olive St., Fl. 4, St. Louis, MO 63103
Ronald J. Himes
Tel: (314) 534-3807 Fax: (314) 534-4035
ronh@theblackrep.org
www.theblackrep.org
 Est. 1976. Response Time: 2 mos. **Preference.** Length: full length plays and musicals. Style: comedy, drama, musical. Subject: T.Y.A., writers of color. **Application.** What to submit: query, synopsis, 5-pg sample, resume.

**Stages Repertory Theatre**
3201 Allen Pkwy., #101
Houston, TX 77019
Tel: (713) 527-0220 Fax: (713) 527-8669
www.stagestheatre.com
Est. 1978. Production: cast limit 6
Response Time: 9 mos. **Preference.**
Length: full length plays. Style:
comedy, drama. Subject: T.Y.A.
**Application.** What to submit: full
script.

**Stages Theatre Center**
1540 N. McCadden Pl.
Hollywood, CA 90028
Paul Verdier
Tel: (323) 463-5356 Fax: (323) 463-3904
ask@stageshollywood.com
www.stagestheatrecenter.com
Est. 1982. Response Time: 1 yr.
**Preference.** Length: full length plays.
Subject: T.Y.A. **Application.** What to
submit: full script. Spanish and French
texts encouraged.

**Stages Theatre Company**
1111 Main St., Hopkins, MN 55343
Bruce Rowan
Tel: (952) 979-1120 Fax: (952) 979-1124
brow@stagestheatre.org
www.stagestheatre.org
Est. 1984. Production: ages 10-21
Response Time: 3 mos. **Preference.**
Subject: T.Y.A. **Application.** What to
submit: query, synopsis, full script,
SASE. Material must have children in
primary roles.

**Stageworks, Inc.**
120 Adriatic Ave., Tampa, FL 33606
Anna Brennen
Tel: (813) 215-8984
anna.brennen@stagworkstheatre.org
www.stageworkstheatre.org
For FL playwrights only. Prefer multi-
racial casts, not to exceed 6. Unit set.
Stageworks is a minority issues driven
theatre. **Consideration.** Opportunity/
Award: Reading with nationally
known dramaturg. **Preference.**
Length: full length plays. Style:
Comedy, Drama, Variety. Subject:
woman, writers of color, disabled, gay/
lesbian. **Application.** What to submit:
Full-Length script. Author must be
21 or older. FL resident. Material
must be unproduced. How to submit:
Unsolicited. Deadline: 5/15/2009.

**Stageworks/Hudson**
41-A Cross St., Hudson, NY 12534
Laura Margolis
Tel: (518) 828-7843 Fax: (518) 828-4026
contact@stageworkstheater.org
www.stageworkstheater.org
Est. 1993. Equity SPT, spring-fall
season. Production: cast limit 8, unit
set, no fly. Response Time: 8 mos.
**Preference.** Length: full length plays.
Style: adaptation, comedy, drama.
**Application.** What to submit: query,
synopsis, submissions not returned.

**Stamford Theatre Works (STW)**
307 Atlantic St., Stamford, CT 06901
Steve Karp
Tel: (203) 359-4414 Fax: (203) 353-8018
www.stamfordtheatreworks.org
Est. 1988. Production: small cast, unit
set. Response Time: 2 mos query, 6
mos script. **Preference.** Length: full
length plays. **Application.** How to
submit: professional recommendation.

**Steppenwolf Theatre Company**
758 W. North Ave., 4th Fl.
Chicago, IL 60610
Edward Sobel
Tel: (312) 335-1888
www.steppenwolf.org
Est. 1976. 1985 Regional Theater Tony
winner. Formed by an actors collective,
Steppenwolf is now an ensemble of
41, performing in 3 spaces: 515-seat
Downstairs (CAT-6); 299-seat Upstairs
(CAT-3, CAT-5); 88-seat Garage (CAT-
3). Production: cast limit 10. Response
Time: Response time is 6-8 months.
**Preference.** Length: full length plays.
Style: adaptation, drama. **Application.**
What to submit: query, synopsis,
10-pg sample, resume. Material
must be unproduced. How to submit:
Full scripts via agent only. If not
represented, follow guidelines posted
on website.

**Stepping Stone Theatre for Youth Development**
55 Victoria St. N, St. Paul, MN 55104
Richard Hitchler
Tel: (651) 225-9265 Fax: (651) 225-1225
www.steppingstonetheatre.org
>Est. 1987. Production: youth cast of 10-20. Response Time: 6 mos. **Application.** What to submit: full script, audio. Material must be unoptioned, unproduced.

**Stoneham Theatre**
395 Main St, Stoneham, MA 02180
Weylin Symes
weylin@stonehamtheatre.org
www.stonehamtheatre.org
>Est. 2000. Equity theatre located 8 miles north of Boston. NEAT contract. Production: cast limit 12 (play) or 18 (musical), orchestra limit 7. Response Time: 4 mos. **Preference.** Length: full length plays and musicals. **Application.** What to submit: query, synopsis, 20-pg sample, audio, submissions not returned.

**Stray Dog Theatre (SDT)**
2348 Tennessee Ave., St. Louis, MO 63104
Gary F. Bell
Tel: (314) 865-1995 Fax: (314) 865-1995
straydogtheatre@aol.com
www.straydogtheatre.org
>Est. 2003. Production: cast limti 15, no fly. Response Time: 2 mos query, 6 mos script. **Preference.** Length: full length plays. **Application.** What to submit: query, synopsis, 20-pg sample, audio, resume, SASE.

**StreetSigns Center for Literature and Performance**
204 Harlands Creek Dr.
Pittsboro, NC 27312
>Est. 1992. Founded in Chicago, Street Signs now works with Georgetown Univ. in Washington and UNC Chapel Hill to develop and present new literary adaptations, company-created works, new plays, and re-imaginings of classics. Staff: Derek Goldman (Artistic Dir), Joseph Megel (Assoc Artistic Dir).

**Studio Arena Theatre**
710 Main St., Buffalo, NY 14202
Kathleen Gaffney
Tel: (716) 856-8025 Fax: (716) 856-3415
www.studioarena.org
>Est. 1965. Equity LORT B. Production: cast limit 6, no fly. Response Time: 6 mos. **Preference.** Length: full length plays. Style: adaptation, comedy, drama. **Application.** What to submit: 1-pg synopsis. How to submit: agent.

**Studio Theatre**
1501 14th St. NW, Washington, DC 20005
Danielle Amato
literary@studiotheatre.org
www.studiotheatre.org
>Est. 1978. Equity SPT. Rarely produces world premieres. Response Time: 6 mos. **Consideration.** Opportunity/Award: royalty. **Preference.** Length: full length plays. **Application.** What to submit: full script, SASE. How to submit: professional recommendation.

**SummerNITE**
NIU School of Theater, DeKalb, IL 60115
Tel: (815) 753-1334 Fax: (815) 753-8415
cmarkle@niu.edu
www.niu.edu/theatre/summernite/playwrights.htm
>Premieres (US or Chicago) of innovative and intellectually stimulating stage works. **Application.** How to submit: agent.

**Sundog Theatre**
Box 10183, Staten Island, NY 10301
Susan Fenley
sfenley@sundogtheatre.org
www.SundogTheatre.org
>Production: cast of 2-10, orchestra limit 4, minimal set. **Preference.** Length: full length plays. **Application.** Author must be resident or citizen of US. Material must be unoptioned. How to submit: professional recommendation. Deadline for 10-20 minute plays: Dec 15, 2008.

**Sweetwood Productions**
3406 Riva Ridge Rd., Austin, TX 78764
Pat Hazell
Tel: (512) 383-9498 Fax: (512) 383-1680
pat@sweetwoodproductions.com
www.sweetwoodproductions.com
> **Consideration.** Opportunity/Award: Production. **Preference.** Style: comedy or variety, drama, musical. Subject: All subjects. **Application.** What to submit: Query, synopsis or treatment, full script. Material must be unoptioned, unpublished. How to submit: professional recommendation.

**Synchronicity Performance Group**
Box 6012, Atlanta, GA 31107
Rachel May
Tel: (404) 523-1009
info@sychrotheatre.com
www.synchrotheatre.com
> Est. 1997. Dedicated to strong women characters, scripts with depth, meaning and social content, and powerful stories. Production: cast limit 12, no fly. Response Time: only if interested. **Preference.** Length: full length plays. Style: no musical. Subject: woman, T.Y.A. **Application.** What to submit: query, synopsis, 5-pg sample, SASE.

**Syracuse Stage**
820 E. Genesee St., Syracuse, NY 13210
Nichole Gantshar
ngantshar@aol.com
www.syracusestage.org
> Est. 1974. Production: small cast. **Preference.** Length: full length plays. **Application.** What to submit: query, synopsis, 10-pg sample, resume, list of characters, SASE. How to submit: professional recommendation, agent.

**Teatro Dallas**
1331 Record Crossing Rd.
Dallas, TX 75235
Jessica McCartney
teatro@airmail.net
www.teatrodallas.org
> Est. 1985. Classical and contemporary Latino playwrights. Production: cast limit 8, unit set. **Preference.** Style: no musical. Subject: T.Y.A., writers of color. **Application.** What to submit: query, synopsis, SASE. How to submit: professional recommendation.

**Teatro Vision**
1700 Alum Rock Ave., San Jose, CA 95116
Elisa Marina Alvarado
Tel: (408) 928-5582 Fax: (408) 928-5589
elisamarina@teatrovision.org
www.teatrovision.org
> Est. 1984. Equity BAT-2. 3-play season in 500-seat theater. Production: age 18 and older, cast limit 12, orchestra limit 4, flexible set. Response Time: 1 mo. **Consideration.** Opportunity/Award: royalty. **Preference.** Subject: writers of color. **Application.** What to submit: query, synopsis, SASE. Author must be age 18 or older.

**Theater for the New City (TFNC)**
155 1st Ave., New York, NY 10003
Crystal Field
Tel: (212) 254-1109 Fax: (212) 979-6570
www.theaterforthenewcity.net
> Est. 1970. Equity Showcase. Experimental new works. **Preference.** Length: full length plays. **Application.** What to submit: synopsis, 10-pg sample, SASE. Material must be unproduced.

**Towne Street Theatre (TST)**
4101 Budlong Ave., #4
Los Angeles, CA 90037
Nancy Cheryll Davis
Tel: (213) 624-4796
www.townestreet.org
> Est. 1992. The premiere African-American theater in L.A., producing and developing original works by local playwrights on the African-American experience. **Preference.** Style: original. **Application.** What to submit: query, 5-pg sample, resume. Material must be in standard format.

**Transport Group**
265 Riverside Dr. #3f
New York, NY 10025
Jack Cummings III
Tel: (212) 560-4372 Fax: (212) 678-9594

info@transportgroup.org
www.transportgroup.org

**Writers' Theatre**
376 Park Ave., Glencoe, IL 60022
Jimmy McDermott
Tel: (847) 242-6001 Fax: (847) 242-6011
info@writerstheatre.org
www.writerstheatre.org
> Est. 1992. Response Time: 6 mos. **Preference.** Length: full length plays. Style: all styles, no musical. **Application.** What to submit: synopsis, 10-pg sample, SASE. How to submit: professional recommendation.

**Teatro Vista**
3712 N Broadway, #275
Chicago, IL 60613
Laura Wurz
Tel: (312) 666-4659 Fax: (312) 666-4659
info@teatrovista.org
www.teatrovista.org
> We focus on works by, about or for Latinos. **Consideration.** Opportunity/ Award: Reading, Workshop, Production. **Preference.** Length: full length plays. Style: All. **Application.** What to submit: Synopsis or treatment, 10-page sample. How to submit: unsolicited, agent.

**Tectonic Theater Project**
204 W 84th St., New York, NY 10024
Jimmy Maize
Tel: (212) 579-6111 Fax: (212) 579-6112
literary@tectonictheaterproject.org
www.tectonictheaterproject.org
> Est. 1992. Lab led by Moisés Kaufman. Response Time: 1 month. **Preference.** Length: full length plays and musicals. Style: all styles, daring/ experimental in form/structure. **Application.** What to submit: synopsis, full script, SASE. How to submit: agent.

**Ten Grand Productions**
123 E 24th St., New York, NY 10010
Jason Hewitt
Tel: (212) 253-2059
jhewitt@tengrand.org
www.tengrand.org

> Est. 2003. **Preference.** Style: drama. **Application.** What to submit: 20-pg sample, SASE.

**Tennessee Repertory Theatre**
161 Rains Ave., Nashville, TN 37203
Rene D. Copeland
Tel: (615) 244-4878
www.tennesseerep.org
> Est. 1985. Production: small cast, small orchestra Response Time: 1 yr. **Preference.** Length: full length plays. **Application.** What to submit: query, synopsis, dialogue sample, audio, SASE.

**Thalia Spanish Theatre**
41-17 Greenpoint Ave.
Sunnyside, NY 11104
Angel Gil Orrios
Tel: (718) 729-3880 Fax: (718) 729-3388
info@thaliatheatre.org
www.thaliatheatre.org
> Est. 1977. Response Time: 3 mos. **Preference.** Length: full length plays. Style: no musical. Subject: writers of color. **Application.** What to submit: full script.

**The Flea Theater**
41 White St., New York, NY 10013
Tel: (212) 226-0051 Fax: (212) 965-1808
garyw@theflea.org
www.theflea.org
> Est. 1996. Produces 3 original shows/ yr plus theater, music, dance, and cross-disciplinary pieces in a second space. Also offers mini-fests and regular ongoing programs, incl. Pataphysics playwriting workshops. Production: ages 20-30 Response Time: 1 yr. **Preference.** Length: full length plays. **Application.** How to submit: agent.

**The Human Race Theatre Company**
126 N. Main St., #300, Dayton, OH 45402
Kevin Moore
contact@humanracetheatre.org
www.humanracetheatre.org
> Est. 1986. Opportunities incl. Musical Theatre Workshops. Production: small cast, touring set, no fly. Response

Time: 6 mos. **Preference.** Length: full length plays. Style: Regional Theatre mix: Contemporary, Classics, Original. Subject: T.Y.A. **Application.** What to submit: For Musicals: Refer to Submission guideline on our Website For Plays: Letter of Introduction with synopsis & history. Author must be resident of OH. How to submit: By regular mail or email.

**The New Group**
410 W. 42nd St., New York, NY 10036
Ian Morgan
Tel: (212) 244-3380 Fax: (212) 244-3438
info@thenewgroup.org
www.thenewgroup.org
   Est. 1991. Opportunities incl. workshops and readings. We do not respond to electronic submissions. Response Time: 2 mos for samples, 9 mos for full scripts. **Preference.** Length: full length plays. **Application.** What to submit: query, synopsis, 10-pg sample, resume, SASE. How to submit: mail.

**The Side Project**
1439 W. Jarvis Ave., Chicago, IL 60626
Adam Webster
Tel: (773) 973-2150 Fax: (312) 335-4277
info@thesideproject.net
www.thesideproject.net
   Submissions considered on a rolling basis for staged reading, workshop and productions. Deadline by March 1 for following season. Focus is on world, U.S. and/or Midwest premieres. **Preference.** Length: full length plays. Subject: All subjects. **Application.** Material must not be optioned or produced.

**The Theatre @ Boston Court**
Box 60187, Pasadena, CA 91116
Aaron Henne
Tel: (626) 683-6883 Fax: (626) 683-6886
AaronH@BostonCourt.com
www.BostonCourt.org
   Est. 2003. Equity 99-seat. Production: cast limit 12 Response Time: 6 wks query, 6 mos script. **Preference.** Length: full length plays. **Application.** What to submit: query, synopsis, 10-pg sample, audio, SASE. Author must be Southern California writers only. We are unable to accept unsolicited queries from non-local writers. How to submit: professional recommendation.

**Theater at Monmouth**
Box 385, Bethlehem, CT 04259
David Greenham
TAMOffice@TheaterAtMonmouth.org
www.theateratmonmouth.org
   Est. 1970. Only adaptations of popular classics for adults and children. Response Time: 2 mos. **Preference.** Length: full length plays. Style: Adaptation or new play in classic style. Subject: T.Y.A. **Application.** What to submit: query, synopsis, SASE. How to submit: E-mail or mail, no phone calls, please. Deadline: ongoing.

**Theater Breaking Through Barriers**
306 W. 18th St., New York, NY 10011
Ike Schambelan
Tel: (212) 243-4337 Fax: (212) 243-4337
ischambelan@nyc.rr.com
www.tbtb.org
   Est. 1979. Equity Tier LOA. Staff: George Ashiotis (Co-Artistic Dir). Production: cast of 1-6 Response Time: 2 mos. **Consideration.** Opportunity/Award: $1,000 honorarium. **Preference.** Subject: disabled. **Application.** What to submit: full script, SASE.

**Theater Catalyst**
2030 Sansom St., Philadelphia, PA 19103
Joe Koroly
Tel: (215) 563-4330 Fax: (215) 563-4843
tcatalyst@hotmail.com
www.theatercatalyst.org
   Est. 1998. Supports diverse and underserved theater artists in the Philadelphia area. Production: cast limit 6 Response Time: 6 mos. **Application.** What to submit: synopsis, SASE.

**Theater IV**
7 1/2 West Marshall St.
Richmond, VA 23220
Janine Serresseque
Tel: (804) 7831688
TheatreIVandBarksdale@gmail.com
www.theatreiv.org

Est. 1975. Production: cast of 3-5, touring set Audience: Grades K-12 Response Time: 2 mos query, 2 yrs script. **Preference.** Style: fairy tales, folk tales, fables, history, African American history, safety, outreach, science. **Application.** What to submit: query, synopsis. Material must be 50 minutes to 1 hour in length. How to submit: email, regular mail.

**Theater J**
1529 16th St. NW, Washington, DC 20036
Ari Roth
Tel: (202) 777-3228 Fax: (202) 518-9421
shirleys@washingtondcjcc.org
www.theaterj.org
Est. 1991. Offers readings, workshops, and productions. Response Time: 6 mos. **Preference.** Length: full length plays and musicals. **Application.** What to submit: synopsis, full script, SASE.

**Theater of the Seventh Sister**
Box 276, Lancaster, PA 17608
Gary Smith
Tel: (717) 396-7764 Fax: (717) 509-4662
theseventhsister@mac.com
www.seventhsister.com
Opportunities incl. Project Genesis reading series. Local/regional work preferred. Frequency: semiannual. **Consideration.** Opportunity/Award: production, reading. **Preference.** Length: full length plays. Style: all styles. Subject: All subjects. **Application.** What to submit: synopsis. Material must be unproduced. How to submit: unsolicited.

**Theater Previews at Duke**
Box 90680, 209 Bivins Build.
Durham, NC 27708
Miriam Sauls
Tel: (919) 660-3346 Fax: (919) 684-8906
mmsauls@duke.edu
www.duke.edu/web/theaterstudies
Est. 1986. Response Time: 3 mos query, 6 mos script. **Preference.** Length: full length plays. **Application.** How to submit: agent.

**Theater Ten Ten**
1010 Park Ave., New York, NY 10028
Judith Jarosz
www.TheaterTenTen.com
Est. 1955. Production: small cast Response Time: 1 yr. **Preference.** Subject: woman. **Application.** What to submit: synopsis, 10-pg sample. Material must be for/by women. How to submit: submit character break down, synopsis, and ten page sample via email to theatr1010@aol.com.

**Theatre Ariel**
Box 0334, Merion, PA 19066
Deborah Baer Mozes
Tel: (215) 7359481
theatreariel@netreach.net
www.wjt.ca/mem/ariel.htm
Est. 1990. Production: cast limit 5, touring set. Response Time: 1 mo query, 9 mos script. **Preference.** Length: full length plays. Style: adaptation, comedy, drama. Subject: T.Y.A. **Application.** What to submit: query, synopsis, 10-pg sample, resume.

**Theatre at the Center / Lawrence Arts Center**
940 New Hampshire St.
Lawrence, KS 66044
Ric Averill
Tel: (785) 843-2787 Fax: (785) 843-6629
lacdrama@sunflower.com
www.lawrenceartscenter.com
Est. 1973. Production: cast limit 6 adults or 30 youth. Response Time: 6 wks query, 3 mos script. **Preference.** Subject: T.Y.A. **Application.** What to submit: full script. Material must be original.

**Theatre Company**
4001 W. McNichols, Detroit, MI 48208
Melinda Pacha
Tel: (313) 993-1130 Fax: (313) 993-6465
pachamj@udmercy.edu
libarts.udmercy.edu/dep/thr
Est. 1972. **Application.** What to submit: synopsis, 30-pg writing sample, SASE. How to submit: unsolicited.

**Theatre de la Jeune Lune**
105 N. 1st St., Minneapolis, MN 55401
Dominique Serrand
Tel: (612) 332-3968 Fax: (612) 332-0048
www.jeunelune.org
> Est. 1979. 2005 Regional Theater Tony winner. **Preference.** Length: full length plays. Style: no musical. **Application.** What to submit: query, synopsis.

**Theatre in the Square**
11 Whitlock Ave., Marietta, GA 30064
Jessica West
Tel: (770) 422-8369 Fax: (770) 422-7436
www.theatreinthesquare.com
> Est. 1982. Equity SPT. Production: cast limit 5, unit set, no fly. Response Time: 6 mos. **Preference.** Length: full length plays. Subject: T.Y.A. **Application.** What to submit: query, synopsis, 10-pg sample, resume, submissions not returned. Material must be unproduced in Southeast.

**Theatre of Yugen**
2840 Mariposa St.
San Francisco, CA 94110
Libby Zilber
Tel: (415) 621-0507 Fax: (415) 621-0223
Libby@theatreofyugen.org
www.theatreofyugen.org
> Est. 1978. Non-Equity. Traditional and new works of East-West fusion primarily based on Noh forms. **Preference.** Style: experimental, movement based. **Application.** What to submit: query, SASE.

**Theatre Outlet**
Box 715, Allentown, PA 18105
George Miller
Tel: (610) 820-9270 Fax: (610) 820-9130
theatero@aol.com
www.theatreoutlet.org
> Est. 1988. Response Time: 1 mo query, 2 mos script. **Preference.** Length: full length plays. Style: no musical. **Application.** What to submit: query, synopsis.

**Theatre Rhinoceros**
2926 16th St., San Francisco, CA 94103
John Fisher
Tel: (415) 552-4100 Fax: (415) 558-9044
www.therhino.org
> Est. 1977. Response Time: 6 mos. **Preference.** Length: full length plays. Subject: gay/lesbian. **Application.** How to submit: agent.

**Theatre Three, Inc.**
2800 Routh St., Dallas, TX 75201
Jac Alder
admin@theatre3dallas.com
www.theatre3dallas.com
> Est. 1961. Equity SPT. 14 shows/yr in 2 spaces. Production: cast limit 20, small orchestra. Response Time: 3 mos. **Preference.** Length: full length plays. **Application.** What to submit: query, sample, SASE. How to submit: professional recommendation.

**TheatreWorks**
Box 50458, Palo Alto, CA 94303
Kent Nicholson
Fax: (650) 463-1963
kent@theatreworks.org
www.theatreworks.org
> Est. 1970. LORT B. Staff: Robert Kelley (Artistic Dir.). Response Time: 8 wks query, 8 mos script. **Preference.** Length: full length plays and musicals. Subject: All subjects, writers of color, disabled. **Application.** What to submit: query, synopsis, 10-pg sample, audio, SASE. Material must be unoptioned. How to submit: agent.

**Theatrical Outfit**
Box 1555, Atlanta, GA 30301
Jill Jane Clements
Tel: (678) 528-1490 Fax: (404) 577-5259
www.theatricaloutfit.org
> Est. 1976. **Application.** How to submit: **not accepting unsolicited manuscripts at this time.**

**This Women's Work Theatre Co. (TWWTC)**
Box 20290, Greeley Sq. Sta.
New York, NY 10001

www.newperspectivestheatre.org
Specializes in original plays by emerging female writers, emphasizing works that liberate characters from outdated stereotypes. For specific requirements see website.

**Touchstone Theatre**
321 E. 4th St., Bethlehem, PA 18015
Mark McKenna
Tel: (610) 867-1689 Fax: (610) 867-0561
touchstone@nni.com
www.touchstone.org
Est. 1981. Only accepts proposals for collaborative work with company ensemble. Response Time: 8 mos. **Application.** What to submit: query.

**Town Hall Theatre Company (THT)**
3535 School St., Lafayette, CA 94549
Clive Worsley
Fax: (925) 283-3481
thtmanager@comcast.net
www.thtc.org
Est. 1944. Formerly Dramateurs (1944-92). Equity BAT. **Assistance:** room/board, travel. Production: teen cast of 2-8, orchestra limit 3, unit set. Response Time: 3 mos. **Consideration.** Opportunity/Award: 8% royalty. **Preference.** Length: full length musicals. Style: comedy, drama, musical. **Application.** What to submit: query, submissions not returned. Author must be resident of CA. Material must be unpublished.

**Triangle Productions!**
3430 SE Belmont St., Portland, OR 97214
Donald L. Horn
Tel: (503) 230-9404 Fax: (503) 230-9303
trianglepro@juno.com
www.tripro.org
Est. 1989. Production: cast limit 4, touring set. Response Time: 1 mo query, 7 mos. **Preference.** Length: full length musicals. Style: comedy, musical. Subject: T.Y.A., gay/lesbian. **Application.** What to submit: query. How to submit: email.

**TriArts at the Sharon Playhouse**
Box 1187, Sharon, CT 06069
Michael Berkeley
Tel: (860) 364-7469 Fax: (860) 3648043
info@triarts.net
www.triarts.net
Est. 1989. Bryan L. Knapp New Works series. Production: no fly. Response Time: 2 mos, query 6 mos. **Preference.** Style: comedy, drama, musical. Subject: T.Y.A. **Application.** What to submit: query, synopsis, audio.

**Trinity Repertory Company**
201 Washington St., Providence, RI 02903
Craig Watson
cwatson@trinityrep.com
www.trinityrep.com
Est. 1964. Equity LORT. 1981 Regional Theater Tony winner. Staff: Curt Columbus (Artistic Dir), Michael Gennaro (Exec Dir). Response Time: 4 mos. **Preference.** Length: full length plays. **Application.** What to submit: query, synopsis, 10-pg sample.

**Trustus Theatre**
Box 11721, Columbia, SC 29211
Sarah Hammond
Tel: (803) 254-9732 Fax: (803) 771-9153
trustus@trustus.org
www.trustus.org
Est. 1985. Late-night series for open-minded audiences. Production: cast limit 6, unit set. **Preference.** Style: comedy. Subject: All subjects, woman, writers of color, gay/lesbian. **Application.** What to submit: full script, SASE. How to submit: Electronic submissions strongly encouraged to Sarahkhammond@gmail.com.

**Turtle Shell Productions**
300 W. 43rd St., #403
New York, NY 10036
John Cooper
Tel: (646) 765-7670
lacoopster@aol.com
www.turtleshellproductions.com
Equity showcase. **Consideration.** Opportunity/Award: Production.

**Preference.** Style: Unsolicited. Subject: All subjects. **Application.** What to submit: Full script. Material must not be published or produced. Deadline: 4/9/2009.

**Two River Theatre Company (TRTC)**
21 Bridge Ave., Red Bank, NJ 07701
Aaron Posner
Tel: (732) 345-1400 Fax: (732) 345-1414
info@trtc.org
www.trtc.org
Est. 1994. Production: cast limit 10 Response Time: 10 mos. **Preference.** Length: full length plays. Style: adaptation, comedy, drama. **Application.** What to submit: synopsis, 10-pg sample, SASE. How to submit: agent.

**Unicorn Theatre**
3828 Main St., Kansas City, MO 64111
Herman Wilson
Tel: (816) 531-7529 ext. 23
Fax: (816) 531-0421
clevin@unicorntheatre.org
www.unicorntheatre.org
Est. 1974. One new play each year is developed and produced in the Unicorn's regular season. Fees: 2% subsidiary rights for 5 yrs. Production: cast limit 10. Response Time: 8 mos. **Consideration.** Opportunity/Award: $1,000 in lieu of royalty. **Preference.** Length: full length plays. Style: comedy, drama. Subject: woman, writers of color, disabled, gay/lesbian. **Application.** What to submit: query, synopsis, script, bio, cast list, submissions not returned clevin@unicorntheatre.org. Material must be unpublished, professionally unproduced. How to submit: by mail, see address above.

**Unity Theatre Ensemble**
P.O. Box 2466, St. Louis, MO 63031
Ralph E. Green
Tel: (314) 355-3586
www.utensemble.org
Check website for details.

**Utah Shakespearean Festival**
351 W. Center St., Cedar City, UT 84720
www.bard.org
Accepts scripts through its New American Playwrights Project (NAPP).

**Valley Youth Theatre (VYT)**
807 N. 3rd St., Phoenix, AZ 85004
Bobb Cooper
Tel: (602) 253-8188 Fax: (602) 253-8282
bobb@vyt.com
www.vyt.com
Est. 1989. Response Time: 2 wks query, 2 mos script. **Preference.** Style: comedy, drama, musical. Subject: T.Y.A. **Application.** What to submit: query, audio.

**Victory Gardens Theater**
2257 N. Lincoln Ave., Chicago, IL 60614
Aaron Carter
Tel: (773) 549-5788 Fax: (773) 549-2779
adymond@victorygardens.org
www.victorygardens.org
Est. 1974. Equity CAT-4. 2001 Regional Theater Tony winner. 6 productions/season. Staff: Dennis Zacek (Artistic Dir.). Response Time: 6 mos. **Preference.** Length: full length plays. Subject: woman, writers of color, disabled, gay/lesbian. **Application.** What to submit: Chicago area residents: full script, SASE. All others: query, synopsis, 10-pg sample, SASE. Author must be resident of Chicago area. Material must be original. VG primarily produces world or regional premieres. How to submit: hardcopy, no electronic submissions. Deadline: Accepts submissions January through June only.

**Victory Theatre Center**
3326 W. Victory Blvd.
Burbank, CA 91505
Maria Gobetti
Tel: (818) 841-4404 Fax: (818) 841-6328
thevictory@mindspring.com
www.thevictorytheatrecenter.org
Est. 1979. Incl. 99-seat Big Victory and 50-seat Little Victory theaters. Production: unit set. Response Time:

1 yr. **Consideration.** Opportunity/ Award: royalty. **Preference.** Length: full length plays and musicals. Subject: woman, writers of color, gay/lesbian. **Application.** What to submit: full script, SASE.

**Village Theatre**
303 Front St. N., Issaquah, WA 98027
Robb Hunt
Tel: (425) 392-1942 Fax: (425) 391-3242
www.villagetheatre.org
Est. 1979. Equity LOA. Readings, workshops, and productions of new musicals. Staff: Steve Tomkins (Artistic Dir), Blythe Phillips (Artistic Admin) Production: cast limit 20 Response Time: 6 mos. **Consideration.** Opportunity/Award: royalty. **Preference.** Length: full length musicals. Style: musical. **Application.** What to submit: full script, audio, SASE. How to submit: professional recommendation, agent.

**Vineyard Theatre**
108 E. 15th St., New York, NY 10003
Sarah Stern
Tel: (212) 353-3366 ext. 215
Fax: (212) 353-3803
literary@vineyardtheatre.org
www.vineyardtheatre.org
Est. 1981. Response Time: 1 yr query. **Preference.** Length: full length plays and musicals. **Application.** What to submit: query, synopsis, 10-pg sample, audio, resume, submissions not returned.

**Virginia Premiere Theatre**
PO Box 84, Foster, VA 23056
Robert Ruffin
Tel: (804) 725-3645
info@vptheatre.com
www.vptheatre.com
**Consideration.** Opportunity/Award: production, reading, workshop. **Preference.** Length: full length plays and musicals. Style: All. Subject: All subjects. **Application.** What to submit: query, synopsis or treatment, 10 page sample. Author must not be published. How to submit: Unsolicited.

**Virginia Stage Company (VSC)**
Box 3770, Norfolk, VA 23514
Patrick Mullins
Tel: (757) 627-6988 ext. 309
Fax: (757) 628-5958
pmullins@vastage.com
www.vastage.com
Est. 1979. Equity LORT C. Production: cast limit 8. Response Time: 1 mo query, 6 mos script. **Preference.** Length: full length plays. **Application.** What to submit: query, synopsis. Author must be resident of VA. Material must be unproduced.

**VS. Theatre Company**
Box 2293, Los Angeles, CA 91610
Johnny Clark
Tel: (323) 816-2471
info@vstheatre.org
www.vstheatre.org
Est. 2003. Production: cast limit 6. Response Time: 6 mos. **Preference.** Length: full length plays. Style: no musical. **Application.** What to submit: agent only submissions. How to submit: online.

**Walnut Street Theatre**
825 Walnut St., Philadelphia, PA 19103
Beverly Elliott
Tel: (215) 574-3550 ext. 515
Fax: (215) 5743598
literary@walnutstreettheatre.org
www.walnutstreettheatre.org
Est. 1809. Equity LORT A, D. Production: cast limit 4 (studio), 14 (play) or 20 (musical) Response Time: 3 mos query, 6 mos script. **Preference.** Length: full length plays and musicals. **Application.** What to submit: query, synopsis, 20-pg sample, audio, SASE. How to submit: Send synopsis package via mail.

**Watertower Theatre, Inc.**
15650 Addison Rd., Addison, TX 75001
Terry Martin
Tel: (972) 450-6230 Fax: (972) 450-6244
www.watertowertheatre.org
Est. 1976. Production: medium cast Response Time: 4 mos query, 6 mos script. **Preference.** Length: full length

musicals. Style: comedy, musical. **Application.** What to submit: query, synopsis, SASE. Author must be represented by an agent. How to submit: agent only.

**Wellfleet Harbor Actors Theater**
Box 797, Wellfleet, MA 02667
Daniel Lombardo
Tel: (508) 349-3011 ext. 107
Fax: (508) 349-9082
djlombardo@juno.com
www.what.org
> Est. 1985. Response Time: 3 mos query, 6 mos script. **Preference.** Length: full length plays. Style: adventurous. **Application.** What to submit: synopsis, 20p. excerpt, bio. How to submit: professional recommendation.

**West Coast Ensemble**
Box 38728, Los Angeles, CA 90038
Les Hanson
Tel: (323) 876-9337 Fax: (323) 876-8916
www.wcensemble.org
> Est 1982. 99-seat. Response Time: 9 mos. **Application.** What to submit: full script, SASE.

**Western Stage**
156 Homestead Ave., Salinas, CA 93901
Jon Selover
Tel: (831) 755-6987 Fax: (831) 755-6954
www.westernstage.org
> Est. 1974. Production: large cast. Response Time: 6 mos query, 3 mos script. **Preference.** Length: full length musicals. Style: adaptation, musical. **Application.** What to submit: query, synopsis, audio. Material must be plays for young performers or with strong roles for women.

**Weston Playhouse**
703 Main St., Weston, VT 5161
www.westonplayhouse.org
> Est. 1935. Staff: Malcolm Ewen, Tim Fort, Steve Stettler (Producing Dirs).

**Westport Arts Center**
51 Riverside Ave., Westport, CT 6880
www.westportartscenter.org
> Programs in visual and performing arts. Ongoing exhibits. Chamber music, jazz and folk concerts, literary and film events performed in area venues.

**Westport Country Playhouse**
25 Powers Ct., Westport, CT 6880
Tazewell Thompson
Tel: (203) 227-5137
www.westportplayhouse.org
> Est. 1931. 578-seat year-round Equity theater with 75-yr summer program. Staff: Jodi Schoenbrun Carter (Managing Dir). Production: ages 12 and older, cast of 2-10, orchestra of 4-8. Response Time: 9 mos. **Consideration.** Opportunity/ Award: royalty. **Preference.** Length: full length plays and musicals. **Application.** What to submit: full script, SASE. How to submit: professional recommendation.

**White Horse Theater Company**
205 3rd Ave., #6-N, New York, NY 10003
Cyndy A. Marion
www.whitehorsetheater.com
> Est. 2002. Equity Showcase or staged reading. Response Time: 4 mos. **Preference.** Length: full length plays. Style: adaptation, comedy, drama. **Application.** What to submit: SASE. Author must be resident of US. Material must be unproduced. How to submit: see website for procedure.

**Will Geer Theatricum Botanicum**
Box 1222, Topanga, CA 90290
Ellen Geer
Tel: (310) 455-2322 Fax: (310) 455-3724
info@theatricum.com
www.theatricum.com
> Est. 1973. Production: cast limit 10, simple set. Response Time: 1 mo query, 6 mos script. **Preference.** Length: full length plays. **Application.** What to submit: query, synopsis, 10-pg sample, full script, audio. Material must be suitable for outdoor space.

**Williamstown Theatre Festival**
229 W. 42nd St. #801
New York, NY 10036
Justin Waldman
Tel: (212) 395-9090 Fax: (212) 395-9099
sagins@wtfestival.org
www.wtfestival.org
> Est. 1955. 2002 Regional Theater Tony winner. New Play Staged Reading Series offers 7 works/season. Frequency: annual. **Consideration.** Opportunity/Award: reading. **Preference.** Length: full length plays. **Application.** What to submit: query, SASE. How to submit: agent only.

**Willows Theatre Company**
1425 Gasoline Alley, Concord, CA 94520
Alexandra Elliott
Tel: (925) 798-1824
alex@willowstheatre.org
www.willowstheatre.org
> Est. 1974. Equity LORT D, LOA. Frequency: annual. Production: less than 15. Response Time: 3 mos. **Preference.** Style: comedy, drama. **Application.** What to submit: full script. Material must be unproduced. How to submit: unsolicited. Deadline: 5/8/2009.

**Wilma Theater**
265 S. Broad St., Philadelphia, PA 19107
Walter Bilderback
Tel: (215) 893-9456 Fax: (215) 893-0895
wcb@wilmatheater.org
www.wilmatheater.org
> Est. 1979. Equity LOR C. Production: cast limit 8. Response Time: 1 yr. **Preference.** Length: full length plays. **Application.** What to submit: please check our website for past seasons and Artistic Statement. How to submit: agent, otherwise, professional reccomendation, query, and 10-pg. sample.

**Wings Theatre Company, Inc.**
154 Christopher St.
New York, NY 10014
Jeffery Corrick
Tel: (212) 627-2960 Fax: (212) 462-0024
jcorrick@wingstheatre.com
www.wingstheatre.com
> Est. 1986. Equity Tier III. Gay Play Series (major gay characters & themes) and New Musical Series (any theme). **Preference.** Length: full length plays. **Application.** What to submit: full script, audio. Material must be unproduced.

**Women's Project & Productions**
55 West End Ave., New York, NY 10023
Megan Carter
www.womensproject.org
> Est. 1978. Equity ANTC contract. Oldest and largest US theater dedicated to producing and promoting theater created by women. Response Time: 1 yr. **Preference.** Length: full length plays. **Application.** Material must be unproduced in NYC. How to submit: professional recommendation, agent.

**Woolly Mammoth Theatre Company**
641 D St. NW, Washington, DC 20004
Elissa Goetschius
Tel: (202) 349-1281 Fax: (202) 289-2446
elissa@woollymammoth.net
www.woollymammoth.net
> Est. 1980. Equity SPT. Production: cast limit 6. Response Time: 1 yr. **Preference.** Length: full length plays. Style: no musical. **Application.** How to submit: professional recommendation.

**Working Theater**
Box 892, New York, NY 10002
Connie Grappo
Tel: (212) 539-5675
www.theworkingtheater.org
> Est. 1985. Equity LOA. New plays that appeal to the diverse communities of working people in NYC. Frequency: semiannual. Production: 6 max. Response Time: 6 mos. **Preference.** Length: full length plays. Style: all styles. Subject: woman, writers of color, disabled, gay/lesbian. **Application.** What to submit: synopsis, sample, full script, SASE. Material must be unproduced. How to submit: unsolicited, professional recommendation, agent.

**Xoregos Performing Company**
496 9th Ave., #4-A
New York, NY 10018
Shela Xoregos
Tel: (212) 239-8405
www.xoregos.com
> Est. 2001. Equity Showcase and non-Equity. **Application.** What to submit: query, submissions not returned. How to submit: professional recommendation.

**Yale Repertory Theatre**
Box 208244, New Haven, CT 6520
Catherine Sheehy
Tel: (203) 432-1591
catherine.sheehy@yale.edu
www.yale.edu/yalerep
> Est. 1965. 1991 Regional Theater Tony winner. Response Time: 2 mos query, 3 mos script. **Preference.** Length: full length plays. Style: no musical. **Application.** What to submit: query, SASE. How to submit: agent.

**Yangtze Repertory Theatre of America**
22 Howard St., #3-B New York, NY 10013
Dr. Joanna Chan
Tel: (914) 941-7575 Fax: (914) 923-0733
joanawychan@juno.com
www.yangtze-reptheatre.org

**York Shakespeare Company**
Box 720, JAF Sta., New York, NY 10116
Seth Duerr
Tel: (646) 6237117
sduerr@yorkshakespeare.org
www.yorkshakespeare.org
> Est. 2001. **Preference.** Length: full length plays. **Application.** What to submit: full script. Material must be unoptioned. How to submit: professional recommendation.

**York Theatre Company**
619 Lexington Ave., New York, NY 10022
Tel: (212) 935-5824 Fax: (212) 832-0037
mail@yorktheatre.org
www.yorktheatre.org
> Est. 1985. Equity Off-Broadway. Opportunities incl. developmental reading series. Production: cast of 3-6, piano only. Response Time: 6 mos. **Preference.** Length: full length musicals. Style: musical. **Application.** What to submit: full script, audio, SASE. Material must be unproduced.

## THEATERS (*FEE CHARGED*)

**Attic Theatre and Film Center**
5429 W. Washington Blvd.
Los Angeles, CA 90016
Kacey Camp
Tel: (323) 525-0600
litmanager@attictheatre.org
www.attictheatre.org
> Est. 1987. LA 99-seat. Production: simple set, no fly or wing space. Response Time: 3 mos query, 6 mos script. **Preference.** Length: full length plays. **Application.** What to submit: query, synopsis, sample, SASE. Submission application fee: $15.

**Play With Your Food**
PO Box 2161, Westport, CT 06880
Carole Schweid
Tel: (203) 247-4083
carole@playwithyourfood.org
www.playwithyourfood.org
> Looking for first rate one-act plays for popular lunchtime play-reading series. **Consideration.** Opportunity/Award: Reading/Royalty. **Application.** What to submit: Full Script. Submission application fee: $50.

**Theatre Alliance of Michigan**
22323 Cedar St.
St. Clair Shores, MI 48081
Mary Lou Britton
mellbee@earthlink.net
www.theatreallianceofmichigan.org
> Annual contest. Written by adults; performed by children for children. See website for more information and rules. **Consideration.** Opportunity/Award: $300; exposure to members seeking scripts for young audiences. Award/Grant/Stipend: $300. **Preference.** Length: full length plays. Style: Comedy, Drama, Musical. Subject: All subjects, T.Y.A., writers of color, disabled. **Application.** What to submit: Full Script. CD/Tape of songs if Musical. Author must be Teen or adult, living anywhere. Material must be properly typed and formatted. How to submit: U.S. Mail. See website for details. Submission application fee: $20. Deadline: 12/31/2009.

**Two Chairs Theater Company**
Box 3390, Grand Junction, CO 81502
James Garland
Tel: (970) 263-7920
submit@twochairs.org
www.twochairs.org
> Acts of Brevity Short Play Fest Production: cast limit 5. **Application.** What to submit: synopsis, full script, production history. Please see website for submission details. How to submit: email (pdf, doc, fdr). Submission application fee: $10.

# Educational Opportunities

## COLLEGES AND UNIVERSITIES

### MFA Programs

**Arizona State University**
Ms. Karla Elling, Program Manager
Arizona State University
Virginia G. Piper Creative Writing
MFA Creative Writing
Box 875002, Tempe, AZ 85387
Tel: (602) 965-6018
karla.elling@asu.edu
www.asu.edu
- Degrees Offered: MFA in Creative Writing with Playwriting emphasis
- Program Length: 3 years
- Represented Faculty: Christopher Danowski, Gus Edwards, Pamela Sterling
- Production Opportunities: Staged Readings to Full Student
- Other highlights: KCACTF, New Works Festival (internal)

**Arkansas at Fayetteville, University of**
Dr. Andrew Gibbs, Chair
University of Arkansas at Fayetteville
Department of Drama
619 Kimpel Hall, Fayetteville, AR 72701
Tel: (479) 575-2953
drama@cavern.uark.edu
www.uark.edu
- Degrees Offered: BA, MFA in Playwriting
- Program Length: 60 hours
- Students per Class: 25 max
- Represented Faculty: Roger Gross, Chuck Gorden

**Brooklyn College**
Mr. Mac Wellman, Coordinator of Playwriting MFA
Brooklyn College CUNY
English Department
2900 Bedford Ave., Brooklyn, NY 11210
Tel: (718) 951-5000
www.depthome.brooklyn.cuny.edu
- Degrees Offered: BA, BFA, MFA in Playwriting
- Program Length: 2 years
- Represented Faculty: Erin Courtney, Alison Solomon

**Brown University**
Mr. Brian Evenson, Director
Brown University
Literary Arts Program
Box 1923, Providence, RI 2912
Tel: (401) 863-3260, (401) 863-9408
Brian_Evenson@brown.edu
www.brown.edu
- Degrees Offered: BA, MA, MFA in Literary Arts: Playwriting; AB English/Creative Writing
- Program Length: 2 years
- Students per Class: ~3
- Represented Faculty: Paula Vogel, Aishah Rahman, Guests

**University of California - Riverside**
Mr. Eric Barr, Chair
University of California at Riverside
Department of Theatre - 093
Riverside, CA 92521
Tel: (951) 827-6488
eric.barr@ucr.edu
www.performingarts.ucr.edu
- Degrees Offered: BA, MFA in Creative Writing and Writing for the Performing Arts
- Program Length: 6 Quarters/ 48 hours
- Students per Class: ~4
- Represented Faculty: Eric Barr, Rickerby Hinds, Robin Russin, Guests
- Production Opportunities: Various
- Other highlights: Playworks (internal)

**University of California - San Diego**
Ms. Naomi Iizuka, Head of Playwriting
University of California at San Diego
Department of Theatre and Dance
9500 Gilman Drive MCO344
La Jolla, CA 92093
Tel: (858) 534-3791
www.theatre.ucsd.edu
   Degrees Offered: MFA Playwriting
   Program Length: 3 years
   Represented Faculty: Naomi Iizuka,
   Allan Havis
   Other highlights: Baldwin New Play
   Festival

**California State University - Long Beach**
Ms. Joanne Gordon, Chair
California State University - Long Beach
Department of Theatre Arts
1250 Bellflower Boulevard
Long Beach, CA 90840
Tel: (562) 985-7891
jgordan@csulb.edu
www.csulb.edu
   Degrees Offered: MFA in Theatre
   Arts with option in Dramatic Writing
   Program Length: 2 years
   Students per Class: 6
   Other highlights: Cal Rep

**Carnegie Mellon University School of Drama**
Mr. Milan Stitt, Coordinator
Carnegie Mellon University School
of Drama
Dramatic Writing, Purnell Center for
the Arts
5000 Forbes Ave., Pittsburgh, PA 15213
Tel: (412) 268-2398
Milan@andrew.cmu.edu
www.cmu.edu
   Degrees Offered: MFA Dramatic
   Writing
   Program Length: 2 years
   Students per Class: ~5
   Represented Faculty: Milan Stitt,
   Guests
   Production Opportunities: Staged
   Readings to Experimental
   Other highlights: KCACTF, Winter/
   Summer New Play Festival (sponsor),
   Playground (internal)

**Columbia University**
Mr. Steven Chaikelson, Chair
Columbia University
School of the Arts, Theatre Division
601 Dodge Hall
2960 Broadway, New York, NY 10027
Tel: (212) 854-3408
theatre@columbia.edu
www.columbia.edu
   Degrees Offered: BA, MA, MFA in
   Playwriting, PhD
   Program Length: 3 years
   Represented Faculty: Charles Mee,
   Kelly Stuart, Tina Landau, Guests
   Production Opportunities: Staged
   Readings to Limited Student

**Florida State University**
Mr. Timothy Long, Head of Writing Area
Florida State University
Film School
University Center 3100A
PO Box 3062350, Tallahassee, FL 32306
Tel: (850) 644-2907
tlong@film.fsu.edu
www.film.fsu.edu
   Degrees Offered: MFA in Writing for
   the Stage & Screen
   Program Length: 2 years and 2
   Summers
   Students per Class: 6
   Represented Faculty: Timothy Long,
   Victoria Meyer
   Production Opportunities: Full
   Production
   Other highlights: KCACTF

**University of Hawaii - Manoa**
Mr. Gregg Lizenbery, Chair
University of Hawaii at Manoa
Department of Theatre and Dance
Kennedy Theatre
1770 East-West Rd., Honolulu, HI 96822
Tel: (808) 956-2464
lgreg@hawaii.edu
www.hawaii.edu
   Degrees Offered: BA, MA, MFA in
   Playwriting, PhD
   Program Length: 60 hours
   Students per Class: ~2

# Educational Opportunities : Colleges and Universities

**Hollins University**
Mr. Todd Ristau, Program Director
Hollins University
Graduate Center
PO Box 9603, Roanoke, VA 24020
Tel: (540) 362-6386
tristau@hollins.edu
www.hollins.edu
    Degrees Offered: MFA in Playwriting
    Program Length: 4-5 Summers, 60 hours
    Represented Faculty: Todd Ristau, Jonathan Dorf, Ruth Margraff, Stephen Sossaman
    Other highlights: Mill Mountain Theatre, No Shame Theatre

**Iowa, University of**
Mr. Art Borreca, Head of Playwrights Workshop
University of Iowa
Department of Theatre Arts
200 North Riverside Drive 107 TB
Iowa City, IA 52242
Tel: (319) 353-2401
art-borreca@uiowa.edu
www.uiowa.edu
    Degrees Offered: BA, MFA in Playwriting
    Program Length: 3 years
    Students per Class: 11
    Represented Faculty: Art Borreca, Dare Clubb, Artist in Residence, Kate Aspengren, Sydne Mahone, Guests
    Other highlights: Iowa New Play Festival (internal)

**Juilliard School**
Mr. Christopher Durang, Co-Director, American Playwrights
The Julliard School
Drama Division,
60 Lincoln Ctr. Plaza
New York, NY 10023
Tel: (212) 799-5000 x251
www.juilliard.edu
    Degrees Offered: Non-degree program in Playwriting (1 yr. Fellowship, 2nd year invite), MFA equivalent
    Program Length: 1 to 2 years
    Represented Faculty: Christopher Durang, Marsha Norman

**University of Nevada - Las Vegas (UNLV)**
Mr. KC Davis, Graduate Coordinator, Playwriting
University of Las Vegas at Nevada
Department of Theatre
4505 S. Maryland Parkway
Box 455036, Las Vegas, NV 89154
Tel: (702) 895-3666
kc.davis@unlv.edu
www.theatre.unlv.edu
    Degrees Offered: BA, MFA in Playwriting
    Students per Class: ~8
    Represented Faculty: KC Davis

**University of New Mexico**
Ms. Judith Bennahum, Chair
University of New Mexico
Theatre Arts
Fine Arts Center, Rm. 1412
Albuquerque, NM 87131
Tel: (505) 277-4332
theatre@unm.edu
www.unm.edu
    Degrees Offered: BA, MFA in Dramatic Writing
    Program Length: 3 years
    Represented Faculty: James Linnell
    Production Opportunities: Staged Readings to Full Student
    Other highlights: Words Afire Festival (internal)

**New School University**
Mr. Pippin Parker, Chair, Playwriting MFA
The New School University
The New School for Drama
151 Bank St., New York, NY 10014
Tel: (212) 229-5859
www.newschool.edu
    Degrees Offered: MFA in Playwriting
    Program Length: 3 years
    Represented Faculty: Pippin Parker, Nicole Burdette, Laura Maria Censabella, Frank Pugliese, Christopher Shinn, Michael Weller, John Patrick Shanley (in residence)
    Production Opportunities: Staged Readings to Full Student

**New York University, Tisch School of the Arts**
**Dramatic Writing Program**
Mr. Richard Wesley, Chair
NYU, Tisch School of the Arts
Goldberg Department of Dramatic Writing
721 Broadway, 7th Floor
New York, NY 10003
Tel: (212) 998-1535
rew3@nyu.edu
www.nyu.edu
> Degrees Offered: BFA in Dramatic Writing, MFA in Dramatic Writing with a Concentration in Playwriting, Screenwriting, or Television Writing.
> Program Length: 2 years
> Students per Class: ~20
> Represented Faculty: Richard Wesley, Walter Bernstein, Sabrina Dhawan, Jeremy Pikser, Charlie Rubin, Marsha Norman, Janet Neipris, Rinne Groff, Guests
> Production Opportunities: Student Readings to Full Student
> Other highlights: KCACTF, ATHE, UG Ten Minute Play Festival, Ten Minute Play Festival, Festival of New Work

**New York University, Tisch School of the Arts**
**The Graduate Musical Theatre Writing Program**
Ms. Sarah Schlesinger, Chair
NYU, Tisch School of the Arts
Goldberg Department of Dramatic Writing
113-A 2nd Avenue, 1st Floor
New York, NY 10003
Tel: (212) 998-1830
musical.theatre@nyu.edu
www.gmtw.tisch.nyu.edu
> Degrees Offered: MFA in Musical Theatre Writing
> Program Length: 2 years
> Students per Class: 22~30
> Represented Faculty: Sarah Schlesinger, Fred Carl, Robert Lee, Mel Marvin, Sybille Pearson, Martin Epstein, Adjuncts, Guests
> Production Opportunities: Staged reading of a one-act musical and a staged-reading of a final thesis musical
> Other highlights: Various musical workshop opportunities

**Northwestern University**
Mr. David Tolchinsky, Director
Northwestern University
MFA Writing for the Screen and Stage, Dept of Radio-TV-Film
1800 Sherman Avenue, Ste. 106
Evanston, IL 60201
Tel: (847) 491-2252
write@northwestern.edu
www.write.northwestern.edu
> Degrees Offered: BA Creative Writing for the Media, MFA in Writing for the Screen and Stage
> Program Length: 2 years
> Represented Faculty: Bill Bleich, Jay Bonansinga, Shawn Douglass, Paul Edwards, Kat Falls, Rebecca Gilman, David Kukoff, Penny Penniston, Ana Puga, Anna Shapiro, Dave Tolchinsky, Barbara Wallace and Tom Wolfe, Harvey Young, Mary Zimmerman, Guests
> Production Opportunities: Full Support, multi-media, including $5000 Grant
> Other highlights: Cinestory, Flicker Festival (film)

**Ohio University**
Mr. Charles Smith, Head of MFA Playwriting Program
Ohio University
MFA Playwriting Program, School of Theatre
Kantner Hall 307, Athens, OH 45701
Tel: (740) 593-4818
ohioplaywriting@gmail.com
www.finearts.ohio.edu
> Degrees Offered: BA, BFA, MFA, BFA in Playwriting, MFA Playwriting
> Program Length: 3 years
> Students per Class: ~2 to 4
> Represented Faculty: Charles Smith, Erik Ramsey
> Production Opportunities: Staged Readings to Full Student
> Other highlights: Annual Playwrights Festival (internal)

**Rutgers University - New Brunswick**
Mr. Lee Blessing, Head of Playwriting Program
Rutgers University
Mason Gross School of the Arts, Department of Theatre Arts
33 Livingston Ave.
New Brunswick, NJ 8901
Tel: (201) 932-1766
contactus@masongross.rutgers.edu
www.masongross.rutgers.edu
> Degrees Offered: BA, BFA, MFA in Playwriting
> Program Length: 3 years
> Students per Class: 2
> Represented Faculty: Joseph Hart, Lee Blessing, Guests
> Production Opportunities: Staged Readings to Full Professional

**San Francisco State University**
Mr. Roy Conboy, Head of Playwriting Program
San Francisco State University
College of Humanities - Department of Creative Writing
1600 Holloway Ave.
San Francisco, CA 94132
Tel: (415) 338-1891
rconboy@sfsu.edu or cwriting@sfsu.edu
www.online.sfsu.edu
> Degrees Offered: BA, MA in English: Creative Writing, MFA in Creative Writing - Playwriting
> Program Length: 30 hours MA, 59 hours MFA
> Represented Faculty: Michelle Carter, Roy Conboy, Anne Galjour, Brian Thorstensen
> Production Opportunities: Staged Readings to Full Student
> Other highlights: KCACTF, GreenHouse Productions, One-Act Festival (internal), One-Act Fringe (internal), Bay Area Playwrights Festival

**University of Southern California**
Ms. Madeline Puzo, Dean
University of Southern California
School of Theatre
1029 Childs Way, Los Angeles, CA 90089
Tel: (213) 821-2744
thtrinfo@usc.edu
www.theatre.usc.edu
> Degrees Offered: BA, BFA, MA, MFA in Dramatic Writing
> Program Length: 3 years
> Students per Class: ~13
> Represented Faculty: Velina Hasu Houston, Oliver Mayer, Luis Alfaro, Paula Cizmar Guests

**Southern Illinois University - Carbondale**
Dr. David A. Rush, Head of Playwriting Program
University of Southern Illinois at Carbondale
Department of Theatre and Dance
Carbondale, IL 62901
Tel: (618) 453-4757
darush@siu.edu
www.siuc.edu
> Degrees Offered: BA, MFA in Playwriting, PhDin Playwriting (Doctor of Philosophy in conjunction with Speech Communication)
> Program Length: 60 hours
> Represented Faculty: Dr. David A. Rush, Guests
> Production Opportunities: Staged Readings to Full Student
> Other highlights: Various, Script Camp (sponsor)

**University of Texas - Austin**
Ms. Susan Zeder, Area Head, Playwriting
University of Texas at Austin
Department of Theatre and Dance
1 University Station D3900
Austin, TX 78712
Tel: (512) 232-5325
suzanz@mail.utexas.edu
www.utexas.edu
> Degrees Offered: BA in Theatre and Dance with Playwriting concentration, MFA in Playwriting
> Program Length: 3 years
> Students per Class: 2
> Represented Faculty: Suzan Zeder, Ruth Margraff
> Production Opportunities: Staged Readings to Full Student
> Other highlights: KCACTF, Cohen New Works Festival (internal)

**University of Texas - El Paso (UTEP)**
Dr. Joel K. Murray, Key Contact
University of Texas at El Paso
Theatre, Dance & Film Department
500 W. University Ave.
El Paso, TX 79968
Tel: (915) 747-7854
jmurray@utep.edu
www.academics.utep.edu
    Degrees Offered: BA, MA Theatre with a specialization in Playwriting
    Represented Faculty: Joel Murray, Guests
    Production Opportunities: Experimental no readings
    Other highlights: New Voices Play Festival (internal)

**Yale School of Drama**
Mr. James Bundy, Dean
Yale University, Yale School of Drama
PO Box 208244, New Haven, CT 6520
Tel: (203) 432-1505
james.bundy@yale.edu
www.yale.edu
    Degrees Offered: MFA in Playwriting
    Program Length: 3 years
    Students per Class: ~11
    Represented Faculty: John Guare, Michael Korie, Lisa Kron, Tina Landau, Lindsay Law, Richard Nelson, Lynn Nottage, Peter Parnell and Adam Rapp.
    Production Opportunities: Staged Readings to Full Student
    Other highlights: New Play Festival (internal)

## NON-DEGREE PROGRAMS

**Adelphi University**
Ms. Judith Baumel, Director
English Department
Adelphi University
PO Box 701, Garden City, NY 11530
Tel: (516) 877-4031
BAUMEL@adelphi.edu
academics.adelphi.edu
    Degree Offered: BA, MFA in Creative Writing
    Represented Faculty: Anton Dudley, Kermit Frazier

**Arizona State University**
Mr. Guillermo Reyes, Head of Playwriting
Theatre Department
Arizona State University - Herberger College of the Arts
Box 872002, Tempe, AZ 85287
Tel: (602) 965-5351, (602) 965 0517
guillermo.reyes@asu.edu
www.theatre.asu.edu
    Degree Offered: BA
    Represented Faculty: Guillermo Reyes, Jeff McMahon, Pamela Sterling, Phillip Taylor, Guests
    Production Opportunities: Staged Readings to Full Student
    Other Highlights: KC/ACTF

**Bennington College**
Ms. Sherry Kramer, Key Contact
Dance/Drama
Bennington College
One College Dr., Bennington, VT 5201
Tel: (802) 442-5401
skramer@bennington.edu
    Degree Offered: BA
    Represented Faculty: Sherry Kramer, Jean Randich, Guests
    Production Opportunities:

**Chapman University**
Mr. Thomas Bradac, Chair
Department of Theatre
Chapman University
One University Dr., Orange, CA 92866
Tel: (714) 744-7016
bradac@chapman.edu
www.chapman.edu
    Degree Offered: BA

**College of Charleston**
Mr. Todd McNerny, Chair
Theatre Department, School of the Arts
College of Charleston
66 George St., Charleston, SC 29424
Tel: (843) 953-6306
oleksiakm@cofc.edu
www.cofc.edu
    Degree Offered: BA
    Represented Faculty: Dr. Franklin Ashley, Guests
    Production Opportunities: Staged Readings to Experimental
    Other Highlights: KC/ACTF, ATHE

# Educational Opportunities : Colleges and Universities

**Chicago State University**
Songodina Ifatunji, Key Contact
Breakey Theater
Chicago State University
9501 South King Dr., Chicago, IL 60628
Tel: (773) 995-2419
s-ifatunji@csu.edu
www.csu.edu
   Degree Offered: BA

**Dartmouth College**
Mr. Dan Kotlowitz, Director
Department of Theatre
Dartmouth College
Box 6204 Hopkins Center
Hanover, NH 3755
Tel: (603) 646-3104
Department.of.Theater@Dartmouth.EDU
www.dartmouth.edu
   Degree Offered: BA
   Represented Faculty: Joe Sutton, Guests

**Duke University**
Mr. John M. Clum, Chair
Department of Theatre Studies
Duke University
206 Bivins Building
Box 90680, Durham, NC 27708
Tel: (919) 660-3343
jclum@duke.edu
www.duke.edu
   Degree Offered: BA
   Represented Faculty: John Clum, Neal C. Bell, Elisabeth Benfey, Guests

**George Mason University**
Ms. Heather McDonald, Instructor
Department of Theatre, College of Visual and Performing Arts
George Mason University
4400 University Dr., MSN 3E6
Fairfax, VA 22030
Tel: (703) 993-1120
dulcinae@earthlink.net
www.gmu.edu
   Degree Offered: BA
   Represented Faculty: Heather McDonald

**Georgetown University**
Dr. Derek Goldman, Artistic Director
Program in Performing Arts
Georgetown University
Davis Performing Arts Center
Box 571063, Washington, D.C. 20057
Tel: (202) 687-3838
dag45@georgetown.edu
www.performingarts.georgetown.edu
   Degree Offered: BA, MFA

**Houston, University of**
Dr. Steven W. Wallace, Director
School of Theatre and Dance
University of Houston
133 CWM, Houston, TX 77204
Tel: (713) 743-3003
swwallace@UH.edu
www.theatre.uh.edu
   Degree Offered: BA, MA, MFA
   Represented Faculty: Steven W. Wallace, Dr. Syndey Berger
   Other Highlights: Edward Albee Playwrights Workshop, Ostrow Musical Theatre Lab

**Howard University**
Mr. Joe Selmon, Chair
Department of Theatre Arts
Howard University
Room 2101 Childers Hall
Washington, D.C. 20059
Tel: (202) 806-7050
jselmon@howard.edu
www.howard.edu
   Degree Offered: BA, MFA

**Livingstone College**
Dr. Eddie P. Bradley,
Theatre Arts Department
Livingstone College, Salisbury, NC 28144
Tel: (704) 216-1849
www.livingstone.edu
   Degree Offered: BA, BFA
   Represented Faculty: Dr. Eddie P. Bradley

**Louisiana - Monroe, University of**
Dr. Roger Held, Chair
TheatreWorks, ULM
University of Louisiana at Monroe
400 University Ave., Monroe, LA 71209
Tel: (318) 342-1413

spheld@ulm.edu
www.nlu.edu
    Degree Offered: BA, MA
    Represented Faculty: Dr. Roger Held, Guests
    Production Opportunities: Staged Readings to Full Student
    Other Highlights: KCACTF

**Louisiana State University**
Mr. Michael S. Tick, Chair
Department of Theatre
Louisiana State University
217- Dramatic Arts Building
Baton Rouge, LA 70803
Tel: (225) 578-3531
mtickl@lsu.edu
www.theatre.lsu.edu
    Degree Offered: BA
    Represented Faculty: Femi Euba

**Metropolitain State University**
Ms. Suzanne Walfoort, Chair
Communication, Writing, and the Arts Department
Metropolitain State University
Suite 205, Energy Park Place
1380 Energy Lane, St. Paul, MN 55108
Tel: (651) 999-5947
suzanne.walfoort@metrostate.edu
www.metrostate.edu
    Degree Offered: BA Theatre

**Miami University of Ohio**
Dr. Howard A. Blanning, Key Contact
Department of Theatre
Miami University of Ohio
212 Hiestand Hall, Oxford, OH 45056
Tel: (513) 529-1270
blanniha@muohio.edu
www.fna.muohio.edu
    Degree Offered: BA, MA
    Represented Faculty: Dr. Howard Blanning, Guests
    Production Opportunities: Staged Readings to Experimental
    Other Highlights: KCACTF

**Michigan - University of**
Mr. Gregory Poggi, Chair
Department of Theatre and Drama
University of Michigan
1226 Murfin Avenue
Walgreen Drama Center
Ann Arbor, MI 48109
Tel: (734) 764-5350
theatre.info@umich.edu
www.music.umich.edu
    Degree Offered: BA
    Represented Faculty: OyamO
    Production Opportunities: Limited Productions

**Northern Kentucky University**
Mr. Ken Jones, Key Contact
Department of Theatre and Dance
Northern Kentucky University
Fine Arts- 205
Nunn Dr., Highland Heights, KY 41099
Tel: (859) 572-6362
jonesk@nku.edu
www.nku.edu
    Degree Offered: BA, BFA
    Represented Faculty: Ken Jones, Guests
    Production Opportunities: Staged Readings to Limited Productions
    Other Highlights: KC/ACTF, KTA, Y.E.S. Festival (sponsor, contact Sandra Forman)

**Occidental College**
Ms. Susan Gratch, Chair
Theater Department
Occidental College
1600 Campus Rd.
Los Angeles, CA 90041
Tel: (323) 259-2771
beatrice@oxy.edu
www.departments.oxy.edu
    Degree Offered: BA
    Represented Faculty: Laurel Meade
    Production Opportunities: Limited Productions
    Other Highlights: New Play Festival (internal)

**San Diego, University of**
Dr. David Hay, Director
Department of Theatre Arts
University of San Diego
Camino Hall, C130
5998 Alcala Park, San Diego, CA 92110
Tel: (619) 260-7763
dhay@sandiego.edu
www.sandiego.edu

Degree Offered: BA, MFA
Represented Faculty: Evelyn Diaz Cruz
Production Opportunities: Staged Readings to Experimental
Other Highlights: Student Lab

**Texas A&M University - Commerce**
Mr. Jim Tyler Anderson, Key Contact
Theatre
Texas A&M University at Commerce
Performing Arts Center 103
Commerce, TX 75429
Tel: (903) 886-5338
jim_anderson@tamu-commerce.edu
www.tamu-commerce.edu
Degree Offered: BA, MA
Represented Faculty: Jim Tyler Anderson, Dr. John Hanners
Production Opportunities: Staged Readings to Full Student
Other Highlights: KCACTF, Texas Institute for Educational Parnerships (sponsor)

**Tulsa, University of**
Mr. Michael Wright, Dirctor of the Interdisciplinary Program in Creative Writing
Department of Theatre and Musical Theatre, Kendall Hall
University of Tulsa
600 S. College Ave., Tulsa, OK 74104
Tel: (918) 631-3174
michael-wright@utulsa.edu
www.cas.utulsa.edu
Degree Offered: BA Theatre
Represented Faculty: Michael Wright
Production Opportunities: Staged Readings, Film, to Full Student
Other Highlights: KCACTF

**Washington University**
Mr. Robert Henke, Chair
Performing Arts Department
Washington University
Campus Box 1108, St. Louis, MO 63130
Tel: (314) 935-4473
rhenke@artsci.wustl.edu
www.artsci.wustl.edu
Degree Offered: BA
Represented Faculty: Carter W. Lewis
Other Highlights: A.E. Hotchner Playwriting Competition (internal)

**Western Washington University**
Mr. Gregory Lawrence Pulver, Chair
Theatre Arts Department
Western Washington University
Bellingham, WA 98225
Tel: (360) 650-6862
Gregory.Pulver@wwu.edu
www.wwu.edu
Represented Faculty: Bryan Willis

**Wichita State University**
Dr. Steve Peters, Director
School of Performing Arts
Wichita State University
1845 Fairmount, Wichita, KS 67260
Tel: (316) 978-3360
steve.peters@wichita.edu
www.webs.wichita.edu
Degree Offered: BA, BFA, MFA
Production Opportunities: Staged Readings to Experimental
Other Highlights: KC/ACTF, National Playwriting Contest (Open, Host)

**William and Mary, College of**
Mr. Steve Holliday, Chair
Department of Theatre, Speech and Dance
College of William and Mary
PO Box 8795, Williamsburg, VA 23187
Tel: (757) 221-2664
seholl@wm.edu
www.wm.edu
Degree Offered: BA
Represented Faculty: M. Fonkijom Fusi, Francis Tanglao-Aguas, Laurie Wolf

## OTHER PROGRAMS

**Agnes Scott College**
Mr. David S. Thompson, Chair
Department of Theatre and Dance
Agnes Scott College
141 E. College Ave., Decatur, GA 30030
Tel: (800) 868-8602
www.agnesscott.edu
Degree Offered: BA Theatre, emphasis in dramatic writiing

**Bard College**
Ms. JoAnne Akalaitis, Director
Theatre Department
Bard College
PO Box 5000
Annandale-on-Hudson, NY 12504
Tel: (845) 758-7936
akalaiti@bard.edu
www.bard.edu
    Degree Offered: BA Theatre,
    emphasis in playwriting

**Brigham Young University**
Mr. Eric Samuelsen, Key Contact
Theatre & Media Arts
Bringham Young University
D-581B HFAC, Provo, Utah 84602
Tel: (801) 422-3305
eric_samuelsen@byu.edu
tma.byu.edu
    Degree Offered: BA in Theatre Arts
    with an area of interest in playwriting,
    MFA
    Represented Faculty: Eric Samuelson

**California - Santa Barbara, University of**
Mr. Simon Williams, Chair
Department of Theatre and Dance
University of California at Santa Barbara
Mail Code 7060
552 University Road
Santa Barbara, CA 93106
Tel: (805) 893-5515
williams@theaterdance.ucsb.edu
www.dramadance.ucsb.edu
    Degree Offered: BA Emphasis in
    Playwriting, MA, PhD
    Program Length: 2 years
    Students per class: <20
    Represented Faculty: Naomi Iizuka,
    Dr. Carlos Martin, Robert Potter
    Production Opportunities: Staged
    Readings to Experimental
    Other Highlights: KCACTF, ATHE,
    New Play Festival (internal)

**Campbell University**
Mr. Stephen J. Larson, Chair
Department of Theatre Arts
Campbell University
PO Box 776, Buies Creek, NC 27506
Tel: (910) 893-1507
www.campbell.edu
    Degree Offered: BA in Playwriting
    Represented Faculty: Herald Heno
    Production Opportunities: Full
    Student no readings
    Other Highlights: no

**Case Western Reserve**
Ms. Catherine Albers, Academic
Representative
Department of Theatre and Dance
Case Western Reserve
10900 Euclid Ave., Cleveland, OH 44106
Tel: (216) 368-4868
catherine.albers@case.edu
www.case.edu
    Degree Offered: BA in Dramatic
    Writing
    Represented Faculty: Jon Orlock

**Columbia College Chicago**
Mr. Randall Albers, Chair
Fiction Writing Department
Columbia College Chicago
600 South Michigan Avenue
Chicago, IL 60605
Tel: (312) 344-7616
ralbers@colum.edu
www.fiction.colum.edu
    Degree Offered: BA Playwriting, BFA
    Playwriting
    Represented Faculty: Randy Albers,
    Joe Meno, Lisa Schlesinger
    Other Highlights: Hair Trigger -
    anthology (internal publication)

**DePaul University**
Mr. Dean Corrin, Head of Playwriting
The Theatre School
DePaul University
2135 N. Kenmore, Chicago, IL 60614
Tel: (773) 325-7932, (773) 325-7999
dcorrin@depaul.edu
theatreschool.depaul.edu
    Degree Offered: BFA in Playwriting
    Program Length: 4 years
    Represented Faculty: Dean Corrin,
    Reginald Lawrence, Carlos Murillo,
    Guests
    Production Opportunities: Staged
    Readings to Full Students

# Educational Opportunities : Colleges and Universities

**Drexel University**
Ms. Sharon Walker, Key Contact
Antoinette Westphal College of Media Arts and Design
Drexel University
Nesbitt Hall, 33rd and Market Streets
Philadelphia, PA 19104
Tel: (215) 895-2408
cinetv@drexel.edu
www.drexel.edu
    Degree Offered: BS in Screenwriting & Playwriting
    Represented Faculty: Bruce Graham, Joseph Stinson
    Other Highlights: High School Ten-minute Play Contest

**Emerson College**
Dr. Daniel Tobin, Chair
Department of Writing, Literature & Publishing
Emerson College
120 Boylston St., Boston, MA 2116
Tel: (617) 824-8750
www.emerson.edu
    Degree Offered: MFA in Creative Writing (focus in min. 2 areas can include playwriting)
    Program Length: 52 hours
    Represented Faculty: Andrew Clarke

**Fordham University**
Mr. Matthew Maguire, Head of Playwriting Program
Fordham Univ. Theatre Program
Fordham University
Lincoln Center Campus
113 W. 60th St. Room 423
New York, NY 10023
Tel: (212) 636-6306
mmaguire@fordham.edu
www.fordham.edu
    Degree Offered: BA in Playwriting
    Represented Faculty: Matthew Maguire, Michael John Garces, Guests

**Georgia, University of**
Dr. David Saltz, Department Head
Department of Theatre and Film Studies
University of Georgia
203B Fine Arts, Athens, GA 30602
Tel: (706) 542-2836
saltz@uga.edu
www.drama.uga.edu
    Degree Offered: BA Drama with a concentration in writing
    Represented Faculty: Dr. Antje Ascheild, George Contini, Dr. Phillip Auslander
    Production Opportunities: Staged Readings to Full Student
    Other Highlights: various student related

**Independence Community College**
Mr. Peter Ellenstein, Director
William Inge Center for the Arts
Independence Community College
PO Box 708, 1057 W. College Ave.
Independence, KS 67301
Tel: (800) 842-6063 ext.5490
pellenstein@ingecenter.org
www.ingefestival.org
    Degree Offered: Professional Playwriting Certificate Program, AA
    Represented Faculty: Various Playwrights in Residence
    Production Opportunities:
    Other Highlights: William Inge Theatre Festival

**Kansas State University**
Ms. Kate Anderson, Director of Theatre
Department of Speech Communication, Theatre and Dance
Kansas State University
Nichols Hall 129, Manhattan, KS 66506
Tel: (785) 532-6769
Katjef@k-state.edu
www.k-state.edu
    Degree Offered: BA Theatre, Concentration in Playwriting
    Represented Faculty: Charlotte MacFarland, Sally Bailey
    Production Opportunities: Staged Readings to Full Student
    Other Highlights: KCACTF

**Marymount Manhattan College**
Ms. Mary Fleischer, Chair
Fine and Performing Arts
Marymount Manhattan College
221 East 71st St., New York, NY 10021
Tel: (212) 774-0761
mfleischer@mmm.edu

www.marymount.mmm.edu
   Degree Offered: BA inTheatre Arts
   concentration in Writing for the Stage

**University of Missouri - Kansas City**
Dr. Felicia Hardison Londre`, Curators'
Professor of Theatre
UMKC Theatre
University of Missouri at Kansas City
5100 Rockhill Rd., Kansas City, MI 64110
Tel: (816) 235-2781
LondreF@umkc.edu
www.umkc.edu
   Degree Offered: BA, MA in Theatre
   History, Lit. or Playwriting
   Program Length:
   Students per class: ~8

**State University of New York - Purchase**
Ms. Kathleen Tolan, Chair
Dramatic Writing Program
SUNY Purchase
735 Anderson Hill Rd.
Purchase, NY 10577
Tel: (914) 251-6830
www.purchase.edu
   Degree Offered: BFA in Dramatic
   Writing
   Program Length: 4 years
   Students per class: ~20
   Represented Faculty: Kathleen Tolan,
   A. Dean Bell, Iris Cahn, Madeleine
   George, Part-time and Guests

**Roosevelt Universtity**
Ms. Janet Wondra, Coordinator of
Creative Writing
Department of Literature and Languages
Roosevelt University
430 S. Michigan Ave., Chicago, IL 60605
Tel: (312) 341-3770
jwondra@roosevelt.edu
www.roosevelt.edu
   Degree Offered: MFA in Creative
   Writing

**Sarah Lawrence College**
Ms. Shirley Kaplan, Director
Sarah Lawrence College
One Mead Way, Bronxville, NY 10708
Tel: (914) 395-2430
slcadmit@mail.sic.edu
www.slc.edu
   Degree Offered: BFA, MFA (self-
   designed, can focus on playwriting)

   Program Length: 2 years
   Represented Faculty: Allan Baker,
   Cassandra Medley, Earnest H. Abuba,
   Amlin Gray, Stuart Spencer
   Production Opportunities: Staged
   Readings to Full Student
   Other Highlights: Theatre Outreach

**University of Virginia**
Mr. L. Douglas Grissom, Playwriting
Department of Drama
University of Virginia
PO Box 400128, Charlottesville, VA 22904
Tel: (804) 924-1447
ldg2h@virginia.edu
www.virginia.edu
   Degree Offered: BA in Drama
   (Playwriting), MFA
   Represented Faculty: Doug Grissom,
   Guests
   Production Opportunities: Staged
   Readings to Full Student
   Other Highlights: KCACTF

**Western Washington University**
Mr. Gregory Lawrence Pulver, Chair
Theatre Arts Department
Western Washington University
519 High Street/ PA 395B
Bellingham, WA 98225
Tel: (360) 650-6862
Gregory.Pulver@www.edu
www.wwu.edu
   Degree Offered: BA in Theatre with a
   concentration in Dramatic Writing
   Represented Faculty: Bryan Willis
   Other Highlights: KCACTF

**Wyoming, University of**
Mr. William M. Downs, Professor
Department of Theatre and Dance
University of Wyoming
1000 E. University Ave., Dept. 3951
Laramie, WY 82071
Tel: (307) 766-2198
downs@uwyo.edu
www.uwyo.edu
   Degree Offered: BA, BFA Theatre
   with Playwriting Concentration
   Represented Faculty: William Downs
   Production Opportunities: Staged
   Readings
   Other Highlights: KCACTF, RMTF,
   URTA

## DRAMATIC WRITING INSTRUCTION ABROAD
### (Canada, London, Ireland)

## CANADA

**University of British Columbia**
Bryan Wade, Advisor
UBC Creative Writing Program
Buchanan Room E462
1866 Main Mall
Vancouver, BC, Canada V6T 1Z1
Tel: (604) 822-2042
bwade@interchange.ubc.ca
www.creativewriting.ubc.ca
    Degrees Offered: MFA in Stage Playwriting
    Program Length: 2 years
    Students per Class: Not Specified

**University of Calgary**
James Dugan, Department Head
FASST (Fine Arts Student Success Team)
CH D100
Faculty of Fine Arts, University of Calgary
2500 University Drive NW
Calgary, Alberta, Canada T2N 1N4
Tel: (403) 220-5313
fasst@ucalgary.ca
www.finearts.ucalgary.ca
    Degrees Offered: MFA in Drama with Playwriting emphasis
    Program Length: 2 years
    Students per Class: Not Specified

**Dalhousie University**
Darryl Whetter, Department of English.
6135 University Avenue
Room 1186
Halifax, NS, Canada B3H 4P9
Tel: (902) 494-3384
dr344618@dal.ca
www.english.dal.ca
    Degrees Offered: Creative Writing Concentration to be counted as a Double Major in student's BA field of study
    Program Length: 4 years
    Students per Class: 15 (playwriting)

**University of Guelph**
Constance Rooke, Director
School of English & Theatre Studies
University of Guelph
Guelph, ON, Canada N1G 2W1
Tel: (416) 798-1331 x6235
cwmfa@uoguelph.ca
www.arts.uoguelph.ca
    Degrees Offered: MFA in Creative Writing with Playwriting concentration
    Program Length: 2 years
    Students per Class: not specified
    Highlights: Harbourfront's International Festival of Authors and its year-long Reading Series

**Memorial University of Newfoundland**
Dr. Larry Mathews
Department of English Language and Literature
St. John's, NL, Canada A1C 5S7
Tel: 709-737-8049
lmathews@mun.ca
www.mun.ca
    Degrees Offered: Creative Writing Diploma
    Program Length: 24 credit hours
    Students per Class: Not Specified

**University of New Brunswick**
Ross Leckie, Director of Creative Writing
Carleton Hall
University of New Brunswick
P.O. Box 4400
Fredericton, NB, Canada E3B 5A3
Tel: (506) 453-4676
leckie@unb.ca
www.unbf.ca
    Degrees Offered: MA in Creative Writing
    Program Length: 2 years
    Students per Class: Not specified
    Highlights: various journals

**University of Northern British Columbia**
Stan Beeler, Associate Professor, and Program Chair
Prince George Campus
3333 University Way
Prince George, BC, Canada V2N 4Z9
Tel: (250) 960-6619
stan@unbc.ca
www.unbc.ca
> Degrees Offered: MA in English (UNBC does not offer degrees in Creative Writing, however the English Program will offer a limited number of MA candidates the opportunity to complete a 12-credit creative thesis in lieu of an academic thesis.)
> Students per Class: Not Specified

**Vancouver Island University**
Richard Dunstan, Chair
Department of Creative Writing and Journalism,
Vancouver Island University,
900 5th St.,
Nanaimo, BC, Canada V9R 5S5
Tel: (250) 753-3245 Local 2786
moherf@viu.ca
www.viu.ca
> Degrees Offered: BFA in Creative Writing
> Program Length: 4 years
> Students per Class: not specified
> Highlights: Portal Magazine, Incline Magazine

**University of Victoria**
Dr. Lynne Van Luven, Graduate Advisor
Department of Writing
University of Victoria
P.O. Box 1700, STN CSC
Victoria, BC, Canada V8W 2Y2
Tel: (250) 721-7307
lvluven@finearts.uvic.ca
www.finearts.uvic.ca
> Degrees Offered: MFA in Writing with Playwriting focus
> Program Length: 2 years (full time students only)
> Students per Class: Not specified

**University of Windsor**
Dr. Karl Jirgens, Head
2-104 Chrysler Hall North
Windsor, ON, Canada N9B 3P4
Tel: (519) 253-3000 ext. 2289
englishmail@uwindsor.ca
www.uwindsor.ca
> Degrees Offered: M.A. in English: Literature and Creative Writing with Playwriting Focus
> Program Length: 3 years
> Students per Class: not specified
> Highlights: Publication opportunities in The Windsor Review, Rampike Magazine, Generation

**York University**
Shawn Kerwin, Chair
Department of Theatre
Faculty of Fine Arts
4700 Keele St.
Toronto, ON, Canada M3J 1P3
Tel: (416) 736-5172
theatre@yorku.ca
www.yorku.ca
> Degrees Offered: MFA in Theatre with Playwriting emphasis
> Program Length: 2 years
> Students per Class: Not Specified
> Production Opportunities: plays will be presented in the department's annual New Play Workshop

## OTHER WRITING PROGRAMS, COURSES, AND WORKSHOPS.

**Alberta Playwrights Network**
Val Lieske, Administrator
2633 Hochwald Avenue SW
Calgary, Alberta, Canada T3E 7K2
Tel: (403) 269-8564
admin@albertaplaywrights.com
www.albertaplaywrights.com
Offers: programs for new play development

**Great Canadian Theatre Company**
Lise Ann Johnson, Artistic Director
910 Gladstone Ave. Ottawa
Ottawa, ON, Canada K1R 6Y4
Tel: (613) 236-5192 x227

# Educational Opportunities : Dramatic Writing Instruction Abroad

artisticdirector@gctc.ca
www.gctc.ca
    Offers: play development program, workshops, gives playwrights the opportunity to work with a dramaturg during the development process of their piece, performance venue rental

**OIW - Ottawa Independent Writers**
George Laidlaw, President
P.O. Box 23137
Ottawa, ON, Canada K2A 4E2
laidlaw@iosphere.net
www.oiw.ca
    Offers: workshops

**The Writers' Circle of Durham Region**
Sue Reynolds, President
Bayly Postal Outlet
Health Rite Pharmacy
P.O. Box 14558
75 Bayly Street West
Ajax, ON, Canada L1S 7K7
Tel: (905) 686-0211
www.wcdr.org
    Offers: workshops, education, and networking, both independently and in co-operation with existing organizations.

## LONDON

**Angila Ruskin University**
Contact through main Email
East Road
Cambridge CB1 1PT
Tel: 0845-271-3333
answers@anglia.ac.uk
www.anglia.ac.uk
    Degrees Offered: Writing and Drama BA (Hons)
    Program Length: 6 years
    Highlights: local and national networks for developing performance writing

**Birbeck University of London**
Matthew Innes, Faculty of Arts Dean
Malet Street, Bloomsbury Professor
London, UK WC1E 7HX
Tel: 0845-601-0174
info@bbk.ac.uk
www.bbk.ac.uk
    Degrees Offered: Creative Writing (general) Certificate of Higher Learning (playwriting courses offered), Creative Writing (general) Certificate of Higher Education
    Program Length: 1 year
    Students per Class: not specified

**The Central School of Speech and Drama University of London**
Professor Gavin Henderson CBE, Senior Team Principal
Embassy Theatre
Eton Avenue, Swiss Cottage
London, UK NW3 3HY
Tel: +44 (0) 20-7722-8183
enquiries@cssd.ac.uk
www.cssd.ac.uk
    Degrees Offered: MA Writing for Stage and Broadcast Media, Postgraduate Diploma Writing for Stage and Broadcast Media
    Program Length: One year, full-time; two years, part-time.

**Goldsmiths University of London**
John Ginman, Convenor
Department of Drama
Goldsmiths, University of London
New Cross, London, UK SE14 6NW
Tel: +44 (0)20-7717-2251
drama@gold.ac.uk
www.goldsmiths.ac.uk
    Degrees Offered: MA in Writing for Performance
    Program Length: 1 year full-time or 2 years part-time
    Students per Class: not specified

**Royal Academy of Dramatic Art in Collaboration with King's College, London**
Lloyd Trott, Academy Dramaturg
Royal Academy of Dramatic Art
62-64 Gower Street,
London, UK WC1 6ED
Tel: 020-7636-7076
info@theplace.org.uk
www.rada.org
www.kcl.ac.uk
    Degrees Offered: MA Text and Performance with playwriting offered
    Highlights: The Sara Sugarman Bursaries will provide the opportunity

for two writers to be attached to the Royal Academy of Dramatic Art for a year. They can receive free script writing tuition and script development support from a series of specialist tutors.

**Royal Holloway, University of London**
Liz Schafer, MA Coordinator
Department of Drama & Theatre Studies
Royal Holloway
University of London
Egham, Surrey, UK TW20 0EX
Tel: 44 (0) 1784-443922
drama@rhul.ac.uk
www.rhul.ac.uk
> Degrees Offered: MA in Theatre with a pathway in Playwriting
> Program Length: 50 weeks full-time; 102 weeks part-time.
> Students per Class: Not Specifed
> Production Opportunities: Students have access to all the facilities within the department, including the Studio Theatre (a traditional black-box structure), the Handa Noh Theatre (a unique feature of Royal Holloway), and The Boilerhouse

## OTHER WRITING PROGRAMS, COURSES, AND WORKSHOPS.

**Cambridge Wordfest**
Cathy Moore, Director and Founder
Bick Barn, Royston Lane, Comberton, Cambridge, CB23 7EE
Tel: 01223-264404
admin@cambridgewordfest.co.uk
htwww.cambridgewordfest.co.uk
> Offers: workshops and readings

**Euroscript Development Workshops**
Charles Harris, Course Director
The Drill Hall
16 Chenies Street
London, UK WC1E 7EX
Tel: 0207-435-1330
enquiries@euroscript.co.uk
www.euroscript.co.uk
> Offers: Workshops to help you take an individual project to treatment, first draft or further drafts in a flexible time period.

> Students per Class: 5-6
> Highlights: On-going flexible help with your script

**Tamasha New Writing**
Zoe Cooper, main contact
Tamasha
Unit 220 Great Guildford Business Square
30 Great Guildford Street
London, UK SE1 0HS
Tel: 44 (0) 20-7633-2270
info@tamasha.org.uk
www.tamasha.org.uk
> Offers: an intensive two-week course which seeks to develop the artistic individuality of its participants
> Highlights: mentoring, guest lecturers, networking opportunities, membership for Tamasha Developing Artists

**Warehouse Theatre Summer Writing Course**
Ken Christiansen, Main Contact/Workshop Leader
Dingwall Road
UK CR0 2NF
Tel: 020-8681-1257
croydonwww@aol.com
www.warehousetheatre.co.uk
> Program Length: Summer (July-August)
> Students per Class: 18
> Offers: The course will cover creating a character, dramatic action, obstacles and themes.

**WordPlay - FairGround's Playwriting Course, London**
Adam Peck, main contact
PO Box 23595
UK EH6 7YX
Tel: 07816-787-124
adzpeck@hotmail.com
www.literaturetraining.com
> Offers: 12-week, part time playwriting course aimed at anyone interested in writing for the theatre. Open to anyone with little or no prior knowledge of playwriting, but with some prior experience of theatre-making.

# IRELAND

**University College Cork**
Dr. Ger FitzGibbon, Co-ordinator
Department of English,
University College Cork,
Cork, Ireland
Tel: 353 (0) 21-4902591
g.fitzgibbon@ucc.ie
www.ucc.ie
    Degrees Offered: MA in Drama & Theatre Studies with Playwriting focus

**Mary Immaculate College**
Dr. Eugene O'Brien, Head of English Department
South Circular Road
Limerick, Ireland
Tel: 353-61-204989
eugene.obrien@mic.ul.ie
www.mic.ul.ieCreativeWriting3.htm
    Degrees Offered: Mary Immaculate College Creative Writing Course

**National University of Ireland, Galway**
Dr. Adrian Frazier, Director
School of Humanities
University Road
Galway, Ireland
Tel: 00-353-91-49-31-29
adrian.frazier@nuigalway.ie
www.go4th.ie
    Degrees Offered: MA in Writing
    Program Length: 1 year
    Students Per Class: 15

**Oscar Wilde Centre for Irish Writing**
Mr. Gerald Dawe, Director
School of English Trinity College Dublin
21 Westland Row, Dublin 2, Ireland
Tel: 353-1-8961346 / 8962897
gdawe@tcd.ie
www.tcd.ie
    Degrees Offered: M.Phil. in Creative Writing

**University College Dublin**
Ms Hilary Gow, Administrator
School of English, Drama, and Film
Belfield, Dublin 4, Ireland
Tel: 353-1-716-1174
englishdramafilm@ucd.ie
www.ucd.ie
    Degrees Offered: MA Creative Writing
    Program Length: 1 year

**Warnborough College, Ireland**
Dr Maria Jacketti
All Hallows
Grace Park Road
Drumcondra, Dublin 9, Ireland
Tel: +353 (0) 1-857-1964
cwriting@warnborough.edu *or*
admissions@warnborough.edu
www.warnborough.ie
    Degrees Offered: MFA in Creative Writing (The program is conducted via distance learning. Students work independently, with the guidance of an allocated mentor. Cohort-based learning is conducted via the Online Moodle. Occasionally, there are optional summer workshops.)
    Program Length: four terms (16 months) or less

## OTHER WRITING PROGRAMS, COURSES, AND WORKSHOPS

**Derry Playhouse Writers Workshop**
Aisling Doherty, Main Contact
The Playhouse
Artillery Street
Derry, Ireland
aislingdoherty@btconnect.com
www.derryplayhousewriters.org
    Offers: playwriting workshops
    Program Length: Workshops run each Wednesday from 12 to 4pm

**Fishamble Theatre Company**
Gavin Kostick, Main Contact
Fishamble
Shamrock Chambers
1 – 2 Eustace Street
Temple Bar
Dublin 2, Ireland
Tel: 01-6704018
gavin@fishamble.com
www.fishamble.com
    Offers: weekend and evening courses
    Program Length: nine-week evening course or weekend course
    Students per Class: 10

**Gaiety School of Acting**
Patrick Sutton, Director
Gaiety School of Acting
Sycamore Street
Temple Bar
Dublin 2, Ireland
Tel: 353 (0) 1-679-9277
info@gaietyschool.com
www.gaietyschool.com
   Offers: playwriting workshops and courses
   Program Length: 10 weeks
   Students per Class: not specified

**Irish Writers' Centre**
19 Parnell Square
Dublin 1, Ireland
Tel: 353 1 872 1302
info@writerscentre.ie
www.writerscentre.ie
   Offers: creative writing courses in a wide range of genres at Beginner, Intermediate and Advanced levels
   Program Length: 10 weeks, 2 mornings, or 5 days

**Literature East Midlands**
Naomi Wilds, Coordinator
31 Granby Street
Loughborough
LE11 3DU
Tel: 01-509-268010
naomiw@charnwood-arts.org.uk
www.literatureeastmidlands.co.uk
   Offers: critical feedback and workshops

## WORKSHOPS

**Academy for New Musical Theatre (ANMT)**
5628 Vineland Ave.
North Hollywood, CA 91601
Scott Guy
Tel: (818) 506-8500 Fax: (818) 506-8500
academy@anmt.org
www.anmt.org
    Est. 1981. Supports wide array of programs to further artistic creation of new musical stage works, incl. workshops (Lehman Engel curriculum), readings, and commercial development. Staff: John Sparks (Artistic Dir), Elise Dewsberry (Assoc Artistic Dir). Fees: $895 (Intro Workshop), $695 (Lab), $395 (Fast Track Lab), $75 (Cabaret Workshop). **Consideration.** Opportunity/Award: query via email. **Application.** What to submit: query, SASE. How to submit: Visit www.anmt.org .

**Advanced Playwriting Workshop**
Box 5134, New York, NY 10185
Sheri Goldhirsch
Tel: (212) 594-5440 Fax: (212) 684-4902
admin@youngplaywrights.org
www.youngplaywrights.org
    Deadline: Postmarked by 9/20/09
The Advanced Playwriting Workshop meets in midtown Manhattan every Tue, 4:30-7:00pm, October 14 – April 28. Exercises help members develop and revise new plays. Members also attend Broadway and Off-Broadway productions, and receive a staged reading of one of their plays in April. **Preference.** Style: comedy, drama. **Application.** What to submit: application, sample, teacher/mentor recommendation, submissions not returned. Author must be age 18 or younger. Material must be original. How to submit: Visit our website at www.youngplaywrights.org for application instructions. Deadline: 11/1/2009.

**Broadway Tomorrow Musical Theatre**
191 Claremont Ave., #53
New York, NY 10027
Elyse Curtis
Tel: (212) 531-2447
solministry@juno.com
www.solministry.com
    Est. 1983. New musicals on new age, transformative or spiritual themes with redeeming value given self-contained concert readings with writer/composer involvement. Staff: Norman Curtis (Musical Dir). Response Time: 6 mos. **Preference.** Length: full length musicals. Style: adaptation, musical, translation. **Application.** What to submit: synopsis, audio or CD (3 songs), SASE. Author must be resident of NYC area.

**Charles Maryan's Playwrights/ Directors Workshop**
777 West End Ave., #6-C
New York, NY 10025
Charles Maryan
Tel: (212) 864-0542
cmaryan@pace.edu
    Est. 1982. Fees: $250/sem Response Time: 2 wks.

**Around the Block Urban Playwriting Workgroup**
Around the Block, 5 E. 22nd St., #9-K
New York, NY 10010
Carlos Jerome
Tel: (212) 673-9187
info@aroundtheblock.org
www.aroundtheblock.org
    Est. 2001. Focusing on (but not restricted to) the life & aspirations of urban communities, particularly NYC. Group meets every 2 wks. No fee. Membership in ATB not required. Staff: Gloria Zelaya, Louis (Co-dir, Theater Arts). See also: Raymond J Flores Short Play Series Response Time: 2 wks. **Consideration.** Opportunity/Award: reading. **Application.** How to submit: contact us to arrange participation.

**ASCAP Musical Theatre Workshop [NY]**
1 Lincoln Plaza, Fl. 7
New York, NY 10023
Michael A. Kerker
Tel: (212) 621-6234 Fax: (212) 621-6558
mkerker@ascap.com
www.ascap.com
   Directed by Stephen Schwartz, program of 50-min from works-in-progress before a panel of professional directors, musical directors, producers, critics and fellow writers. All sessions begin 7pm, May-Jun. **Application.** What to submit: synopsis, audio (4 songs), bios, song descriptions.

**ASCAP/Disney Musical Theatre Workshop**
7920 W. Sunset Blvd., Fl. 3
Los Angeles, CA 90046
Tel: (323) 883-1000 Fax: (323) 883-1049
mkerker@ascap.com
www.ascap.com
   Directed by Stephen Schwartz, 50-min presentation of works-in-development before a professional panel. All sessions begin 7pm, Jan-Feb. **Application.** What to submit: synopsis, audio (4 songs), bios, song descriptions. Deadline: 12/27/2009.

**Cape Cod Theatre Project**
Box 410, Falmouth, MA 2541
Andrew Polk
Tel: (508) 457-4242
andrew@capecodtheatreproject.org
www.capecodtheatreproject.org
   Est. 1995. Equity LOA. **Preference.** Length: full length plays. Style: others. **Application.** What to submit: query, synopsis, submissions not returned. Author must be resident or citizen of US. Material must be unpublished, unproduced. Deadline: 2/1/2009.

**Cherry Lane Theatre Mentor Project**
38 Commerce St., New York, NY 10014
James King
Tel: (212) 989-2020
company@cherrylanetheatre.org
www.cherrylanetheatre.org
   Est. 1997. Pairs young writers with master to work on scripts for full season, ending with Equity Showcase. Staff: Angelina Fiordellis (Artistic Director), Michael Weller (Supervising Mentor) Frequency: annual Production: medium cast size, no orchestra. **Preference.** Length: full length plays. **Application.** What to submit: submissions not returned. Material must be unoptioned, unproduced. How to submit: professional recommendation.

**Colorado New Play Summit**
1101 13th St., Denver, CO 80204
Douglas Langworth
Tel: (303) 893-4000 Fax: (303) 825-2117
www.dcpa.org
   DCTC (est. 1979; 1998 Regional Theater Tony winner) presents the Colorado New Play Summit (est. 2005), which offers rehearsed reading of new work for industry and general audience. Assistance: room/board, travel Frequency: annual Response Time: 6 mos. **Preference.** Length: full length plays. **Application.** What to submit: full script, SASE. Material must be unoptioned, unproduced. How to submit: unsolicited (AZ, CO, MT, NM, UT, WY residents only), agent.

**Composers & Lyricists Workshop**
320 W. 57th St., New York, NY 10019
Jean Banks
Fax: (212) 262-2508
jbanks@bmi.com
www.bmi.com
   Weekly 2-hr sessions (Sep-May). Frequency: annual. **Preference.** Style: musical. **Application.** What to submit: application, sample, audio. Deadline: 8/1/2009.

**David Henry Hwang Writers Institute**
120 N. Judge John Aiso St.
Los Angeles, CA 90012
Jeff Liu
Tel: (213) 625-7000 ext. 27
Fax: (213) 625-7111
jliu@eastwestplayers.org
www.eastwestplayers.org

# Educational Opportunities : Workshops

Est. 1991. 2 workshops/yr (fall, spring). Fees: $400. **Application.** What to submit: query.

**Fieldwork**
161 6th Ave, Fl. 14, New York, NY 10013
Michael Helland
Tel: (212) 691-6969 Fax: (212) 255-2053
michael@thefield.org
www.thefield.org

Est. 1986. 10-wk workshop to create original material, share work, and receive peer feedback. Fees vary: visit us online for current offerings. Assistance: work-study option. Frequency: quarterly.

**Frank Silvera Writers' Workshop**
Box 1791, Manhattanville Sta.
New York, NY 10027
Garland Lee Thompson
Tel: (212) 281-8832 Fax: (212) 281-8839
playrite@earthlink.net
www.fsww.org

Est. 1973. Equity Showcase. Playwright development program. **Consideration.** Opportunity/Award: 6% royalty. **Preference.** Style: Open. Subject: All subjects, writers of color. **Application.** What to submit: full script, SASE. Author must be age 18 or older, resident or citizen of US. Material must be unoptioned, unpublished, unproduced. How to submit: US Postage Mail or hand-delivery.

**Hangar Theatre Lab Company Playwriting Residencies**
Box 205, Ithaca, NY 14851
Literary Asst.
literary@hangartheatre.org
www.hangartheatre.org

4 playwrights offered 2-3 wk residency in Jul-Aug. Full production by Lab Company. The Hangar solicits full-lengths from former winners. Assistance: $200 plus housing and travel. Frequency: annual. Response Time: by 5/1/09. **Application.** What to submit: full script, resume/bio, must be submitted electronically, see website for guidelines. Material must be unproduced. How to submit: online. Deadline: 2/15/2009.

**Harbor Theatre Workshop**
160 W. 71st St., #PH-A
New York, NY 10023
Stuart Warmflash
Tel: (212) 787-1945 Fax: (212) 712-2378
swarmflash@harbortheatre.org
www.harbortheatre.org

Est. 1994. Equity productions. Staff: Julie Carpenter (Producing Dir). Fees: $400 Response Time: 6 wks. **Preference.** Length: full length musicals. Style: comedy, drama, musical. **Application.** What to submit: query, synopsis, SASE. Material must be unoptioned, unpublished, unproduced.

**Jeffrey Sweet's Improv for Playwrights**
250 W. 90th St., #15-G
New York, NY 10024
Kristine Niven
Tel: (212) 875-1857
artnewdir@aol.com
www.artisticnewdirections.org

Est. 1986. Jeffrey Sweet teaches technique for setting up scenes to improvise toward first drafts of one-acts, plus revising, introducing characters, and using improv for full-lengths. Monthly sessions. Fees: vary per length of session.

**Know Theatre of Cincinnati**
1120 Jackson St., Cincinnati, OH 45202
Jason Buffy
Tel: (513) 300-5669 Fax: (513) 421-3235
artistic@knowtheatre.com
www.knowtheatre.com

Est. 1997. Know Theatre produces new works, both plays and musicals, as well as adaptations of classics. Know Theatre also works with new and talented writers to workshop new works for production. **Preference.** Length: full length plays and musicals. Subject: All subjects, woman, writers of color, gay/lesbian. **Application.** What to submit: query, synopsis, 20 page sample. How to submit: unsolicited. Rolling deadline.

## Librettists Workshop
320 W. 57th St., New York, NY 10019
Jean Banks
Tel: (212) 830-2508 Fax: (212) 262-2508
jbanks@bmi.com
www.bmi.com
> Weekly 2-hr sessions (Sep-May) in NYC. Frequency: annual. **Preference.** Style: musical. **Application.** What to submit: application, sample. Deadline: 5/1/2009.

## Manhattan Playwrights Unit (MPU)
338 W. 19th St., #6-B
New York, NY 10011
Saul Zachary
Tel: (212) 989-0948
> Est. 1979. Ongoing biweekly inhouse workshop for professional-level playwrights and screenwriters. Informal and intense. Staff: Stacie Linardos. **Preference.** Style: all styles. **Application.** What to submit: query, resume, submissions not returned. How to submit: unsolicited.

## Missouri Playwrights Workshop (MPW)
129 Fine Arts Bldg., Columbia, MO 65211
David Crespy
Tel: (573) 882-0535
crespyd@missouri.edu
theatre.missouri.edu/mpw/index.htm
> Est. 1998. Weekly salon for developing work by Missouri playwrights. **Application.** What to submit: query, synopsis, submissions not returned. Author must be resident of MO, and attend workshop.

## Musical Theatre Lab
133 Wortham, Houston, TX 77204
Stuart Ostrow
Tel: (713) 743-2912
> Est. 1973. Each fall, 3 works performed by Lab students at Hobby Center. Recent works incl. 'Twas, Doll, Coyote Goes Salmon Fishing, and 1040. Response Time: 1mo. **Preference.** Length: full length musicals. Style: musical. **Application.** What to submit: full script, audio, score, SASE. Material must be unoptioned, original.

## National Theatre Workshop of the Handicapped
535 Greenwich St., New York, NY 10013
John Spalla
Tel: (212) 206-7789 Fax: (212) 206-0200
jspalla@ntwh.org
www.ntwh.org
> Est. 1977. 2-wk summer program at Crosby School in Belfast, Maine, bringing together disabled and able-bodied playwrights and actors to create pieces on themes of disability. Fees: $10 application. **Application.** What to submit: application.

## New Directors/New Works (ND/NW)
520 8th Ave., #320, New York, NY 10018
Roger Danforth
Tel: (212) 244-9494 Fax: (212) 244-9191
directorsproject@dramaleague.org
www.dramaleague.org
> Directors Project program to support new works by directors and collaborating artists. Application must be submitted by the director. Each team works with a professional mentor. Assistance: $1,000 stipend Frequency: annual. **Preference.** Length: full length plays. **Application.** What to submit: application, sample, production budget, two letters of recommendation, SASE. Author must be resident of US. Deadline: 2/1/2009.

## New Harmony Project
Box 441062, Indianapolis, IN 46244
Joel Grynheim
Tel: (317) 464-1103
jgrynheim@newharmonyproject.org
www.newharmonyproject.org
> Est. 1986. Development thru rehearsals and readings in 2½-wk conference of scripts that explore the human journey by offering hope and showing respect for the positive values of life. Assistance: $1,000 stipend, room/board, travel Frequency: annual. **Consideration.** Opportunity/Award: reading. **Application.** What to submit: 2-pg proposal, 10-pg sample, full script, audio, resume. Deadline: 10/1/2009.

**New Play Development Workshop**
Box 1290, Boulder, CO 80306
Tel: (303) 530-2167
playwrightsprogram@athe.org
Playwrights Program develops 7-10 new scripts/yr at the ATHE conference.

**PRTT Playwrights Unit**
304 W. 47th St., New York, NY 10036
Allen Davis III
Tel: (212) 354-1293 Fax: (212) 307-6769
allen@prtt.org
www.prtt.org
Est. 1977. Developmental workshops for beginners and for professionals (Oct-Apr), with readings and staged productions. Fees: $150 Frequency: annual Response Time: 1 mo. **Consideration.** Opportunity/Award: production, reading. **Application.** What to submit: query, full script (professional unit), SASE. Author must be resident of NYC area, Latino/minorities preferred.

**NYC Playwrights Lab**
Box 171, Peck Slip Sta.
New York, NY 10272
Dina von Zweck
www.writerightnyc.com
Small group of professional playwrights meeting weekly to make good scripts great, aiming to produce plays with significant impact in contemporary theater. Fees: $350/10 sessions Response Time: 3 mos. **Preference.** Style: adaptation, comedy, drama, opera, experimental. **Application.** What to submit: application, synopsis, 10-pg sample, submissions not returned. Deadline: 5/30/2009.

**Pataphysics**
41 White St., New York, NY 10013
Tel: (212) 226-0051 Fax: (212) 965-1808
garyw@theflea.org
www.theflea.org
Pataphysics workshops are scheduled sporadically and occur unexpectedly. To receive notification of upcoming classes, please email. Recent master playwrights have incl Lee Breuer, Lisa Kron, Jeffrey M. Jones, Ruth Margraff, Lynn M. Thomson, Paula Vogel, and Mac Wellman. **Application.** What to submit: query, 10-pg sample (4 copies), resume, SASE.

**Penumbra Theatre Company**
270 N Kent St., St. Paul, MN 55102
Dominic Taylor
Tel: (651) 288-6795
www.penumbratheatre.org
**Preference.** Length: full length plays. Style: all styles. Subject: writers of color.

**Playwrights Gallery**
119 W. 72nd St., #2700
New York, NY 10023
Deborah Savadge
www.playwrightsgallery.com
Est. 1989. Company of professional actors reads new work twice monthly. Public readings 2-3 times/yr. Meet Sep-Jun, alt Wed, noon-2pm. Response **Time: 9 mos. Preference.** Style: comedy, drama. **Application.** What to submit: 20-pg sample, SASE. How to submit: professional recommendation. Deadline: 1/15/2009. Second Deadline: 8/1/2009.

**Playwrights' Lab**
266 W. 37th St., Fl. 22
New York, NY 10018
Brian Richardson
Tel: (212) 695-1596
theatre@pulseensembletheatre.org
www.pulseensembletheatre.org
Develops 1 work of each playwright in 4-mo workshop. Group (limit 10) meets 3 hrs/wk to read scenes, with discussion afterward. Presents two showcases of 3 works/year. Some plays selected for further development. Fees $100/month.

**Playwrights' Platform**
398 Columbus Ave #604
Boston, MA 02116-6008
Pat Brennan
membership@playwrightsplatform.org
www.playwrightsplatform.org

Est. 1976. Monthly developmental readings in Boston area and annual festival in Boston, MA. Fees: $35/yr. Response Time: 3 mos. **Application.** Author must be available to attend monthly meetings in Boston area. How to submit: member only submissions online.

**Primary Stages Playwriting Workshops**
307 W. 38th St., #1510
New York, NY 10018
Michelle Bossy
Tel: (212) 840-9705 Fax: (212) 840-9725
michelle@primarystages.com
www.primarystages.com
Est. 2002. Each wk, 8 writers bring 10-15 pgs for instructor feedback and group discussion, completing first draft of new full-length in 8 wks. Fees: $450. **Preference.** Length: full length plays. **Application.** What to submit: let of interest, resume.

**Stage Left Theatre Company**
3408 N. Sheffield Ave.
Chicago, IL 60657
Kevin Heckman
Tel: (773) 883-8830 ext. 3
scripts@stagelefttheatre.com
www.stagelefttheatre.com
Est. 1982. Storefront theatre for plays that raise debate on sociopolticial issues, incl. Downstage Left (or DSL) development program. Staff: Kevin Heckman, Literary Manager Assistance: travel Response Time: 1 yr. **Consideration.** Opportunity/Award: royalty. **Preference.** Length: full length plays. **Application.** What to submit: application, 1-pg synopsis, full script, resume, SASE, development history of piece.

**Sage Theater**
235 W. 48th St., #26B
New York, NY 10036
Diana Blake
Tel: (212) 302-6665 Fax: (212) 3024661
info@sagetheater.us
www.sagetheater.us

Response Time: 4 mos. **Preference.** Style: sketch/musical comedy only. **Application.** What to submit: full script, SASE.

**The Scripteasers**
3404 Hawk St., San Diego, CA 92103
Jonathan Dunn-Rankin
Tel: (619) 295-4040
thescripteasers@msn.com
www.scripteasers.org
Est. 1948. Writers' development group with biweekly readings of original plays and facilitated discussion. Staff: Jonathan Dunn-Rankin (Sec'y). **Application.** What to submit: full script, SASE. Author must be resident of SoCal. Material must be unoptioned, unpublished, unproduced.

**Scripts Up!**
355 South End Ave., #5-N
New York, NY 10280
Janet McCall
Tel: (212) 946-1155
Est. 1999. Small NFP play-development organization specializing in professional full-time workshop stagings with audience feedback. Playwrights should have NYC area residency availabilty during entire process. **Preference.** Length: full length plays. **Application.** What to submit: synopsis, 15-pg sample, resume. Material must be unoptioned, unpublished, unproduced.

**Simon Studio**
Box 231469, Ansonia Sta.
New York, NY 10023
Roger Simon
Tel: (212) 841-0204 Fax: (212) 543-0286
rhsstudio@hotmail.com
www.simonstudio.com
Development through long distance consultation and/or residency of 5-10 weeks or short term intensive (1-5) days in NYC and/or Poughkeepsie/NY. Writers develop and showcase new work for stage, TV/Film, radio. Consideration for Samuel French National Short Play Fest, Simon Studio/Drama Book Shop

Cinema & Theatre Fest. and Time Warner TV's Simon Studio Presents. Service includes ongoing readings and critiques in workshops for in house, public and invited industry. Fees: $15 aplication fee,$225-$450 program fee. **Preference.** Style: all styles. **Application.** What to submit: query letter (note theme addressed), synopsis, 30-pg writing sample, audio, submissions returned with SASE. How to submit: unsolicited.

**Southern Writers Project (SWP)**
1 Festival Dr., Montgomery, AL 36117
Nancy Rominger
Fax: (334) 271-5348
web_swp@asf.net
www.southernwritersproject.net
ASF accepts scripts through its Southern Writers' Project (est. 1991). Up to 6 scripts each year are developed in weeklong workshop, with some chosen for production next season. Assistance: room/board, travel Response Time: 6 mos. **Preference.** Length: full length plays. Subject: writers of color. **Application.** What to submit: full script, SASE. Material must be unproduced.

**Sundance Institute Theatre at White Oak**
8530 Wilshire Blvd., Fl. 3
Beverly Hills, CA 90211
Christopher Hibma
Tel: (310) 360-1981 Fax: (310) 360-1975
theatre@sundance.org
www.sundance.org
Est. 2003. Equity Special Agreement. 2-wk developmental workshop focusing on musical theater and ensemble-created work. Assistance: stipend, room/board, travel Frequency: annual. **Application.** What to submit: synopsis, submissions not returned. Material must be unproduced. How to submit: invite.

**Sundance Institute Theatre Program**
8530 Wilshire Blvd., Fl. 3
Beverly Hills, CA 90211
Christopher Hibma
Tel: (310) 360-1981 Fax: (310) 360-1975
theatre@sundance.org
www.sundance.org
Est. 1981. Equity Special Agreement. Developmental Jul workshops for directors and playwrights in Sundance, UT. Fees: $30 application Assistance: $500, room/board, travel Frequency: annual Response Time: 4 mos. **Preference.** Length: full length plays and musicals. Style: Online at www.sundance.org/theatreapp . Subject: All subjects, woman, T.Y.A., writers of color, disabled, gay/lesbian. **Application.** What to submit: application, full script, audio, video, SASE. Material must be unproduced. How to submit: Online at www.sundance.org/theatreapp . Submission application fee: 35. Deadline: 12/15/2009.

**The Kennedy Center New Visions/New Voices Festival (NVNV)**
Kennedy Center, P.O. Box 101510
Arlington, VA 22210
Kim Peter Kovac
Tel: (202) 416-8830 Fax: (202) 416-8297
kctya@kennedy-center.org
www.kennedycenter.org/education/nvnv.html
Deadline and applications available online summer of 2009. Est. 1991. Biennial (even yrs) weeklong residency in Apr to encourage and support creation of new plays and musicals for young people and families. Assistance: stipend, travel. **Preference.** Subject: All subjects, T.Y.A. **Application.** What to submit: application, synopsis, sample, full script (3 copies), audio, submissions not returned. Material must be unproduced. How to submit: thru sponsoring theater.

**The PlayCrafters Group**
11 Golf View Rd., Doylestown, PA 18901
James Breckenridge
Tel: (888) 399-2506
hbcraft@att.net
Professional play script and screenplay evaluations and consultations for the creative dramatic writer. Fees: $175

and up. **Preference.** Style: all genres. **Application.** What to submit: play scripts & screenplays. Material must be any stage of development. How to submit: please contact by phone or e-mail.

**Theatre Building Chicago Musical Theatre Writers' Workshop**
1225 W. Belmont Ave., Chicago, IL 60657
John Sparks
Tel: (773) 929-7367 ext. 222
Fax: (773) 327-1404
jsparks@theatrebuildingchicago.org
www.theatrebuildingchicago.org
Est. 1984. Formerly New Tuners Workshop. 3-tiered workshop: Intro (1st yr), Intermediate (2nd yr), Advanced (ongoing). Fees: $25 application, $1,000/yr (Intro/ Intermediate), $400/yr (Advanced). **Preference.** Style: Musical theatre (book, music and lyrics). **Application.** What to submit: application, 5-pg sample, audio, SASE. Deadline: 9/1/2009.

**Urban Retreat**
Young Playwrights Inc,
P.O. Box 5134, New York, NY 10185
Sheri Goldhirsch
Tel: (212) 594-5440 Fax: (212) 684-4902
admin@youngplaywrights.org
www.youngplaywrights.org
Early Bird Postmark Deadline: 3/1/2010 Final Deadline: Postmarked by 5/1/2010 July 11-19, 2010, intensive workshop series in NYC. Participants then collaborate with professional dramaturgs, directors, and actors on staged reading of a new play. Fees: $1,650. **Assistance:** room/board, travel, theater tickets. **Preference.** Style: comedy, drama. **Application.** What to submit: application, sample, submissions not returned. Author must be age 14-21. Material must be original. How to submit: Visit our website at www.youngplaywrights.org for application instructions. Deadline: 4/9/2009.

**Writer/Director Lab**
86 Franklin St., Fl. 5
New York, NY 10013
Sarah Benson
Tel: (212) 941-8632 Fax: (212) 941-7148
writerdirector@sohorep.org
www.sohorep.org
Est. 1998. Writers and directors apply separately, then are paired for the workshop. Meet bimonthly Oct-April to read plays aloud and discuss. Each writers brings work in 3 times during workshop. **Application.** What to submit: query, application, full script, resume, SASE. Deadline: 5/15/2009.

# Writer Resources

## EMERGENCY FUNDS

**Entertainment Industry Assistance Program (EIAP)**
729 7th Ave., Fl. 10, New York, NY 10019
Tel: (212) 221-7300 ext. 119
www.actorsfund.org
  Helps working entertainment professionals with: counseling; advocacy and referrals to social services; emergency aid for food, rent, medical care. Chicago: 312-372-0989, Los Angeles: 323-933-9244 x15.

**Authors League Fund**
31 E. 32nd St., Fl. 7, New York, NY 10016
Sarah Heller
Fax: (212) 564-5363
staff@authorsguild.org
www.authorsleaguefund.org
  Interest-free loans for personal emergencies of immediate need (rent, medical, etc.). **Application.** What to submit: application. Author must be produced or published.

**Carnegie Fund for Authors**
1 Old Country Rd., #113
Carle Place, NY 11514
Tel: (516) 877-2141
  Aid to authors (of at least 1 commercially published book) for financial emergency as a result of illness or injury to self, spouse or dependent child, or that has placed author in pressing and substantial verifiable need. **Application.** Author must be age 18 or older.

**Dramatists Guild Fund**
1501 Broadway, #701
New York, NY 10036
Susan Drury
Tel: (212) 391-8384 Fax: (212) 944-0420
sdrury@dramatistsguild.com
www.dramatistsguild.com
  Est. 1962. Grants for personal emergencies such as rent, medical, etc. Also grants to nonprofit US theaters producing new works. **Application.** What to submit: application. Author must be produced or published. How to submit: Call, e-mail, website.

**Mary Mason Memorial Lemonade Fund**
870 Market St, #375
San Francisco, CA 94102
Tel: (415) 430-1140 Fax: (415) 430-1145
dale@theatrebayarea.org
www.theatrebayarea.org/programs/lemonade.jsp

**PEN Writers Fund**
588 Broadway, #303
New York, NY 10012
Andrew Proctor
www.pen.org
  Est. 1921. Emergency fund for professional writers with serious financial difficulties. Assistance: $2,000 limit Response Time: 2 mos. **Preference.** Length: full length plays. **Application.** What to submit: application. Author must be resident of US. Material must be produced or published (not self-published).

## MEMBERSHIP AND SERVICE ORGANIZATIONS

**Actors' Fund of America**
729 7th Ave., Fl. 10, New York, NY 10019
Barbara Davis
Tel: (212) 221-7300 Fax: (212) 764-6404
www.actorsfund.org
> Est. 1882. Human services org for all entertainment professionals. Also makes emergency grants for essential needs.

**ACTS Institute Inc.**
Box 30854
Palm Beach Gardens, FL 33420
Charlotte Plotsky
Tel: (561) 625-2273
actsinstitute@bellsouth.net
> Est. 1981. Nonprofit public foundation and membership group for developing creative artists and projects as a charitable and educational endeavor. Current project is public education (lectures, workshops, etc.) various topics, and publications program. **Application.** What to submit: query.

**Alliance of Artists Communities (AAC)**
255 South Main St., Providence, RI 2903
Tel: (401) 351-4320 Fax: (401) 351-4507
www.artistcommunities.org

**Alliance of Los Angeles Playwrights (ALAP)**
7510 Sunset Blvd., #1050
Los Angeles, CA 90046
Dan Berkowitz, Jon Dorf
Tel: (323) 957-4752
info@laplaywrights.org
www.laplaywrights.org
> Service and support org for professional needs of LA playwrights. Sponsors annual reading series, professional symposia, networking and social events. Also offers phone hotline, email listserv, bimonthly newsletter, resource guide to local theater, model contracts, and annual membership directory. Fees: $40/yr dues, $20 students, $275 lifetime (tax-deductable). **Application.** What to submit: application. How to submit: website.

**Alternate ROOTS Inc.**
1083 Austin Ave., NE, Atlanta, GA 30307
Carolyn Morris
Tel: (407) 577-1079 Fax: (404) 5777991
info@alternateroots.org
www.alternateroots.org
> Service org for playwrights, directors & choreographers creating original, community-based projects. Services incl. newsletter, bulletin, presenters' subsidy, annual meeting, and professional/artistic training and development. Fees: $20/yr (intro), $75/yr. **Application.** What to submit: application. Author must be resident of the South.

**American Assn. of Community Theatre (AACT)**
8402 Briar Wood Cir.
Lago Vista, TX 78645
Bill Muchow
www.aact.org
> Est. 1986.

**American Indian Community House**
11 Broadway, Fl. 2
New York, NY 10004
Jim Cyrus
Tel: (212) 598-0100 ext. 228
Fax: (212) 598-4909
jcyrus@aich.org; www.aich.org
> Fees: $25/yr.

**The Theatre Museum**
723 7th Ave., New York, NY 10019
Helen Marie Guditis
Tel: (212) 764-4112 ext. 201
Fax: (212) 764-0458
www.thetheatremuseum.org
> Est. 1986. Nonprofit organization to preserve, perpetuate and protect the legacy of live theater on Broadway. AKA Direct from Broadway.

**American Music Center (AMC)**
30 W. 26th St., #1001
New York, NY 10010
Maritza Norr
Tel: (212) 366-5260 Fax: (212) 366-5265
center@amc.net
www.amc.net

Est. 1939. Fees: $55/yr, $35/yr (student, senior).

**American Translators Assn. (ATA)**
225 Reinekers Ln., #590
Alexandria, VA 22314
Walter Bacak Jr.
Tel: (703) 683-6100 Fax: (703) 683-6122
ata@atanet.org
www.atanet.org
Est. 1959. Nonprofit to promote, educate and support US translators. Activities incl. conference, 2 awards and several publications. Open to anyone interested in translation and interpretation. Fees: $145/yr dues (associate). **Application.** What to submit: application.

**ASCAP (American Society of Composers, Authors & Publishers)**
1 Lincoln Plaza, New York, NY 10023
Tel: (212) 621-6234 Fax: (212) 621-6558
mkerker@ascap.com
www.ascap.com
Est. 1914. Membership org for composers, lyricists and publishers of musical works. Programs incl. winter and spring Musical Theater Workshops directed by Stephen Schwartz and Songwriters Showcases in NY and LA. **Application.** What to submit: application. Author must be published, recorded or performed.

**Association for Jewish Theatre (AJT)**
444 W. Camelback Rd., #208
Phoenix, AZ 85013
Janet Arnold
www.afjt.com
International network of theatres and playwrights to enhance Jewish theatre. Info and increased visibility of Jewish theater, incl. annual newsletter, website with member pages, annual conference, submissions guide, etc. Exec Director-Kayla Gordon Fees: $80/yr dues (Sep-Aug). **Application.** What to submit: application on website.

**Assn. of Authors' Representatives, Inc.**
676A 9th Avenue, #312
New York, NY 10036
Joanne Brownstein

**Association of Hispanic Arts (AHA)**
Box 1169, New York, NY 10029
Nicholas L. Arture
Tel: (212) 876-1242 Fax: (212) 876-1285
informacion@latinoarts.org
www.latinoarts.org
Est. 1975. Nonprofit advancing Latino arts as integral to the nation's cultural life. Facilitates projects and programs to foster Latino culture, incl. workshops and seminars for artists and organizations, and a directory of Latino arts.

**Association for Theatre in Higher Education (ATHE)**
Box 1290, Boulder, CO 80306
Tel: (888) 284-3737 Fax: (303) 530-2168
info@athe.org
www.athe.org
Org of individuals and institutions promoting excellence in theater education thru its publications, conferences, advocacy, projects, and collaborative efforts with other organizations. Membership year runs Jun-May. Fees: $105/yr (indiv), $80/yr (retiree), $50/yr (student). **Application.** What to submit: application. How to submit: online.

**Austin Script Works (ASW)**
Box 9787, Austin, TX 78766
Christina J. Moore
Tel: (512) 454-9727
info@scriptworks.org
www.scriptworks.org
Est. 1997. Austin Script Works supports playwrights by providing opportunities at all stages of the writing process from inception to production, through a variety of programming. Fees: $45/yr, $35/yr (student, senior). **Application.** What to submit: application. How to submit: online.

**BMI (Broadcast Music Inc)**
320 W. 57th St., New York, NY 10019
Tel: (212) 586-2000 Fax: (212) 262-2824
www.bmi.com
> Est. 1939. Performing rights society that collects royalties from radio, TV, web, restaurants, and other businesses that use music on behalf of songwriters, composers, and music publishers.

**Chicago Dramatists**
1105 W. Chicago Ave., Chicago, IL 60622
Russ Tutterow
Tel: (312) 633-0630
newplays@chicagodramatists.org
www.chicagodramatists.org
> Est. 1979. Developmental theater and playwright workshop. Programs incl. readings, productions, workshops, panels, marketing services, and referrals to producers, etc. Classes and quarterly 10-min workshop open to all playwrights. Quarterly bulletins and website announce all events and programs. Fees: $125/year (National Associate Membership), $200/yar (Chicago Associate Membership), free (Residency). **Application.** How to submit: See "Programs" chapter of web site for full information.

**The National League of American Pen Women, Inc.**
1300 17th St. NW, Washington, DC 20036
N. Taylor Collins
Tel: (202) 785-1997 Fax: (202) 452-8868
nlapw1@verizon.com
www.nlapw.org
> New members in Letters, contact Thelma Urich, 6143 Tennessee Ave., St. Louis, MO 63111, 314-752-5210. New members in Music, contact Eugénie R. Rocherolle, 16 Jericho Dr., Old Lyme, CT 06371, 860-434-0603. Fees: $40/yr.

**Dramatists Guild of America Inc.**
1501 Broadway, #701
New York, NY 10036
Tom Epstein
Tel: (212) 398-9366 Fax: (212) 944-0420
membership@dramatistsguild.com
www.dramatistsguild.com
> Est. 1920. Works for the professional rights of writers of stage works and the conditions under which those works are created and produced. Also fights to secure fair royalties and protect subsidiary rights, artistic control, and copyright ownership. Members receive various services and publications, incl *The Dramatist* magazine, Newsletter, and Resource Directory. Fees: $95/yr (assoc), $150 (active, estate), $35/yr (student). **Application.** What to submit: application, full script. How to submit: online.

**Educational Theatre Association**
2343 Auburn Ave., Cincinnati, OH 45219
David LaFleche
Tel: (513) 421-3900 Fax: (513) 421-7077
dlafleche@edta.org
www.edta.org
> Fees: $75/yr, $25/yr (student). **Application.** What to submit: application.

**The Field**
161 6th Ave., Fl. 14, New York, NY 10013
Michael Helland
Tel: (212) 691-6969 Fax: (212) 255-2053
michael@thefield.org
www.thefield.org
> Est. 1986. Service org offering residencies, creative labs, performance showcases, mgmt workshops, fiscal sponsorship, consultations and more. Fees: $100/$250 a yr. **Application.** What to submit: application.

**FirstStage**
Box 38280, Los Angeles, CA 90038
Dennis Safren
Tel: (323) 850-6271
firststagela@aol.com
www.firststagela.org
> Work must be 30 min. or less. Est. 1983. Develops new work for stage and screen. Do not have to be a member for work to be considered. If you wish to join, dues are $250 per year for local members; $68 per year for non-local members. Response Time: 6 mos. **Application.** What to submit: full script, SASE. Material must be unproduced; 30 minutes or less.

# Writer Resources : Membership and Service Organizations

**The Foundation Center**
79 5th Ave., New York, NY 10003
Maggie Morth
Tel: (212) 807-2415 Fax: (212) 807-3677
fdonline@fdncenter.org
www.fdncenter.org
> Est. 1956. Network of centers with grant info. We do not make grants, do research, consult, make referrals, arrange intros, or write/review proposals. HQ in NY. Regional centers in Atlanta (50 Hurt Plz, #150), Cleveland (1422 Euclid Ave, #1600), DC (1627 K St, NW, 3rd Fl) San Francisco (312 Sutter St, #606).

**Fractured Atlas**
248 W. 35th St., #1202
New York, NY 10001
Adam Natale
Tel: (212) 277-8020 Fax: (212) 277-8025
support@fracturedatlas.org
www.fracturedatlas.org
> Est. 2002. Benefits incl. fiscal sponsorship, low-cost healthcare & Liability insurance, press/publicity services, online classes, calendar, forums, grants. Staff: Adam Huttler (Exec Dir), Adam Natale (Dir, Member Services) Maria Ortiz (Dir, Healthcare), Arwen Lowbridge (Mng Dir.), Alexandra Gray (Dir, Development), Dianne Ebicella (Pgm Assoc). Fees: $75/yr (individual), FREE Associate Membership for Dramatists Guild members.

**Greensboro Playwrights' Forum**
200 N. Davie St., #2
Greensboro, NC 27401
Stephen D. Hyers
Tel: (336) 335-6426 Fax: (336) 373-2659
stephen.hyers@greensboronc.gov
www.playwrightsforum.org
> Est. 1993. Aids area dramatists in publishling, producing, and learning theater writing. Services incl. monthly meetings, workshops, staged readings, newsletter, and studio space. Fees: $25/yr. **Application.** What to submit: application.

**Hatch-Billops Collection**
491 Broadway, Fl. 7.
New York, NY 10012
James V. Hatch
Tel: (212) 966-3231 Fax: (212) 966-3231
hatchbillops@yahoo.com
www.hatch-billopscollection.org
> Est. 1975. Collection of primary and secondary resource materials in the black cultural arts.

**Hispanic Organization of Latin Actors (HOLA)**
107 Suffolk St., #302
New York, NY 10002
Manuel Alfaro
Tel: (212) 253-1015 Fax: (212) 253-9651
holagram@hellohola.org
www.hellohola.org

**Inside Broadway**
630 9th Ave., #802, New York, NY 10036
Michael Presser
Tel: (212) 245-0710 Fax: (212) 245-3018
mpresser@insidebroadway.org
www.insidebroadway.org
> Professional children's theater producing classic musicals in NYC public schools. Also offer hands-on, in-school residencies that enrich core curriculum through drama, dance, and music.

**Institute of Outdoor Drama**
1700 MLK Jr. Blvd., CB-3240
Chapel Hill, NC 27599-3240
Rob Franklin. Cox
Tel: (919) 962-1328 Fax: (919) 962-4212
outdoor@unc.edu
www.unc.edu/depts/outdoor
> Public service agency of UNC at Chapel Hill for consultation, info, publicity, employment advice, conferences and symposia, and research material on every phase of planning and producing outdoor theater. **Application.** What to submit: query, SASE.

**International Women's Writing Guild (IWWG)**
Box 810, Gracie Sta.
New York, NY 10028
Hannelore Hahn
Tel: (212) 737-7536 Fax: (212) 737-7536
www.iwwg.org
 Est. 1976. Network for empowering women thru writing, incl. workshops/courses, submission tip sheet, bi-monthly newsletter, and dental/vision insurance. Fees: $45/yr. **Application.** What to submit: application.

**League of Chicago Theatres/League of Chicago Theatres Foundation**
228 South Wabash #200
Chicago, IL 60604
Tel: (312) 554-9800 Fax: (312) 922-7202
info@chicagoplays.com
www.chicagoplays.com
 Est. 1979.

**League of Professional Theatre Women**
Lynne Rogers, Box 2292
New York, NY 10108
Lenore De Kare
Tel: (212) 414-8048 Fax: (212) 225-2378
id5columbia.edu
www.theatrewomen.org
 Nonprofit advocacy organization promoting visibility and increasing opportunities for women in the professional theater.

**League of Washington Theatres (LOWT)**
Box 21645, Washington, DC 20009
 Est. 1982. Association of nonprofit professional theaters and related organizations in the greater Washington metropolitan area.

**United States Copyright Office**
101 Independence Ave., SE
Washington, DC 20559
Tel: (202) 707-3000
www.copyright.gov
 Though registration isn't required for protection, copyright law provides several advantages to registration. Fees: $45 (basic claim). **Application.** What to submit: application, full script (2 copies), audio (2 copies).

**Literary Managers & Dramaturgs of the Americas (LMDA)**
Box 728, Village Sta.
New York, NY 10014
Louise McKay
Tel: (212) 5610315
lmdanyc@hotmail.com
www.lmda.org
 Est. 1985. Volunteer membership org w/400 members in US/Canada. Current programs and services incl. annual conference, regional meetings/symposia, LMDA Review quarterly journal, Script Exchange newsletter, outreach program, univ./advocacy caucuses, email network, and dramaturgy prize. Annual memberships is Jun-May. Fees: $60/yr, $25/yr (student). **Application.** What to submit: application. How to submit: online.

**Audrey Skirball-Kenis (ASK) Unpublished Play Collection**
630 W. 5th St., Los Angeles, CA 90071
Bette McDonough
Tel: (213) 228-7325
www.lapl.org/central/literature.html
 Service org with over 800 unpublished scripts of plays done in L.A. The collection, located in the Lit/Fiction Dept for reference only, incl. reviews and playwright bios. Open Mon-Thu, 10am-8pm; Fri-Sat, 10am-6pm; Sun, 1pm-5pm.

**LA Stage Alliance**
644 S. Figueroa St.
Los Angeles, CA 90017
Sara Adelman
Tel: (213) 614-0556 Fax: (213) 6140561
info@lastagealliance.com
www.lastagealliance.com
 Est. 1975. Formerly TheatreLA. Nonprofit service org of groups and individuals providing L.A. Stage magazine, networking opportunities, half-price tickets, Ovation Awards, cooperative ads, info and referrals.

# Writer Resources : Membership and Service Organizations

Fees: $35/yr (individual), $20/yr (student). **Application.** What to submit: application. How to submit: online.

**National Audio Theatre Festivals (NATF)**
115 Dikeman St., Hempstead, NY 11550
Sue Zizza
Tel: (516) 483-8321 Fax: (516) 538-7583
www.natf.org

**National Writers Association Foundation (NWAF)**
Box 4187, Parker, CO 80134
Sandy Whelchel
Tel: (303) 841-0246 Fax: (303) 841-2607
authorsandy@hotmail.com
www.nationalwriters.com
Est. 1998. 1-$1,000 scholarship and one Conference scholarship which includes an opportunity to speak with four producers. Frequency: annual Response Time: 4 months. **Consideration.** Opportunity/Award: 1,000. **Preference.** Style: all styles. **Application.** What to submit: application,10 pg. sample, SASE. Material must be unoptioned, unpublished, unproduced. How to submit: unsolicited. Deadline: 12/31/2009.

**New Dramatists**
424 W. 44th St., New York, NY 10036
Emily Morse
Tel: (212) 757-6960 Fax: (212) 2654738
newdramatists@newdramatists.org
www.newdramatists.org
Est. 1949. Service org offering development programs (reading-workshop; literary services; artistic services) and services (readings; nonperformance workshops w/ artistic collaborators; natl Script Share distribution; monthly Member Bulletin; free tickets; intl exchanges; travel grants and other awards). Staff: Todd London (Artistic Dir). Response Time: 9 mos. **Application.** What to submit: application, full script, SASE. Deadline: 9/15/2009.

**New Playwrights Foundation**
608 San Vicente Blvd., #18
Santa Monica, CA 90402
Jeffrey Bergquist
Tel: (310) 393-3682
dialogue@newplaywrights.org
www.newplaywrights.org
Est. 1969. Meets every othe Tursday in Santa Monica. Some members' works have been produced by NPF. Fees: $25/yr. **Application.** Author must be able to attend workshops in Santa Monica.

**NYC Playwrights**
2 12th St., #1013, Hoboken, NJ 07030
Nancy McClernan
info@nycplaywrights.org
www.nycplaywrights.org
Est. 2000. Writers and actors meet each Wed., 7-10 PM at Where Eagles Dare (347 W. 36th St., #12-A) for in-hand readings of works in progress, free and open to the public. Member writers may reserve a 30 min. slot, on a first-come, first-served basis, up to 8 wks in advance. Fees: $55/6 mos. **Application.** What to submit: application,10-pg sample.

**Billy Rose Theatre Division**
40 Lincoln Center Plaza, Fl. 3
New York, NY 10023
Bob Taylor
Tel: (212) 870-1637
rtaylor@nypl.org
www.nypl.org/research/lpa
Research facility with historical and current docs of performing arts and popular entertainment, incl. books, personal papers, scripts and promptbooks from theater, film, TV and radio. Tape archive incl. Broadway, Off-Broadway and regional productions.

**Non-Traditional Casting Project, Inc. (NTCP)**
1560 Broadway, #1600
New York, NY 10036
Sharon Jensen
Tel: (212) 730-4750 Fax: (212) 730-4820

info@ntcp.org
www.ntcp.org
> Est. 1986. Nonprofit advocacy org to address and seek solutions to racism and exclusion in theater, film and TV, working to advance creative participation of US writers of color, female artists, deaf and hard-of-hearing artists, and artists with disabilities. **Application.** Author must be of color, female or disabled.

**North Carolina Playwrights Alliance (NCPA)**
Box 10463, Raleigh, NC 27605
Adrienne Pender
www.ncplaywrightsalliance.org
> Est. 2001. Fees: $20/yr. **Application.** What to submit: application. Author must be resident of NC. How to submit: online.

**North Carolina Writers' Network (NCWN)**
Box 954, Carrboro, NC 27510
Ed Southern
Tel: (919) 967-9540 Fax: (919) 929-0535
mail@ncwriters.org
www.ncwriters.org
> Nonprofit to connect, promote and lead NC writers thru conferences, contests, newsletter, website, member pages, member book catalog, critique and consultation, etc. (some services require addl. fees). Fees: $75/yr, $65/yr (senior), $55/yr (student). **Application.** What to submit: Membership application . How to submit: Online at www.ncwriters.org .

**Ollantay Center for the Arts**
Box 720636, Jackson Heights, NY
Pedro Monge-Rafuls
Tel: (718) 699-6772 Fax: (718) 699-6773
> Each season Ollantay offers playwright workshops with well-known Latin American authors and play-reading programs to help local playwrights. A literature program is dedicated exclusively to the promotion of local writers through conferences and panel discussions. Creators of *Ollantay* magazine, a biannual journal in English and Spanish that publishes at least one play in each issue. Ollantay Press publishes books. Frequency: annual Response Time: 5/15/04. **Consideration.** Opportunity/Award: awards, possible future production, publication, reading. **Preference.** Subject: writers of color. **Application.** What to submit: synopsis, submissions returned with SASE. How to submit: unsolicited.

**OPERA America**
330 7th Ave., Fl. 16, New York, NY 10001
Tel: (212) 796-8620 Fax: (212) 7968631
frontdesk@operaamerica.org
www.operaamerica.org
> National service org promoting creation, presentation and enjoyment of opera. Provides professional development resources for composers, librettists, educators, etc. Composers may subscribe to Opera Source job search ($45/yr). Fees: $60/yr. **Application.** What to submit: application. How to submit: online.

**Orange County Playwrights Alliance (OCPA)**
412 Emerald Place, Seal Beach, CA 90740
Eric Eberwein
firenbones@aol.com
www.ocplaywrights.org
> Est. 1995. Member org. workshop of Orange Co. dramatists. Develops new works, staged readings, occasional productions. Fees: $80/yr. **Application.** What to submit: full script.

**Philadelphia Dramatists Center (PDC)**
c/o CEC, 3500 Lancaster Ave.
Philadelphia, PA 19104
Walt Vail
pdc@usner.org
pdc1.pbwiki.com
> Membership org for improving the craft, opportunities and conditions of dramatic writers, incl. newsletter, emails, readings, writers' circles, workshops, free/discounted space rental, guest speakers, reading library, social events, resource books, and copyright forms. Members may also

# Writer Resources : Membership and Service Organizations

list works on PDC's website. Fees: $40/yr, $20/yr (student). **Application.** What to submit: application.

**Playformers**
20 Waterside Plaza, #11-G
New York, NY 10010
Lynda Crawford
Tel: (917) 825-2663
playformers@earthlink.net
   Est. 1987. Monthy meetings (Sep-May) to read new work by members. Fees: $25/quarter (covering refreshments for actors) Response Time: 2 mos. **Application.** What to submit: full script, SASE.

**The Playwrights Center San Francisco (PCSF)**
588 Sutter St., #430
San Francisco, CA 94102
Laylah Muran
Tel: (415) 8203206
layla@playwrightscentersf.org
www.playwrightscentersf.org
   Est. 1980. Organization of playwrights, directors and actors developing Bay Area writing, audience development and related arts. Weekly events incl. staged readings, scene workshops, classes and panel discussions. Author provieds scripts for actors. No submission process for scene nights. Fees: $60/yr (full), $30/yr (student) Frequency: semiannual for staged and developmental readings Response Time: 3 mos. **Application.** What to submit: application. Author must be resident of Bay Area.

**The Playwrights' Center**
2301 Franklin Ave. E.
Minneapolis, MN 55406
Anna Peterson
Tel: (612) 332-7481 Fax: (612) 332-6037
info@pwcenter.org
www.pwcenter.org
   Provides services that support playwrights and playwriting. Programs incl. listed submission opportunities, fellowships, workshops, readings, classes, and online member-to-member networking services. Fees:

$50/yr . **Application.** What to submit: application. How to submit: online.

**Playwrights Guild of Canada (PGC)**
215 Spadina Ave. Suite 210
Toronto, ON M5T-2C7 Canada
Dian Marie Bridge
Tel: (416) 703-0201 Fax: (416) 703-0059
info@playwrightsguild.ca
www.playwrightsguild.ca
   Est. 1972. Formerly Playwrights Union of Canada. National nonprofit offering triannual directory of Canadian plays/playwrights, contract negotiation with PACT, amateur/professional production administration, and quarterly magazine. Fees: $150/yr (full), $65/yr (assoc) Response Time: 3 wks. **Application.** What to submit: application, resume. Author must be citizen or landed immigrant of Canada.

**Playwrights' Forum**
Box 5322, Rockville, MD 20851
Ernie Joselovitz
Tel: (301) 8160569
pforum@erols.com
www.erols.com/pforum/welcome.htm
   Est. 1991. Tiered options: Forum 2 professional member; Forum 1 apprentice member; Associate member. Fees: $120/session (4 mos). **Application.** What to submit: application. Author must be resident of Mid-Atlantic. How to submit: online. Deadlines: 1/15/2009, 5/15/2009, 9/15/2009.

**The Purple Circuit**
921 N. Naomi St., Burbank, CA 91505
Bill Kaiser
Tel: (818) 953-5096
purplecir@aol.com
www.buddybuddy.com/pc.html
   Service group to promote GLBT performing arts worldwide. Maintains Calif. show listings hotline (818-953-5072), directory of GLBT-friendly venues, and freelisting of playwrights. **Preference.** Subject: gay/lesbian. **Application.** How to submit: email.

**Rodgers & Hammerstein Theatricals**
229 W. 28th St., Fl. 11
New York, NY 10001
Tel: (800) 400-8160 Fax: (212) 268-1245
editor@rnh.com
www.rnhtheatricals.com

**Saskatchewan Writers Guild (SWG)**
Box 3986, Regina, SK Canada
Laura Malhiot
Tel: (306) 757-6310
swg@sasktel.net
www.skwriter.com
> Est. 1969. Membership is open to all writers, teachers, librarians, publishers, booksellers, students, and others interested in Saskatchewan writing. Fees: $65/yr (regular), $45/yr (student, senior).

**Shubert Archives**
149 W. 45th St., New York, NY 10036
www.shubertorganization.com/divisionsandaffiliates/shubertarchive.asp
> Est. 1976. Repository for over 6m docs related to the Shubert brothers and Shubert Org, incl. costume/set designs, scripts, music, publicity, photos, letters, business records, and architectural plans.

**The Songwriters Guild of America (SGA)**
1560 Broadway, #1306
New York, NY 10036
George Wurzbach
Tel: (212) 768-7902 Fax: (212) 768-9048
ny@songwritersguild.com
www.songwritersguild.com
> Est. 1931. Fees: $60/yr (gold), $84/yr (platinum), $108/yr (diamond).

**STAGE (Society for Theatrical Artists' Guidance and Enhancement)**
1106 Lupo Dr., Dallas, TX 75207
Jeff Fenter
Tel: (214) 630-7722 Fax: (214) 6304468
stage@stage-online.org
www.stage-online.org
> Est. 1981. Nonprofit promoting theater, broadcast, and film by serving as info clearinghouse and training center for north central Texas. Fees: $80 (initial), $65/yr (renewal).

**StageSource**
88 Tremont St., #714, Boston, MA 2108
Jeremy Johnson
Tel: (617) 720-6066 Fax: (617) 720-4275
info@stagesource.org
www.stagesource.org
> Est. 1985. Alliance of artists and organizations in New England. Benefits incl. e-newsletters, group health insurance, professional development seminars, job expo, free/discount tickets, talent bank, and networking events. Fees: $115 (initial), $65/yr (renewal).

**International Theatre Institute US Center (ITI/US)**
520 8th Ave., Fl. 24, New York, NY 10018
Emilya Cachapero
Tel: (212) 609-5900 Fax: (212) 609-5901
iti@tcg.org
www.tcg.org
> TCG is the US center of ITI, a UNESCO network of over 90 centers dedicated to cultural exchange and advocacy. TCG/ITI helps intl. theater professionals and scholars with info about US practice, introductions to US professionals, and planning visits. Similar help is offered to Americans traveling and working abroad. Fees: $39.95/year.

**Theatre Communications Group (TCG)**
520 8th Ave., Fl. 24, New York, NY 10018
Teresa Eyring
Tel: (212) 609-5900 Fax: (212) 609-5901
tcg@tcg.org
www.tcg.org
> National service org for nonprofit US professional theater. Services incl. grants, fellowships and awards to artists and institutions; workshops, roundtables and conferences; advocacy; surveys, research and publications, incl. reference, plays and periodicals; US Center for Intl. Theatre Institue. Membership incl. American Theatre magazine subscription, ticket discounts nationwide, savings on TCG resource materials and book discounts from TCG and other select publishers.

Fees: $39.95/yr, $20/yr (student).
**Application.** How to submit: online.

**Theater Instituut Nederland (TIN)**
Box 19304, Amsterdam, Netherlands
Henk Scholten
info@tin.nl
www.tin.nl
Est. 1992. Houses a museum and library, collects current info and documentation and organizes events such as discussions, conferences, workshops, exhibitions and international presentations. It also publishes books, CDs and other materials and participates in various international networks.

**Writers Guild of America, West (WGAW)**
7000 W. 3rd St., Los Angeles, CA 90048
Corinne Tippin
Tel: (323) 782-4532
www.wga.org

**Writers Lounge**
11240 Magnolia Blvd. # 204
North Hollywood, CA 91601
Kaz Matamura
writela@yahoo.com
www.writela.com
Est. 2006. Writers Lounge is an exclusive membership lounge.

**The Writers Room**
740 Broadway, Fl. 12
New York, NY 10003
Donna Brodie
Tel: (212) 2546995
writersroom@writersroom.org
www.writersroom.org
Est. 1978. Large loft with 44 work stations, library, storage area, kitchen/lounge and phone room. Open 24/7. 1 month list for full-time membership; no wait list for part-time. Fees: $75 application,$450/6 mos. (6pm-6am), $550/6 mos. (6pm-11:30am), $650/6 mos. (27/7). **Consideration.** Opportunity/Award: Reading series. **Application.** What to submit: application.

**The Fund for Women Artists**
3739 Balboa St. #181
San Francisco, CA 94121
Martha Richards
Tel: (415) 751-2202 Fax: (650) 2449136
info@womenarts.org
www.womenarts.org
Founded to ensure women have full access to the resources they need, by challenging stereotypes and increasing opportunities.

**The Theatre Museum**
723 7th Ave, 7th Fl.
New York, NY 10019
Helen Marie. Guditis
Tel: (212) 764-4112 Fax: (212) 7640458
information@thetheatremuseum.org
Chartered in 2003 -the only non profit museum in America with the mission to preserve, perpetuate and protect the legacy of the theatre.

**Theatre Bay Area (TBA)**
870 Market St., #375
San Francisco, CA 94102
Brad Erickson
Tel: (415) 430-1140 Fax: (415) 4301145
tba@theatrebayarea.org
www.theatrebayarea.org
Nonprofit of Bay Area individuals and theater companies. Services incl. monthly Theatre Bay Area magazine with listing of writer opportunities, grants of $1,500-$5,000 for artists and $10,000 new works fund. Other publications incl. regional theater directory. Fees: $65/yr, $55/yr (student). **Application.** What to submit: application. Author must be resident of Bay Area.

**Chicago Alliance for Playwrights (CAP)**
1225 W. Belmont Ave., Chicago, IL 60657
Joanne Koch
Tel: (773) 929-7367 ext. 60
Fax: (773) 3271404
info@chicagoallianceforplaywrights.org
www.chicagoallianceforplaywrights.org
Networking org for playwrights, theaters and other individuals and groups. Publishes newsletter and annual directory of members and their

work. Also sponsors seminars and workshops. Fees: $25/yr. **Application.** What to submit: application. Author must be current or former resident of Midwest. How to submit: email.

**Theatre Development Fund (TDF)**
1501 Broadway, Fl. 21
New York, NY 10036
Tel: (212) 221-0885 Fax: (212) 768-1563
www.tdf.org/application
> Est. 1968. Dedicated to the advancement of profit and nonprofit drama, music and dance productions in NYC. Programs incl. TKTS discount booths, TDF membership, Theater Access Project (TAP), Costume Collection. Fees: $25/yr. **Application.** What to submit: application. How to submit: online.

**Theatre Project**
45 W. Preston St., Baltimore, MD 21201
Anne Cantler Fulwiler
Tel: (410) 539-3091
office@theatreproject.org
www.theatreproject.org
> Est. 1971. Introduces Baltimore to those experimenting with new forms, incl. both globally recognized and emerging local artists. Production: small cast, unit set Response Time: 2 mos. **Consideration.** Opportunity/Award: box office percentage. **Preference.** Style: avant garde. **Application.** What to submit: synopsis, video, SASE. Material must be original. How to submit: professional recommendation.

**Theatre West**
3333 Cahuenga Blvd. W.
Hollywood, CA 90068
John Gallogly
Tel: (323) 851-4839 Fax: (323) 851-5286
theatrewest@theatrewest.org
www.theatrewest.org
> Est. 1962. Member org. Mandatory 6 hrs/mo volunterring in 1st year of membership. Fees: $100 application (if accepted),$50/mo. **Consideration.** Opportunity/Award: reading. **Preference.** Length: full length plays. **Application.** What to submit: full script. Author must be resident of S. Calif.

**Theatre for Young Audiences/ USA**
Emerald City Theatre Admin. Offices
2936 N. Southport Ave, 3rd Floor
Chicago, IL 60657
Tel: (703) 403-5820 Fax: (773) 529-2693
info@tyausa.org
www.tyausa.org
> National service org promoting professional TYA across cultural and international boundaries. Services incl semiannual journal and frequent bulletins, member directories. Fees: $75/yr, $40/yr (retiree), $35/yr (student) . **Preference.** Subject: T.Y.A. **Application.** What to submit: application.

**TRU (Theater Resources Unlimited)**
115 MacDougal St., New York, NY 10012
Bob Ost
Tel: (212) 714-7628 Fax: (212) 864-6301
trunltd@aol.com
www.truonline.org
> Est. 1992. Support and educational services for producers, theater companies, and self-producing artists, emphasizing the business side of the arts. Fees: $60/yr (individual).

**V&A Theatre Collections**
23 Blythe Road, Blythe House
London, England W14 OQX UK
Tel: 44-207-471-2697
Fax: 44-207-471-9864
tmenquiries@vam.ac.uk
http://www.vam.ac.uk/collections/theatre_performance

**Women's Theatre Alliance (WTA)**
2936 N. Southport Ave.
Chicago, IL 60657
Katie Carey Govier
womenstheatre@lycos.com
www.wtachicago.org
> Est. 1992. Fees: $25/yr (Jan-Dec).

**The Writers' Guild of Great Britain**
15 Britannia St.
London, England WC1X 9JN UK
Anne Hogben
Tel: 44-20-7833-0777
Fax: 44-20-78334777
anne@writersguild.org.uk
www.writersguild.org.uk
   TUC-affiliated union for professional writers living or working in UK. Fees: £100 yr (candidate), £150/yr (full).

**Young Playwrights Inc. (YPI)**
P.O. Box 5134, New York, NY 10185
Sheri Goldhirsch
Tel: (212) 594-5440 Fax: (212) 6844902
admin@youngplaywrights.org
www.youngplaywrights.org
   Est. 1981 by Stephen Sondheim and Dramatists Guild members, YPI identifies and develops young US playwrights by involving them as active participants in the highest quality professional productions of their plays. Consideration. Opportunity/Award: Winning playwrights receive a trip to New York City to participate in the Young Playwrights Conference and an off-broadway staged reading of their work. Preference. Style: All except musicals or adaptations. Application. What to submit: submissions not returned. Author must be age 18 or younger. Material must be original. How to submit: Visit our website at www.youngplaywrights.org for details Check Website for details. Deadline: 1/2/2009.

## ONLINE SCRIPT WRITING SOFTWARE

As most Dramatists Guild members know, commercial script writing software (Final Draft and Movie Magic 6) is offered to the membership at a much reduced price. But for some members, even a reduced price is still too much. How about something that's just for free?

We scoured the internet to find script writing programs that could be available to anyone, at anytime, free of charge. Some programs will add features to your software for a minimal cost.

### Distinguishing Features Key for all Programs Listed

1. What formats can I import my script from into the program?
2. What format can I export my script from?
3. Is it a web-based program, a stand-alone program, or a program that works within another program?
4. What script formats does it provide?
5. Are there features for collaboration, comments, or other people viewing my script? What are they?
6. What kind of computer is this program compatible with?
7. Any other key features that may factor into my decision?

The description of each software is provided on-line at the website, reproduced here for your understanding of what's out there and available to you.

**Cinergy Script Editor** by Mindstar
http://www.mindstarprods.com/cinergy/scripteditor.html

Available as a stand-alone program, or built-in to the larger Cinergy Motion Picture Production System. The script editor creates industry standard formatting for motion picture scripts. Scripts created with the Cinergy Script Editor are immediately compatible with the production management features of Cinergy Version 5.

Distinguishing Features

1. You can import a script already written on Final Draft, Movie Magic, Screenwriter 2000, Scriptware, Rich Text Format (RTF) Files, and even plain text.
2. You can export and save your script as an RTF or PDF document.
3. It is a stand-alone program. However, it is also available as a part of the Cinergy Motion Picture Production System.
4. It provides the format for a Screenplay.
5. Your script can only be viewed by you—there is no collaboration element, web-based or otherwise.

Educational Opportunities : Online Script Writing Software    197

6. Compatible with Windows 98SE/Me/2000/XP, 233 MHz Pentium or higher, 10-30MB of available hard disk space, Internet access for online updates. Minimum system RAM: 32MB. Also, Macintosh G3, G4 or G5 with Virtual PC. The pure Macintosh Version (not yet released) will require OS X.
7. Updates are continuously available for download through the Cinergy Update Wizard.

**ScriptSmart**
http://www.bbc.co.uk/writersroom/scriptsmart/index.shtml

Script Smart is the generic name given to a collection of templates for Microsoft Word which automatically format your script to industry specifications as you type. Several layouts are available depending on which version of Script Smart you are using..

Distinguishing Features

1. Does not support import, only new documents.
2. Allows for export as DOC files.
3. Works within Microsoft Word.
4. Depending on the version (see number 7), provides formats for Screenplay; TV Tape-Live; TV Three-Camera; Radio; Stage; Comic Book (alternative), TV Taped Drama; TV Taped Sitcom; Radio Drama; Radio Sketch; Stage; Comic Book.
5. No collaboration features.
6. Depending on the version (see number 7), ScriptSmart is compatible with MS Word 7 (95) on Windows 95, Windows: MS Word 2000 on Windows 98, and MS Word 2001 on Mac OS9.
7. Three versions with varying templates and features:
   a. **ScriptSmart 97** works on MS Word 7 (95) on Windows 95, and provides layouts for Screenplay, Television (Sitcom), and Radio
   b. **ScriptSmart Plus** works on MS Word 7 (95) on Windows 95, with the same layouts as ScriptSmart 97, adding a few added special features and a built-in help guide.
   c. **ScriptSmart Gold** works on Windows: MS Word 2000 on Windows 98.
      Mac: MS Word 2001 on Mac OS9. It is available in both UK and US editions, offering numerous special features and equivalent formats for both sides of the Atlantic. The UK version provides formatting for Screenplay; TV Taped Drama; TV Taped Sitcom; Radio Drama; Radio Sketch; Stage; Comic Book. The US version provides formatting for Screenplay; TV Tape-Live; TV Three-Camera; Radio; Stage; Comic Book (alternative).

**Plotbot**
http://www.plotbot.com/

Plotbot is a web-based collaborative screenwriting application where you can write a screenplay with as many or as few people as you like. Adopting the wiki approach to screenwriting, each element is editable by any member of a project. You can also comment on, delete or restore any element. You can quickly and easily write your screenplay from almost any browser. You just click to edit any element and push submit to store it—no cumbersome page reloads!

"We realize that writing online opens a whole different can of worms than writing on your laptop in a coffee shop, and we've been careful to preserve the privacy of your writing. Our system is constructed such that even the administrators of the site cannot read your private screenplays, and we back up our data every day to insure that you won't lose your work."

Distinguishing Features

1. No ability to import.
2. You can download and export your script as XML or RTF in order to continue your work offline (such as into Final Draft).
3. Web-based program accessible from almost any browser on any computer with an internet connection
4. Provides a Screenplay format.
5. Created with partnerships in mind, allowing multiple writers to add, edit, and comment on one screenplay, while keeping track of who did what. You can designate your script as "private",so no one can see your work, or "public", which allows other writers to see your script.
6. Compatible with Firefox 1.5 and 2.0 for both PC and the Mac, and the most recent version of Safari, and IE 6 and 7 for the PC.
7. An automatic copyright is provided for every script

**RoughDraft**
http://www.salsbury.f2s.com/rd.htm

RoughDraft is a freeware word processor for Windows 95, 98, ME, NT, 2000 and XP. Although suitable for general use, it has features specifically designed for creative writing: novels, short stories, articles, plays and screenplays. It's designed to be as practical as possible, offering all the features you need, but without being complicated or awkward to use.

Distinguishing Features

1. Allows you to import your files from Microsoft Work 6.0, Microsoft Word 97, and HTML.
2. Saves files as RTF and HTML.
3. RoughDraft is a stand-alone program.
4. Provides formats for Normal, Screenplay, and Stage/Radio Play
5. No collaboration features.
6. Compatible with Windows 95, 98, ME, NT, 2000 and XP, not Mac.

## Zhura

http://www.zhura.com/

Zhura provides its members with the most powerful scriptwriting application available online. Our advanced editing tool provides all of the important features you need to produce professionally-formatted scripts with ease. No more software to download, no more applications to upgrade, no more emailing scripts to yourself to get them on your other computer, and no more printing out hardcopies to collaborate with friends.

Zhura provides the most advanced online screenwriting tool in the industry, plus the ability to connect with the global writing community. On Zhura, you can work privately on your own projects, collaborate in private with your friends, or collaborate with the global public community.

Distinguishing Features

1. Allows import and export into Final Draft, Movie Magic, etc., as well as into PDF files.
2. See number 1.
3. Web-based program, so available from any computer with internet access
4. Provides formats for Screenplays, Stage, Radio Dramas, and Television.
5. Three different ways to work: Personal, Private Groups, and Public.
6. Personal allows complete privacy and security for a solitary writer. Provides numerous revision tools and nightly backups.
7. Private Groups allows a fully collaborative workspace, only available for viewing, editing, comments, etc. to invited members.
8. Public allows every member to view your script. When members create a "Script", they are required to answer two questions: 1) Allow commercial use of your work? and 2) Allow modifications of your work? And based on their answers to these questions a specific Creative Commons License is assigned, which allows other members to see, comment, and even edit your work.
9. Available on any computer with internet access.
10. Changes and edits are constantly tracked. Also provides discussion boards, user profiles, internal mail, and instant messaging.

## Celtx

http://www.celtx.com/index.html

Celtx is the world's first all-in-one media pre-production software. It has everything you need to take your story from concept to production. Celtx replaces 'paper, pen & binder' pre-production with a digital approach that's more complete, simpler to work with, and easier to share.

Distinguishing Features

1. Allows for import of any document (including PDF, budget spreadsheets, images, and scripts written in other applications)

2. Provides export as a PDF file.
3. Includes both a stand-alone system as well as a web-based element, where you can save and access your script from any computer.
4. Includes formats for Screenplay, Stage (US and International), AV Scripts (including documentary, music video, and advertising), Audio Play (including radio and podcast), Comic Book, and Plaintext.
5. Allows you to add members to the online Celtx Server so that your team members can comment, edit, add, or just view your script. Your script can also be uploaded to the Project Central, where it can be viewed and commented on by other Celtx users.
6. Supports Microsoft Windows: NT, 2000, XP, Vista, Mac OS X, and Linux
7. Available in numerous different languages.

**Scripped**

Scripped Writer is a free web-based script writing software application you can use right in your web browser. Unlike other screenwriting software, Scripped Writer is built specifically with the needs of the writer in mind. That means it has all the functionality you need without the clutter of features you'll never use.

With a browser based web application you can use Scripped Writer without downloading software and installing it on your machine. Just like Google Docs®, you can use Scripped Writer from any computer with an internet connection. Simply log in to your Scripped user account and get to writing.

Distinguishing Features

1. Allows for import from Final Draft and Microsoft Word.
2. Allows for export as PDF files, as well as into other industry supported software.
3. Online-based web program, so you can access from any computer with internet access.
4. Provides a format for Screenwriting.
5. Although your script is only visible to you, you can use the online community to create a unique profile, interact with your peers, send messages, post articles, and join discussions, find a writing partner, build your network, and improve your visibility as a creative talent.
6. Works on Firefox (2 & up) and Internet Explorer 7 on a Windows based PC and Firefox (2 & up) on a Mac.

# GLOSSARY OF TERMS OF PLAYWRITING & MUSICAL COMPOSITION

DG members often write in after reading a particular article in *The Dramatist* or a feature in an e-newsletter and comment on words, phrases or concepts discussed in the article that are new to them. We've compiled a glossary of these words and phrases to share with you and for your quick reference.

**11:00 Number** - A song that occurs at the climax of a musical theatre production. See also "climactic scene."

**"A" Page** - A revised page of dramatic text that extends onto a second typed page, as indicated by adding an "A" to the page number (i.e. 1, 1A, 2, 3, 4, 4A, etc.)

**Action** - A dramatic event or series of events that form the spine of the plot of a play or musical.

**Adaptation** - A play that is adapted from a previous story; taken from an already existing piece and modified to a particular dramatist's point of view. For more information on how to adapt refer to the article "Adapting Material for the Stage" moderated by Nagle Jackson from the September/October 2000 issue of *The Dramatist*. http://www.dramaguild.com/lounge/articles/adaptsem.pdf

**Antagonist** - The character who provides a dramatic obstacles to the protagonist's primary objective in a play or musical.

**Aristotle's Six Elements of Drama** - From Aristotle's treatise "The Poetics," based on the ancient Greek belief that tragedy was the highest form of theatre.
1. Plot—what happens in a play; the order of dramatic events; the story as opposed to the theme; what happens in the story rather than its interpretive meaning.
2. Theme – what the play means as opposed to what happens (plot); the main idea within the play.
3. Character – the personality an actor represents in a play.
4. Diction/Language/Dialogue – the word choices made by the dramatist and the enunciation of the actors delivering the lines.
5. Music/Rhythm – by music Aristotle meant the sound, rhythm and melody of the speeches.
6. Spectacle – the visual elements of the production of a play; the scenery, costumes and theatrical effects in a production.

**Aside** - A comment or observation made by a character to the audience not heard by other characters onstage.

**Back-story** - Experiences a character has had prior to the main action of the play which add to character motivations and actions.

**Ballad** - In a musical, a romantic song usually in a slow tempo and generally contrasted with an up-tempo song.

**Beat** - A noted pause which interrupts dialogue for the purpose of indicating a significant shift in the direction of a scene.

**Blocking** - The planned physical movement by a director and executed in a scene by actors; sometimes represented as stage directions in a script. Usually during a block rehearsal, the stage manager takes notes about where the actors are positioned and their movement patterns on stage. See also "stage directions".

**Book** - The story and non-musical text of a musical (including dialogue, stage directions, etc.)

**Cadence** - Rhythmic flow of a sequence of sounds or words. In a play, it is often paired with describing the tone and the dialogue of the piece. In music, the series of intervals or chords that ends a phrase or section.

**Caricature** - In a play, a two-dimensional character that exhibits stock character traits; someone drawn from a stereotype or idea of a certain kind of individual.

**Character Arc** - The emotional progress of a given character during the course of the dramatic story.

**Character-driven *vs.* Plot-driven** - A character-driven play is driven by the actions of its characters as opposed to developed plot points that push the story forward, as in a plot-driven play.

**Character Name** - When any character speaks, his or her name appears on the line preceding the dialogue. In screenplays, the name is tabbed to a location that is roughly in the center of the line. In playwriting, typically the name is centered, but with the advent of screenwriting software that automatically positions the character name correctly, it has become acceptable to use a similar format for character names in stage plays.

**Charm Song** - In musical theater, this kind of song allows a character to beguile the audience. An example of a charm song would be "Wouldn't It be Loverly" from *My Fair Lady*.

**Known circumstances** - Specific, defining elements of a character and his or her situation garnered from the exposition in the play.

**Climactic Scene** - The heightened moment in a play where the character makes a decision that will affect the rest of the course of the play as well as his/her life. For a musical, see also "11:00 number".

**Co-Author** - One who is co-credited in the creation of a script or musical score, lyrics or book.

**Complication** - A series of dramatic events that literally "complicate" the story, often appearing in the second act of a three-act dramatic structure, in which "the plot thickens" and pushes towards some sort of inevitable climax.

**Composer** - In musical theatre, a person who writes music with a specific musical notion or voice so that others can weave that music into a theatrical story of sorts. Usually, in musical theater a composer and a lyricist will come together to create a work. For more words of wisdom on collaboration refer to *The Dramatist* article "How To Collaborate" by Betty Comden from the January/February 2007 issue. http://www.dramaguild.com/lounge/articles/howtocollab.pdf

**Continuing Dialogue** - Dialogue spoken by the same character that continues uninterrupted onto the next page, marked with a (cont'd) in a stage play.

**Craft** - The skills, tools and tactics used to write a play or musical; the dramaturgical resources a dramatist uses to create a full and rich theatrical experience.

**Denouement** - The "wrapping up" of dramatic events after the climax of a play or musical; a notion or projection of "life after."

**Dialogue Pages** - The pages in the play which contain dialogue.

**Diction**
1. The word choices made by the playwright
2. The enunciation of the actors speaking the lines

3. The fourth of Aristotle's Six Elements of Drama

**Draft** - A version of a play. One goes through one draft or many drafts before concluding the work on a project.

**Dramaturgy** - The craft or techniques of analyzing the dramatic composition of a play or musical. A "dramaturg" is often a person assigned to work with the writer on clarifying the text and/or an artist who provides historical context for the story in a play or musical. For more information on dramaturgs you can visit the web site for LMDA (Literary Managers and Dramaturgs of the Americas): http://www.lmda.org/blog See also "development".

**Emotional through-line** - The emotive journey that a character makes throughout the course of the story in a play or musical.

**Exploratory Writing** - Exercises a writer does to illuminate certain scenarios in a play or musical currently being constructed or crafted that do not appear in the final dramatic work; informal writing that emphasizes thinking and invites expression—more about discovering ideas as opposed to presenting them.

**Exposition** - Information revealed through the dialogue and dramatic action early on in a play or musical that reveals character background information, basic conflict and the physical setting of the story (time and place).

**Foreshadowing** - Story suggestions or clues given to the audience about upcoming dramatic events in the play.

**Genre** - A specific category to classify a piece of literature. Major classical genres were epic, tragedy, lyric, comedy and satire.

**"I Am" Songs** - In musical theatre, a song that explains a character, a group of characters or a situation.

**"I Want" Songs** - In musical theater, songs that tell us what characters desire and motivate them. Most love songs fit in this category. In *West Side Story* examples include "Something's Coming" and "Tonight." Also, the reprise of "Tonight" is an opportunity for each character to simultaneously express what they want.

**Inciting Incident** - A dramatic exchange (action or dialogue) that introduces the major conflict of the play.

**Impulse** - The instinct that a dramatist follows when writing a play or musical; an initial instinct when beginning the process of story or character creation.

**Interrupt** - When one character cuts off another character's dialogue, sometimes marked with an ellipsis (...), but better marked with a dash (-).

**Leitmotif** - A recurring theme that is used to describe a person, place, or thing. Most often the term is used to describe a recurring musical motif in operas or musicals, but its definition also extends into film scores, video game soundtracks, and other instrumental scores. The term comes from the German "leit", or "to lead", and the French "motif", or theme; the term essentially can be translated as "leading theme."

**Lights Fade** - A common stage direction to end a scene or an act. Involves the onstage lights fading to black.

**Lyricist** - A writer of song lyrics. Often, a lyricist will collaborate with a composer in the writing of an original song, although at times a lyricist can be brought in to put words to previously composed music.

**Metadrama** *or* **Metatheatre** - A dramatic technique in theatre in which the play comments on itself. It can be as small as a moment (for example, referring to an actor as an actor rather than a character), or encompass the entire theme of the play (for example, a play about plays). Plays-within-a-play are also included in metadrama.

**Musical Numbers Page** - A page in a musical script, usually following the cast page, that lists the musical numbers, divided by act, and the characters that sing in them.

**Obstacles** - A dramatic "hurdle" in the story that a character must surpass to reach his objective.

**Parenthetical** - A comment written in parentheses. A parenthetical adds supplementary information or an after-thought to the primary object of discussion, such as: "My mother's hair (which she took such care to curl) became frizzy from the rain."

**Performance** - Any presentation before an audience, invited or paid, including previews and/or rehearsals.

**Plot** - The dramatic events that construct the spine of the story of the play or musical; not to be confused with theme—plot is what happens rather than what it means.

**Plot Point** - A piece of information that furthers the plot.

**Preaching** - Forcing a point of view in the dramatic story that serves the politics and ideas of the dramatist. This is often seen in didactic or agitprop plays.

**Preliminary Pages** - The information pages which precede your play, consisting of a title page, character page, a page denoting setting and time, and optional scene breakdown and quote pages.

**Premise** - To set forth beforehand, as by way of introduction or explanation, the condition(s) for conflict in the world of the dramatic story.

**Props** - Objects used by characters on stage during a play – i.e., a newspaper, shirt, bowl of fruit.

**Hand Prop** - An object small enough to be carried easily.

**Protagonist** - The principal character of a play or musical around which the dramatic action revolves.

**Quote Page** - A page usually following the title page in a play wherein the dramatist acknowledges an influence on their play by placing a quote. Typical sources of these quotes:
 1. The work of another—and often well-known—writer:
    *A solitude ten thousand*
    *fathoms deep*
    *Sustains the bed on which*
    *we lie, my dear;*
    *Although I love you, you will*
    *have to leap;*
    *Our dream of safely has to*
    *disappear.*
       —W.H. Auden, from Craig Lucas in *Reckless*.
 2. A lyric or phrase from a song:
    "*I could escape the feeling. With my China girl...*"
       —David Bowie & Iggy Pop, from David Henry Hwang in *M. Butterfly*
 3. A folk or common saying:
    ALWAYS BE CLOSING
       —Practical Sales Maxim, from David Mamet in *Glengarry Glen Ross*.

**Resolution** - The dramatic moment in a play or musical at which the conflict comes to some kind of conclusion where the protagonist either gets what they want or doesn't.

**Reveal** - A key element about a character or the plot that is released through exposition at a pivotal moment in the text.

**Reversal** - A moment in the plot where a character achieves the opposite of their aim, resulting in a change from good to bad or bad to good.

**Running Time** - The amount of time a play or scene takes to perform.

**Scene Breakdown** - Breaking down each act and scene into sections, which are then briefly described. A scene breakdown can include information for each scene such as setting, time, characters present, page numbers, and any other information the playwright finds relevant. For a short play, or a play with very few locations or times, a scene breakdown is probably unnecessary.

**Score** - The written form of a musical composition.

**Setting** - The environment of the story in a play or musical; the time and place the story takes place in.

**Setting and Time Page** - A page which indicates the time and place the story takes place in. This can be as detailed or as simple as necessary.

**Showtune Structure** - Most show tunes have a verse and a chorus (or "refrain"). The **verse** sets up the premise of a song and can be of most any length, while the **chorus** states the main point of the lyric.

The structure is thirty-two bars long, usually divided into four sections of eight bars a piece in the **AABA** form.
1. *A is the main melody*, repeated twice.
2. *B is the release* or bridge that should contrast with A.
3. *Then A is repeated a third time*, usually with a melodic twist to give the final bars more interest.

From Cohan to Larson, all modern Broadway composers have worked within this structure. Those showtunes that do not use AABA tend to use a slight variation of the form, (AABC) – but the AABA structure and proportions remain the norm. For more information on musical theater visit the web site: http://www.musicals101.com/

**Simultaneous Dialogue** - When two characters speak at the same time with the dialogue written in two side by side columns on the same page. Some playwrights choose to use diagonal slashes to indicate the interruption of speech.

**Source Material** - Original or basic materials of research such as diaries or manuscripts that inform the dramatic story.

**Spine** - The core or center of a dramatic story; a succession of plot points that total up the large arc of the dramatic conflict.

**Status** - A character's relative rank in relation to other characters. Status can include such elements as social standing, wealth, age, health, or any other indicator that places individuals in some sort of hierarchy. Defining a character as high status or low status through their behavior, attitude, or the way they speak is an effective way to heighten the dramatic stakes and create conflict.

**Structure** - The organization or arrangement of sequences of dramatic events in the storytelling of the play or musical that build suspense and arrest an audience's attention. Aristotle (384-322 B.C.) expounded on a long used set of precepts that have been come to be known as the three-act structure.

**Subplot** - The secondary plot to a story that develops the goals, wants and objectives of the secondary characters.

**Subtext** - Subtext is the unspoken thoughts and motives of a characters, the emotional content underneath spoken dialogue.

**Synopsis** - A description of a play or musical which illuminates the primary plot points of the story, often contained in one sentence, a paragraph or a page of narrative.

**Tactics** - Strategies a character uses to reach his or her objective.

**Theme** - What the play is intended to mean as opposed to what happens (plot)—the main idea or message within the play.

**Time** - The time of day, month, and/or year in which your story takes place.

**Title Page** - The first page of a manuscript which includes the title of play or musical, the dramatist's name and contact information.

**Transition** - A moment of change in the flow of storytelling within the play or musical.

**Tone** - A particular emotional quality or intonation in the storytelling that expresses a specific meaning or spirit.

**Universality** - The wide appeal of a story to many different kinds of people and groups that does not only interest a specific demographic.

**Urgency** - The dire need of a character to attain his/her goal in the story, creating conflict and drama.

**Voice** - A trait distinct to each writer; the way the dramatist personally tells a story to the world with a specific aesthetic sensibility; a combination of the writer's syntax, diction, punctuation, character development, and dialogue.

## FORMATTING & SUBMISSION

**Blind Submission** - Having no personal identification on the script itself. Many writing contests will ask the writer to include personal information on a separate title page so the script remains anonymous while in competition.

**Commission** - A play or musical for which a theater company gives a playwright money to write, typically with the understanding that the theater will have the right of first refusal to premiere it.

**Coverage** - The notes prepared by script readers at literary agency, film production company, theater company or script competition.

**Direct Solicitation** - When a theater contacts a dramatist or his agent about submitting a script. Theaters that use this method typically do not want the playwright to initiate the contact.

**Manuscript Format** - Accepted format to use when submitting a script to theatre companies, contests, publishers, agents and other theatre opportunities.

**Professional Recommendation** - A letter of recommendation from a theater professional (director, artistic director, literary manager, etc.) that is often requested when applying or submitting to certain theatres, residencies and development groups.

**SASE** - Self-Addressed Stamped Envelope. Many playwriting competitions will ask the writer to enclose a SASE to acknowledge the receipt of the play.

**SASP** - A Self-Addressed Stamped Postcard is returned to the writer by a theater to acknowledge that they have received the script.

**Submission Fees** - An amount of money that a contest or theater requires in order to enter a script for a festival, contest, or other such theatrical events. In certain instances it is a legitimate cost used to pay readers. For more thoughts on submission fees refer to the article "Playing The Odds" by Steven Ginsberg from the January/February 2007 edition of *The Dramatist*. http://www.dramaguild.com/lounge/articles/playingodds.pdf

**Unsolicited Scripts** - Scripts that are not sent by an agent. If you wish to submit to a specific theater that only requests submission by agents, a viable option would be to send a letter of inquiry.

## Business and Industry Terms

**99-Seat Theatre** - A classification of theater qualified for "showcase" treatment by equity. See Showcase.

**AEA (Actors' Equity Association)** - The labor union that represents more than 45,000 Actors and Stage Managers in the United States. Equity negotiates wages and working conditions and provides a wide range of benefits, including health and pension plans, for its members. Actors' Equity is a member of AFL-CIO, and is affiliated with FIA, an international organization of performing arts unions.

**AEA Approved** - Having submitted the proper contracts, and having been approved ("approving" is defined by Webster's Dictionary as "to give formal or official sanction to") you may place an Actors Equity Association logo on your program and call yourself AEA Approved.

**A.R.T./NY (Alliance of Resident Theatres/New York)** - The umbrella organization that promotes and supports New York's Off-Broadway theatres. It supports nearly 400 not-for-profit New York Off-Broadway theatres and provides workshops, cash grants, loans, and affordable rehearsal and meeting space, as well as increases visibility and marketing for the theatres.

**ASCAP (The American Society of Composers, Authors and Publishers)** - ASCAP is a membership association of more than 275,000 U.S. composers, songwriters, lyricists, and music publishers of every kind of music. Through agreements with affiliated international societies, ASCAP also represents hundreds of thousands of music creators worldwide. ASCAP is the only U.S. performing rights organization created and controlled by composers, songwriters and music publishers, with a Board of Directors elected by and from the membership. ASCAP protects the rights of its members by licensing and distributing royalties for the non-dramatic public performances of their copyrighted works. ASCAP's licensees encompass all who want to perform copyrighted music publicly. ASCAP makes giving and obtaining permission to perform music simple for both creators and users of music.

**Code Production** - Also called "showcase," any production mounted under the terms of the Equity Basic Showcase Code.

**Commercial Use Products** - Various physical property representing a character in a play or using the name, character or the title of the play or otherwise connected with the play or its title.

**Copyright** - Copyright is a form of protection provided by the laws of the United States (title 17, U. S. Code) to the authors of "original works of authorship," including literary, dramatic, musical, artistic, and certain other intellectual works. This protection is available to both published and unpublished works. It is illegal for anyone to violate any of the rights provided by the copyright law to the owner of copyright. These rights, however, are not unlimited in scope. Sections 107 through 121 of the 1976 Copyright Act establish limitations on these rights. In some cases, these limitations are specified exemptions from copyright liability. One major limitation is the doctrine of "fair use," which is given a statutory basis in section 107 of the 1976 Copyright Act. In other instances, the limitation takes the form of a "compulsory license" under which certain limited uses of copyrighted works are permitted upon payment of specified royalties and compliance with statutory conditions. For further information about the limitations of any of these rights, consult the copyright law or write to the Copyright Office.

**Copyright Notice** - A copyright notice is an identifier placed on copies of the work to inform the world of copyright ownership.

**Derivative Work** - A work based upon one or more pre-existing works. A work consisting of editorial revisions, annotations, elaborations, or other modifications which, as a whole, represent an original work of authorship.

**Equity's Defaulting Employers List** - A producer is responsible for ensuring that when an Equity actor is hired, he or she will be able to pay said actor the appropriate amounts, as well as provide the actor with all the necessary benefits as detailed by Actor's Equity. If he or she does not do this, the producer is called a defaulting employer. Equity maintains a defaulting employers list, which can be accessed through the union. No actor, without the consent of Equity, may work with any producer who has been placed on the defaulting employers list (or anyone who has a connection to a defaulting employer), nor can the actor work with any organization or production which violates Equity codes, and therefore could be placed on the list.

**International Federation of Actors (FIA)** - The non-government, independent umbrella organization that represents performers' unions, guilds, and associations internationally. The FIA lobbies for the rights of performers and advocates for the interests of the unions it represents.

**The League of American Theatres and Producers (now, The Broadway League)** - The trade organization for the commercial theater industry in North America, it represents theatre owners, operators, producers, presenters, and suppliers of goods and services to the theatre community. It was founded in 1930 as The League of New York Theatres. The League has jointly presented and administered the Tony Awards with The American Theatre Wing since 1967.

**LORT (League Of Resident Theatres)** - A collective association of 76 not-for-profit theatres throughout the country that has negotiated collective bargaining agreements with Actors' Equity Association, the Society of Stage Directors & Choreographers, and United Scenic Artists. www.lort.org.

**LMDA (Literary Managers and Dramaturgs of America)** - A national network for dramaturgs and literary managers to expand the field of dramaturgy and literary development. http://www.lmda.org/ SEE ALSO "dramaturgy."

**MPC (Members Project Code)** - An Actors' Equity Association contract.

**The National Endowment For The Arts** - A public agency dedicated to supporting excellence in the arts, both new and established, bringing the arts to all Americans, and providing leadership in arts education. Established by Congress in 1965 as an independent agency of the federal government, the Endowment is the nation's largest annual funding organizations of the arts, bringing great art to all 50 states, including rural areas, inner cities, and military bases.

## Educational Opportunities : Glossary

**PAC** - Performing Arts Center.

**Royalties** - Payments made by a licensee (e.g., a publisher or producer) to a licensor (e.g., a playwright) based upon the continued use of an asset (e.g., a play). This is often, but not always, in the form of a percentage of the gross weekly box office receipts from a theater.

**Signatory** - One who signs a contract, either as an individual, or on behalf of an entity (e.g., a CEO who signs for the employer corporation).

**Single-Unit Production** - A single production presented by an individual or group, without benefit of an organization which survives the production, and expressly excludes any individual or group that regularly produces under an Equity contract.

**Showcase** - Any production mounted under the terms of the Equity Basic Showcase Code. See also "Code Production" and "Production."

**SSD&C (Society of Stage Directors and Choreographers)** - An independent labor union for stage directors and choreographers.

**Subsidiary Rights** - Dispositions of a property, such as a play or musical, that are made subsequent to the production for which one is contracting.

**Theatre Communications Group** - The national organization for the American Theatre. http://www.tcg.org/

**Theater for Young Audiences (TYA)** - The United States chapter of the Association International du Theatre pour l'Enfance et la Jeunesse ("ASSITEJ"). TYA is a national service organization whose mission is to promote and support professional theatre for young audiences internationally. This organization works to connect artists, theatres, and other professionals in the promotion of the cause of theatre for a young audience, supports festivals and productions, prints publications about theatre for young audiences for the entire American theatre community, and represents the United States within the ASSITEJ.

**TKTS** - Booths in New York City (Times Square, South Street, and Downtown Brooklyn) founded by the Theatre Development Fund ("TDF") where you can get half-priced and discounted tickets for Broadway and Off-Broadway shows. Established 1973.

**West End Theatre** - First-class commercial theater district in London, analogous to Broadway.

**Work for Hire** - When an employer is considered the author of a work created by another.

# Special Interests

## TEN-MINUTE AND SHORT PLAY OPPORTUNITIES

Because of the popularity of the ten-minute play, we thought it might serve a lot of you to list those opportunities that are particular to short plays and ten-minute plays. *If the submission is in italics, review dates and submission procedures on the website of the sponsoring organization; at press time, we weren't able to verify the information posted.*

### General Sites

http://www.burryman.com/submissions.html#sub
http://www.aact.org/cgi-bin/webdata_contests.pl?cgifunction=Search
http://enavantplaywrights.yuku.com/forums/3/t/Opportunities-10-Minute-amp-Other-Short-Plays.html

### Publishers Of Ten-Minute Plays

**Brooklyn Publishers** - www.brookpub.com. Please send a query letter and sample pages either via email to submissions@brookpub.com (preferred) or via postal mail to: Brooklyn Publishers, Attn: Editor, 1841 Cord St., Odessa, TX 79762. Please provide a brief description of the play, cast size and gender breakdown, running time, and any production history or awards. As a writing sample, feel free to attach the first 10 pages of the play (5 pages for plays with running times of 10 minutes or less) in PDF or Microsoft Word format.

**Big Dog Plays** - www.bigdogplays.com "We publish short plays (under 30 minutes) only as collections. Therefore, the playwright should send several short plays together as one submission. We prefer produced works. We need to see the entire script. Also, we like playwrights to include a cover letter, production history, all music for musicals (CD and score), and a SASE. We don't accept email submissions. Response time is 2-3 months."

**Meriweather** – a query letter is suggested, but ten-minute plays should be appropriate for the school or church market and most should be in a collection of plays. Production tested plays are encouraged. Editor, Contemporary Drama Service, 885 Elkton Drive, Colorado Springs, CO 80907. Or e-mail query letters (no attachments) to: editor@meriwether.com www.meriwetherpublishing.com/school.aspx

**NewPlays -** All plays to be considered for publication must have been successfully produced for their intended audience, directed by someone other than the author. A simple cover letter with a production history, and perhaps a program or review, is appropriate. Multiple submissions are acceptable; and should be so noted in your cover letter. Patricia Whitton Forrest, Editor and Publisher, New Plays Incorporated, Box 5074, Charlottesville, VA 22905.

**One Act Play Depot** - oneactplays.net. $30 royalties per performance with standard contract. Submit through submissions@oneactplays.net or One Act Play Depot, Box 335, Spiritwood, SK, Canada, S0J 2M0

**Pioneer Drama Service** - www.pioneerdrama.com/playwrights/submit.asp - A query letter or email is suggested: http://www.pioneerdrama.com//contactus.asp?ID=5 . Plays must be accompanied by a Synopsis/Description, Cast List and Breakdown (i.e. 5M, 6W), Running Time, Set Design, Prop List, Recording of Music (when applicable). All plays received will be considered for publication and will usually be accepted or rejected within four months. Send submissions to: Editor, Pioneer Drama Service, Post Office Box 4267, Englewood, CO 80155-4267

## CALENDAR LISTINGS

### January

**Inspirato Festival, Toronto Ten Minute Play Festival**
Inspirato Festival
www.inspiratofestival.ca
http://www.inspiratofestival.ca/write-a-play.php
   **Consideration.** Remuneration: $100, production. **Preference.** Length: 8-12 minutes. Content/Subject Matter: sense of taste must be an important element of your play. **Application.** See website for online submission (www.inspiratofestival.ca/write-a-play2.php). Attach script in a WORD Document. The cover page should only have the title of the play, the playwright's name and the list of characters. The pages should be numbered. **Deadline:** January 4.

**Premiere One-Act Competition**
Moving Arts
www.movingarts.org/submission_guidelines.html
   **Consideration.** $10 entry fee* per script (made out to Moving Arts). Remuneration: $200. **Preferences.** One-Acts. **Application.** Submit script, cover letter, SASE to Moving Arts, Premiere One-Act Competition, P.O. BOX 481145, Los Angeles, CA 90048. Playwright's name should appear only on the cover letter and nowhere on the script. Scripts must be three-hole punched, preferably with a cover--please do not send loose sheets or spiral bound scripts. **Deadline:** Nov 1 - Jan 31 (postmark).

### February

**10-minute Play Festival**
Heartland Theatre Company
P. O. Box 1833, Bloomington, IL 61702
(309) 452-8709
www.heartlandtheatre.org
playfest@heartlandtheatre.org
   **Consideration.** Fees: $25 **Preference.** Length: 10-Minute. Content/Subject Matter: Yearly theme, check website. Material Must Be: unproduced. **Application.** Submit play by e-mail or a hard copy to Heartland Theatre Company, P. O. Box 1833, Bloomington, IL 61702, (Attention: Play Fest 2008) and see online entry form at: www.heartlandtheatre.org. **Deadline:** February 1, 2008.

**Theatre Oxford 10-Minute Play Contest**
Theatre Oxford
10 Minute Play Contest
P. O. Box 1321, Oxford, MS 38655
Dinah Swan, Contest Director: (662) 236-5052
www.10minuteplays.com
> **Consideration.** production, contest. Fees: $10 made out to Theatre Oxford. Remuneration: $1000 prize. **Preference.** Length: max 10 pages. Material Must Be: unproduced. **Application.** Assemble script as follows: Optional cover letter; a title page with the play's title, author's name, address, phone number, and email address. (This is the only place the author's name should appear.) The second page should contain a cast of characters list and time and place information. Do not include a synopsis or any directorial information. The third page will be the first page of the script. Write the play's title at the top of this page. The other pages of the play follow. Staple or paper clip the play. Do NOT use binders or folders of any kind. Plays cannot be returned. Enclose a SASP if you want assurance that your play was received. Submit to: Theatre Oxford 10 Minute Play Contest, P. O. Box 1321, Oxford, MS 38655. **Deadline:** February 15, postmarked.

**10 by 10 in the Triangle**
The Arts Center
300-G East Main Street, Carrboro, NC 27510
(919) 929-2787
www.artscenterlive.org
infor@artscenterlive.org
> **Remuneration.** $100 plus travel stipend. **Preference.** 10 minute plays. **Application.** For each play, send two separate emails to theatre@artscenterlive.org. The first e-mail regards playwright contact information and the second regards contents of the play. E-mail 1 – the subject line and the attached file retain the same name, which is the title of the play followed by the phrase "contact info." For example, if the name of the play is *Poker Face*, the subject line and attached file would read "Poker Face contact info". The attached file only contains the title page with contact information. Please use the full title of the play as numerous plays with similar titles are often received. Email 2 – the subject line and the attached file retain the same name, which is the title of the play. For example, the subject line of this email is Poker Face and the attached file is Poker Face. This file contains cast, set requirements, and script. No contact information, please. If you are submitting two scripts, please send four separate emails. Please do not zip the files. **Submission period:** January-February 15, 2009.

MARCH

**10-Minute International Play Competition**
Fire Rose Productions
10-Minute Play Competition
11246 Magnolia Blvd., NoHo Theatre & Arts District, CA 91601
(818) 766-3691
www.fireroseproductions.com
info@fireroseproductions.com
> **Consideration.** Fees: $5 each play. Remuneration: production, cash prize.
> **Preference.** Length: 10 minutes. **Application.** Submit unbound play, fee, and

application (see website) to 10-Minute Play Competition, Fire Rose Productions, 11246 Magnolia Blvd., NoHo Theatre & Arts District, CA 91601. **Deadline:** March 2009, postmarked

**Ten-Minute Play Contest**
Princeton University Ten-Minute Play Contest
Theater and Dance Program
185 Nassau Street, Princeton University, Princeton NJ 08544
(609) 258-8562
www.princeton.edu
> **Consideration.** Youth award. Remuneration: First Prize: $500.00; Second Prize: $250.00; Third Prize: $100.00. **Preference.** Length: 10-Minute. Author Must Be: Any student who is in the eleventh grade. **Application.** Submit one copy of play, include name, address, and phone number on submission and online form, www.princeton.edu/~visarts/tenminply.htm. Submit to: Princeton Ten-Minute Play Contest, Theater and Dance Program, 185 Nassau Street, Princeton University, Princeton NJ 08544. **Deadline:** March 1, postmarked

**Estrogenius Short Play Showcase**
EstroGenius/Manhattan Theatre Source
177 MacDougal Street, NY, NY 10011
(212) 260-4698
www.estrogenius.org
estrogenius.festival@gmail.com
> **Preferences.** Only new short plays by female writers, no monologues. Length: 10-15 minutes. Simple production values. **Application.** See website for "cover sheet." Submit play, completed cover sheet, and character breakdown to Manhattan Theatre Source, Attn: ESTROGENIUS SHORT PLAY SHOWCASE - play selection, 177 MacDougal Street, NY, NY 10011. **Deadline:** January 15 - March 15, 2009.

**Hurricane Season Playwriting Competition**
The Eclectic Theatre Company
5312 Laurel Canyon Boulevard, Valley Village, CA 91607
(818) 508-3003
www.hurricaneseasontheatre.com
> **Consideration.** Fees: $10 before Feb 15th, $15 before March 15, (processing fee). Remuneration: (6) $75 prizes will be awarded to semi-finalists restaged in the 5th or 6th weekend, (3) $125 prizes (in addition to other winnings) will be awarded to finalists restaged in the 7th weekend, (1) $500 prize (in addition to other winnings) will be awarded as determined by audience voting of the 7th weekend. **Preference.** Length: 15-35 minutes. Minimal set. No one-person plays. Material Must Be: unpublished, unproduced in California. **Application.** Submit two (2) paper copies of your script (no personal info on the script), accompanied by a cover letter that includes name, address, phone number, e-mail, and source along with a check payable to The Eclectic Company Theatre. Submit to: Hurricane Season 2008,C/O The Eclectic Company Theatre, 5312 Laurel Canyon Blvd., Valley Village, CA 91607. **Deadline:** March 15, 2008.

**"Summer Shorts" Festival**
Theatre Limina
www.theatrelimina.org
> **Consideration.** Production. **Preference.** Length: 20 minutes. Production: 4 actors or fewer. Content/Subject Matter: theme for 2008 is "Summer Shorts: Bermuda Shorts." **Application.** Include two electronic copies of each script in Microsoft Word format (.doc) as E-mail attachments, one bearing your name and contact information, the other completely devoid of any identifying information. In the text of the E-mail message, include performance history for each script. If desired, include a brief statement about yourself as a playwright and what you hope to extract from this experience. Submit to: Eric Nelson at SummerShorts08@gmail.com. **Deadline:** March 30th

**Beyond Convention**
Hunger Artists Theatre Company
699-A S. State College Blvd, Fullerton, California 92831
(714) 680-6803
www.hungerartists.com
beyondconvention@gmail.com
> **Consideration.** Remuneration: production. **Preference.** Length: approximately ten minutes. Content/Subject Matter: challenge normal theatre conventions. **Application.** Submit script (a doc or pdf), a cast list, title page including your contact information, and bio to beyondconvention@gmail.com. **Deadline:** March 31

## APRIL

**EATfest**
EATheatre, Emerging Artists Theatre
464 W. 25th St. #4, New York, NY 10001-6501
(212) 247-2429
EATheatre.org
www.EATheatre.org/submissions.php
> **Consideration.** Remuneration: production. **Preferences.** No monologues. Length: 10 to 20 minutes. Material Must Be: unproduced in NYC, unpublished. **Application.** Submit online via website (preferred), or send play to Emerging Artists Theatre, Attention: Playwrights Manager, 464 W. 25th St. #4, New York, NY 10001-6501. Include play and a letter including your name, telephone number, address and e-mail address. **Deadline:** April 1.

**li'l sticky, the 10-minute bar play series**
Blue Box Productions
blueboxworld@gmail.com
http://web.mac.com/blueboxworld
> **Consideration.** Remuneration: production. **Preference.** Length: no more than 10 pages. Content/Subject Matter: plays must be set in a bar, 4 characters or less. **Application.** Each play must have: a title page with title, writer's name(s) and contact information, production history and page numbers must be on each page. Plays must be in pdf, final draft or word format. Submit to: blueboxworld@gmail.com, with subject line ' Li'l Sticky 10-minute play submission.' **Deadline:** rolling

**Festival of Originals**
Theatre Southwest
944 Clarkcrest, Houston, Texas 77063
www.theatresouthwest.org
http://www.theatresouthwest.org
> **Consideration.** Remuneration: production, $100. **Preference.** No Monologues. Length: 20 minutes. Material Must Be: unproduced. **Application.** Submit script, $5 fee, plot summary to Theatre Southwest, 944 Clarkcrest, Houston, Texas 77063,Attention: Festival Submissions; or email mimi@theatresouthwest.org. **Deadline:** April 1

**Moments of Play: A Festival of One-Acts**
Salem Theatre Company
Catherine Bertrand
(978) 790-8546
info@salemtheatre.com
www.salemtheatre.com
> **Consideration.** Remuneration: production only. **Preference.** Length: not longer than 10 minutes. Minimal scene set up. **Application.** Submit the play, brief synopsis not exceeding one page, and character breakdown to: info@salemtheatre.com; or mail to P.O. Box 306, Salem, MA 01970. **Deadline:** April 2

**Salute UR Shorts New Play Festival**
Rapscallion Theatre Collective
1111 Putnam Ave #2, Brooklyn, NY 11221
www.rapscalliontheatrecollective.com
rapscalliontheatre@gmail.com
> **Consideration.** production. Preference. Length: 10-15 minutes. **Application.** Submit play to rapscalliontheatre@gmail.com (preferred method), or mail to 1111 Putnam Ave #2, attn: Rey Hewitt, Brooklyn, NY 11221. **Deadline:** April 15th

## MAY

**Ten Minute New Play Festival**
FUSION Theatre
700 1st Street NW, Albuquerque, New Mexico 87102
www.fusionabq.org
jeng@fusionabq.org
> **Consideration.** production, award. Fees: $5. Disclosure: offset printing costs, Remuneration: jury prize. **Preference.** Length: 10 pages or less, Content/Subject Matter: see website. Material Must Be: unproduced, not previously submitted. **Application.** Play with title page and contact info, fee with e-submission at: http://thecell.fatcow.com/store/page6.html, or mail to: FUSION Theatre Co., Attn: Jen Grigg, 700 1st Street NW, Albuquerque, New Mexico 87102. **Deadline:** May, exact deadline and theme announced in February, check website.

**New Rocky Mountain Voices Competition**
The Westcliffe Center for the Performing Arts
Steve Miller, New Rocky Mountain Voices Program Coordinator
(719) 783-9344
smiller012@centurytel.net
www.jonestheater.com/NRMV-2008.htm
    **Consideration.** Fees: $5 for each play submitted (check out to "WCPA").
**Preference.** Length: not exceeding 30 minutes; 6 or fewer actors. Author Must Be: currently residing in or attending an educational institution in Arizona, Colorado, or New Mexico. Material Must Be: unpublished. **Application.** Send four copies of the manuscript with no mention of the author's name or contact information anywhere in the manuscript, fee, cover letter to include a summary of the author's theater and playwriting experience and goals, mailing address, email address, telephone number and other pertinent contact information. Send to: New Rocky Mountain Voices, C/O Custer County Library, PO Box 689, Westcliffe, CO, 81252 (for United States Postal Service); or New Rocky Mountain Voices, C/O Custer County Library, 209 Main Street, Westcliffe, CO, 81252 ( for UPS or FEDEX). **Deadline:** May 1.

**Rogue Valley 10-Minute Plays Festival**
Art Work Enterprises
www.ashlandnewplays.org
www.ashlandnewplays.org/participate-tmpf-playwrights.html
    **Consideration.** Production and development. **Preference.** Length: 12 pages or less. **Application.** E-mail script as pdf or word file with a subject line of "TMPF Submission" to info@AshlandNewPlays.org. **Deadline:** February 1 - May 1.

**The Chameleon Theatre Circle 10th Annual New Play Contest**
The Chameleon Theatre Circle
819 E. 145th St., Burnsville, MN 55337
(952) 937-5645
www.chameleontheatre.org
chameleon@seetheatre.org
    **Consideration.** Remuneration: 3-5 Winners will receive $25, reading. **Preference.** Length: 15 pages or less. Material Must Be: unproduced. **Application.** See website http://www.seetheatre.org/newplay/NPC9-EntryForm.pdf Submit three (3) copies of each script to 9th Annual New Play Contest, The Chameleon Theatre Circle, 819 E. 145th St.; Burnsville, MN 55337. Do not bind any author identification with your scripts. Include the show's title on at least the first bound page. **Deadline:** Rolling until May 4, 2009.

**Young Playwrights 10-Minute Play Contest**
The Image Theater
Ten Minute Play Contest Entry
68 Oakland Street, Lowell, MA 01851
(978) 441-0102
www.imagetheater.com
    **Consideration.** Type of Opportunity: youth award, production. Remuneration: First prize $100 and a full production; Second Prize, $50 and a staged reading; Third Prize: $25 and a staged reading. **Preference.** Length:10 pages. Production: 6 characters or less, simple set. Author Must Be: 14-18 years old and live near Lowell, Mass. **Application.** Submissions must be bound, with a cover page including your name, address, phone number, and e-mail, if applicable. Submit to: The Image Theater, Ten Minute Play Contest Entry, 68 Oakland Street, Lowell, MA 01851. **Deadline:** May 25.

## June

**The Actors' Theatre 15th Annual Ten-Minute Play Contest**
The Actors' Theatre
1001 Center St., Suite 12, Santa Cruz, CA 95060
(831) 425-1003
www.actorssc.org
www.actorssc.org/contests.php#810s
    **Consideration.** Fees: $10 per play. **Preference.** Length: 10 pages maximum. Minimal set requirements. Material Must Be: unproduced, unpublished. **Application.** Submit 5 copies of your play (securely bound, preferably in a soft cover). Two types of cover pages: 1) a separate cover letter, which includes your name, address, phone number, e-mail and the play title. 2) the play title on each copy. No identifying information on the script other than the title. Submission: mail five hard copies (see address above) to TEN-MINUTE PLAY CONTEST. **Deadline:** June 1.

**One Act Play Festival**
Circus Theatricals
(310) 226-6144 ext. 1
info@circustheatricals.com
www.circustheatricals.com/playwrights.html
www.circustheatricals.com
    **Preference.** Length: 15 pages or less, simple production value. **Application.** Submit three copies of full script, typed and securely bound. No contact info on script/ separate title page with contact info. Short bio. Previous production history. Submit to: Circus Theatricals, Attn: One Act Plays Festival 2008, PO Box 586, Culver City, CA 90232. **Deadline:** June 30, 2008

**At Play(s) 4**
Women At Play(s)
www.womenatplays.com
mariannesawchuk@hotmail.com
    **Consideration.** Remuneration: depends on box office. **Preference.** Length: 20 minutes or less. Content/Subject Matter: All characters must be female. Author Must Be: female. Material Must Be: unproduced and unpublished. **Application.** Submit play with contact info to: mariannesawchuk@hotmail.com. **Deadline:** June 30

## July

**Future 10**
Future Tenant
Stacey Vespaziani
Future 10 Play Submissions
3251 Pinehurst Ave., Pittsburgh, PA 15216
svespaz@mac.com
www.futuretenant.org/programs_FutureTen.html
    **Consideration.** Production. **Preference.** Length: approx 10 pages. Theme: "Life in Pittsburgh." Production: Cast size 2-6, limited set/prop requirements. **Application.** Submit four copies of play, plus a cover letter with all contact info and title of play. No contact info or name should be on submitted scripts. **Deadline:** July 15

## August

Pick of the Vine
Little Fish Theatre
www.littlefishtheatre.org
> **Preference.** Minimal set requirements, 6 or fewer characters. **Application.** Email script with contact info to melanie@littlefishtheatre.org or mail hard copy to: Melanie Jones, Little Fish Theatre, 619 West 38th St, San Pedro CA 90731. http://www.littlefishtheatre.org/scripts.html

## September

**IN10 National Play Competition**
UMBC Department of Theatre
1000 Hilltop Circle, Baltimore, MD 21250
www.umbc.edu/theatre/In10.html
> **Consideration.** Remuneration: $1,000 prize and a staged reading. **Preference.** Length: 10 minutes. Content/Subject Matter: "plays written for female characters age 16 to 30" **Application.** See website. Submit play and application to: Professor Susan McCully, 10-Minute Play Competition, UMBC Department of Theatre, 1000 Hilltop Circle, Baltimore, MD 21250. **Deadline:** September 1st

**Festival of One-Act Plays**
Theatre Three
P.O. Box 512, Port Jefferson, NY 11777-0512
(631) 928-9202
www.theatrethree.com
www.theatrethree.com/oneactsubmissionguidelines.htm
> **Consideration.** Remuneration: small stipend, production. **Preference.** Length: 40 minutes maximum. Simple set, 8 actors or less. Material Must Be: unproduced, no adaptations, musicals, or children's plays. **Application.** Submit a cover letter, a synopsis, and a resume along with one copy of the play. Cover sheet of play should have title, author, author's address, author's telephone number, and author's email address (if available). Plays should be neatly bound or stapled on the left-hand corner. (No loose pages and no binders, please.) All submissions must include a standard SASE for correspondence. Submit to The 13th Annual Festival of One-Act Plays, Attn: Jeffrey Sanzel, Artistic Director, THEATRE THREE, P.O. Box 512, Port Jefferson, NY 11777-0512. **Deadline:** September 30 (postmark).

## October

**Kansas City Women's Playwriting Festival**
Potluck Productions
7338 Belleview, Kansas City, MO 64114
www.kcpotluckproductions.com
> **Consideration.** Remuneration: production. **Preference.** Length: 10-20 minutes. Author Must Be: female. Material Must Be: unpublished. **Application.** Send two (2) paper copies of your script (bound), a show synopsis, resume, and cover letter. Enclose two (2) SASE envelopes or postcards. Submit to: Potluck Productions,

7338 Belleview, Kansas City, MO 64114. **Deadline:** Oct. 1 2008. http://www.kcpotluckproductions.com/script_submissions.htm

**ShowOff! Camino Real International Playwriting Festival**
Camino Real Playhouse
ShowOff!
31776 El Camino Real, San Juan Capistrano, CA 92675
www.caminorealplayhouse.org/ShowOffs.html
info@city-theater.org, pantheater@comcast.net
> **Consideration.** Contest, production. Fees: $10 per play. Disclosure: for use as winner stipends. Remuneration: not specified. **Preference.** Length: 10 minutes. **Application.** Submit plays unbound (stapled is OK) with your full contact info on the cover or title page to: ShowOff!, Camino Real Playhouse, 31776 El Camino Real, San Juan Capistrano, CA 92675. **Deadline:** October 15th each year

## NOVEMBER

**Source Festival**
1835 14th St., NW, Washington, DC 20009
(202) 315-1305
www.sourcedc.org/sourcefestival/html/10minute.html
www.sourcedc.org/sourcefestival/html/submissions.html
> **Consideration.** Remuneration: production. **Preference.** Length: 10 minutes. Material Must Be: unpublished. **Application.** Submit play with contact info on title page and submission form on website. Plays only accepted in following formats: .doc, .pdf, or .rtf. All pages must have number and include title of play and name of playwright. One submission per applicant. **Deadline:** November, check website for details

**National Ten-Minute Play Contest**
Actors Theatre of Louisville
www.actorstheatre.org
www.actorstheatre.org/humana_contest.htm
> **Consideration.** Remuneration: $1000, production. **Preference.** Length: 10 pages or less. Author Must Be: US citizen. Material Must Be: unproduced, not previously submitted. **Application.** Submit play with contact info to: National Ten-Minute Play Contest, Actors Theatre of Louisville, 316 West Main Street, Louisville, KY 40202-4218. **Deadline:** November 2009, check website for details

**Snowdance 10 Minute Comedy Festival**
Over Our Head Players
SNOWDANC
c/o Sixth Street Theatre
318 6th St., Racine, WI, 53403
www.overourheadplayers.org
> **Consideration.** production, prize. Remuneration: A cash award of $300.00, $100.00 to second and third place. **Preference.** Length: 10 minutes. Content/Subject Matter: comedy. Material Must Be: unpublished. **Application.** Submit play with contact info to SNOWDANCE, c/o Sixth Street Theatre, 318 6th St.,Racine, WI, 53403. **Deadline:** November, check website for details.

**Ten-Minute Play Contest**
Lakeshore Players
Outreach Committee
4820 Stewart Ave, White Bear Lake, MN 55110
www.lakeshoreplayers.com
>**Consideration.** Remuneration: production, $10 per performance. **Preference.** Length: 10 minutes. Production: 5 or fewer characters. **Application.** Submit two copies of script (One with contact information, one with title only) to: Lakeshore Players Outreach Committee, 4820 Stewart Ave. White Bear Lake, MN 55110. **Deadline:** November, check website for details

## December

**Queer Shorts**
StageQ
Queer Shorts, c/o StageQ
PO Box 8876, Madison, WI. 53708-8876
www.stageq.com
>**Preference.** Length: 5-15 minutes. Content/Subject Matter: queer lifestyle.
>**Application.** Email play, paragraph synopsis, production requirements, cast breakdown, and if there are any queer characters or nudity to QueerShorts@stageq.com, or mail to: Queer Shorts, c/o StageQ, PO Box 8876, Madison, WI. 53708-8876.
>**Deadline:** October, check website for details

**6 Women Play Festival**
6 Women Play Festival
c/o Pikes Peak Arts Council
PO Box 1073, Colorado Springs, CO 80901
www.sixwomenplayfestival.com
www.sixwomenplayfestival.com/guidelines.html
>**Remuneration.** $100 and a travel stipend to attend the festival. **Preference.** Length: 10 pages. Content/Subject Matter: theme of "changes and transitions." Author Must Be: female. Material Must Be: unpublished, unproduced. **Application.** Submit three copies of play (bound with staple only) with title only. Include one unbound sheet which includes title of play, author's name and address, email, and phone number.
>**Submission period:** September 1 -December 31.

## Rolling Deadline

**Annual Jersey Voices Festival**
Chatham Playhouse
23 North Passaic Avenue, Chatham, New Jersey 07928
(973) 635-7363
www.chathamplayers.org/jerseyvoices.html
jerseyvoices@chathamplayers.org
> **Preference.** Length: 20 minute or less. Author Must Be: New Jersey playwright. **Application.** Submit play to Jersey Voices c/o CCP, P.O. Box 234, Chatham, NJ 07928 or email (in Word of PDF format) to jerseyvoices@chathamplayers.org. **Deadline:** rolling

**Chester Horn Short Play Festival**
TheatreRats
www.theatrerats.com
> **Consideration.** Remuneration: production. **Preference.** Length: no more than 15 pages. **Application.** Submit script (PDF or Word) to scripts@theatrerats.com. **Deadline:** rolling.

**Quickies - the annual festival of shorts**
Live Girls! Theater
www.livegirlstheater.org
> **Consideration.** production or reading. **Preferences.** Small cast and low production requirements. Length: 10-minute. Author Must Be: Female. **Application.** Email plays and include your bio\resume, production history for plays submitted to: submissions@livegirlstheater.org. Attach plays as Word docs. **Deadline:** ongoing.

**SAS PlayFEST**
Atlantis Playmakers
4611 Monroe St., Hollywood FL, 33021
www.atlantisplaymakers.com
> **Consideration.** reading/production. Remuneration: award. **Preference.** Length: 15 minutes or less. Production: 2-5 actors, simple set. Content/Subject Matter: theme-based, see website. Material Must Be: unproduced. **Application.** Submit to 4611 Monroe St Hollywood FL, 33021, or email Word format ONLY to kdb@AtlantisPlaymakers.com. Entries must include a cover page with the playwright's name, address, phone, and e-mail. **Deadline:** rolling, see website

## INTERNATIONAL SUMMER THEATRE FESTIVALS THAT PRODUCE NEW WORK

We thought it would be of interest to you to know the various festivals around the world that you can certainly visit, should you be in that part of the world, and perhaps more importantly (and in many cases) submit your work to – therefore giving you a very good reason to travel!

### AUSTRALIA

**ASSITEJ World Congress and Performing Arts Festival for Young People**
www.assitej2008.com.au
   A festival of children's theatre organized by ASSITEJ, the International Association of Theatre for Children and Young People. The festival occurs in different locations in the world once every three years (2008's Festival was in Adelaide, while 2011's will be in Copenhagen, Denmark, and Malmo, Sweden).

**Brisbane Festival**
Box 3943, South Brisbane, Qld 4101.
(61) 7-833-5400
www.brisbanefestival.com.au
   A festival held biennially that showcases theatre, dance, music, circus, opera, and multimedia performances in numerous venues across Brisbane. The goal is to create new work, foster exchanges between local, national, and international companies and artists, and involve the community by sponsoring debates, dialogues, and fostering grassroots support.

**Melbourne Fringe Festival**
Box 2953, Fitzroy Victoria 3065.
(61) 3-8412-8788
www.melbournefringe.com.au
   The goal of this annual, open-access festival is to bring creative, innovative, and contemporary works by independent artists to broader Melbourne audiences.

### AUSTRIA

**Bregenz Festival**
Platz der Wiener Symphoniker 1, A-6900 Bregenz. (43) 5574-407-0
www.bregenzerfestspiele.com
   This summer festival of music, opera, and theatre involves numerous different venues, including the famed "Floating Stage", a 700-seat outdoor theatre where large-scale musical performances and operas are performed. Bregenz's smaller theatres house operettas and contemporary theatre, often premieres.

**Salzburg Festival**
Hofstallgasse 1, Box 140, A-5010 Salzburg. (43) 662-8045-500.
www.salzburgfestival.com
   This festival features performances of opera, music, and theatre, from classical works to avant-garde experimentation, all performed in the numerous beautiful theatres of Salzburg. According to Hugo von Hoffmansthal, a founding member of the festival, "Dramatic play-acting in the strongest sense is our intention; routine, run-of-the-mill performances have no place here."

**Wiener Festwochen**
Lehárgasse 11, A-1060 Vienna.
(43) 589-22-0
www.festwochen.at
   This annual summer festival involves hundreds of events, comprised of music, theatre, and dance. The performances range from antiquity and classical works to premieres and new works from outstanding artists in twenty countries.

## Belgium

**Momentum Festival**
Bains::Connective, Berthelot 34, 1197
Brussels, Vorst/Forest. (32) 2-534-48-55
www.momentum-festival.org
    This annual summer festival aims to promote and express the artistic form of performance art. It is a forum for performance artists to share their work (because it cannot exist if it is not shared), and for audiences to become more familiar with the art form and the international artists of very high caliber.

## Bosnia and Herzegovina

**Teatarfest Sarajevo**
Fehim Serdarevic, Pruscakova 12, 71 000
Sarajevo. (387) 33-442-958
www,tf.com.ba
    This annual summer festival provides a forum for international theatre groups to come together and share their artistic experience. It aims to showcase unique and creative projects, while researching the artistic and technical elements, as well as to promote works that explore new spaces and media. The festival explores the technical possibilities of the theatre, the cooperation of numerous artists and theatre groups, and provides a meeting place for the exchange of theatrical experiences.

## Brazil

**Festival Internacional de Londrina**
Rua Senador Souza Naves, 75, Sala 42,
Cep 86010, Londrina, Parana.
(55) 43-3322-1787
www.filo.art.br
    This festival showcases theatrical work from premiere artists both nationally and internationally with the theme of tolerance and cultural difference. It supports the communication and exchange between artists with different techniques and aesthetics, brought together through the transformative power of the "theatrical act."

**Festival Internacional de Teatro de São José do Rio Preto**
Praça Jornalista Leonardo Gomes, n° 01
(Praça Cívica), Centro-15015-110, São
José do Rio Preto / SP. (55) 17-3215-1830
www.festivalriopreto.com.br
    This festival delves into the conception, process, and strategies of contemporary theatre, supporting inquisitive, provocative, and exciting new works. It encourages the deconstruction of boundaries between art forms—such as dance, visual arts, music, literature, and technology—as well as taking risks and reaching out of comfortable territory.

**Festival Internacional de Teatro de Bonecos**
Rua Francisco Bicalho, 1912, Caicara,
Belo Horizante, MG Cep 30720-340.
(55) 52-614-600
www.festivaldebonecos.com.br
    During this summer festival, puppetry companies (from Brazil, as well as internationally) perform in numerous different venues. The festival also involves workshops, film showings, book releases, a parade, and numerous other activities.

## Canada

**Banff Summer Arts Festival**
The Banff Centre, Box 1020, Banff AB
T1L 1H5. (403) 762-6100
www.banffcentre.ca
    This annual summer arts festival showcases the talent and artistic work created and nurtured by the Banff Centre. Featuring theatre, dance, music, visual and literary arts, mountain culture, and film screenings, the festival includes more than 160 events from artists from all over the world.

**Festival TransAmériques**
C.P. 1206, Succursale Desjardins,
Montréal, QC H5B 1C3. (514) 842-0704
www.fta.qc.ca

The artists who are represented in this festival range from the emerging to the established, come from all over the world, and present new work in theatre and dance that is original, boundary-breaking, and possesses a powerful message. The festival also involves workshops, discussions, and roundtables to promote the communication both between artists and between artists and their audiences.

**Luminato**
111 Queen St. East, Suite 502, Toronto, ON M5C 1S2. (416) 368-3100
www.luminato.ca

This festival is comprised of work done by artists both from Canada and internationally in the forms of theatre, dance, music, literature, film, and visual arts. Collaboration between artists from different cultures and genres is embraced by the festival, and participants are encouraged to participate and explore their own creativity through their experience.

**SummerWorks Theatre Festival**
Box 12, Station C, Toronto, ON M6J 3M7. (647) 267-7673
www.summerworks.ca

This juried festival encourages both new and remounted productions of Canadian plays that have a clear vision and a specific aesthetic. It works to create an environment where professional artists can take risks and explore new theatrical territory, while maintaining professionalism and accessibility.

**Théâtres d'Ailleurs**
Carrefour International de Théâtre de Québec, 369, Rue de la Couronne, 4e etage, Québec, QC G1K 6E9.
(418) 692-3131
www.carrefourtheatre.qc.ca

This annual spring festival is comprised of contemporary foreign theatre work (which consists of about half of the program), as well as both new and revived work from Quebec (which comprises the other half). The aim is to promote and explore the current trends in contemporary theatre by encouraging collaboration and risk-taking by professional artists, as well as discussion and dialogue among both artists and audiences.

**Uno Festival of Solo Performance**
Intrepid Theatre, 3rd Floor, 1014 Government St. Victoria, BC V8W 1X7.
(250) 383-2663
www.intrepidtheatre.com

This is an annual festival of solo performances by artists from all over the world. It features comedy, drama, readings, dance, spoken word, and workshops, all performed solo.

**Victoria Fringe Theatre Festival**
Intrepid Theatre, 3rd Floor, 1014 Government St. Victoria, BC V8W 1X7.
(250) 383-2663
www.intrepidtheatre.com

This non-juried festival features theatre, dance, spoken word, cabaret, and other areas from innovative artists from all over the world.

**Vancouver Fringe Festival**
1398 Cartwright St. Vancouver, BC V6H 3RH. (604) 257-0350
www.vancouverfringe.com

This un-juried festival, the largest in British Columbia, is a part of the large network of North American Fringe festivals. It features over 600 performances from local, national, and international theatre artists, presenting a broad smattering of new work in live theatre, dance, performance art, multimedia, street performance, and more.

**Winnipeg Fringe Theatre Festival**
174 Market Ave. Winnipeg, MB R3B OP8. (204) 956-1340.
www.winnipegfringe.com

This non-juried summer festival is the second-largest in North America. It supports artistic innovation between both established and emerging artists from around the world, and encourages communication and discussion between these artists and their audiences.

## Cape Verde

**Festival Mindelact**
Association Mindelact, C.P. 734, Ilha de S. Vicente. (238) 232-41-11.
www.mindelact.com

Both Cape Verdian and international companies are invited to participate in this festival, which works to promote cultural growth in Cape Verde and encourage exchange with local and international artists. The festival involves both performances by the invited companies, as well as training in theatre, visual arts, music, design, and other artistic areas. The festival also includes a "Festival Off" alternative and specific programming for children.

## China

**Hong Kong International Arts Carnival**
Level 5, Administration Building, Hong Kong Cultural Centre, 10 Salisbury Rd. Tsimshatsui, Kowloon, Hong Kong.
(852)2370-1044.
www.hkiac.gov.hk

This festival includes events in acrobatics, theatre, dance, puppetry, music, film, and other areas by artists and companies from all over the world. Focused towards children and families, the festival also includes workshops, cultural tours, and exhibitions.

## Croatia

**Dubrovnik Summer Festival**
Od Siguarte 1, 20 000 Dubrovnik.
(385) 20-326-100.
www.dubrovnik-festival.hr

This festival features work from the top artists and companies from all over the world, performing classics as well as new work in the areas of music, dance, opera, and theatre. In venues all over the walled city, both indoors and outdoors, the festival encourages the synthesis of the historical atmosphere with the living spirit of art.

**Eurokaz Festival**
Dezmanov prilaz 3, 10 000 Zagreb.
(385) 1-48-47-856
www.eurokaz.hr

This festival of new work is comprised of theatre, dance, and other various performance arts by over 300 artists from Croatia and internationally. It often focuses parts of the program on specific themes in contemporary theatre, such as body art, iconoclastic, and new dramaturgy, or on the situation of theatre and dance in various geographical regions. The festival encourages innovation, risk-taking, and the movement forward in contemporary art. It also involves discussions, workshops, screenings, readings, and other events, as well as dabbling in publishing.

**International Puppet Theatre Festival**
Meunarodni centar za usluge u kultri, B. Magovca 17, HR-10010, Zagreb.
(385) 1-66-01-626.
public.carnet.hr/pif-festival

This festival is mostly comprised of professional puppet theatre artists from over 450 theatres from all continents performing classical to contemporary work for both adults and children. Two juries exist, and awards are presented for the best work overall, the best work in children's theatre, as well as awards for individual achievement.

## Czech Republic

**4 + 4 Days in Motion**
Celetná 17,110 00 Prague 1.
(420) 224-809-116
www.ctyridny.cz

This festival features work in all genres of contemporary art—theatre, dance, music, film, and visual art—with a specific theme, or *leitmotif,* such as Demolition or Hibernation, in order to connect all visitors to the events, no matter what genre they attend. The festival aims to connect pieces of architecture in Prague with each performance, thereby enlightening the Czech cultural artistry through the work.

**Mezinarodni Festival Divadlo Theatre**
Prokopova 14, 301 35 Plzen.
(420) 377-227-548
www.festivaltheatre.cz
    This festival is comprised of both professional Czech productions, as well as the most outstanding foreign productions over a large range of styles and themes in the genres of drama, music, dance, puppetry, and street theatre. The festival aims to promote the collaboration between artists, as well as to encourage dialogue between the over fifteen different countries represented.

**Prague Fringe Festival**
Budecská 16 Vinohrady, 120 00 Prague 2.
(420) 602-549-008
www.praguefringe.com
This annual fringe festival is comprised of new work in Czech and English from artists and companies from all over the world. Genres presented include theatre, cabaret, music, dance, and comedy whose aim is to provide accessible and exciting theatre for both the Czech citizens and visitors from around the globe.

## ENGLAND

**24:7 Theatre Festival**
Box 247, Machester M60 2ZT.
(44) 8454-084101
www.247theatrefestival.co.uk
    This festival presents new, vibrant plays of under 60 minutes by contemporary artists in non-theatre venues throughout Manchester. The festival assists in the development of the new work, and seeks to encourage artistic partnerships between all artists and technicians while creating exciting, accessible new work for audiences.

**Brighton Festival**
12a Pavilion Buildings, Castle Sq.
Brighton BN1 1EE. (44) 1273-709709
www.brightonfestival.org
    This annual summer festival brings together works of theatre, music, dance, children's and family entertainment, books and debate, and outdoor spectacle in numerous theatrical and non-theatrical locations. Including premieres and commissions from both the UK and worldwide, as well as other events of small and large scale, the festival aims to promote innovation and exploration.

**Brightonfestival Fringe**
12a Pavilion Buildings, Castle Sq.
Brighton BN1 1EE. (44) 1273-260804
www.brightonfestivalfringe.org.uk
    England's oldest and largest fringe festival is an open access event, allowing any artists to list their production (in any area of performing and visual arts) in the brochure and on the website. The festival aims to encourage, help develop, and make accessible new work, as well as to encourage both artists and audiences to take risks and create a forum for exploration and no judgement.

**National Theatre: Watch This Space**
South Bank, London SE1 9PX.
(44) 20-7452-3000
www.nt-online.org/wts
    This festival takes place outside the entrance to the National Theatre, where during the summer months Astroturf and oversized furniture is set up to create an inviting outdoor space. The festival offers about 600 free performances, ranging from international and local world premieres to street entertainments, cabarets, dance, and bands.

## ESTONIA

**Baltoscandal**
Kreutzwaldi 2a, 44314 Rakvere.
(372) 32-95-420
www.baltoscandal.ee
    This biennial international theatre festival was the first in the Baltic region and remains the largest. It showcases contemporary and innovative work in theatre, dance, music, and audio-visual forms that it refers to as "non-existent theatre." The festival also includes discussions, film screenings, and a lively festival club with food, drinks, and live music.

## Finland

**Helsinki Festival**
Lasipalatsi, Mannerheimintie 22-24,
FIN-00100 Helsinki. (358) 9-61-26-5100
www.helsinkifestival.fi
   The largest arts festival in Finland is comprised of ticketed and free performances in the areas of music, theatre, dance, visual arts, and film, as well as outdoor events and cultural activities throughout the city. The aim is to make and promote art that is accessible to all.

**Jyvaskyla Festival**
Asemakatu 6, 40100 Jyväskylä.
(358) 014-624-378
www.jyvaskylankesa.fi
   This arts festival features performances by international artists in the areas of circus, comedy, mime, underground films, and physical theatre. The festival also features programs of new and early music, seminars on various topics like chaos theory, and children's programming.

**Tampere Theatre Festival**
Tullikamarinaukio 2, FIN-33100
Tampere. (358) 3-222-8536
www.teatterikesa.fi
   This festival combines the most interesting productions from the current season of professional theatre in Finland, as well as distinguished invited performances from other countries. In addition to the main performances (which include about 25 productions), the festival produces a variety of other performances, events, and seminars which take place outdoors, in restaurants, and in other theatrical venues around the city.

## France

**Chalon dans la Rue**
52, quai Saint Cosme, 71 100 Chalon sur Saône. (33) 3-85-90-94-70
www.chalondanslarue.com
   France's largest and most prestigious street festival, Chalon dans la Rue is comprised of performances from international artists in street operas, puppetry, live music, circus, dance, theatre, and many other art forms. The festival celebrates diversity of art form, connections between artists and audiences, and the reinvention of public spaces as a place of creativity and artistic exploration.

**Festival d'Anjou**
49, boulevard du Roi René, 49100 Angers.
(33) 2-41-88-14-14
www.festivaldanjou.com
   This annual festival features dozens of theatrical performances by important French artists in such areas as classical and contemporary theatre, workshops, and dramatic readings. The performances take place in many of the most beautiful and historic locations throughout the city.

**Festival d'Avignon**
5, rue Ninon Vallin, 84 000 Avignon.
(33) 4-90-27-66-50
www.festival-avignon.com
   The largest and most famous of France's theatre festivals, the Festival d'Avignon showcases both French and international contemporary theatre, dance, and other performances in theatrical and non-theatrical venues around the area. The pieces which are selected to be a part of the festival (about 40 performances annually) have usually never been performed in front of an audience, and so receive their first production at the festival. With the goal of supporting exciting contemporary work and encouraging the exploration and risk-taking of emerging theatre artists, the festival also includes workshops, discussions, and film screenings.

**Festival de Marseille**
6, Place Sadi Carnot BP 52414, 13215
Marseille, Cedez 02. (33) 4-91-99-00-20
www.festivaldemarseille.com
This festival, inspired by and deeply connected to the city and locations it takes place in, is a multidisciplinary festival of performing arts, including theatre,

dance, music, and cinema. The festival fosters relationships between artists and cultural institutions both nationally and internationally, and aims to bring the most innovative, culturally rich performances to the widest number of people—a goal which the festival encourages by keeping ticket prices low.

**FURIES**
BP101-51007, Châlons-en-Champagne, Cedex. (35) 3-26-65-90-06
www.festival-furies.com

This summer festival of circus and street theatre aims to support the creation and exploration of emerging artists both from France and internationally. The festival is focused on the "firsts", or premieres, and seeks to foster a sense of chaos and creativity.

**OFF Festival of Avignon**
5, rue Ninon Vallin, 84 000 Avignon.
(33) 4-90-85-13-08
www.avignonfestivaletcompagnies.com

This un-juried fringe festival features exciting and contemporary theatrical performances by artists from all over France. Temporary stages are set up in unlikely locations throughout the city, and visitors may stumble upon any number of performances of "Living Art."

**Paris Quartier de'Été**
5, rue Boudreau, 75009 Paris
(33) 1-4-94-98-00
www.quartierdete.com

This summer festival is comprised of free performances in the areas of opera, dance, theatre, film, music, circus, and more, which take place in numerous outdoor green areas throughout the city. The festival encourages exploration, experimentation, and openness between artists and accessibility to audience members.

# GERMANY

**Autorentheatertage**
Alstertor, 20095 Hamburg
(49) 40-32-81-44-44
www.thalia-theater.de

This festival features workshop performances and staged readings of four new plays annually, as selected by a single juror. The plays selected express urgency and importance, and two are selected as winners (based upon audience approval and the vote of an independent jury), and grants are given to the writers. Discussions and talk-backs round out the experience.

**Biennale Bon**
Am Michaelshof 9, D-53177 Bonn
(49) 228-77-85-92
www.biennale-bon.de

This festival celebrates a specific area and its culture through the performances of individual artists and national and state companies in the areas of music, dance, theatre, film, readings, and visual art (2008's area was Turkey). The festival aims to ask questions about the culture selected, as well as to celebrate and share the culture with the audiencs through artistic performances and events.

**New Plays from Europe**
Christian-Zais-Str. 3, D-65189
Wiesbaden. (49) 611-132-398
www.staatstheater-wiesbaden.de/biennale

Considered the most important contemporary theatre festival in Europe, this festival showcases about thirty of the best new plays from numerous European nations, as selected by the artistic direction team. Introductions and post-show discussions are provided for each performance, which is performed in its original language as well as with a simultaneous German translation. Workshops, readings, seminars, parties, concerts, and more are also a part of this celebration of exciting contemporary European drama.

**Ruhrfestspiele Recklinghausen**
Otto-Burmeister-Allee I, 45657
Recklinghausen. (49) 2361-918-0
www.ruhrfestspiele.de
This festival of contemporary theatre brings together artists from around the world—including famous directors and actors—to perform in different theatrical venues throughout the city. The festival aims to connect international artists and companies by creating and performing art under a specific theme.

**Tollwood Sommerfestival**
Waisenhausstr, 20 (Nordflügel), 80637 Munich. (49) 89-383-85-00
www.tollwood.de
This summer festival, which takes place on the Olympic Park Grounds, features international performances in theatre and music, as well as numerous free performances and the selling of handcrafted art and fully organic food. A wide variety of theatre is presented, from physical theatre, to clowning, to circus, and is always geared towards exploration and adventure.

## GREECE

**Athens Festival and Epidaurus Festival**
23, Hadjichristou and Makriyanni St., GR-117 42 Athens. (30) 210-92-82-000
www.greekfestival.gr
This two-month summer festival brings together the best artistic performances from all over the world, collaborations between international artists and companies, as well as world premieres of brand-new Greek work in the realms of music, theatre, and dance. The festival also features staged readings, exhibitions, debates, and summer programs, as well as provides tours around Athens and into jails and drug rehabilitation centers.

## HUNGARY

**Gyula Castle Theatre**
H-5700 Gyula, Kossuth u. 13.
(36) 66-463-148
www.gyulaivaszinhaz.hu
This festival takes place primarily in the only surviving Gothic brick fortress, as well in locations around the city. The festival features historical dramas, Shakespeare, the best theatrical productions from Hungary and abroad, contemporary prosaic theatre, medieval, classical, and jazz music, folk and ballet dance, opera, and more.

## ICELAND

**Reykjavik Arts Festival**
Lækjargata 3b, Box 88 121 Reykjavik.
(354) 561-2444
www.artfest.is
This festival features both classical and brand-new productions of opera, theatre, music, dance, and contemporary art exhibitions as presented by both Icelandic and international artists. The festival's main goal is to promote and expand Icelandic arts and culture, as well as to present outstanding international performances.

## INDIA

**Summer Theatre Festival—Ansda**
Bahawalpur House, 1 Bhagwandas Rd., New Delhi 110 001. (91) 11-23382821
nsd.gov.in/festivals.htm
This annual festival seeks to present and support local artists—both those with renown as well as newcomers, providing a fascinating synthesis of experience. The selected plays vary widely in language, genre, theme, and style, demonstrating and exploring the vast range of theatre happening in India.

## Ireland

**Dublin Theatre Festival**
44 East Essex St., Temple Bar, Dublin 2. (353)1-677-8439
www.dublintheatrefestival.com
    The oldest specialized theatre festival in Europe, the Dublin Theatre Festival combines the best of international theatre with Irish productions, especially the premieres of new plays.

**Galway Arts Festival**
Black Box Theatre, Dyke Rd., Galway. (353) 91-509700
www.galwayartsfestival.com
    This annual festival brings together artists from around the world to create, commission, and present new work in the areas of theatre, music, literature, street art, spectacle, music and comedy.

**International Dublin Gay Theatre Festival**
179 South Circular Rd., Dublin 8. (353) 87-6573732
www.gaytheatre.ie
    This festival aims to both showcase the best of historical gay theatre through the new openness provided, as well as to provide opportunities for emerging gay artists. The performances presented include works by gay authors, works with gay themes or relevance, and works that include participation (in performance or production) by gay artists.

**Kilkenny Arts Festival**
9/10 Abbey Business Centre, Abbey St., Kilkenny. (353)56-775-2175
www.kilkennyarts.ie
    This festival aims to present unique and inspiring works in the areas of theatre, classical, jazz, and folk music, visual art, film, and street and children's programming to the widest possible audience. The festival provides both work that would not be seen otherwise in Kilkenny, as well as commissions and presents new work by Irish artists.

## Israel

**Israel Festival Jerusalem**
Box 4408, Jerusalem 91044/20 Marcus St., Jerusalem. (02) 5663198
www.israel-festival.org.il
    This festival presents performances in the areas of music, dance, and theatre in venues across the historic city of Jerusalem. The program combines both international performances as well as premieres of new Israeli work and tributes to important Israeli artists.

## Italy

**es.terni Festival**
Centro Multimediale p.le Bosco 3/a, 05100 Terni. (39) 333-2907070
www.exsiriterni.it
    This festival presents contemporary creative work by international artists in the forms of theatre, installations, video, and other performance. The work, which involves experimentation and collaboration, takes place in venues and historical locations throughout the city.

**Ombre International Theatre Festival**
Poggibonsi, U.R.P., (39) 0577-986203
www.festivalombre.it
    This festival stages performances by national and international artists in venues throughout the beautiful city of Poggibonsi.

**Ravenna Festival**
Via Dante Alighieri 1, 48100 Ravenna. (39) 0544-249211
www.ravennafestival.org
    This festival features theatre, opera, dance, film, and music that range from the ancient to the contemporary, performed in venues and historic locations around the city. The festival also features a "Roads of Friendship" tour, which brings performances to other nations and cities in order to reach out and promote friendship through art.

**Short Theatre Rome**
Teatro India, Lungotevere dei Papareschi, botteghino, Rome. (39) 06-68400030011
www.shorttheatre.com
 This festival features twelve days of nonstop short performances of theatre, dance, performance art, discussions, meetings, and lectures.

## LATVIA

**International Festival Theatre Methods**
c/o International University Global Theater Experience, 24 Kugu St., Radisson SAS Daugava Hotel, Magnet Business Centre, Riga, LV-1048. (44) 20-8133-2593
www.iugte.com/projects/TM08.php
 This festival aims to unify artists from all over the world who are interested in the research and exploration of traditional and contemporary theatre methods. The festival involves workshops, demonstrations, videos, lectures, readings, and performances.

## MEXICO

**Festival Internacional de Teatro Carmen**
Calle 33 A No. 212 Fraccionamiento Justo Sierra, Carmen, Campeche.
(52) 938-13-489-58
www.artesescenicasrayuela.org
 This festival brings together independent theatre groups and artists from all over the world who are working outside of major cultural and government institutions to explore, create, and present the different styles, genres, and techniques of contemporary work that are being used. It also seeks to enhance the cultural movement in the southeastern part of Mexico—an area that is disparate from the centralized cultural and theatrical movements in the country.

## THE NETHERLANDS

**Festival ad Werf**
Boorstraat 107, 3513 SE Utrecht. (31) 30-231-5355
www.festivalaandewerf.nl
 This festival provides a platform for both the creation and presentation of new work by guest companies and artists. When the festival takes place in May, many of these performances, in the areas of music, theatre, and visual arts, are presented in surprising locations indoors and outdoors throughout the city,

**Holland Festival**
Piet Heinkade 5, 1019 BR Amsterdam. (31) 20-7882100
www.hollandfestival.nl
 The largest international performing arts festival in the Netherlands, the Holland festival brings together the best opera, theatre, music, and dance performances and premieres from international artists and companies. The festival also features a fringe festival, which includes "Eyefuel" (contemporary visual arts), "Earfuel" (contemporary music), and "Mindfuel" (debates and lectures related to festival programming).

**Terschellings Oerol Festival**
Zuid-Midslandweg 4, 8891 GH, Terschelling-Midsland. (31) 562-448-448.
www.oerol.nl
 This festival uses the numerous locations on the island of Terschelling to inspire and present works in the areas of theatre, modern dance, art, and music by international artists. A theme is decided upon annually, and all pieces are connected to that theme, as well as to the varied and surprising locations in which they are performed.

**Theater Festival Groningen**
Box 1736, 9701 BS Groningen. (31) 50-314-02-78.

This annual festival provides performances by exciting international companies in the areas of theatre, dance, multimedia, film, video, and circus (and often interdisciplinary), as well as by up-and-coming pop stars, local celebrities, and children's programming. There are numerous locations, both in theaters and non-traditional performance spaces.

## NORWAY

**Porsgrunn International Theatre Festival**
Grenland Friteater, Huken 3 D, N-3921 Porsgrunn. (47) 35-93-21-00
www.pit.no

This festival brings together international artists to present contemporary theatre in all its varied styles and genres. The festival also features the Street of Fools, an annual festival of street theatre and art.

## POLAND

**International KONTAKT Theatre Festival**
87-100 Torun, Plac Teatralny 1.
(48) 56-6225222
www.teatr.torun.pl

This festival features the most interesting contemporary theatre by the most renowned international artists and companies in Central and Eastern Europe, involving both premieres and adaptations.

## PORTUGAL

**Alkantara Festival**
Rua do Forno do Tijolo, 54 - 5°Esq, 1170-138 Lisbon. (351) 213-152-267
www.alkantara.pt

This dance and theatre festival aims to bring together local and international artists to explore and present their new vision of the world. The festival aims to bridge the gap between cultures, art forms, and artists.

**Altitudes Festival**
Teatro Regional da Serra do Montemuro, Travessa Principal, n.1, Campo Benefeito, 3600-371 Gosende, Castro Daire.
(351) 254-689-352
www.teatrodomontemuro.com

This festival presents productions by international artists in the areas of theatre, music, and dance, as well as supports workshops, residencies, exhibitions, film screenings, and a parade. The festival encourages diversity of both artists and audience members.

**Festival de Almada**
Av. Professor Egas Moniz, 2804 503 Almada. (351) 212-739-360
www.ctalmada.pt

This festival is comprised of innovative, challenging, and diverse contemporary theatre performances by local, national, and international artists and companies in various locations throughout the city. The festival also sponsors numerous supplementary talks, and dance and street theatre performances.

## ROMANIA

**Sibiu International Theatre Festival**
Corneliu Coposu, nr. 550245 Sibiu.
(40) 269-210092
www.sibfest.ro

This festival brings together the best international artists and companies to perform both traditional and new works in the areas of theatre, dance, music, street performances, and exhibitions. The festival aims to be a platform for different cultures to express, present, and interact artistically.

## Scotland

**Edinburgh Fringe Festival**
180 High St., Edinburgh EH1 1QS. (44) 131-226-0026
www.edfringe.com
Officially the largest festival in the world, the Edinburgh Fringe Festival is solely comprised of premieres (world, European, and UK) in the areas of comedy, theatre, music, dance, physical theatre, and exhibitions. These works are presented in about 250 locations throughout the city.

## Serbia

**Belgrade International Theatre Festival**
Terazije 29/1, 11000 Belgrade.
(381) 11-32-43-108
www.bitef.co.yu
This competitive festival aims to support and present works that are exploring the new international and Serbian theatrical trends—experimental, avant-garde, re-interpretations, and more. The festival brings together both masters and upcoming artists and companies who perform works centered around a primary theme.

## South Africa

**National Arts Festival**
Box 304, Grahamstown, 6140, Eastern Cape, RSA. (27) 46-603-1103
www.nafest.co.za
The largest and most diverse of South Africa's arts festivals, the National Arts Festival is comprised of a Main Programme (selected by a jury), and a Fringe Festival (open to all). The festival presents both contemporary and traditional theatre, music, dance, and visual arts by local and international artists, as well as activities like craft fairs, raves, walking tours, and more.

## South Korea

**Keochang International Festival of Theatre**
750-3 Hwangsan-ri, Wecheon-myun, Keochang-goon, Kyungnam, 670-853.
(82) 55-943-415
www.kift.or.kr
This festival presents theatrical works focused on the relationship between man and nature by local and international artists in open-air venues. A main focus of the festival is to promote and present work by local playwrights to an international audience.

**Seoul Fringe Festival**
(121-869) 564-35, Yeonnam-dong, Mapo-gu, Seoul. (82) 2-325-8150
www.seoulfringe.net
This fringe festival features new, innovative, and creative performances in the areas of theatre, film, music, visual arts, and street performance. The goal of the festival is to encourage and showcase the work of independent artists.

## Spain

**Barcelona Summer (Grec) Festival**
Palau de la Virreina La Rambla 99, 08002 Barcelona. (34) 93-316-10-00
www.barcelonafestival.com
Barcelona's main cultural event, this summer festival features performances of theatre, music, film, and dance by the best artists from around the world. The festival encourages the productions of local artists, while also providing a platform for new productions by major international companies.

**Festival Internacional de Teatro Contemporaneo**
Lazarillo t.c.e. c/ Carmen 10, 13200, Manzanares, Ciudad Real.
(34) 618-520876
www.fitzclarzarillo.com
This festival is comprised of both the best contemporary productions, as well as premieres by artists from Europe and

Latin America. The festival also provides a children's theatre festival which runs parallel to the main program.

**Marató de L'Espectacle**
Trafalgar 78, 11, 08010 Barcelona. (34) 936-268-18-68
www.marato.com

This festival presents selections (10 minutes maximum) of experimental, innovative, and risky contemporary theatre by artists and companies from all over the world over the course of two days. The festival aims to attract new audiences of contemporary theatre, foster communication between artists, and support and promote the artists by inviting numerous theatrical promoters, as well as by providing information about rehearsal spaces, training centers, and more.

## SWEDEN

**Götenborgs Dans & Teater Festival**
Norra Hamngatan 8, SE-411 14 Götenborg. (46) 8-31-368-32-69
www.festival.gotenborg.se

Occurring every two years, this festival brings together the best contemporary theatre, dance, and new circus by international artists and companies. It aims to provide a cultural boost to the city and surrounding Nordic region, as well as to encourage the new forms of contemporary theatre and dance. The festival also offers workshops and seminars.

## SWITZERLAND

**Zürcher Theater Spektakel**
Stadthausquai 17, CH-8001 Zürich. (41) 44-412-35-51
www.theaterspektakel.ch

Annually, festival directors invite 25 to 30 international artists who are making waves in the contemporary performing arts world to present projects that are innovative, independent, and unusual, including theatre, dance, music, film, and numerous interdisciplinary fields. The festival also sponsors its own new productions and co-productions.

## TURKEY

**International Istanbul Theatre Festival**
Istanbul Foundation for Culture and Arts, Astiklal Caddesi 64 Beyoglu 34425 Istanbul.
(90) 212-334-07-77
www.iksv.org/tiyatro/english

This biennial festival brings together contemporary theatre performances by Turkish theatre companies as well as selected artists and companies from around the globe. The festival has produced experimental collaborations between Turkish companies and international festivals, and aims to foster further collaboration between Turkish and international artists. The festival also feature lectures, discussions, workshops, exhibitions, and other programming for artists and their audiences.

# INDEX OF SPECIAL INTERESTS

### DISABLED

Actor's Express ..................................................91
Allenberry Playhouse ......................................93
Alley Theatre .....................................................93
Annual Black Theatre Festival ......................42
Boomerang Theatre Company ..................... 44
Canadian Jewish Playwriting Competition ...59
Childsplay .......................................................103
Dramatics Magazine ......................................29
Dream Theatre ..............................................108
Emerging Artists Theatre (EAT) ................109
Enrichment Works ........................................110
Ensemble Theatre of Cincinnati ..................110
Firehouse Center for the Arts ........................61
Fort Wayne Civic Theatre-Northeast
   Indiana Playwright Contest ......................61
Fresh Fruit Festival ........................................ 44
Halcyon Theatre............................................ 114
Hubris Productions ...................................... 116
Interborough Repertory Theater Inc. .......... 118
Jane Chambers Playwriting Award ...............74
Judith Shakespeare Company NYC ............120
Laity Theatre Company ..................................72
McCarter Theater Center..............................124
Meet the Composer Grant Programs............ 84
Milwaukee Chamber Theatre ......................125
Mixed Blood Theatre Company ..................125
National Theatre of the Deaf .......................126
New American Playwrights Project
   (NAPP).........................................................48
New Jersey Repertory Company ..................127
New Perspectives Theatre Company ...........127
New Theatre ...................................................128
Next Generation Playwriting Contest............85
Not Merely Players .......................................130
Old Opera House Theatre Company New
   Voice Play Festival....................................55
OpenStage Theatre & Company ..................131
Original Works Publishing .............................31
Pasadena Playhouse ......................................132
Pillsbury House Theatre ...............................134
Reverie Productions........................................77
Signature Theatre Company ........................ 141
Stageworks, Inc............................................. 143
Sundance Institute Theatre Program........... 181
Ten Minute Musicals Project, The .................69
Theater Breaking Through Barriers ............ 147

Theater Resources Unlimited (TRU)/TRU
   Voices .........................................................56
Theatre Alliance of Michigan .....................156
Theatre Building Chicago .............................51
TheatreWorks ................................................149
Unicorn Theatre ............................................151
Victory Gardens Theater .............................151
VSA arts Playwright Discovery Program .....69
Women's Work Project ..................................41
Woodstock Fringe ..........................................52
Working Theater ...........................................154

### GAY / LESBIAN

About Face Theatre (AFT) ........................... 90
Actor's Express ..............................................91
Alley Theatre ..................................................93
Annual Black Theatre Festival ......................42
Arch & Bruce Brown Foundation .................58
Bailiwick Repertory Theatre .........................98
Boomerang Theatre Company ..................... 44
Canadian Jewish Playwriting Competition ...59
Celebration Theatre ......................................102
Curan Repertory Company ..........................106
Diversionary Theatre ....................................108
Dramatics Magazine.......................................29
Dream Theatre ..............................................108
Emerging Artists Theatre (EAT) ................109
Ensemble Theatre of Cincinnati ..................110
Eric Bentley New Play Competition..............73
Firehouse Center for the Arts ........................61
Fort Wayne Civic Theatre-Northeast
   Indiana Playwright Contest ......................61
Fresh Fruit Festival ........................................ 44
GableStage .................................................... 112
GAYFEST NYC ............................................ 46
Halcyon Theatre............................................ 114
Hubris Productions ...................................... 116
Jane Chambers Playwriting Award ...............74
Judith Shakespeare Company NYC ............120
Juneteenth Legacy Theatre ............................53
Know Theatre of Cincinnati ........................177
Lavender Footlights Festival .........................47
McCarter Theater Center..............................124
Meet the Composer Grant Programs............ 84
Milwaukee Chamber Theatre ......................125
Mixed Blood Theatre Company ..................125

New American Playwrights Project (NAPP) ..........48
New Conservatory Theatre Center ..............126
New Jersey Repertory Company ..................127
New Theatre ..........128
Next Generation Playwriting Contest ............76
Old Opera House Theatre Company New Voice Play Festival ..........55
OpenStage Theatre & Company ..................131
Original Works Publishing ............31
Pasadena Playhouse ..........132
Perseverance Theatre (PT) ..........133
Phoenix Theatre ..........134
Pillsbury House Theatre ..........134
Pittsburgh New Works Festival (PNWF) ......54
Plan-B Theatre Company ............128
Playwrights' Forum ..........135
Purple Circuit, The ..........191
Robert Chesley Award ............67
Reverie Productions ..........77
Signature Theatre Company ........141
Sinister Wisdom Journal ..........33
Stageworks, Inc. ..........143
Sundance Institute Theatre Program ..........181
Ten Minute Musicals Project, The ..........69
Theater Resources Unlimited (TRU)/TRU Voices ..........56
Theatre Building Chicago ..........51
Theatre Rhinoceros ..........149
Triangle Productions! ..........150
Trustus Theatre ..........150
Unicorn Theatre ..........151
Victory Gardens Theater ..........151
Victory Theatre Center ..........151
Women's Work Project ............41
Woodstock Fringe ............52
Working Theater ..........154

**T.Y.A. (THEATRE FOR YOUND AUDIENCES)**

Actors' Playhouse National Children's Theatre Festival ............42
All Arts Matter ............92
Allenberry Playhouse ............93
American Stage ............94
Anchorage Press Plays Inc. ............27
Anna Zornio Memorial Children's Theatre Playwriting Award ..........57
Annual Black Theatre Festival ............42
Arkansas Arts Center Children's Theatre .....96
ArtsPower National Touring Theatre ..........97
Aurand Harris Fellowship ............80

Aurand Harris Memorial Playwriting Award ............72
Aurora Theatre, Inc. ............97
b current ............98
Baker's Plays ............28
Beverly Hills Theatre Guild Youth Theatre Marilyn Hall Awards ............58
Black Rep ............99
Brooklyn Publishers ............28
California Theatre Center ..........101
Canadian Jewish Playwriting Competition ...59
Children's Theatre Company (CTC) ..........103
Childsplay ..........103
Columbus Children's Theatre (CCT) ..........105
Contemporary Drama Service ............29
Coterie Theatre ..........106
CTA Crossroads Theatre ..........106
Cumberland County Playhouse ..........106
Cunningham Commission for Youth Theatre ............60
Dallas Children's Theater ..........107
Danisarte ..........107
Dell'Arte Company ..........107
Discovery Theater ..........107
Dramatics Magazine ............29
El Centro Su Teatro ..........109
Eldridge Publishing Company Inc. ............29
Enrichment Works ..........110
Ensemble Theatre, The ..........110
Ensemble Theatre of Cincinnati ..........110
Express Children's Theatre ..........111
First Stage Children's Theater ..........111
Flat Rock Playhouse ..........111
Florida Repertory Theatre ..........111
Freed-Hardeman Univ. ..........112
Freelance Press ............30
Fresh Fruit Festival ............44
Greenbrier Valley Theatre ..........114
Growing Stage - The Children's Theatre of New Jersey ..........114
Halcyon Theatre ..........114
Hangar Theatre KIDDSTUFF ..........115
Harwich Junior Theatre (HJT) ..........115
Honolulu Theatre for Youth ..........116
Human Race Theatre Company, The ..........146
Imagination Stage ..........103
Interborough Repertory Theater Inc. (IRT) 118
Jane Chambers Playwriting Award ............74
Kennedy Center New Visions/New Voices Festival (NVNV), The ..........181
Laity Theatre Company ............72
LaMicro Theater ..........121

## Special Interests

Lost Nation Theater ............................... 122
Macy's New Play Prize for Young
   Audiences ................................................ 64
Meet the Composer Grant Programs ............ 84
Merry-Go-Round Playhouse ...................... 124
Metro Theater Company ............................. 124
Mu Performing Arts ................................... 125
National Theatre of the Deaf ...................... 126
New Conservatory Theatre Center .............. 126
New Plays Inc. ............................................ 31
Old Opera House Theatre Company New
   Voice Play Festival .................................. 55
Omaha Theater Company ........................... 131
Pasadena Playhouse .................................... 132
Penumbra Theatre Company ...................... 133
Pillsbury House Theatre ............................. 134
Round House Theatre ................................. 138
Sacramento Theatre Company ................... 138
Seattle Children's Theatre .......................... 139
Shadowlight Productions ............................ 140
Smith and Kraus .......................................... 33
South Coast Repertory Theatre ................... 142
Springer Opera House ................................ 142
St. Louis Black Repertory Company ........... 142
Stage One: The Louisville Children's
   Theater ................................................... 136
Stages Repertory Theatre ........................... 143
Stages Theatre Center ................................. 143
Stages Theatre Company ............................ 143
Story Time Stories That Rhyme ................... 34
Sundance Institute Theatre Program ........... 181
Synchronicity Performance Group .............. 145
Teatro Dallas .............................................. 145
Ten Minute Musicals Project, The ................ 69
Theater at Monmouth ................................. 147
Theatre Alliance of Michigan ..................... 156
Theatre Ariel .............................................. 148
Theatre at the Center / Lawrence
   Arts Center ............................................. 148
Theatre Building Chicago ............................ 51
Theatre for Young Audiences/ USA ............ 194
Theatre in the Square ................................. 149
Theatrefolk ................................................. 34
Triangle Productions! ................................ 150
TriArts at the Sharon Playhouse ................. 150
Valley Youth Theatre (VYT) ...................... 151
Women's Work Project ................................ 41

### WOMEN

Abingdon Theatre Company ........................ 90
About Face Theatre (AFT) .......................... 90
All Arts Matter ............................................ 92
Allenberry Playhouse ................................... 93
Alley Theatre .............................................. 93
Annual Black Theatre Festival .................... 42
Babes With Blades - Joining Sword
   and Pen .................................................... 58
Boomerang Theatre Company ..................... 44
Canadian Jewish Playwriting Competition ... 59
Christopher Brian Wolk Award .................... 59
Contemporary Drama Service ..................... 29
Danisarte .................................................. 107
Dramatics Magazine .................................... 29
Dream Theatre .......................................... 108
Electric Theatre Company ......................... 109
Emerging Artists Theatre (EAT) ............... 109
Enrichment Works .................................... 110
Ensemble Theatre, The .............................. 110
Ensemble Theatre of Cincinnati ................. 110
Firehouse Center for the Arts ...................... 61
Florida Repertory Theatre ......................... 111
Fort Wayne Civic Theatre-Northeast Indiana
   Playwright Contest .................................. 61
Freed-Hardeman University ...................... 112
Fresh Fruit Festival ..................................... 44
Green Light ................................................ 62
Greenbrier Valley Theatre ......................... 114
Halcyon Theatre ........................................ 114
Hubris Productions .................................... 116
Jane Chambers Playwriting Award ............... 74
Jane Chambers Student Playwriting Award .. 74
Judith Shakespeare Company NYC ............ 120
Juneteenth Legacy Theatre .......................... 53
Know Theatre of Cincinnati ...................... 177
Laity Theatre Company ............................... 72
LaMicro Theater ....................................... 121
Looking Glass Theatre .............................. 122
Main Street Theater .................................. 123
McCarter Theater Center .......................... 124
Meet the Composer Grant Programs ............ 84
Milwaukee Chamber Theatre ..................... 125
New American Playwrights
   Project (NAPP) ....................................... 48
New Jersey Repertory Company ................ 127
New Perspectives Theatre Company .......... 127
New Theatre ............................................. 128
Next Generation Playwriting Contest ........... 76
Not Merely Players ................................... 130
Old Opera House Theatre Company New
   Voice Play Festival .................................. 55
OpenStage Theatre & Company ................ 131
Original Works Publishing .......................... 31
Pasadena Playhouse .................................. 132

Phoenix Arts Association Theatre ............. 133
Phoenix Theatre .................................................. 134
Pillsbury House Theatre ............................... 134
Pittsburgh New Works Festival (PNWF) ...... 54
Playwrights' Forum ........................................ 135
Reverie Productions ......................................... 77
Signature Theatre Company ........................ 141
South Coast Repertory Theatre .................... 142
Stageworks, Inc. ............................................... 143
Sundance Institute Theatre Program ........... 181
Synchronicity Performance Group ............. 145
Ten Minute Musicals Project, The ................. 69
Theater Resources Unlimited (TRU)/TRU
   Voices ............................................................. 56
Theater Ten Ten .............................................. 148
Theatre Building Chicago ............................... 51
Trustus Theatre .............................................. 150
Unicorn Theatre .............................................. 151
Victory Gardens Theater ............................... 151
Victory Theatre Center .................................. 151
Women's Work Project .................................... 41
Woodstock Fringe ............................................. 52
Working Theater ............................................ 154

## WRITERS OF COLOR

Abingdon Theatre Company .......................... 90
About Face Theatre (AFT) ............................. 90
Actor's Express ................................................. 91
African Continuum Theatre Co. (ACTCo) .... 92
Allen Lee Hughes Fellowship Program ........ 79
Alley Theatre ..................................................... 93
Anchorage Press Plays Inc. ............................. 27
Annual Black Theatre Festival ...................... 42
Arte Publico Press ............................................ 27
Asian American Theater Company ............... 97
Asian Theatre Journal ..................................... 28
Aurora Theatre, Inc. ......................................... 97
Baldwin New Play Festival ............................. 43
Bilingual Foundation of the Arts (BFA) ....... 43
Black Ensemble Theater .................................. 99
Black Rep ........................................................... 99
Boomerang Theatre Company ....................... 44
Canadian Jewish Playwriting Competition ... 59
Caribbean American Repertory Theatre ..... 102
Childsplay ........................................................ 103
Christopher Brian Wolk Award ..................... 59
Contemporary Drama Service ........................ 29
Crossroads Theatre Company ...................... 106
Danisarte ......................................................... 107
Dramatics Magazine ........................................ 29
Dream Theatre ............................................... 108

East West Players ........................................... 109
El Centro Su Teatro ....................................... 109
Electric Theatre Company ............................ 109
Emerging Artists Theatre (EAT) ................. 109
Enrichment Works .......................................... 110
Ensemble Theatre, The ................................. 110
Ensemble Theatre of Cincinnati .................. 110
eta Creative Arts Foundation Inc. ............... 111
Firehouse Center for the Arts ........................ 61
Fort Wayne Civic Theatre-Northeast
   Indiana Playwright Contest ....................... 61
Frank Silvera Writers' Workshop ................ 177
Freedom Repertory Theatre ......................... 112
Fremont Centre Theatre New Playwright
   Contest ........................................................... 73
Fresh Fruit Festival ......................................... 44
GableStage ...................................................... 112
Genesis Festival ............................................... 46
Greenbrier Valley Theatre ............................ 114
Halcyon Theatre ............................................. 114
Honolulu Theatre for Youth ......................... 116
Hubris Productions ........................................ 116
InnerAct Productions .................................... 117
INTAR (International Arts Relations)
   Theatre ......................................................... 118
Jane Chambers Playwriting Award .............. 74
Japan Foundation ............................................. 82
Judith Shakespeare Company NYC ............ 120
Juneteenth Legacy Theatre ............................ 53
Know Theatre of Cincinnati ......................... 177
Laity Theatre Company .................................. 72
LaMicro Theater ............................................. 121
Latin American Theater Ensemble
   (LATE) / El Portón del Barrio ................ 121
Lorraine Hansberry Theater ........................ 122
Ma-Yi Theatre Company .............................. 123
McCarter Theater Center ............................. 124
Meet the Composer Grant Programs ............ 84
Met Life Nuestras Voces Playwriting
   Competition ................................................. 64
Milwaukee Chamber Theatre ....................... 125
Miracle Theatre Group ................................. 125
Mu Performing Arts ...................................... 125
New American Playwrights Project
   (NAPP) ........................................................... 48
New Federal Theatre ..................................... 126
New Jersey Repertory Company ................. 127
New Jomandi Productions, Inc. ................... 127
New Perspectives Theatre Company .......... 127
New Theatre ................................................... 128
Next Generation Playwriting Contest .......... 76

## Special Interests

Old Opera House Theatre Company
  New Voice Play Festival ............................ 55
Ollantay Center for the Arts ........................ 190
OpenStage Theatre & Company .................. 131
Original Works Publishing ........................... 31
Pacific Rim Prize ............................................ 65
Pan Asian Repertory Theatre ...................... 127
Pasadena Playhouse ..................................... 132
Passage Theatre ........................................... 132
Penumbra Theatre Company ....................... 133
Phoenix Theatre ........................................... 134
Pillsbury House Theatre .............................. 134
Pittsburgh New Works Festival (PNWF) ...... 54
Playwrights' Forum ..................................... 135
Political Theatre Festival .............................. 50
Reverie Productions ...................................... 77
Sacramento Theatre Company .................... 138
Signature Theatre Company ........................ 141
South Coast Repertory Theatre ................... 142
Southern Writers Project (SWP) ................. 181
St. Louis Black Repertory Company ........... 142
Stageworks, Inc. ........................................... 143
Sundance Institute Theatre Program ........... 181
Teatro Dallas ................................................ 145
Teatro Vision ............................................... 145
Ten Minute Musicals Project, The ................ 69
Thalia Spanish Theatre ................................ 146
Theater Resources Unlimited (TRU)/TRU
  Voices ......................................................... 56
Theatre Alliance of Michigan ..................... 156
Theatre Building Chicago ............................. 51
TheatreWorks ............................................... 149
Theodore Ward Prize .................................... 69
Trustus Theatre ............................................ 150
Unicorn Theatre ........................................... 151
Victory Gardens Theater ............................. 151
Victory Theatre Center ................................ 151
Women's Work Project .................................. 41
Woodstock Fringe .......................................... 52
Working Theater .......................................... 154

# Submission Calendar

These opportunities accept submissions year-round. Consult the company website for the most up to date information. Also, consult the Dramatists Guild website for new opportunities, changes in rules and deadlines, and for ongoing opportunities not listed in this year's directory.

## January

| | | |
|---|---|---|
| 1/1/2008 | Berlin Artists-in-Residence | 80 |
| 1/1/2009 | Carnegie Mellon University | 158 |
| 1/1/2009 | Yaddo | 41 |
| 1/2/2008 | Hawai'i Prize | 62 |
| 1/2/2009 | National Playwriting Competition | 65 |
| 1/2/2009 | Pacific Rim Prize | 65 |
| 1/2/2009 | Resident Prize | 68 |
| 1/5/2009 | Utah Arts Council | 88 |
| 1/9/2009 | Women's Work Project | 41 |
| 1/12/2009 | Camargo Foundation | 36 |
| 1/12/2009 | Grawemeyer Award for Music Composition | 74 |
| 1/13/2009 | Theater Resources Unlimited (TRU)/TRU Voices | 56 |
| 1/15/2009 | Ashland New Plays Festival | 52 |
| 1/15/2009 | Laity Theatre Company | 72 |
| 1/15/2009 | Literature Fellowships: Translation Projects | 83 |
| 1/15/2009 | Perishable Theatre Women's Playwriting Festival | 55 |
| 1/15/2009 | Phoenix Theatre | 134 |
| 1/15/2009 | Playwrights Gallery | 179 |
| 1/15/2009 | Premiere Stages Play Festival | 50 |
| 1/15/2009 | Ragdale Foundation | 40 |
| 1/15/2009 | Southern Playwrights Competition | 68 |
| 1/15/2009 | Summerfield G. Roberts Award | 69 |
| 1/15/2009 | Virginia Center for the Creative Arts (VCCA) | 41 |
| 1/15/2010 | CEC ArtsLink | 80 |
| 1/16/2009 | PEN/Laura Pels Foundation Awards for Drama | 67 |
| 1/18/2009 | Helene Wurlitzer Foundation of New Mexico | 37 |
| 1/19/2008 | Jewel Box Theatre Playwriting Award | 75 |
| 1/28/2009 | Humanities Projects in Media | 82 |
| 1/30/2009 | Baldwin New Play Festival | 43 |
| 1/30/2009 | Dr. Floyd Gaffney PLaywriting Award on the African-American Experience | 60 |
| 1/31/2009 | Kenyon Review | 30 |
| 1/31/2009 | National One-Act Playwriting Contest | 76 |
| 1/31/2009 | PEN Center USA Literary Awards | 77 |

## February

| | | |
|---|---|---|
| 2/1/2009 | Blue Mountain Center | 35 |
| 2/1/2009 | Cape Cod Theatre Project | 176 |
| 2/1/2009 | Hall Farm Center for Arts and Education | 37 |
| 2/1/2009 | Indiana Arts Commission (IAC) | 82 |

| | | |
|---|---|---|
| 2/1/2009 | Kitchen Dog Theater (KDT) New Works Festival | 47 |
| 2/1/2009 | Last Frontier Theatre Conference | 47 |
| 2/1/2009 | Moving Arts Premiere One-Act Competition | 76 |
| 2/1/2009 | New Directors/New Works (ND/NW) | 178 |
| 2/1/2009 | Public Access Television Corporation PATV | 67 |
| 2/1/2009 | Vermont Playwrights Award | 70 |
| 2/1/2009 | Yale University School of Drama | 162 |
| 2/1/2010 | City Attic Theatre CAT Tales Festival | 60 |
| 2/14/2009 | Penobscot Theatre | 49 |
| 2/15/2009 | Djerassi Resident Artists Program | 36 |
| 2/15/2009 | Francesca Primus Prize | 73 |
| 2/15/2009 | Fresh Fruit Festival | 44 |
| 2/15/2009 | Hangar Theatre Lab Company Playwriting Residencies | 177 |
| 2/15/2009 | Jane Chambers Playwriting Award | 74 |
| 2/15/2009 | Marin Arts Council Fund for Artists | 84 |
| 2/15/2009 | North Dakota Council on the Arts | 86 |
| 2/15/2009 | Theatre Oxford 10-Minute Play Contest | 78 |
| 2/15/2009 | Travel & Study Grant Program | 88 |
| 2/16/2009 | Isle Royale National Park Artist-in-Residence | 38 |
| 2/20/2009 | Artist Trust | 80 |
| 2/25/2009 | Jane Chambers Student Playwriting Award | 74 |
| 2/28/2009 | Babes With Blades - Joining Sword and Pen | 58 |
| 2/28/2009 | Beverly Hills Theatre Guild Youth Theatre Marilyn Hall Awards | 59 |
| 2/28/2009 | McLaren Memorial Comedy Playwriting Competition | 75 |

## MARCH

| | | |
|---|---|---|
| 3/1/2009 | Alabama State Council on the Arts | 79 |
| 3/1/2009 | Alaska State Council on the Arts (ASCA) | 79 |
| 3/1/2009 | Arthur W. Stone New Play Award | 58 |
| 3/1/2009 | Byrdcliffe Arts Colony Artist-in-Residence (AIR) | 35 |
| 3/1/2009 | Centre Stage South Carolina New Play Festival | 44 |
| 3/1/2009 | Edward Albee Foundation | 36 |
| 3/1/2009 | Kimmel Harding Nelson (KHN) Center for the Arts | 38 |
| 3/1/2009 | Old Opera House Theatre Company New Voice Play Festival | 55 |
| 3/1/2009 | ReOrient Golden Thread Fest | 50 |
| 3/1/2009 | South Dakota Arts Council | 88 |
| 3/1/2009 | Ucross Foundation Residency Program | 41 |
| 3/3/2009 | Anna Zornio Memorial Children's Theatre Playwriting Award | 57 |
| 3/3/2009 | Louisiana Division of the Arts | 83 |
| 3/15/2009 | Arts & Letters Prize in Drama | 71 |
| 3/15/2009 | Barnstormers Theatre | 43 |
| 3/15/2009 | Blank Theatre Company Young Playwrights Festival | 44 |
| 3/15/2009 | Colorado Council on the Arts | 81 |
| 3/15/2009 | Downstage Left (DSL) | 108 |
| 3/15/2009 | Juneteenth Legacy Theatre | 53 |
| 3/15/2009 | Lamia Ink! Intl. One-Page Play Competition | 53 |
| 3/15/2009 | Plays for the 21st Century | 77 |
| 3/15/2009 | Short Attention Span PlayFEST | 50 |
| 3/31/2009 | Appalachian Festival of Plays and Playwrights | 42 |
| 3/31/2009 | Envision Retreat | 36 |
| 3/31/2009 | Fire Rose Prods. 10-Min. Play Festival | 53 |
| 3/31/2009 | None of the Above Playwriting Contest | 66 |

## April

| | | |
|---|---|---|
| 4/1/2008 | Iowa Arts Council | 82 |
| 4/1/2009 | National Children's Theatre Festival | 72 |
| 4/1/2009 | New York Mills Arts Retreat | 40 |
| 4/1/2009 | Pittsburgh New Works Festival (PNWF) | 54 |
| 4/1/2009 | Rhode Island State Council on the Arts | 87 |
| 4/6/2009 | Nevada Arts Council | 85 |
| 4/9/2009 | Turtle Shell Productions | 70 |
| 4/9/2009 | Urban Retreat | 182 |
| 4/10/2009 | New Hampshire State Council on the Arts | 85 |
| 4/11/2009 | Write a Play! NYC Contest | 71 |
| 4/15/2009 | Hambidge Center | 37 |
| 4/15/2009 | John Gassner Memorial Playwriting Award | 75 |
| 4/15/2009 | Luna Stage | 122 |
| 4/15/2009 | MacDowell Colony | 39 |
| 4/15/2009 | Montana Artists Residency | 40 |
| 4/15/2009 | New Rocky Mountain Voices | 76 |
| 4/15/2009 | VSA arts Playwright Discovery Program | 69 |
| 4/23/2009 | Essential Theatre Playwriting Award | 61 |
| 4/30/2009 | Aurand Harris Fellowship | 80 |
| 4/30/2009 | Fremont Centre Theatre New Playwright Contest | 73 |
| 4/30/2009 | Green Light | 62 |
| 4/30/2009 | International Radio Playwriting Competition | 62 |

## May

| | | |
|---|---|---|
| 5/1/2009 | Actors' Playhouse National Children's Theatre Festival | 42 |
| 5/1/2009 | Aurand Harris Memorial Playwriting Award | 72 |
| 5/1/2009 | Eric Bentley New Play Competition | 73 |
| 5/1/2009 | Lewis Galantiere Award | 63 |
| 5/1/2009 | Librettists Workshop | 178 |
| 5/1/2009 | W. Keith Hedrick Playwriting Contest | 78 |
| 5/1/2009 | Ungar German Translation Award | 70 |
| 5/2/2009 | Fiscal Sponsorship | 81 |
| 5/8/2009 | Willows Theatre Company | 154 |
| 5/15/2009 | Jacksonville University | 63 |
| 5/15/2009 | Community Theatre Association of Michigan | 72 |
| 5/15/2009 | FUSION Theatre Co. | 73 |
| 5/15/2009 | Jacksonville University Helford Prize | 63 |
| 5/15/2009 | LiveWire Chicago Theatre | 64 |
| 5/15/2009 | Stageworks, Inc. | 143 |
| 5/15/2009 | Writer's Digest Writing Competition | 78 |
| 5/15/2009 | Writer/Director Lab | 182 |
| 5/30/2009 | NYC Playwrights Lab | 179 |
| 5/31/2009 | Award Blue | 58 |
| 5/31/2009 | Das Goldkiel | 72 |
| 5/31/2009 | Prix Hors Pair | 77 |

## June

| | | |
|---|---|---|
| 6/1/2009 | Actors' Theatre Ten-Minute Play Contest | 71 |
| 6/1/2009 | Charles M. Getchell Award, SETC | 57 |
| 6/1/2009 | American Scandinavian Foundation Translation Prize | 57 |
| 6/1/2009 | California Young Playwrights Contest | 59 |

# Submission Calendar

| | | |
|---|---|---|
| 6/1/2009 | Christopher Brian Wolk Award | 59 |
| 6/1/2009 | Jackie White Memorial National Children's Play Writing Contest | 63 |
| 6/1/2009 | New Professional Theatre Writers Festival | 48 |
| 6/2/2009 | Headlands Center for the Arts | 37 |
| 6/2/2009 | Turtle Shell Productions | 70 |
| 6/12/209 | Maine Arts Commission | 83 |
| 6/13/2009 | New York Television Festival | 49 |
| 6/15/2009 | Institute of Gunnar Gunnarsson - Klaustrid | 38 |
| 6/15/2009 | L. Arnold Weissberger Award | 63 |
| 6/15/2009 | Lanesboro Residency Program Fellowships | 39 |
| 6/15/2009 | Teatro del Pueblo | 51 |
| 6/15/2009 | Towson University Prize for Literature | 69 |
| 6/30/2009 | Brevard Little Theatre New-Play Competition | 57 |
| 6/30/2009 | Canadian Jewish Playwriting Competition | 59 |
| 6/30/2009 | Festival of New American Plays | 45 |

## July

| | | |
|---|---|---|
| 7/1/2009 | Aurora Theatre Company: Global Age Project | 58 |
| 7/1/2009 | Global Age Project (GAP) | 46 |
| 7/1/2009 | Henrico Theatre Company One-Act Playwriting Competition | 62 |
| 7/1/2009 | Theodore Ward Prize | 69 |
| 7/8/2009 | New Jersey State Council on the Arts | 85 |
| 7/25/2009 | Many Voices Playwriting Residency Awards | 83 |

## August

| | | |
|---|---|---|
| 8/1/2009 | Composers & Lyricists Workshop | 176 |
| 8/1/2009 | Delaware Division of the Arts | 81 |
| 8/1/2009 | Fulbright Program for US Scholars | 81 |
| 8/1/2009 | The Kennedy Center New Visions/New Voices Festival (NVNV) | 181 |
| 8/1/2009 | National New Play Network | 76 |
| 8/1/2009 | Pennsylvania Council on the Arts | 86 |
| 8/1/2009 | Playfest - Harriett Lake Festival of New Plays | 49 |
| 8/1/2009 | Political Theatre Festival | 50 |
| 8/1/2009 | Virginia Commission for the Arts | 89 |
| 8/8/2009 | Firehouse Center for the Arts | 61 |
| 8/15/2009 | David C. Horn Prize | 72 |
| 8/31/2009 | The Ten Minute Musicals Project | 69 |

## September

| | | |
|---|---|---|
| 9/1/2009 | Connecticut Commission on Culture & Tourism (CCT) | 81 |
| 9/1/2009 | Fort Wayne Civic Theatre-Northeast Indiana Playwright Contest | 61 |
| 9/1/2009 | Jewish Ensemble Theater Festival of New Plays | 47 |
| 9/1/2009 | Jewish Ensemble Theatre | 119 |
| 9/1/2009 | Mississippi Theatre Association | 75 |
| 9/1/2009 | New Playwrights Competition | 65 |
| 9/1/2009 | Next Act Theatre | 129 |
| 9/1/2009 | Ohio Arts Council | 86 |
| 9/15/2009 | John Simon Guggenheim Memorial Foundation | 83 |
| 9/15/2009 | New Dramatists | 189 |
| 9/15/2010 | Kleban Award | 83 |
| 9/17/2009 | Wisconsin Arts Board | 89 |

| Date | Event | Page |
|---|---|---|
| 9/20/2009 | Susan Smith Blackburn Prize | 69 |
| 9/30/2009 | Baltimore Playwrights Festival | 52 |
| 9/30/2009 | Hawthornden Castle International Retreat for Writers | 37 |
| 9/30/2009 | John D. and Catherine T. MacArthur Fund Grant | 83 |
| 9/30/2009 | Long Beach Playhouse New Works Festival | 54 |
| 9/30/2009 | Theatre Three One-Act Play Festival | 52 |

## OCTOBER

| Date | Event | Page |
|---|---|---|
| 10/1/2009 | Actors' Theatre Full-Length Play Contest | 71 |
| 10/1/2009 | New Generations Program: Future Collaborations | 85 |
| 10/1/2009 | New Harmony Project | 178 |
| 10/1/2009 | Radcliffe Institute Fellowships | 87 |
| 10/1/2009 | South Carolina Arts Commission | 87 |
| 10/1/2009 | Theatre Building Chicago | 51 |
| 10/1/2009 | U.S. Dept. of State Fulbright Program for US Students | 88 |
| 10/1/2009 | Vermont Arts Council | 88 |
| 10/3/2009 | Artists' Fellowships | 80 |
| 10/5/2009 | American Antiquarian Society Fellowships | 79 |
| 10/15/2009 | Hedgebrook | 37 |
| 10/15/2009 | National Playwrights Conference (NPC) | 54 |
| 10/15/2009 | Playwrights First Award | 67 |
| 10/15/2009 | ShowOff! Playwriting Festival | 55 |
| 10/15/2009 | Valencia Character Company | 70 |
| 10/26/2009 | TCG/ITI Intl. Fellowship | 88 |
| 10/31/2009 | Cultural Conversations | 45 |
| 10/31/2009 | FutureFest | 46 |
| 10/31/2009 | Irish American Theatre Co. | 74 |
| 10/31/2009 | Little Theatre of Alexandria National One-Act Playwriting Competition | 64 |
| 10/31/2009 | Mildred & Albert Panowski Playwriting Award | 64 |
| 10/31/2009 | Reva Shiner Full-Length Play Contest | 77 |
| 10/31/2009 | Southern Appalachian Playwrights' Conference | 51 |

## NOVEMBER

| Date | Event | Page |
|---|---|---|
| 11/1/2008 | American-Scandinavian Foundation (ASF) | 79 |
| 11/1/2009 | Actors Theatre of Louisville | 92 |
| 11/1/2009 | Advanced Playwriting Workshop | 175 |
| 11/1/2009 | Beverly Hills Theatre Guild Julie Harris Playwright Awards | 59 |
| 11/1/2009 | Black Box New Play Festival | 53 |
| 11/1/2009 | Coe College Playwriting Festival & Symposia | 45 |
| 11/1/2009 | National Ten-Minute Play Contest | 65 |
| 11/1/2009 | Rome Prize | 87 |
| 11/15/2009 | Asian Cultural Council | 80 |
| 11/15/2009 | Beverly Hills California Musical Theatre Award | 59 |
| 11/15/2009 | Boston Theater Marathon | 44 |
| 11/15/2009 | First Light Festival | 111 |
| 11/15/2009 | FirstStage One-Act Play Contest | 73 |
| 11/15/2009 | Nebraska Arts Council | 85 |
| 11/15/2009 | Playwrights' Week | 50 |
| 11/20/2009 | Ledig House Writers Residency Program | 39 |
| 11/25/2009 | Tennessee Williams/New Orleans Literary Festival | 56 |

## Submission Calendar

| | | |
|---|---|---|
| 11/30/2009 | Edgar Allan Poe Award for Best Play | 60 |
| 11/30/2009 | International Mystery Writers' Festival | 47 |
| 11/30/2009 | Poems & Plays | 32 |
| 11/30/2009 | Raymond J. Flores Short Play Festival | 55 |

### DECEMBER

| | | |
|---|---|---|
| 12/1/2009 | American College Theater Festival (ACTF) | 52 |
| 12/1/2009 | Cunningham Commission for Youth Theatre | 60 |
| 12/1/2009 | Electric Theatre Company | 109 |
| 12/1/2009 | Georgia College and State University | 73 |
| 12/1/2009 | High School New Play Award | 74 |
| 12/1/2009 | National Music Theater Conference (NMTC) | 54 |
| 12/1/2009 | New American Playwrights Project (NAPP) | 48 |
| 12/1/2009 | One-Act Playwriting Competition | 67 |
| 12/1/2009 | Rocky Mountain National Park Artist-in-Residence Program | 40 |
| 12/5/2009 | Pew Fellowships in the Arts (PFA) | 86 |
| 12/15/2009 | New Play Festival | 76 |
| 12/15/2009 | Next Generation Playwriting Contest | 76 |
| 12/15/2009 | PEN Translation Prize | 77 |
| 12/15/2009 | Reverie Productions | 77 |
| 12/15/2009 | Sketchbook Festival | 56 |
| 12/15/2009 | Sundance Institute Theatre Program | 181 |
| 12/16/2009 | Burning Coal Theatre Company | 101 |
| 12/21/2009 | STAGE International Script Competition | 68 |
| 12/27/2009 | ASCAP/Disney Musical Theatre Workshop | 176 |
| 12/31/2009 | Alden B. Dow Creativity Center | 35 |
| 12/31/2009 | Attic Theatre One-Act Marathon | 43 |
| 12/31/2009 | Cincinnati Fringe Festival | 53 |
| 12/31/2009 | Genesis Festival | 46 |
| 12/31/2009 | Goshen College Peace Playwriting Contest | 62 |
| 12/31/2009 | Harold Morton Landon Translation Award | 62 |
| 12/31/2009 | Lavender Footlights Festival | 47 |
| 12/31/2009 | Little Festival of the Unexpected | 48 |
| 12/31/2009 | Mountain Playhouse Playwriting Contest | 64 |
| 12/31/2009 | Nathan Miller History Play Contest | 65 |
| 12/31/2009 | National Writers Association Foundation (NWAF) | 189 |
| 12/31/2009 | New York City 15-Minute Play Fest | 49 |
| 12/31/2009 | Ohioana Career Award | 66 |
| 12/31/2009 | Ohioana Citations | 66 |
| 12/31/2009 | Ohioana Pegasus Award | 66 |
| 12/31/2009 | Robert J. Pickering Award for Playwriting Excellence | 67 |
| 12/31/2009 | Seven Devils Playwrights Conference | 56 |
| 12/31/2009 | Theatre in the Raw Play Writing Contest | 78 |

### OTHER

| | | |
|---|---|---|
| rolling | Hubris Productions | 116 |
| see website | Stage Left Theatre Company | 180 |
| rolling | The Side Project | 147 |
| rolling | Virginia Premiere Theatre | 152 |
| see website | Wichita State University New Play Competition | 70 |

# INDEX

3S Theatre Collective .............................................. 90
5th Avenue Theatre................................................. 90
6 Women Playwriting Festival .............................42
12 Miles West Theatre Company .........................89
16th St. Theater.........................................................89
40th Street Stage...................................................... 90
1812 Productions .....................................................89

## A

Abingdon Theatre Company ................................. 90
About Face Theatre (AFT)...................................... 90
Absinthe-Minded Theatre Company .................... 90
Academy for New Musical Theatre (ANMT)....... 175
Act II Playhouse ...................................................... 90
Acting Company......................................................91
Actors Art Theatre (AAT).......................................91
Actors Collective .....................................................91
Actor's Express ........................................................91
Actors' Fund of America......................................184
Actors' Guild of Lexington ....................................91
Actors' Playhouse National Children's Theatre
 Festival .................................................................42
Actors' Theatre Full-Length Play Contest.............71
Actors Theatre of Louisville...................................92
Actors Theatre of Louisville, Humana Festival......42
Actors Theatre of Phoenix .....................................92
Actors' Theatre Ten-Minute Play Contest ............71
ACTS Institute Inc..................................................184
ACT Theater (A Contemporary Theatre)..............91
Adelphi University.................................................162
Adirondack Theatre Festival ..................................92
A. D. Players ............................................................91
Advanced Playwriting Workshop........................ 175
Adventure Stage Chicago (ASC)............................92
African Continuum Theatre Co. (ACTCo) ..........92
AfroSolo Theatre Company ...................................92
Agnes Scott College ..............................................165
Alabama Shakespeare Festival ..............................42
Alabama State Council on the Arts ......................79
Alaska Quarterly Review (AQR)...........................27
Alaska State Council on the Arts (ASCA)............79
Alberta Playwrights Network............................... 170
Alden B. Dow Creativity Center ............................35
Alfreda's Reader's Theater......................................27
Algonkuin Theatre Company.................................92
All Arts Matter ........................................................92
Allenberry Playhouse ..............................................93
Allen Lee Hughes Fellowship Program .................79
Alley Theatre ............................................................93
Alliance of Artists Communities (AAC) .............184
Alliance of Los Angeles Playwrights (ALAP) .....184
Alliance Theatre .......................................................93

Allied Theater Group/Stage West .........................93
Altarena Playhouse / Alameda Little Theater ........93
Alternate ROOTS Inc.............................................184
Altos de Chavon.......................................................35
Amas Musical Theatre ............................................93
American Antiquarian Society Fellowships...........79
American Assn. of Community Theatre (AACT) 184
American College Theater Festival (ACTF)...........52
American Folklore Theatre (AFT) .........................93
American Indian Community House ...................184
American Musical Theatre of San Jose (AMT)..... 94
American Music Center (AMC).............................184
American Repertory Theatre ................................. 94
American-Scandinavian Foundation (ASF) ..........79
American Scandinavian Foundation Translation
 Prize .....................................................................57
American Stage ....................................................... 94
American Theater Company ................................. 95
American Theatre of Actors, Inc. (ATA) ...............95
American Translators Assn. (ATA)...................... 185
Amherst Players/Upstage NY ................................95
Amphibian Productions...........................................95
Anchorage Press Plays Inc. .....................................27
Angila Ruskin University ...................................... 171
Animated Theaterworks Inc...................................95
Anna Zornio Memorial Children's Theatre
 Playwriting Award .............................................57
Annual Black Theatre Festival...............................42
Appalachian Festival of Plays and Playwrights......42
Aquila Theatre Company .......................................95
Araca Group .............................................................25
Arch & Bruce Brown Foundation .........................58
Arden Theatre Company ........................................95
Arena Players Repertory Theatre...........................96
Arena Stage..............................................................96
Arizona Commission on the Arts (ACA)..............79
Arizona State University ............................... 157, 162
Arizona Theatre Company .....................................96
Arkansas Arts Center Children's Theatre..............96
Arkansas Arts Council............................................79
Arkansas at Fayetteville, University of ................157
Arkansas Repertory Theatre ..................................96
Around the Block Urban Playwriting
 Workgroup........................................................ 175
Ars Nova...................................................................96
Arte Publico Press....................................................27
Arthur W. Stone New Play Award .......................58
Artists' Fellowships................................................. 80
Artists Repertory Theatre .......................................96
Artist Trust............................................................... 80
Arts & Letters Prize in Drama................................71
ArtsPower National Touring Theatre................... 97

246

# Index

ART Station ............................................................. 96
Artward Bound Residency Program ....................... 35
ASCAP (American Society of Composers,
  Authors & Publishers) ........................................ 185
ASCAP/Disney Musical Theatre Workshop ......... 176
ASCAP Musical Theatre Workshop ...................... 176
Ashland New Plays Festival .................................... 52
Asian American Theater Company ........................ 97
Asian American Writers Workshop ....................... 27
Asian Cultural Council ............................................ 80
Asian Theatre Journal ............................................. 28
Asolo Repertory Theatre ......................................... 97
Assn. of Authors' Representatives, Inc. ............... 185
Association for Jewish Theatre (AJT) ................. 185
Association for Theatre in Higher Education
  (ATHE) ............................................................... 185
Asylum Theatre ....................................................... 97
Atlantic Center for the Arts .................................... 35
Atlantic Theater Company ..................................... 97
Attic Ensemble ........................................................ 97
Attic Theatre and Film Center .............................. 156
Attic Theatre One-Act Marathon ........................... 43
Audience .................................................................. 28
Audrey Skirball-Kenis (ASK) Unpublished
  Play Collection ................................................... 188
August Wilson New Play Initiative ........................ 97
Aurand Harris Fellowship ....................................... 80
Aurand Harris Memorial Playwriting Award ........ 72
Aurora Theatre Company: Global Age Project ..... 58
Aurora Theatre, Inc. ................................................ 97
Austin Playhouse ..................................................... 98
Austin Script Works (ASW) ................................. 185
Authors League Fund ............................................ 183
Award Blue .............................................................. 58
Axis Theatre Company ........................................... 98

## B

Babes With Blades Joining Sword and Pen .......... 58
Bailiwick Repertory Theatre .................................. 98
Baker's Plays ........................................................... 28
Baker's Plays High School Playwriting Contest ... 58
Baldwin New Play Festival ..................................... 43
Baltimore Playwrights Festival .............................. 52
Bard College .......................................................... 165
Barksdale Theatre .................................................... 98
Barnstormers Theatre ............................................. 43
Barrington Stage Company .................................... 98
Barrow Group .......................................................... 98
Barter Theatre ......................................................... 99
Bay Area Playwrights Festival (BAPF) ................ 43
Bay Street Theatre .................................................. 99
b current .................................................................. 98
Bennington College .............................................. 162
Berkeley Repertory Theatre ................................... 99
Berkshire Theatre Festival ..................................... 99
Berlin Artists-in-Residence .................................... 80
Beverly Hills California Musical Theatre Award ... 59

Beverly Hills Theatre Guild Julie Harris
  Playwright Awards ............................................... 59
Beverly Hills Theatre Guild Youth Theatre
  Marilyn Hall Awards ............................................ 59
Big Dog Publishing ................................................. 28
Bilingual Foundation of the Arts (BFA) ............... 43
Billy Rose Theatre Division ................................. 189
Birbeck University of London .............................. 171
Black Box New Play Festival ................................. 53
Black Ensemble Theater ......................................... 99
Black Playwrights Festival ..................................... 44
Black Rep ................................................................. 99
Black Spectrum Theatre ......................................... 99
Black Swan Theater ................................................ 99
Blank Theatre Company Young Playwrights
  Festival ................................................................. 44
Blinn College Theatre Arts Program .................. 100
Bloomsburg Theatre Ensemble (BTE) ................ 100
Blowing Rock Stage Company ............................ 100
Blue Coyote Theater Group (BCTG) .................. 100
Blue Mountain Center ............................................ 35
BMI (Broadcast Music Inc) .................................. 186
BoarsHead Theatre: Michigan Public Theater .... 100
Bond Street Theatre .............................................. 100
Boomerang Theatre Company ............................... 44
Borderlands Theater .............................................. 100
Boston Playwrights' Theatre ................................ 100
Boston Theater Marathon ....................................... 44
Brat Productions ...................................................... 94
Brava! for Women in the Arts ................................ 94
Breaking Ground Festival ...................................... 42
Brevard Little Theatre New-Play Competition .... 57
Brigham Young University .................................. 166
Bristol Riverside Theatre ....................................... 94
Broadway Play Publishing Inc. (BPPI) ................. 27
Broadway Tomorrow Musical Theatre ................ 175
Broken Watch Theatre Company ........................ 101
Brooklyn College .................................................. 157
Brooklyn Publishers ................................................ 28
Brown University .................................................. 157
Bryant-Lake Bowl Theater ................................... 101
B Street Theatre ...................................................... 98
Buntville Crew ...................................................... 101
Burning Coal Theatre Company .......................... 101
Byrdcliffe Arts Colony Artist-in-Residence
  (AIR) .................................................................... 35

## C

Caffeine Theatre ................................................... 101
Caldwell Theatre Company ................................. 101
California - Santa Barbara, University of ........... 166
California State University - Long Beach .......... 158
California Theatre Center .................................... 101
California Young Playwrights Contest ................. 59
Callaloo ................................................................... 28
Camargo Foundation .............................................. 36
Cambridge Wordfest ............................................ 172
Cameron Mackintosh Inc. ...................................... 25

Campbell University..............................................166
Canadian Jewish Playwriting Competition.............59
Cape Cod Theatre Project.....................................176
Capilano Review TCR.............................................28
Capital Repertory Theatre....................................102
Caribbean American Repertory Theatre..............102
Carnegie Fund for Authors...................................183
Carnegie Mellon University School of Drama.....158
Carole Shorenstein Hays Prods. (CSHP).................25
Casa Karina.............................................................36
Casa Manana Inc...................................................102
Case Western Reserve..........................................166
CEC ArtsLink..........................................................80
Celebration Theatre..............................................102
Center Stage..........................................................102
Center Stage Community Playhouse....................102
Center Theatre Group (CTG)................................102
Central School of Speech and Drama
   University of London, The................................171
Centre Stage South Carolina New Play Festival....44
Centrum Creative Residencies Program.................36
Chameleon Theatre Company Ltd.........................94
Chapman University.............................................162
Charles Maryan's Playwrights/Directors
   Workshop...........................................................175
Charles M. Getchell Award, SETC..........................57
Charleston Stage.....................................................94
Cherry Lane Theatre Mentor Project...................176
Chicago Alliance for Playwrights (CAP)..............193
Chicago Dramatists...............................................186
Chicago State University......................................163
Children's Theatre Company (CTC).....................103
Childsplay.............................................................103
Chinese Theatre Works........................................103
Christopher Brian Wolk Award..............................59
Cincinnati Black Theatre Company.....................103
Cincinnati Fringe Festival......................................53
Cincinnati Playhouse in the Park.........................103
Cincinnati Playhouse in the Park Mickey
   Kaplan New American Play Prize......................60
Cinnabar Theater..................................................104
Circle Theatre of Forest Park.................................45
City Attic Theatre CAT Tales Festival...................60
City Theatre..........................................................104
City Theatre Company.........................................104
Clarence Brown Theatre (CBT)............................104
Classical Theatre of Harlem.................................104
Cleveland Play House...........................................104
Cleveland Public Theatre.....................................104
Clubbed Thumb....................................................104
Coe College Playwriting Festival & Symposia......45
Colony Theatre Company....................................105
Colorado Council on the Arts................................81
Colorado New Play Summit.................................176
Columbia College Chicago...................................166
Columbia University............................................158
Columbus Children's Theatre (CCT)....................105
Commonweal Theatre Company.........................105
Community Theatre Association of Michigan......72

Composers & Lyricists Workshop........................176
Conejo Players Theatre........................................105
Coney Island, USA...............................................105
Congo Square Theatre Company.........................105
Connecticut Commission on Culture & Tourism
   (CCT)...................................................................81
Contemporary American Theater Festival
   (CATF)...............................................................105
Contemporary American Theatre Company
   (CATCO)............................................................102
Contemporary Drama Service................................29
Cornerstone Theater Company...........................105
Coterie Theatre....................................................106
Court Theatre......................................................103
Creative Evolution...............................................106
Crossroads Theatre Company..............................106
CTA Crossroads Theatre......................................106
Cultural Conversations..........................................45
Cumberland County Playhouse...........................106
Cunningham Commission for Youth Theatre.......60
Curan Repertory Theatre....................................106
Cyrano's Theatre Company (CTC)......................106

**D**

Dad's Garage Theatre Co.....................................106
Dalhousie University...........................................169
Dallas Children's Theater....................................107
Dallas Theater Center..........................................107
Danisarte..............................................................107
Dartmouth College..............................................163
Das Goldkiel..........................................................72
David C. Horn Prize...............................................72
David Henry Hwang Writers Institute................176
Delaware Division of the Arts...............................81
Delaware Theatre Company...............................107
Dell'Arte Company..............................................107
DePaul University...............................................166
Derry Playhouse Writers Workshop....................173
Detroit Repertory Theatre..................................107
Detroit Repertory Theatre/Millan Theatre
   Company...........................................................107
Direct Plays............................................................29
Discovery Theater................................................107
District of Columbia Arts Center (DCAC)..........107
Diversionary Theatre..........................................108
Dixon Place..........................................................108
Djerassi Resident Artists Program........................36
Dobama Theatre..................................................108
Dodger Properties..................................................25
Do Gooder Productions.......................................108
Doorway Arts Ensemble......................................108
Dorothy Silver Playwriting Competition..............60
Double Edge Theatre...........................................108
Downstage Left (DSL).........................................108
Drama Source........................................................29
Dramatic Publishing Company.............................29
Dramatics Magazine..............................................29
Dramatists Guild Fund........................................183
Dramatists Guild of America Inc........................186

# Index

Dramatists Play Service, Inc. ...29
Dream Theatre ...108
Drexel University ...167
Dr. Floyd Gaffney PLaywriting Award on the African-American Experience ... 60
Drilling Company ...109
Duke University ...163

## E

East West Players ...109
Edgar Allan Poe Award for Best Play ... 60
Educational Theatre Association ...186
Edward Albee Foundation ...36
Egyptian Theatre Company ...109
Eileen Heckart Drama For Seniors Competition ...61
El Centro Su Teatro ...109
Eldridge Publishing Company Inc. ...29
Electric Theatre Company ...109
Emelin Theatre for the Performing Arts ...109
Emerging Artists Theatre (EAT) ...109
Emerson College ...167
Empire Publishing Service ...30
Encompass New Opera Theatre ...110
Enrichment Works ...110
Ensemble Theater ...110
Ensemble Theatre Company of Santa Barbara ...110
Ensemble Theatre of Cincinnati ...110
Ensemble Theatre, The ...110
Entertainment Industry Assistance Program (EIAP) ...183
Envision Retreat ...36
Eric Bentley New Play Competition ...73
Essential Theatre Playwriting Award ...61
eta Creative Arts Foundation Inc. ...111
Euroscript Development Workshops ...172
Express Children's Theatre ...111

## F

Festival of New American Plays ...45
Field, The ...186
Fieldwork ...177
Firehouse Center for the Arts ...61
Fire Rose Prods. 10-Min. Play Festival ...53
First Light Festival ...111
FirstStage ...186
First Stage Children's Theater ...111
FirstStage One-Act Play Contest ...73
Fiscal Sponsorship ...81
Fishamble Theatre Company ...173
Flat Rock Playhouse ...111
Flea Theater, The ...146
Florida Repertory Theatre ...111
Florida Stage ...111
Florida State University ...158
Florida Studio Theatre ...111
Florida Studio Theatre's Richard & Betty Burdick New Play Reading Series ...45
Foothill Theatre Company ...112

Fordham University ...167
Ford's Theatre Society ...112
Fort Wayne Civic Theatre-Northeast Indiana Playwright Contest ...61
Foundation Center, The ...187
Fountainhead Theatre ...112
Fountain Theatre ...112
Fractured Atlas ...187
Francesca Primus Prize ...73
Frankel-Baruch-Viertel-Routh Group ...25
Frank Silvera Writers' Workshop ...177
Fred Ebb Award ...61
Freed-Hardeman Univ. ...112
Freedom Repertory Theatre ...112
Freelance Press ...30
Free Street Programs ...112
Fremont Centre Theatre New Playwright Contest ...73
Fresh Fruit Festival ... 44
Fringe of Toronto Theatre Festival ...45
Fulbright Program for US Scholars ...81
Full-Length Play Competition ...70
Fund for New Work ...81
Fund for Women Artists, The ...193
FusionFest ... 46
FUSION Theatre Co. ...73
FutureFest ... 46

## G

GableStage ...112
Gaiety School of Acting ...174
GAYFEST NYC ... 46
Geffen Playhouse ...112
Gell Center of the Finger Lakes ...37
Genesis Festival ... 46
Genesis Repertory Ensemble ...113
George Bennett Fellowship ...81
George Mason University ...163
George Street Playhouse ...113
Georgetown University ...163
Georgia College and State University ...73
Georgia Shakespeare ...113
Georgia, University of ...167
Germinal Stage Denver ...113
Geva Theatre Center ...113
Global Age Project (GAP) ... 46
Golden Fleece Ltd. ...113
Goldsmiths University of London ...171
Goodman Theatre ...113
Goodspeed Musicals ...114
Goshen College Peace Playwriting Contest ...62
Grawemeyer Award for Music Composition ...74
Great Canadian Theatre Company ...170
Great Lakes Theater Festival ...114
Greenbrier Valley Theatre ...114
Green Integer ...30
Green Light ...62
Greensboro Playwrights' Forum ...187
Gretna Theatre ...114

Growing Stage The Children's Theatre of New
  Jersey .................................................................. 114
Gumbo Media ......................................................... 30
Guthrie Theater .................................................... 114

## H

Hadley Players ..................................................... 114
Halcyon Theatre .................................................. 114
Hall Farm Center for Arts and Education ............. 37
Hambidge Center ................................................... 37
Hangar Theatre KIDDSTUFF ............................. 115
Hangar Theatre Lab Company Playwriting
  Residencies ........................................................ 177
Harbor Theatre Workshop .................................. 177
Harlem Stage at The Gatehouse ......................... 115
Harlequin Productions ........................................ 115
Harold Morton Landon Translation Award ......... 62
Harold Prince ........................................................ 25
Hartford Stage .................................................... 115
Harwich Junior Theatre (HJT) ........................... 115
Hatch-Billops Collection .................................... 187
HaveScripts.com ................................................... 30
Hawai'i Prize ........................................................ 62
Hawthornden Castle International Retreat
  for Writers ........................................................... 37
Headlands Center for the Arts ............................. 37
Hedgebrook ........................................................... 37
Hedgerow Theatre .............................................. 115
Helene Wurlitzer Foundation of New Mexico ........ 37
Henrico Theatre Company One-Act
  Playwriting Competition .................................... 62
High School New Play Award ............................. 74
Hip Pocket Theatre ............................................. 115
Hippodrome State Theatre ................................. 115
Hispanic Organization of Latin Actors (HOLA) .. 187
Hodder Fellowship ............................................... 82
Hollins University .............................................. 158
Honolulu Theatre for Youth ............................... 116
Horizon Theatre Rep .......................................... 116
Horse Trade Theater Group ............................... 116
Houston, University of ....................................... 163
Howard University ............................................. 163
Hubris Productions ............................................. 116
Hudson Theatres ................................................. 116
Humanities Projects in Media ............................. 82
Human Race Theatre Company, The ................ 146
Hyde Park Theatre ............................................. 116
Hypothetical Theatre Company .......................... 116

## I

Idaho ................................................................... 117
Illinois Theatre Center ....................................... 103
Illusion Theater .................................................. 103
Imagination Stage .............................................. 103
Immigrants' Theatre Project .............................. 117
Impact Theatre Company ................................... 117
Independence Community College .................... 167
Indiana Arts Commission (IAC) .......................... 82

Indiana Repertory Theatre ................................ 117
Infamous Commonwealth Theatre .................... 117
InnerAct Productions ......................................... 117
Inside Broadway ................................................. 187
Inspirato Festival ................................................. 47
Institute of Gunnar Gunnarsson -Klaustrid ......... 38
Institute of Outdoor Drama ................................ 187
INTAR (International Arts Relations) Theatre .... 118
InterAct Theatre Company ................................ 118
Interborough Repertory Theater Inc. (IRT) ........ 118
International City Theatre ................................. 118
International Mystery Writers' Festival .............. 47
International Radio Playwriting Competition ..... 62
International Theatre Institute US Center
  (ITI/US) ............................................................. 192
International Women's Writing Guild (IWWG) ... 187
International Writing Program (IWP) ................. 38
Interplayers Ensemble Theatre .......................... 118
Intersection for the Arts James D. Phelan
  Literary Award .................................................. 63
Intiman Theatre .................................................. 118
Iowa Arts Council ................................................. 82
Iowa, University of ............................................. 159
Irish American Theatre Co. ................................. 74
Irish Classical Theatre Company (ICTC) ........... 118
Irish Repertory Theatre ..................................... 119
Irish Writers' Centre .......................................... 174
Irondale Ensemble Project ................................. 119
Isle Royale National Park Artist-in-Residence .... 38

## J

Jackie White Memorial National Children's Play
  Writing Contest ................................................. 63
Jacksonville University ....................................... 63
Jacksonville Univ. Helford Prize ......................... 63
Jane Chambers Playwriting Award ..................... 74
Jane Chambers Student Playwriting Award ....... 74
Jane Harmon Associates ...................................... 25
Japan Foundation ................................................. 82
Jefferson Performing Arts Society ..................... 119
Jeffrey Sweet's Improv for Playwrights ............ 177
Jerome Playwright-in-Residence Fellowships .... 82
Jewel Box Theatre Playwriting Award ................ 75
Jewish Ensemble Theater Festival of New Plays .... 47
Jewish Ensemble Theatre .................................. 119
Jewish Theater of New York .............................. 119
John Capo Productions ....................................... 119
John D. and Catherine T. MacArthur Fund Grant .. 83
John Gassner Memorial Playwriting Award ....... 75
John Simon Guggenheim Memorial Foundation .... 83
Jubilee Theatre ................................................... 119
Judith Shakespeare Company NYC .................... 120
Juilliard School ................................................... 159
Juneteenth Legacy Theatre ................................. 53

## K

Kairos Italy Theater (KIT) ................................. 120
Kalani Oceanside Retreat Village ........................ 38

Kalliope: A Journal of Women's Literature & Art.30
Kansas City Repertory Theatre..............................120
Kansas State University..........................................167
Karamu House Inc....................................................120
Kavinoky Theatre.....................................................120
Kennedy Center New Visions/New Voices
 Festival (NVNV), The........................................181
Kentucky Repertory Theatre at
 Horse Cave..........................................................120
Kenyon Review..........................................................30
Kidworks Touring Theatre Co. ..............................120
Killing Kompany......................................................120
Kimmel Harding Nelson (KHN) Center for
 the Arts..................................................................38
Kitchen Dog Theater (KDT) New Works
 Festival..................................................................47
Kleban Award............................................................83
Know Theatre of Cincinnati....................................177
Kumu Kahua Theatre..............................................121
Kuntu Repertory Theatre........................................121
Kuumba Ensemble Heritage House Community
 Theater................................................................121

L

Laguna Playhouse....................................................121
Laity Theatre Company............................................72
La Jolla Playhouse...................................................121
La MaMa Experimental Theater Club...................121
Lamia Ink! Intl. One-Page Play Competition.........53
LaMicro Theater......................................................121
Lanesboro Residency Program Fellowships...........39
L. Arnold Weissberger Award..................................63
LA Stage Alliance...................................................188
Last Frontier Theatre Conference............................47
L.A. Theatre Works (LATW).................................121
Latin American Theater Ensemble (LATE) /
 El Portón del Barrio..........................................121
Lavender Footlights Festival....................................47
Lazy Bee Scripts.......................................................30
League of Chicago Theatres/League of
 Chicago Theatres Foundation..........................188
League of Professional Theatre Women...............188
League of Washington Theatres (LOWT).............188
Ledig House Writers Residency Program...............39
Leighton Artists' Colony for Independent
 Residencies...........................................................39
Lewis Galantiere Award...........................................63
Librettists Workshop...............................................178
Lifeline Theatre.......................................................122
Lillenas Publishing Company..................................31
Limelight Scripts.......................................................31
Lincoln Center Theater...........................................122
Literary Managers & Dramaturgs of the
 Americas (LMDA)............................................188
Literature East Midlands........................................174
Literature Fellowships: Translation Projects..........83
Little Festival of the Unexpected............................48
Little Fish Theatre (LFT).......................................122

Little Theatre of Alexandria National One-Act
 Playwriting Competition....................................64
Live Bait Theater....................................................122
LiveWire Chicago Theatre.......................................64
Livingstone College................................................163
Long Beach Playhouse New Works Festival..........54
Looking Glass Theatre...........................................122
Lorraine Hansberry Theater..................................122
Lost Nation Theater................................................122
Louisiana Division of the Arts.................................83
Louisiana - Monroe, University of........................163
Louisiana State University.....................................164
Ludwig Vogelstein Foundation, Inc. .......................83
Luna Stage..............................................................122
Lyric Stage Company of Boston............................123

M

MacDowell Colony...................................................39
Macy's New Play Prize for Young Audiences........64
Madison Repertory Theatre...................................123
Magic Theatre.........................................................123
Maine Arts Commission...........................................83
Main Street Theater................................................123
Manhattan Playwrights Unit (MPU).....................178
Many Voices Playwriting Residency Awards.........83
Margery Klain...........................................................25
Margo Lion Ltd.........................................................26
Marin Arts Council Fund for Artists.......................84
Marin Theater Company (MTC)...........................123
Mary Anderson Center for the Arts.........................39
Mary Immaculate College......................................173
Mary Mason Memorial Lemonade Fund..............183
Marymount Manhattan College.............................167
Massachusetts Cultural Council (MCC..................84
Maxim Mazumdar New Play Competition.............75
Ma-Yi Theatre Company........................................123
McCarter Theater Center........................................124
MCC Theater...........................................................123
McKnight Advancement Grants..............................84
McKnight National Playwriting Residency
 and Commission..................................................84
McLaren Memorial Comedy Playwriting
 Competition.........................................................75
Meadow Brook Theatre..........................................124
Meet the Composer Grant Programs.......................84
Melting Pot Theatre Company...............................124
Memorial University of Newfoundland...............169
Merrimack Repertory Theatre...............................124
Merry-Go-Round Playhouse..................................124
Met Life Nuestras Voces Playwriting
 Competition.........................................................64
Metropolitain State University...............................164
MetroStage..............................................................124
Metro Theater Company........................................124
Miami University of Ohio......................................164
Michener Center for Writers...................................85
Michigan - University of.......................................164
Mildred & Albert Panowski Playwriting Award...64
Milk Can Theatre Company...................................124

Millay Colony for the Arts .........................................39
Mill Mountain Theatre ..............................................125
Milwaukee Chamber Theatre....................................125
Milwaukee Repertory Theater ...................................125
Miracle Theatre Group ..............................................125
Mississippi Theatre Association ...............................75
Missouri Playwrights Workshop (MPW) .............. 178
Mixed Blood Theatre Company ...............................125
Montana Artists Residency ......................................40
Montana Repertory Theater .....................................125
Moose Hide Books ....................................................31
Mountain Playhouse Playwriting Contest............... 64
Moving Arts................................................................125
Moving Arts Premiere One-Act Competition..........76
Mu Performing Arts ..................................................125
Musical Theatre Lab..................................................178
Music Theatre International (MTI) ........................31

# N

NACL Theatre (North American Cultural
   Laboratory)..............................................................126
Naples Players ETC ..................................................65
Nathan Miller History Play Contest.........................65
National Audio Theatre Festivals (NATF) ............189
National Children's Theatre Festival .......................72
National League of American Pen Women,
   Inc., The...................................................................186
National Music Theater Conference (NMTC)........54
National New Play Network......................................76
National New Play Network NNPN Smith Prize ...65
National One-Act Playwriting Contest ....................76
National Playwrights Conference (NPC)................54
National Playwriting Competition ...........................65
National Ten-Minute Play Contest ...........................65
National Theatre of the Deaf....................................126
National Theatre Workshop of the
   Handicapped ........................................................178
National University of Ireland, Galway .................173
National Writers Association Foundation
   (NWAF) ...................................................................189
Near West Theatre (NWT)........................................126
Nebraska Arts Council ..............................................85
Nebraska Theatre Caravan ......................................126
Nederlander Organization........................................26
Negro Ensemble Company......................................126
Nevada Arts Council .................................................85
New American Playwrights Project (NAPP)..........48
New Conservatory Theatre Center..........................126
New Directors/New Works (ND/NW) ....................178
New Dramatists .........................................................189
New Federal Theatre .................................................126
New Generations Program: Future
   Collaborations......................................................85
New Georges...............................................................126
New Ground Theatre .................................................127
New Group, The .........................................................147
New Hampshire State Council
   on the Arts.............................................................85
New Harmony Project................................................178

New Jersey Playwrights Festival of New Plays ......48
New Jersey Repertory Company.............................127
New Jersey State Council on the Arts....................85
New Jomandi Productions, Inc. ..............................127
New Perspectives Theatre Company ....................127
New Play Development Workshop.........................179
New Play Festival ......................................................76
New Plays Inc .............................................................31
New Playwrights Competition ................................65
New Playwrights Foundation ..................................189
New Professional Theatre Writers Festival ..........48
New Repertory Theatre.............................................128
New Rocky Mountain Voices....................................76
New School University ............................................159
New South Play Festival...........................................48
New Stage Theatre ....................................................128
New Theatre ...............................................................128
New Time Productions..............................................26
New WORLD Theater (NWT) ..................................129
New York City 15-Minute Play Fest ........................49
New York Mills Arts Retreat ..................................... 40
New York Stage and Film (NYSAF) .......................129
New York State Council on the Arts (NYSCA)......86
New York State Theatre Institute (NYSTI)..........129
New York Television Festival...................................49
New York Theatre Workshop (NYTW).................129
New York Theatre Workshop (NYTW)
   Playwriting Fellowship ......................................86
New York University, Tisch School of
   the Arts ........................................................ 159, 160
Next Act Theatre .......................................................129
Next Generation Playwriting Contest ....................76
Next Theater Company.............................................129
Noise Within (ANW) .................................................130
None of the Above Playwriting Contest................ 66
Non-Traditional Casting Project, Inc. (NTCP).....189
Norman Maine Publishing.......................................32
North Carolina New Play Project (NCNPP).......... 66
North Carolina Playwrights Alliance (NCPA) .....190
North Carolina Writers' Network (NCWN) .........190
North Dakota Council on the Arts ........................86
Northern Kentucky University ...............................164
Northern Stage...........................................................130
Northlight Theatre.....................................................130
North Shore Music Theatre (NSMT)....................130
Northside Theatre Company ...................................130
Northwestern University .........................................160
Not Merely Players ....................................................130
NYC Playwrights........................................................189
NYC Playwrights Lab ...............................................179

# O

Obsidian Theatre Company.....................................130
Occidental College ....................................................164
Off-Off-Broadway Original Short-Play Festival ....49
Ohioana Career Award.............................................66
Ohioana Citations......................................................66
Ohioana Pegasus Award..........................................66
Ohio Arts Council ......................................................86

# Index

Ohio University .................................................. 160
OIW - Ottawa Independent Writers ....................... 171
Oklahoma Arts Council ........................................ 86
Oldcastle Theatre Company ................................ 131
Old Globe ............................................................ 130
Old Log Theater .................................................. 131
Old Opera House Theatre Company New
   Voice Play Festival ............................................ 55
Ollantay Center for the Arts ................................ 190
Olney Theatre Center for the Arts ...................... 131
Omaha Theater Company .................................. 131
One-Act Playwriting Competition ......................... 67
Open Circle Theater (OCT) ................................. 131
Open Eye Theater ............................................... 131
OpenStage Theatre & Company ........................ 131
OPERA America ................................................. 190
Opera Cleveland ................................................. 131
Orange County Playwrights Alliance (OCPA) ..... 190
Oregon Shakespeare Festival ............................ 132
Organic Theater Company ................................. 127
Original Works Publishing .................................... 31
Oscar Wilde Centre for Irish Writing ................... 173

## P

P73 Playwriting Fellowship ................................... 85
Pacific Rim Prize ................................................... 65
PAJ: A Journal of Performance and Art .............. 32
Pan Asian Repertory Theatre ............................. 127
Pangea World Theater ....................................... 132
Pasadena Playhouse .......................................... 132
Passage Theatre ................................................. 132
Pataphysics ......................................................... 179
PCPA Theatrefest ............................................... 132
Pegasus Players ................................................. 132
Pegasus Theater Company ................................ 133
PEN Center USA Literary Awards ........................ 77
Pendragon Theatre ............................................. 133
Penguin Repertory Company ............................. 133
PEN/Laura Pels Foundation Awards
   for Drama ........................................................... 67
Penn State New Musical Theatre Festival ........... 49
Pennsylvania Council on the Arts ........................ 86
Penobscot Theatre ................................................ 49
PEN Translation Prize ........................................... 77
Penumbra Theatre Company ..................... 133, 179
PEN Writers Fund ............................................... 183
People's Light and Theatre Company ................ 133
Performance Network Theatre ........................... 133
Perishable Theatre Women's Playwriting
   Festival ............................................................... 55
Perseverance Theatre (PT) ................................ 133
Pew Fellowships in the Arts (PFA) ....................... 86
Philadelphia Dramatists Center (PDC) ............... 190
Philadelphia Theatre Company (PTC) ............... 133
Phoenix Arts Association Theatre ...................... 133
Phoenix Theatre ................................................. 134
Pier One Theatre ................................................ 134
Pilgrim Project ...................................................... 87
Pillsbury House Theatre ..................................... 134

Pioneer Theatre Company ................................. 134
Pittsburgh New Works Festival (PNWF) .............. 54
Pittsburgh Public Theater ................................... 128
Piven Theatre ..................................................... 128
Plan-B Theatre Company ................................... 128
PlayCrafters Group, The .................................... 181
Players Press Inc. ................................................ 32
Playfest -Harriett Lake Festival of
   New Plays ......................................................... 49
Playformers ........................................................ 191
Playhouse on the Square ................................... 134
PlayMakers Repertory Company ....................... 134
Playscripts, Inc. .................................................... 32
Plays for the 21st Century ................................... 77
Play With Your Food ........................................... 156
Playwrights Center San Francisco (PCSF), The ... 191
Playwrights' Center, The .................................... 191
Playwrights First Award ....................................... 67
Playwrights' Forum .................................... 135, 191
Playwrights Gallery ............................................ 179
Playwrights Guild of Canada (PGC) .................. 191
Playwrights Horizons .......................................... 134
Playwrights' Lab ................................................. 179
Playwrights' Platform ......................................... 179
Playwrights' Week ............................................... 50
Poems & Plays ..................................................... 32
Polarity Ensemble Theatre ................................. 135
Political Theatre Festival ...................................... 50
Popular Play Service ............................................ 32
Porchlight Music Theatre Chicago ..................... 135
Portland Center Stage ....................................... 135
Portland Stage Company .................................. 135
Premiere Stages Play Festival ............................. 50
Primary Stages ................................................... 135
Primary Stages Playwriting Workshops ............. 180
Prime Stage Theatre .......................................... 135
Prince Music Theater ......................................... 136
Princess Grace Foundation USA Playwriting
   Fellowship ......................................................... 87
Prism International ............................................... 33
Prix Hors Pair ....................................................... 77
Prop Thtr ............................................................. 128
Prospect Theater Company ............................... 128
Providence Black Repertory Company .............. 128
PRTT Playwrights Unit ....................................... 179
Public Access Television Corporation PATV ....... 67
Public Theater .................................................... 136
Public Theater/Emerging Writers Group, The ..... 88
Puerto Rican Traveling Theatre ......................... 136
Purple Circuit, The ............................................. 191
Purple Rose Theatre Company ......................... 136

## Q

Queens Theatre in the Park ............................... 136

## R

Radcliffe Institute Fellowships .............................. 87
Ragdale Foundation ............................................. 40

Rainbow Dinner Theatre...137
Raymond J. Flores Short Play Festival...55
Red Barn Theatre...137
Red Bull Theater...137
Red Orchid Theatre...137
ReOrient Golden Thread Fest...50
Repertory Theatre of St. Louis...137
Resident Prize...68
Resource Publications, Inc...33
Reva Shiner Full-Length Play Contest...77
Reverie Productions...77
Rhode Island State Council on the Arts...87
Riant Theatre...137
Richard Rodgers Awards for Musical Theater...68
Rick Hobard...26
Riverlight and Company...137
Riverside Theatre...138
Robert Chesley Award...67
Robert J. Pickering Award for Playwriting Excellence...67
Rocky Mountain National Park Artist-in-Residence Program...40
Rodger Hess Productions Inc...26
Rodgers & Hammerstein Theatricals...192
Rome Prize...87
Roosevelt Universtity...168
Roots & Branches Theater...138
Ross Valley Players...138
Round House Theatre...138
Roxbury Crossroads Theatre...138
Royal Academy of Dramatic Art in Collaboration with King's College, London...171
Royal Court Theatre...138
Royal Holloway, University of London...172
Ruby Lloyd Apsey Award...68
Rutgers University - New Brunswick...161
Ryan Repertory Company Inc...138

## S

Sacramento Theatre Company...138
Sage Theater...180
Salt Lake Acting Company...138
Samuel French Inc...33
San Diego Repertory Theatre...139
San Diego, University of...164
San Francisco State University...161
San Jose Repertory Theatre...139
Santa Monica Playhouse...139
Sarah Lawrence College...168
Saskatchewan Writers Guild (SWG)...192
Scratch Pad Festival...50
Scripteasers, The...180
Scripts Up!...180
Seacoast Repertory Theatre...139
Seaside Music Theater (SMT)...139
Seattle Children's Theatre...139
Seattle Repertory Theatre...139
Second Stage Theatre...140
Seltaeb Music Pty. Ltd...33

Serendipity Theatre Company...140
Seven Angels Theatre...140
Seven Devils Playwrights Conference...56
Seventh Street Playhouse, LLC...140
ShadowBox: The Sketch Comedy Rock 'n' Roll Club...140
Shadowlight Productions...140
Shakespeare & Company...140
Shakespeare Festival at Tulane...141
Shakespeare Theatre Company...136
Short Attention Span PlayFEST...50
Shotgun Productions Inc...136
ShowOff! Playwriting Festival...55
Shubert Archives...192
Shubert Organization...26
Side Project, The...147
Signature Theatre...141
Signature Theatre Company...141
SignStage...141
Simon Studio...180
Simpatico Theatre Project...141
Sinister Wisdom Journal...33
SITI Company...141
Sketchbook Festival...56
Skylight...141
Slavic and East European Performance...33
Smith and Kraus...33
Society Hill Playhouse...141
SoHo Repertory Theatre Inc...142
Songwriters Guild of America (SGA), The...192
Sonoma County Repertory Theater...142
South Camden Theatre Company...142
South Carolina Arts Commission...87
South Coast Repertory Theatre...142
South Dakota Arts Council...88
Southern Appalachian Playwrights' Conference...51
Southern Illinois University - Carbondale...161
Southern Playwrights Competition...68
Southern Writers Project (SWP)...181
Speert Publishing...33
Springer Opera House...142
Square Mama Productions...142
STAGE International Script Competition...68
Stage Left Theatre Company...180
Stage One: The Louisville Children's Theater...136
STAGE (Society for Theatrical Artists' Guidance and Enhancement)...192
StageSource...192
Stages Repertory Theatre...143
Stages Theatre Center...143
Stages Theatre Company...143
Stageworks/Hudson...143
Stageworks, Inc...143
Stamford Theatre Works (STW)...143
State University of New York - Purchase...168
Steppenwolf Theatre Company...143
Stepping Stone Theatre for Youth Development...144
Stewart F. Lane...26
St. Louis Black Repertory Company...142

# Index

Stoneham Theatre ................................................. 144
Story Time Stories That Rhyme ............................. 34
Stray Dog Theatre (SDT) ..................................... 144
StreetSigns Center for Literature and
   Performance ...................................................... 144
Studio Arena Theatre ........................................... 144
Studio for Creative Inquiry .................................... 40
Studio Theatre ...................................................... 144
Summerfield G. Roberts Award ............................. 69
SummerNITE ....................................................... 144
Summer Writing Workshops .................................. 51
Sundance Institute Playwrights Retreat ................. 40
Sundance Institute Theatre at White Oak ............ 181
Sundance Institute Theatre Program .................... 181
Sundog Theatre .................................................... 144
Susan Gallin Productions Inc. ................................ 26
Susan Smith Blackburn Prize ................................. 69
Sweetwood Productions ....................................... 145
Synchronicity Performance Group ....................... 145
Syracuse Stage .................................................... 145

## T

Tamasha New Writing ......................................... 172
Tams-Witmark Music Library Inc. ......................... 34
TCG/ITI Intl. Fellowship ........................................ 88
Teatro Dallas ....................................................... 145
Teatro del Pueblo .................................................. 51
Teatro Vision ....................................................... 145
Teatro Vista ........................................................ 146
TeCo Theatrical Productions New Play
   Competition ........................................................ 78
Tectonic Theater Project ..................................... 146
Ten Grand Productions ....................................... 146
Ten Minute Musicals Project, The ......................... 69
Tennessee Repertory Theatre .............................. 146
Tennessee Williams/New Orleans Literary
   Festival ............................................................... 56
Texas A&M University - Commerce .................... 165
Thalia Spanish Theatre ....................................... 146
Theater 150 Ten-Minute Play Festival ................... 51
Theater at Monmouth ......................................... 147
Theater Breaking Through Barriers ..................... 147
Theater Catalyst .................................................. 147
Theater for the New City (TFNC) ........................ 145
Theater Instituut Nederland (TIN) ....................... 193
Theater IV .......................................................... 147
Theater J ............................................................. 148
Theater Magazine ................................................. 34
Theater Museum, The ......................................... 184
Theater of the Seventh Sister ............................. 148
Theater Previews at Duke ................................... 148
Theater Resources Unlimited (TRU)/TRU
   Voices ................................................................ 56
Theater Ten Ten .................................................. 148
Theatre Alliance of Michigan .............................. 156
Theatre Ariel ....................................................... 148
Theatre at the Center / Lawrence Arts Center ...... 148
Theatre Bay Area (TBA) ..................................... 193
Theatre @ Boston Court, The .............................. 147

Theatre Building Chicago ...................................... 51
Theatre Building Chicago Musical Theatre
   Writers' Workshop ........................................... 182
Theatre Communications Group (TCG) ......... 34, 192
Theatre Company ............................................... 148
Theatre de la Jeune Lune ................................... 149
Theatre Development Fund (TDF) ...................... 194
Theatrefolk .......................................................... 34
TheatreForum ....................................................... 34
Theatre for Young Audiences/ USA .................... 194
Theatre in the Raw Play Writing Contest ............. 78
Theatre in the Square ........................................ 149
Theatre Museum, The ........................................ 193
Theatre of Yugen ................................................ 149
Theatre Outlet .................................................... 149
Theatre Oxford 10-Minute Play Contest ............... 78
Theatre Project ................................................... 194
Theatre Rhinoceros ............................................. 149
Theatre Three, Inc. ............................................. 149
Theatre Three One-Act Play Festival .................... 52
Theatre West ...................................................... 194
TheatreWorks ..................................................... 149
Theatrical Outfit ................................................. 149
Theatrical Rights Worldwide ................................. 34
Theodore Ward Prize ............................................ 69
This Women's Work Theatre Co. (TWWTC) ....... 149
Touchstone Theatre ............................................ 150
Towne Street Theatre (TST) ............................... 145
Towngate Theatre Playwriting Contest ................. 66
Town Hall Theatre Company (THT) .................... 150
Towson Univ. Prize for Literature ......................... 69
Transport Group ................................................. 145
Travel & Study Grant Program ............................. 88
Triangle Productions! ......................................... 150
TriArts at the Sharon Playhouse ......................... 150
Trinity Repertory Company ................................ 150
Trustus Playwrights' Festival ................................ 56
Trustus Theatre .................................................. 150
TRU (Theater Resources Unlimited) ................... 194
Tulsa, University of ............................................ 165
Turtle Shell Productions ............................... 70, 150
Two Chairs Theater Company ............................. 156
Two River Theatre Company (TRTC) ................. 151
Tyrone Guthrie Centre ......................................... 40

## U

Ucross Foundation Residency Program ................ 41
Ungar German Translation Award ........................ 70
Unicorn Theatre ................................................. 151
Unity Theatre Ensemble ..................................... 151
University College Cork ...................................... 173
University College Dublin ................................... 173
University of British Columbia ............................ 169
University of Calgary .......................................... 169
University of California - Riverside ..................... 157
University of California - San Diego ................... 158
University of Guelph .......................................... 169
University of Hawaii - Manoa ............................. 158
University of Missouri - Kansas City ................... 168

University of Nevada - Las Vegas (UNLV) ........... 159
University of New Brunswick ............................... 169
University of New Mexico ..................................... 159
University of Northern British Columbia ............. 169
University of Southern California .......................... 161
University of Texas - Austin ................................... 161
University of Texas - El Paso (UTEP) ................... 162
University of Victoria ............................................. 170
University of Virginia ............................................. 168
University of Windsor ............................................ 170
Urban Retreat .......................................................... 182
Urban Stages Emerging Playwright Award ............ 78
U.S. Dept. of State Fulbright Program for US
    Students ............................................................. 88
U.S./Japan Creative Artists' Program ..................... 41
Utah Arts Council ................................................... 88
Utah Shakespearean Festival ................................ 151

## V

Valencia Character Company ................................. 70
Valley Youth Theatre (VYT) ................................. 151
Vancouver Island University ................................. 170
V&A Theatre Collections ....................................... 194
Vermont Arts Council ............................................. 88
Vermont Playwrights Award ................................... 70
Victory Gardens Theater ....................................... 151
Victory Theatre Center .......................................... 151
Village Theatre ...................................................... 152
Villar-Hauser Theatre Development Fund, The ..... 89
Vineyard Theatre ................................................... 152
Virginia Center for the Creative Arts (VCCA) ....... 41
Virginia Commission for the Arts .......................... 89
Virginia Premiere Theatre ..................................... 152
Virginia Stage Company (VSC) ............................ 152
VSA arts Playwright Discovery Program ............... 69
VS. Theatre Company ........................................... 152

## W

Walnut Street Theatre ........................................... 152
Warehouse Theatre Summer Writing Course ....... 172
Warnborough College, Ireland .............................. 173
Washington University .......................................... 165
Watertower Theatre, Inc. ....................................... 152
Weissberger Theater Group .................................... 26
Wellfleet Harbor Actors Theater ........................... 153
West Coast Ensemble ............................................ 153
Western Stage ........................................................ 153
Western Washington University .................... 165, 168

Weston Playhouse .................................................. 153
Westport Arts Center ............................................. 153
Westport Country Playhouse ................................. 153
White Horse Theater Company ............................. 153
Whiting Writers' Awards ........................................ 70
Wichita State University ....................................... 165
Wichita State Univ. (WSU) New Play
    Competition ...................................................... 70
Will Geer Theatricum Botanicum ......................... 153
William and Mary, College of ............................... 165
William Inge Center for the Arts ............................ 38
Williamstown Theatre Festival ............................. 153
Willows Theatre Company .................................... 154
Wilma Theater ....................................................... 154
Wings Theatre Company, Inc. ............................... 154
Wisconsin Arts Board ............................................. 89
W. Keith Hedrick Playwriting Contest ................... 78
Women's Project & Productions ........................... 154
Women's Theatre Alliance (WTA) ........................ 194
Women's Work Project ........................................... 41
Woodstock Fringe ................................................... 52
Woolly Mammoth Theatre Company ................... 154
WordPlay - FairGround's Playwriting
    Course, London ............................................... 172
Working Theater .................................................... 154
Write a Play! NYC Contest .................................... 71
Writer/Director Lab .............................................. 182
Writers' Circle of Durham Region, The ................ 171
Writer's Digest Writing Competition ..................... 78
Writers Guild of America, West (WGAW) ........... 193
Writers' Guild of Great Britain, The ..................... 195
Writers Lounge ...................................................... 193
Writers Room, The ................................................ 193
Writers' Theatre .................................................... 146
Wyoming, University of ........................................ 168

## X

Xoregos Performing Company .............................. 155

## Y

Yaddo ...................................................................... 41
Yale Repertory Theatre ......................................... 155
Yale School of Drama ........................................... 162
Yangtze Repertory Theatre of America ................ 155
York Shakespeare Company ................................. 155
York Theatre Company ......................................... 155
York University ..................................................... 170
Young Playwrights Inc. (YPI) ............................... 195

ANYONE writing for the stage can apply and enjoy the privileges of membership, which include:
- A subscription to *The Dramatist* magazine
- A bimonthly e-Newsletter listing upcoming events, ticket offers, member news, and the latest business affairs news items
- An annual *Dramatists Guild Resource Directory*, a guide to the theatrical marketplace, with comprehensive lists of opportunities and resources
- Model Contracts for all levels of production, plus collaboration agreements and more
- Free business adivce and assistance on many theatre and career-related matters
- Free admission to symposia, seminars, and other events around the country
- Access to the Members Lounge section of the Dramatists Guild website, where you can order contracts, download articles, search the database of resources, view videos and stream audio from past seminars and events
- AND MORE!

## CATEGORIES OF MEMBERSHIP

The Dramatists Guild of America offers membership to all dramatic writers, including playwrights, librettists, lyricists and composers, regardless of their production or publication history.

☐ **Active Members ($150/yr)** have been produced on a First- Class/Broadway or Off-Broadway contract, or on the main stage of a regional LORT theatre. Applications must be accompanied by a copy of a review or program from the qualifying production.

☐ **Associate Members ($95/yr)** are authors of all theatrical works, including plays, librettos, lyrics and musical compositions written for the stage. Applications must be accompanied either by a complete theatrical work of any length written by the applicant or by a program or a review of a stage production.

☐ **Student Members ($35/yr)** must be enrolled in a course of dramatic writing instruction at the time of their application for membership. Applications must be accompanied by a letter from the program's senior administrator, or other proof of enrollment, indicating the expected date of graduation.

College/University _____

Graduation Date _____

**Estate Members ($125/yr)** are the executors of estates of deceased theatrical writers who would have qualified as Active or Associate Members during their lifetime. To become an Estate Member, please call the office at 212-398-9366 and speak with the membership department.

**Subscribers**
If you are not a theatrical writer, you can still obtain certain Guild publications as an Individual Subscriber, an Institutional Subscriber, or a Professional Subscriber. For more information on the various levels of subscription, please call the office at 212-398-9366.

## MEMBERSHIP APPLICATION

Please check all that apply:

☐ Playwright  ☐ Composer  ☐ Lyricist  ☐ Librettist

(Mr./Mrs./Ms.) _____
(Name you use professionally. Please print or type)

Pseudonym(s) _____

Address _____

City _____ State _____ Zip _____

Phone _____

Email _____

Social Security Number _____

Date of Birth _____

(If Applicable) Agent/Agency _____

Agent Address/Phone _____

☐ I authorize the release of my personal information

☐ Enclosed is my check to The Dramatists Guild of America, Inc.

☐ Please bill my credit card:  ☐ MC  ☐ VISA  ☐ AMEX  ☐ DISCOVER

Card Number _____ Exp. Date _____

Signature _____

Unlike other guilds and unions, there is no initiation fee. Residents of Canada, please add $10 to the membership fee. Other residents outside the United States, please add $20 to membership fee. All payments must be in U.S. funds or payable through a U.S. bank.

Mail to: The Dramatists Guild of America
Attn: Membership Department
1501 Broadway, Suite 701, NY, NY 10036.

For more information: 212.398.9366